The Promise of the Land

The Taubman Lectures in Jewish Studies

1. *Biblical Prose Prayer as a Window to the Popular Religion of Ancient Israel*, Moshe Greenberg

2. *Hebrew Poetry in the Middle Ages and the Renaissance*, Dan Pagis

3. *The Promise of the Land: The Inheritance of the Land of Canaan by the Israelites*, Moshe Weinfeld

Moshe Weinfeld

The Promise of the Land

The Inheritance of the Land of Canaan by the Israelites

University of California Press
Berkeley Los Angeles Oxford

University of California Press
Berkeley and Los Angeles, California

University of California Press, Ltd.
Oxford, England

Library of Congress Cataloging-in-Publication Data

Weinfeld, Moshe.
The promise of the land : the inheritance of the land of Canaan by the Israelites / Moshe Weinfeld.
p. cm. — (The Taubman lectures in Jewish studies)
Includes bibliographical references and index.
ISBN 0-520-07510-2
1. Palestine in the Bible. 2. Bible. O.T.—Historiography. 3. Palestine—Boundaries—Biblical teaching. 4. Gentiles in the Old Testament. I. Title. II. Series: Taubman lectures in Jewish studies. Sixth series.
BS1199.P26W45 1993
221.9′5—dc20 91-19827
CIP

Printed in the United States of America
1 2 3 4 5 6 7 8 9

The paper used in this publication meets the minimum requirements of American National Standard for Information Sciences—Permanence of Paper for Printed Library Materials, ANSI Z39.48–1984. ♾

The Taubman Professorship and Lectures

The Herman P. and Sophia Taubman Visiting Professorship in Jewish Studies was established at the University of California, Berkeley, in 1975 by grants from Milton I. Taubman and the Taubman Foundation; an equal sum was contributed by the family of Maurice Amado, Walter A. Haas, Daniel E. Koshland, Madeleine Haas Russell, and Benjamin H. Swig. Distinguished scholars in the fields of Jewish studies are invited to teach at Berkeley for the enrichment of students and to give open lectures for the benefit of the public at large. Publication of the lectures is made possible by a special gift of the Taubman Foundation.

Contents

Acknowledgments

When I was honored to serve as visiting Taubman Professor at the University of California at Berkeley during the spring semester of 1989, one of my duties was to deliver three public lectures. I chose to lecture on the theme of the inheritance of the land of Canaan by the Israelites, a theme that contains a very broad spectrum of issues. Out of the broad range of aspects of this theme that I investigated in the last decade, I decided to take up the following three subjects:

1. the promise of the Land to the Patriarchs and its realization in light of Greek foundation stories;

2. Two Divergent Views concerning the extent of the Promised Land;

3. the ban of the Canaanites, its development, its meaning, and its significance.

I was offered the opportunity to publish these lectures. Since these three lectures are only a part of a very complex subject, I suggested to Professor Z. Brinner, then the head of the department of Near Eastern studies at U.C. Berkeley, that I not limit myself to the publication of the three lectures, but submit for publication the whole theme, including all aspects. This was agreed upon. This book, therefore, contains nine chapters, covering the most significant aspects of the theme.

The three lectures that I delivered at Berkeley served as a point of departure for a comprehensive treatment of the problem of the land of Israel, including a literary investigation and studies of historico-geographical problems, the nature of the historiography, and historical, ideological, and theological dimensions.

I am grateful to my colleagues at Berkeley for the hospitality extended to my wife and me during our stay there. I am grateful to Professor J. Milgrom for the invitation to the Taubman Lectures. Special thanks to Professor Z. Brinner for his initiative in the publishing of the book. I am also deeply grateful to my colleagues D. Asheri of the Hebrew University and E. Gruen of the University of California at Berkeley for their advice concerning the problems connected with the Greek and Roman civilization. Many thanks to my friends Marc Bernstein, John Gee, and P. David Wright for their help in preparing the manuscript for publication, and to Mrs. Rahel Yaniv for her help in preparing the bibliography and for other functions connected with the work.

Many thanks to the publisher E. Peeters for permission to publish here Chapter 1, which has been previously published in *Orientalia Lovaniensia Analecta* 23, Leuven 1988 (edited by M. Heltzer and E. Lipinski). I am also very grateful to E. J. Brill, Leiden, for permission to publish here Chapter 2, which has been published before in *Supplements to Vetus Testamentum* 40 (1988) 270–283 (pages 22–41 here) and in *Vetus Testamentum* 38 (1988) 324–332 (pages 41–51 here). I am also most grateful to my student Paul Friedfertig for his help in preparing the indexes for this book. Last, but not least, thanks are due to the personnel of the University of California Press for their dedication and efficiency in preparing the manuscript for publication.

Abbreviations

AASOR	*Annual of the American Schools of Oriental Research*
AB	Anchor Bible
AcOr	*Acta Orientalia*
AfO	*Archiv für Orientforschung*
ANET	J. B. Pritchard (ed.), *Ancient Near Eastern Texts*
AOAT	Alter Orient und Altes Testament
ARM	Archives royales de Mari
ArOr	*Archív Orientální*
ARu	J. Kohler and A. Ungnad, *Assyrische Rechtsurkunden*
ARW	*Archiv für Religionswissenschaft*
AT	D. J. Wiseman, *The Alalaḫ Tablets*
BA	*Biblical Archaeologist*
BASOR	*Bulletin of the American Schools of Oriental Research*
BBSt	L. W. King, *Babylonian Boundary Stones and Memorial Tablets*
Bib	*Biblica*
BibOr	*Biblica et Orientalia*

BIES	*Bulletin of the Israel Exploration Society (=Yediot)*
BKOT	*Biblischer Kommentar, Altes Testament*
BO	*Bibliotheca Orientalis*
BT	Babylonian Talmud
BZ	*Biblische Zeitschrift*
CAD	*The Chicago Assyrian Dictionary*
CAH	*Cambridge Ancient History*
CBQ	*Catholic Biblical Quarterly*
CTA	A. Herdner, *Corpus des tablettes en cunéiformes alphabétiques*
D	Deuteronomy
EA	J. A. Knudtzon (ed.), *Die El-Amarna Tafeln*
EHAT	Exegetisches Handbuch zum Alten Testament
EI	*Eretz Israel*
FRLANT	Forschungen zur Religion und Literatur des Alten und Neuen Testaments
GAG	W. von Soden, *Grundriss der akkadischen Grammatik*
HAT	Handbuch zum Alten Testament
HKAT	Handkommentar zum Alten Testament
HSS	Harvard Semitic Studies
HTR	*Harvard Theological Review*
HUCA	*Hebrew Union College Annual*
ICC	International Critical Commentary
IEJ	*Israel Exploration Journal*
JANES	*Journal of the Ancient Near Eastern Society of Columbia University*
JAOS	*Journal of the American Oriental Society*
JBL	*Journal of Biblical Literature*

JCS	*Journal of Cuneiform Studies*
JE	Jahwistic-Elohistic source
JESHO	*Journal of the Economic and Social History of the Orient*
JHS	*Journal of Hellenic Studies*
JJS	*Journal of Jewish Studies*
JNES	*Journal of Near Eastern Studies*
JPS	Jewish Publication Society
JQR	*Jewish Quarterly Review*
KAI	H. Donner and W. Röllig, *Kanaanäische und aramäische Inschriften*
KBo	*Keilschrifttexte aus Boghazköi*
KeHAT	Kurzgefasstes exegetisches Handbuch zum Alten Testament
KHC	K. Marti (ed.), Kurzer Handkommentar zum Alten Testament
KS	A. Alt, *Kleine Schriften zur Geschichte des Volkes Israel*
KUB	*Keilschrifturkunden aus Boghazköi*
LCL	Loeb Classical Library
LXX	Septuagint
MDOG	*Mitteilungen der deutschen Orient-Gesellschaft*
MDP	*Mémoires de la délégation française en Perse*
MDPV	*Mitteilungen und Nachrichten des Deutschen Palästina-Vereins*
MGWJ	*Monatsschrift für Geschichte und Wissenschaft des Judentums*
MSL	*Materialien zum sumerischen Lexikon*
MT	Masoretic text
MVAeG	*Mitteilungen der vorderasiatisch-ägyptischen Gesellschaft*

NEB New English Bible
OLZ *Orientalistische Literaturzeitung*
P Priestly Code
PRU *Le Palais royal d'Ugarit*
PW Pauly-Wissowa, *Real-Encyclopädie der classischen Altertumswissenschaft*
RA *Revue d'assyriologie et d'archéologie orientale*
RB *Revue biblique*
RÉJ *Revue des études juives*
RHA *Revue hittite et asianique*
RHR *Revue de l'histoire des religions*
SAKI F. Thureau-Dangin (ed.), *Die sumerischen und akkadischen Königsinschriften*
StBot Studien zu den Bogazköi-Texten
SVT Supplements to Vetus Testamentum
TCL Textes cunéiformes. Musée du Louvre
ThStKr *Theologische Studien und Kritiken*
TZ *Theologische Zeitschrift*
UF *Ugarit-Forschungen*
VT *Vetus Testamentum*
VTE D. J. Wiseman, *The Vassal Treaties of Esarhaddon*
WMANT Wissenschftliche Monographien zum Alten und Neuen Testament
WO *Die Welt des Orients*
VAB Vorderasiatische Biliothek
ZA *Zeitschrift für Assyriologie*
ZAW *Zeitschrift für die alttestamentliche Wissenschaft*
ZDPV *Zeitschrift des deutschen Palästina-Vereins*

Introduction

The fate of the land is the focal point of Biblical historiography. Beginning with the patriarchal stories in Genesis and ending with the destruction of Jerusalem in the book of Kings, the historiography of Israel hinges upon the land. The patriarchal stories envision the promise of the Land to Israel, and the remainder of the Pentateuch—the Exodus, the giving of the Law at Sinai and at the Plains of Moab, and the wanderings in the desert—describe a kind of preparation for the entrance into the Land. The historiography of the books of Joshua through Kings was motivated by a need to answer three questions: Why did the Israelites not conquer the Land in its ideal borders? (Compare Josh. 1:1–4 with Josh. 23:4–5, 13; Judg. 2:11–3:4.) Why was the northern land taken away from the Israelites (2 Kings 17:1–23)? And what was the cause of the fall of Jerusalem (2 Kings 21:11–15)? In this study I attempt to consider all the aspects of the theme of inheritance of the land of Israel: literary, historical, geographical, ideological, and theological.

This investigation begins with the issue of the promise of the land in the patriarchal narratives. As we shall see, the story of the settlement of the Israelite tribes in the land of Canaan unfolds in two stages: a first stage telling us about the first ancestor who leaves his homeland with his family to reach the new destined land, and a second stage, which takes place hundreds of years later, depicting the settlement by descendants of the first ancestor in the destined land. In both stages we find rival traditions both about the location of the events and about the identity of the national hero under whom the events take shape. Thus, in the first stage we find two rival cycles of ancestral stories: the cycle of Abraham, which elevates the place of Hebron in the south as the site of the ancestor, and that of Jacob, which identifies Shechem and Bethel in the north as the sites of the first ancestor. Similarly, in the second stage we find competing claims with respect to Gilgal and Shechem as the place of the foundation ceremony when entering the promised land (compare Josh. 3–5 with Josh. 8:30–35). The traditions also vary in specifying the first settler and conqueror: the northern tradition adopts Joshua, the chieftain of Ephraim (Num. 13:8), as first settler and conqueror, whereas the Judahites adopt Caleb, the chieftain of Judah (Num. 13:6), as first settler and conqueror in the area of Hebron (Judg. 1:12–15, 20).

The first stage—the arrival of the first ancestor with his family—is dealt with in Chapter 1, while the second stage—the national enterprise of the settlement—is discussed in Chapter 2.

Both stages have parallels in the Greek pattern of colonization. The first stage, depicting the first ancestor as migrating with his family to a new land and bearing a mission of becoming a great nation and ruling other peoples (Gen. 12:2; 27:29), is clearly reflected in the *Aeneid* epic. This epic, as we shall see, is based on the Greek pattern of foundation of new sites. The second stage, too, parallels the Greek tradition in which a new colony is established by a group of settlers led by the hero-founder. And as in Israel, rival stories are told in Greece concerning the founding of a new city and the identity of its founder.

The basic elements common to Greek and Israelite settlement are as follows:

1. Consultation of the divine oracle before settlement.

2. Central role of the founder in the settlement.

3. Cooperation of the founder with a priest or seer who guides him.

4. Casting of the lot for division of the land.

5. Erection of pillars, stones, and altars in the new territory.

6. Commitment of the settlers to observe the laws of the deity.

7. Interpretation of the new land as given by divine promise.

Chapter 3 addresses two divergent biblical views concerning the extent of the promised land—the borders of the land of Israel. The priestly school, which originated in Shiloh, delineates borders that exclude Transjordan, south of the lake of Kineret (Num. 34), based on the borders of the Egyptian province of Canaan (during the thirteenth century B.C.E.), which did not include Transjordan. This delineation contradicts the sources that describe the land of Israel as stretching from the river Euphrates to the River of Egypt (Gen. 15:18; compare Exod. 23:31; Deut. 1:7; 11:24; Ps. 72:8), including, of course, the territory of Transjordan. The more inclusive view was adopted by the Deuteronomic school, which sees the beginning of the conquest in the passage of the river Arnon in Transjordan, and not just in the passage of the Jordan.

Chapter 4 discusses the ban (*ḥerem*) of the Canaanites that was a theoretical demand raised by the Deuteronomic school of the seventh century B.C.E. The older sources speak about expelling (*grš*) the Canaanites or dispossessing (*hwryš*) them, but never about exterminating (*ḥrm*) them. The genuine *ḥerem* was an ad hoc institution that applied to specific cases of severe enmity involving fighting, such as at Arad (Num. 21:1–3), Jericho (Josh. 6:17), and Amaleq (1 Sam. 15). The Deuteronomic school, however, applied the *ḥerem* theoretically to the pre-Israelite population as a whole (Deut. 7:2; 20:17–18; Josh. 10:40–41, 11:12–15). In reality, the Canaanites were neither completely expelled nor exterminated, as may be deduced from Judg. 1:21–33 and 1 Kings 9:20–21.

Chapter 5 discusses the complex problem of how the Israelites conquered the land of Canaan: by sword, or by gradual, quiet infiltration? Apparently, one means does not exclude the other; the settlement started quietly, but as it expanded settlers became involved in clashes with the Canaanites. On the other hand, some assimilation did occur, as with the tribe of Judah, which expanded through symbiosis with the Calebites, Kenezites, and Yerachmelites.

Chapter 6 is devoted to various views concerning the campaign to conquer the land. According to the tradition of the house of Joseph and Benjamin (Josh. 2–11), the leader of the tribe of Ephraim was the one who led the campaign. In contrast, according to the tradition of Judah, the conquest was led by the tribe of Judah and Caleb the Kenezite (Judg. 1). The Joseph-Ephraimite tradition prevailed, as edited by scribes in accordance with Deuteronomic commands for the total annihilation (*ḥerem*) of the Canaanites. In the view of these scribes the conquest is seen as a blitz campaign, in which Joshua and "all Israel" conquer the whole land from Baal Gad in Lebanon to Mount Halaq in the south. In this campaign Joshua essentially destroyed the entire native population of Canaan and did not leave any survivors in the land (Josh. 10:28–43; 11:11–23)—a utopian conception that developed during King Josiah's time in the seventh century B.C.E.

Chapter 7 deals with the historiosophy of the period of the conquest and the judges, and especially with the sin of the period of the judges. According to the old historiosophy (Judg. 1:1–2:5), the sin of the Israelites during the period of the judges was non-dispossession of the Canaanites, the previous inhabitants of the land, and intermarriage with them (Judg. 3:5–6), which entailed the worshipping of their gods.

In contrast, the Deuteronomic historiographer, who portrayed the conquest as total extermination of the pre-Israelite population, describes the sin of the period of the judges as worship of the gods of Israel's surrounding countries. Within the land itself, no more non-Israelites survived; all had been exterminated following the Deuteronomic law of *ḥerem*. According to the Deuteronomic editor of the book of Judges, the sin of the Israelites in the period of the judges was not the non-dispossession of the Canaanites, since these had already been annihilated by Joshua. Thus, the non-dispossession—according to this view—was not a sin against God but a punishment from God, and it involved non-dispossession of the inhabitants of the "remaining land" in Lebanon and on the Philistine coast (Judg. 3:1–4).

Chapter 8 treats the theological aspect of the promise of the land and its realization. The Land of Israel was considered a great gift bestowed by God upon the people of Israel—hence the importance of the "Promise of the Land" in the faith of Israel. The Israelites deemed the inheritance of their land a privilege for which they must be worthy. Should they fail to be worthy, the land would be taken away from them as it had been from the Canaanites before them. The danger of exile, to which Israel became exposed following the rise of the Assyrian empire in the eighth century B.C.E., opened a process of national self-examination and led to the recognition that maintaining the land was contingent upon the fulfillment of God's will and his commandments. This recognition served as an impetus for the development of the historiography of ancient Israel as presented in the books of Joshua and Kings. The exile of northern Israel as well as that of Judah was explained in these works as resulting from the sins of the people. An intense feeling of guilt prevailed among the people in exile, which caused them to return fervently to God. Their goal was not the renewed conquest of the land but rather the renewal of the religious center in Jerusalem. The Temple and its sanctity, as well as observance of the Torah, were set forth as the primary objective for the people who returned from exile, and for this cause they were prepared to give their lives. Thus "the Land" became the means to an end and not the end itself. Even when proclaiming war on their neighbors, they were motivated not by a need to conquer portions of the promised land but rather by devotion to God, his Temple, and his law.

Furthermore, toward the end of the Second Temple period there developed a process of spiritualization of the concept of "the land," corresponding to a similar development regarding the concept of Jerusalem. "Inheritance of the Land" was interpreted as inheriting "a share in the world to come" (*ḥlq bʿwlm hbʾ*), just as Jerusalem, the city, acquired the meaning of heavenly Jerusalem. However, in contradistinction to the prevailing tendency in Christianity to strip "the Land" and Jerusalem of their realistic, earthly meanings and to see them merely as symbols, in Judaism the real land and physical Jerusalem were always retained as the basis for the spiritual values and symbols mounted upon them. Without the real Land and the earthly city, Messianic redemption was inconceivable in Judaism.

Chapter 9 treats the nature of the divine covenantal promise to the patriarchs concerning the land. In contradistinction to Sinaitic covenant, in which the Israelites pledge to keep the law of God, in the Abrahamic covenant it is God who commits himself to give the land to the Patriarchs and their descendants. Also, the Sinaitic covenant constitutes *an obligation* of the people, who promise to fulfill the Lord's commandments in the future, while the Abrahamic covenant is a *promise* of God based on Abraham having already proved himself in the past as his loyal servant (Gen. 15:6; 22:18; 26:5). A covenant of the same type is concluded with David, who is promised a dynasty forever (2 Sam. 7) since he proved himself as a loyal servant of God in the past (1 Kings 3:14; 8:18; 9:4, etc.). Both contracts, the Abrahamic and the Davidic, constitute a gift forever and without any condition.

Such legal commitments of the sovereign are found in the Hittite and Assyrian royal grants of land to their faithful servants. Like the covenants of God with Abraham and David, these grants are perpetual and unconditional. And like the Davidic covenant in 2 Sam. 7:14–16 that even if the Judean king sins he will be punished but God's grace (=gift) will never be canceled, we find in the Hittite royal land-gifts that the sovereign will punish the vassal for his sins but will not cancel his commitment. Only after the fall of Samaria and the cessation of the Davidic dynasty were the promissory covenants perceived as conditional, a perception that comes to expression in the Deuteronomic literature.

1

The Patriarchal Stories in the Light of Greek Foundation Stories

As is well known, most of the genres of biblical literature have their counterparts in the ancient Near East. Creation stories, genealogies, legal codes, cultic instructions, temple-building accounts, royal annals, prophecies, psalms, wisdom literature of various kinds—all are widely attested in the cognate literatures from Mesopotamia, the Hittites, and the Egyptians. The only genre lacking such counterparts is that of stories about the beginning of the nation and its settlement, which are so boldly represented in the Patriarchal narratives and the accounts of the Exodus and the conquest of the Land. The contrast is especially striking when we compare the first eleven chapters of Genesis with the rest of the book. In Gen. 1–11 we find stories of creation, the flood story, and lists of world ancestors before and after the flood—literary types all well established in Mesopotamian literature. From chapter 12 onward, however, no parallel with the ancient Near East can be shown—not in content, of course, which reflects the particular nature of Israel, but also not in form. This kind of storytelling might be expected in the great cultures of the ancient Near East, but we look for it in vain. The lack of this genre is quite understandable given that, unlike Israel, the large autochthonous cultures were not cognizant of a beginning of their national existence.

On the other hand, this genre *would* be expected in the Greek sphere, which like Israel was based on colonization and founding of new sites. That the genre of foundation stories was widely popular in the Greek world may be learned from Plato's *Hippias Maior* (285D), where, in response to Socrates' question about what the people liked to hear most, the Sophist replies, "stories about heroes and foundation of cities." I have long suspected that this genre of Israelite literature had much in common with the Greek milieu, especially since this type of storytelling, including the David Court story, crystalized in the Davidic period, when there were contacts with elements originating in the Greek sphere, such as Krethi and Plethi.

My thoughts on this problem took further shape when, more than ten years ago, I participated in a seminar on the *Aeneid* conducted by the late H. Wirszubsky. What concerned me especially in the seminar discussion was the central idea of the work: the mission of Aeneas to found a city that would rule the world, an idea strikingly similar to that found in the book of Genesis, in which Abraham and his seed are to become, like Aeneas, a great nation (*gôy gadōl:* Gen. 12:1 ff.) that will rule peoples (Gen. 27:29).

I have been pondering this question ever since. I had the feeling that the composition of the patriarchal stories is based on a model similar to that of Aeneas. Because the *Aeneid* is modeled on foundation stories prevalent in Greek colonies, the so-called *Ktisissagen,* I saw in the patriarchal stories, with their promises for the inheritance of the land of Canaan, a reflection of the same genre.[1]

1. One must consider, of course, that many different stories had circulated before the epic of Virgil took its present form (see below). However, because we are concerned with the typology of the epic rather than its historical development, we have chosen as a point of departure for this study the richest and most elaborate foundation story, that of Virgil.

The antiquity of the connection between Aeneas and Rome is evident in Hesiod: the tale about the birth of Aeneas is followed by the fate about the birth of Latinus (*Theogony* 1008 ff.).

The typological model investigated here is also reflected in the Greek

I was pleased to discover that one of my colleagues at the University of Tel Aviv, Jacob Licht, was elaborating a similar idea and applying it to the Exodus–Sinai cycle. He suggested that I publish his thesis in a journal I edited, *Shnaton* 4 (1980), which I was eager to do. Licht's point of departure was Deut. 27:9: "Today you have become the people of the Lord your God," which he took as a proclamation of establishment. He rightly connected it with the foundation stories so widespread in the Greek world and so boldly expressed in the Roman epic of Virgil. Both Licht and I drew the same analogy, though from different points of departure: I was asking about the patriarchal promises, while he was interested in the Exodus-Covenant traditions. The two approaches could be combined, as they are in the Pentateuch itself, but my main focus in this book is the Aeneas-Abraham analogy.

In chapter 2, I compare the pattern of Israelite settlement to the pattern of foundation of colonies in the Greek world.[2] Here, however, I concentrate on a typological comparison of the Patriarchal traditions with the rich traditions concerning the ancestors of ancient Rome, beginning with the roles of the ancestor in both cultures.

---

traditions about the return of the *Heraklidai* (the Dorian migration), in which we find the same motifs: promised land, exile for several generations, and divine guidance. But here, too, we have only fragmentary evidence, not a crystalized epic comparable to the Patriarchal narratives.

C. H. Gordon ("Vergil and the Near East," *Ugaritica* 7 [1969], pp. 266–88) adduces a range of parallels, from Abraham to Jesus, to show affinities between the Aeneids, the Bible, and the ancient Near East. He provides a list of common motifs, such as the tree of life (cf. Aen. 6:138 f.); the master who ties his yoked team with reins of vine-leaves (Aen. 6:804 f.; compare Gen. 49:11; *CTA* 19; II:53–55 = *Aqht*); and the offering of seven sacrificial bullocks (Aen. 6:38 f.; compare Num. 23:4, 14, 29). However, in the absence of integration and critical analysis of the material he adduces, his thesis is unconvincing.

2. First published in my article, "The Pattern of the Israelite Settlement in Canaan," in *Congress Volume, Jerusalem 1986,* ed. by J. A. Emerton, pp. 270–83 (Supplements to Vetus Testamentum 40; Leiden, 1988).

1. A Man Leaving a Great Civilization and Charged with a Universal Mission. Aeneas leaves famous Troy and stays for a while in Carthage, which later becomes Rome's great enemy; finally, his son Ascanius reaches Lavinium, and later his son gets to Alba-Longa.[3] His descendants reach Rome, which is destined to rule the world.[4] Similarly, Abraham leaves the great civilization of Mesopotamia, Ur of the Chaldaeans,[5]

3. Virgil begins the poem with a reference to Lavinium (*Aen.* 1:2–3), but when Aeneas's destination is named, it is the Tiber (2:781–82; cf. 7:157 ff.). In *Aen.* 1:267 ff., Jupiter proclaims that Lavinium will be *sedes regni* for thirty years, but then the reign will shift to Alba-Longa. On the whole problem, cf. recently G. K. Galinsky, *Aeneas, Sicily and Rome* (Princeton, 1969), pp. 141 ff.

4. "You shall see Lavinium's city and its promised walls, and you shall raise on high to the starry heavens . . . your son . . . shall crush proud nations . . ." (*Aen.* 1:57 ff.); "from this noble line shall be born the Trojan Caesar who shall limit his empire with ocean, his glory with the stars . . . welcome to heaven, laden with Eastern spoils" (1:286 ff.); "there the house of Aeneas shall rule over all lands" (3:97); "he was to rule over Italy, a land teeming with empire . . . to head on a race from Teucer's noble blood and bring all the world beneath his laws" (4:229 ff.); "remember, you, O Roman, to rule the nations with your sway . . . to impose peace with law . . ." (6:775 ff.).

5. Gen. 11:28–31; 15:7; Neh. 9:7. This is an anachronism, because the Chaldaeans appear in the Mesopotamian documents for the first time in the ninth century B.C.E., and they became rulers of Babylon only in the seventh and sixth centuries. The city of Ur, however, was already known in the third millennium as the center of a great Sumerian empire that reached its peak during the third dynasty of Ur (twenty-first–twentieth centuries B.C.E.). It seems that in the original version of the Patriarchal narratives the Patriarchs came from Haran; Ur of the Chaldaeans, as the place of their origin, was incorporated in a later stage. In fact, according to the ancient (J) layer of the Patriarchal stories, Abraham received the call to leave his homeland (Gen. 12:1) in *Haran* (cf. Gen. 11:31b–32) and not in *'Ur Kasdim;* see my forthcoming commentary on Genesis. From the point of view of typology and pattern, which is the main point of our study, Ur and Haran serve the same purpose: to indicate that the father of the nation comes from a known civilization. Both Ur and Haran served as great centers of culture, and both were associated with the worship of the moongod Sin.

stays for a while in Aram, which later becomes Israel's enemy, and reaches Canaan, the Land of promise, out of which his descendants will rule other peoples.[6]

In both cases we have examples of an ethnic tradition later developed into an imperial ideology; in both, we are presented with a divine promise given to the father of a nation who later becomes a messenger for a world mission. The ancient traditions of Israel, originally bound to the settlement in Canaan, were applied during the Davidic period to the rule of an empire, stretching from the Euphrates to the River of Egypt (Gen. 15:18).[7] By the same token, the traditions about settlement in Latium were applied, during the time of Augustus, to the Roman Empire—Aeneas became not only the father of Rome itself but also a prefiguration of the ruler of the entire world. The prophecy of Poseidon in the *Iliad* 20:307 that Aeneas will rule over the Trojans, *νύν δὲ δὴ* Αἰνείαο *βίη* Τρώεσσιν ἀνάξει (cf. Homeric Hymns, *AD Venerem* 3:196–97), is indeed recorded (reinterpreted) in an oracle in *Aen.* 3:97–98 saying that the house of Aeneas shall rule "over all lands": *hic domus Aeneae cunctis dominabitur oris.*[8]

Before us, then, lies a typological parallel: a man escapes the

6. "I make you the father of a multitude of nations" (Gen. 17:5); "peoples shall serve you and nations bow down to you" (Gen. 27:29); "and the homage of peoples be his" (Gen. 49:10); cf. also Gen. 12:3 and parallels.

7. For *gôy gadôl* implying the Davidic empire, see my article, "The Old Testament: The Discipline and Its Goals," in *Congress Volume, Vienna 1980,* ed. by J. A. Emerton, pp. 423–34 (Supplements to Vetus Testamentum 32; Leiden, 1981). For the Davidic background of the Patriarchal stories, see B. Mazar, "The Historical Background of the Book of Genesis," in *JNES* 28 (1969), pp. 73–83.

8. Strabo, *Geography* 13 1:53 (608) quotes a reading in the *Iliad* 20:307; *πάντεσσΙν* for Γ*ρώεσσιν*: Αἰνείαο γένος πάντεοοιν ἀνάξει; cf. L. Malten, "Aineias," *Archiv fur Religionswissenschaft* 29 (1931), p. 53, and see P. M. Smith, "Aeneadae as Patrons in Iliad XX," *Harvard Studies in Classical Philology* 85 (1981), pp. 17–58.

land of a major civilization and departs with his wife and his father—Abraham with Sarah and Terah; Aeneas with his wife, Creusa, his father, Anchises, and his son, Ascanius[9]—in order to establish a new nation and a new culture. This concept is well expressed by the prophets: "Abraham was but one man, yet he possessed the land" (Ezek. 33:25), and "Look back to Abraham your father . . . for he was only one when I called him, but I blessed him and made him many" (Isa. 51:2). It is interesting that just as Isa. 51:2 and later Jewish tradition refer to Abraham as "father," Virgil calls Aeneas "*pater*" (e.g., 2:2).

2. Gap between Migration of the Ancestor and the Actual Foundation. The Israelites were aware that many years intervened between the promise given the ancestor at the beginning of his migration and the realization of the promise. This lengthy gap is invoked when Abraham is told that 400 or 430 years will pass before his descendants will inherit the promised land (Gen. 15:13; cf. Exod. 12:41). Similarly, Aeneas is told, in the prophecy of Jupiter (1:270 ff.), that 333 years will pass before the birth of the twins—in other words, before the foundation of Rome.[10] The lengthy interval between the stories about the first heroes and the real foundation of the *oikist* (see below) existed in both cultures.[11] The older Romulus

9. Creusa died on Aeneas's way from Troy (2:735 ff.), which can be compared with Rachel's death on Jacob's way from Aram (Gen. 35:16–20; 48:7). For the Jacob cycle as paralleling the Abraham cycle, see below.

Aeneas bearing his father from Troy, and accompanied by his wife and a son is represented in many base paintings and statuettes of Etruscan origin; cf. R. G. Austin, *P. Vergili Maronis Aeneidos II* (Oxford, 1964), pp. 286 ff. See the discussion of N. M. Horsfall, "Enea," in *Encyclopedia Virgiliana* 2 (Rome 1985), pp. 221–29.

10. Cf. N. M. Horsfall, "Virgil's Roman Chronography," *Classical Quarterly* 24 (1974), pp. 111–16.

11. Cf. S. A. Brinkman, "The Foundation Legends in Vergil," *Classical Journal* 54 (1958–59), pp. 25–33. See, recently, A. Momigliano, "How to Reconcile Greeks and Trojans?" in *Mededelingen der Koninklijke Nederlandse Akademie van Wetenschappen. Afd. Letterkunde* N.S. 45/9 (Amsterdam, 1982), pp. 231–54.

story was basically a Latin account, while the Aeneas version had its source in the writings of the Greek poets; during the course of the third century, the Aeneas and Romulus legends began to be combined, and to fill the 400-year lacuna after the supposed landing of Aeneas, a long Trojan dynasty was invoked.

A similar situation is encountered in ancient Israel: the birth of the nation is anchored—according to tradition—in the Exodus and the conquest of Canaan, but the remote ancestor of Israel was sought in Ur and in Aram Naharaim,[12] ancient civilizations on the Euphrates. In late Rome, as well as in later Israel, there was a historical awareness of the chronological gap between the two stages of origin. Aeneas could not personally be considered the founder of Rome, because the destruction of Troy was known on the basis of genealogies to have taken place several hundred years before Rome was founded.[13] The Israelites, too, had been aware of the chronological and historical gap between the Exodus and the conquest of Canaan, on the one hand, and the period of their remote ancestors, on the other. Thus we find in 1 Chron. 7:25–27 ten generations between Ephraim and Joshua, and not four generations as in the Pentateuchal stories. Similar inconsistencies exist in the Roman traditions about Aeneas.[14]

12. For Haran and Nahor as important centers in Upper Mesopotamia at the beginning of the second millennium B.C.E., cf., recently, R. De Vaux, *Histoire ancienne d'Israel* 1 (Paris, 1971), pp. 188–90 and the references there.

13. Cf. D. Asheri, "The Dating of the Fall of Troy in Greek Historiography from Herodotus to Timaeus," in A. Rofé and Y. Zakovitch, eds., *Isaac Leo Seeligman Volume: Essays on the Bible and the Ancient World* 2 (Jerusalem, 1983), pp. 509–23 (Hebrew).

14. According to the Sicilian historian Alcimus (fourth century B.C.E.), Romulus, who was the son of Aeneas, had a daughter named Alba, whose son Romus founded Rome (cf. T. S. Cornell, "Aeneas and the Twins: The Development of the Roman Foundation Legend," *Proceedings of the Cambridge Philological Society* 21 (1975), p. 7), but according to Dionysius of Halicarnassus (1:9:4), there were sixteen generations between Aeneas and Romulus.

Abraham in Israel and Aeneas in Rome belonged, then, to the legendary stage of tradition, in contrast to the actual historical stage of settlement.

Furthermore, just as the Romans adopted the Trojan Aeneas legend from the Greeks, as has been demonstrated by the artifacts from Etruria and by the adoption of the Trojan Penates,[15] the Genesis traditions about the nomadic ancestors of Israel in the Syro-Palestinian area, as well as the traditions about their El-worship in Canaan, seem to have been adopted from peoples who lived in the region before the settlement of the Israelite tribes.[16] As is well known, the Pentateuchal traditions themselves attest that the Patriarchs did not know Yahweh, the name of the national God of Israel (Exod. 6:3 ff., cf. Exod. 3:13–15).

The very name *Jacob* may prove the local nature of the patriarchal traditions. R. Weill has hypothesized that the Israelites received the stories about Jacob—a name known to us as a prince of the Hyksos dynasty, *Yaqob-hr*—from the Canaanites.[17] This theory has recently been confirmed by A. Kempinski on the basis of an investigation of the scarab found in Shiqmonah, inscribed with the name Yaqob-hr.[18] Thus, it appears that the Israelites received from the Canaanites the legends about Jacob who went down to Egypt with the Hyksos.

15. Cf. Galinsky, *Aeneas* (n. 3), list of illustrations, pp. xiii–xxii, 154 ff., and plates. Cf., most recently, *Enea nel Lazio, Archeologia e mito: bimillenario virgiliano* (Rome, 1981). I am indebted to Prof. D. Asheri for the reference to this book.

16. Cf. F. M. Cross, *Canaanite Myth and Hebrew Epic* (Cambridge, Mass., 1973), pp. 1–75.

17. R. Weill, *La fin du Moyen Empire égyptien* (Paris, 1918), pp. 188–91.

18. A. Kempinski, "Some Observations on the Hyksos (15th) Dynasty and Its Canaanite Origins," in S. I. Groll, ed., *Pharaonic Egypt, the Bible and Christianity* (Jerusalem, 1985), pp. 129–37; J. Elgavish, "Shiqmonah," *Encyclopedia of Archaeological Excavations in the Holy Land* 4 (Jerusalem, 1978), col. 1101.

From a purely historical view, the patriarchal age reflects the history of the Syro-Palestinian nomads, which was later adopted by the Israelites and incorporated into their national history. By the same token, the stories about Aeneas have nothing to do with the history of Rome proper but were adopted by the Romans after contact with the Greeks of Magna Graecia.

3. *Promise at Stake.* When Jacob is endangered by the threat of Esau's advancing army, he prays: "Save me from my brother Esau; else I fear he may come and strike me down . . . yet, you have said . . . I will make your offspring as the sand of the sea" (Gen. 32:12–13). Similarly, we read in the *Aeneid* epic that when Aeneas was endangered by the sea storms Venus intervened on his behalf and prayed to Jupiter: "O you . . . who [rule] the world of men and gods, what crime . . . could my Aeneas have done. . . . Surely it was your promise . . . that from them the Romans were to rise . . . rulers to hold the sea and all lands beneath their sway, what thought . . . has turned you?" (1:229 ff).

The promise is seen, then, in Israel, as well as in the Roman epic, as something that could not be taken back: a *divine commitment* not to be violated (cf. Exod. 32:11–14).[19] Connected with the promise at stake are the omens that point to certain difficulties in the realization of the divine promise. An example in the *Aeneid* is the episode of the birds of prey at the sacrificial table: when Aeneas and his men sit at the table with Jupiter, the Harpies (raptors) fall upon the table and with their unclean touch contaminate the dish. Aeneas's comrades drive them away with their swords (3:22 ff.). The onslaught of the Harpies was considered a bad omen, and indeed, after this event the seer Celaens predicts that before Aeneas will finish

19. For the importance of the divine promise of the land in Greek colonization, see Chapter 2.

building the promised city, famine will overtake him and his men.[20] A similar phenomenon is encountered in Gen. 15: when Abraham is cutting the pieces of the sacrificial animals of the Covenant, birds of prey come down upon the carcasses, and Abraham drives them away.[21] Immediately afterward, he is informed that his descendants will be enslaved and oppressed in Egypt before they will reach the promised land (Gen. 15:13).

4. The Pious Ancestor. Abraham is described as God-fearing (*yrʾ ʾlhym,* Gen. 22:12), "walking before the Lord" (24:40), and "listening to his voice" (22:8; 26:5; cf. 17:1), much like David, who is depicted as "walking before God with righteousness and perfection" (1 Kings 3:6; 9:4; 14:8; 15:3; cf. Ps. 132:1; 2 Chron 6:42). It was these moral-religious qualities that made Abraham and David worthy of God's promise for land and kingdom, respectively. Both promises—and only these promises—are defined as *hbryt whḥsd* "the covenant of grace." Furthermore, in connection with the promise of descendants we also find identical phraseology not attested elsewhere: "One of your own issue," *ʾšr yṣʾ mmʿyk,* in 2 Sam. 7:12 and Gen. 15:4.[22] The considerable overlap between the two figures has been noted, and, as I have suggested elsewhere,

20. The religious nature of the banquet is reflected in *Aen.* 3:222: "Calling gods and Jove himself to share . . ." and in l. 231: "we spread the tables and renewed the fire of the altars."

The appearance of harpies and hawks as a bad omen during foundation and colonization is indicated in Callimachus, *Aetia* 2:43: "they were building the walls of the city without guarding themselves against the *harpasos* . . . for it has an evil influence . . . the wings of a hawk . . . if you ever lead a people to a colony [in a foreign land]. . . ."

21. For the sacrificial nature of the cut animals in Gen. 15, cf. S. E. Loewenstamm, "Zur Traditionsgeschichte des Bundes zwischen den Stücken," *VT* 18 (1968), pp. 500 ff.

22. On the Abrahamic and Davidic covenants and their affinities, see below, chapter 9.

Abraham the warrior in Gen. 14 behaves quite similarly to David the warrior in 1 Sam. 30.[23] The suggestion that Abraham is a retrojection of David seems quite plausible, therefore.

The same phenomenon is encountered in Virgil's Aeneid. As Galinsky has suggested, the image of pious Aeneas is a back projection from pious Augustus.[24] Like the Abraham-David imagery in Israel, the Aeneas-Augustus imagery in Rome reflects a later stage of the crystallization of the story. As is well known, the Abraham cycle in Genesis represents a later stage than the Jacob cycle, which appears to be closer to the original tradition and less fragmentary than the Abrahamic stories.[25] The Jacob stories contain motifs that are even closer to the foundation traditions of the Greek-Roman world.

5. The Ancestral Gods. Let us first consider the motif of the ancestral gods transferred to the newly founded site, a motif of extremely ancient origin both in Israel and in the Greek-Roman world. In the journey of Aeneas to Latium, the *di penates,* the Numina guardians of the family, play an important role.[26] They already appear in the accounts of *Hellanicus* (fifth century B.C.E.) and Timaeus (third century B.C.E.), and in Virgil's poem, bringing the gods to Italy appears as the purpose of Aeneas's journey (1:6): "Till he should build a city and bring his gods to Latium" (1:5–6). Troy commits the *sancta* and the Penates to Aeneas's case in order to find for them the city that he shall at last establish (2:293 ff.); the Penates accompany Aeneas and comfort him, as is appropriate for tutelary gods (3:147 ff.).

23. See my short commentary on Genesis, (Tel Aviv, 1975), pp. 68–69 (Hebrew), and cf. recently Y. Muffs, "Abraham the Noble Warrior" *Journal of Jewish Studies* 33 (1982), pp. 81–108.

24. Galinsky, *Aeneas* (n. 3), pp. 3 ff.

25. Cf. Z. Weisman, *The Narrative Cycle of the Jacob Stories and their Integration in the History of the Nation* (Jerusalem, 1986) (Hebrew).

26. On the Penates and their becoming the ancestral gods of Rome, see Galinsky, *Aeneas* (n. 3), pp. 148 ff.

Next to Aeneas on the Etruscan amphora of the fifth century B.C.E. is the figure of a woman—his wife, Creusa—carrying an object shaped like a cushion with stripes, which apparently contained the Trojan sacra.[27] This image reminds us of how Rachel, Jacob's wife, takes with her the *teraphim* (protective family numina) in order to bring them to the new land (Gen. 31:19, 34).[28] Indeed, Josephus recounts a story of a woman taking with her the ancestral images of the gods belonging to her husband, and he adds that it was the custom to take along these objects of worship when going abroad (Ant. 18:344).[29]

Furthermore, according to Plutarch (Camillus 20:6 ff.), the sacra of Troy were stolen by Aeneas, much as the teraphim were stolen by Rachel (Gen. 31:19, 34), another parallel that brings the analogy even closer. The Danites, too, on their way to the new territory in the north, steal the teraphim from Micah's house (Judg. 18:4 ff.).[30] The theft of the sacra from Troy is prevalent in the various traditions about Aeneas (cf., e.g., Dionys. Hal. 1:69:3), which may explain the importance of the thefts of the teraphim by Rachel, on her way to the new land, and by the Danites, when they were leaving to settle their new territory. One should add to the Danite story another motif that belongs to the ktisis pattern: in the Aeneas tradition, we find that six hundred men took care of the Penates in Lavinium (Dionys. Hal. 1:67:2). Similarly, in Judg.

27. Ibid., fig. 45b. Cf. N. M. Horsfall, "Steischorus at Bovillae," *JHS* 99 (1979), p. 40.

28. On the teraphim, see, recently, H. Rouillard and J. Tropper, "*trpym,* rituels de guerison et culte des ancêtres d'après 1 Sam. 19:11–17 et les textes parallèles d'Assur et de Nuzi," *VT* 37 (1987), pp. 340–61.

29. Cf. M. Greenberg, "Another Look at Rachel's Theft of the Teraphim," *JBL* 81 (1962), pp. 239–48.

30. It is interesting to note that in both stories we find similar reactions toward the stealing of the "gods." The Israelite narrator, who is critical of the institution of *teraphim,* reacts in a sarcastic manner: "Why did you steal my gods?" (Gen. 31:30); "You have taken . . . the gods that I made" (Judg. 18:24).

18:16 we find that six hundred Danites guarded the men who took the teraphim.

The story about the settlement of the Danites reflects, then, the pattern of the foundation of a new city, a pattern shared by Israel and Greek world. In later Israel, when the motif of carrying the ancestral gods was blurred because of theological developments, we do not find it in the later Abrahamic cycle, which became dominant in the Patriarchal stories. In the older Jacobic cycle, however, the topic of ancestral gods survived not only as teraphim: in Gen. 31:53 we find Laban and Jacob relying on the judgment of the ancestral deities, *ʾlhy ʾbyhm,* which may have been embodied in the teraphim, Rachel's theft of which was mentioned a few verses earlier.[31]

I would argue that both the "foreign gods" (*elohey nekar*) hidden by Jacob when he arrived at Shechem (Gen. 35:4) and the "foreign gods" removed by Joshua in Shechem (Josh. 24:23) should be identified with the teraphim brought from "beyond the river," where the Hebrews had worshipped "foreign gods," as stated by Joshua: "your forefathers [Terah and Nahor] lived beyond the river and worshipped other gods." Indeed, Joshua asks the people at the gathering in Shechem: "Choose this day which ones you are going to worship: the gods that your forefathers worshipped beyond the river or those of the Amorites . . . but I and my household will worship the Lord" (24:15). Like the Penates in Rome, which constituted the chief private cult of every Roman household and also served as the royal *di penates* (like the royal Vesta) and the *Penates publici,*[32] the teraphim served as a house cult (cf. 1 Sam. 19:13–16) and in official worship as well (Hosea 3:4; cf. Judges 17:5; 18:14–17; 18:20).

In the ancient traditions, the teraphim appear as a legitimate

31. In Akkadian the ancestral gods are also called *ilāni;* cf. A. E. Draffkorn and Kilmer, "Ilāni/Elohim," *JBL* 76 (1957), pp. 216–224.

32. Cf. S. Weinstock, "Penates," in col. 429; A. Alföldi, *Early Rome and the Latins* (Ann Arbor, 1966), p. 246 ff.

cultic object, as may be learned from 1 Sam. 19:13–16, in which we find the teraphim in David's house. Furthermore, it seems that they were kept in the same manner as were the Penates: on the Etruscan amphora of the fifth century B.C.E. we find Creusa carrying the Penates in an object shaped like a cushion, and in 1 Sam. 19:13–16 we read that Michal put the teraphim in David's bed with a goat's-hair cushion (*kebir*) at the head—apparently, Michal took the teraphim out of the cover in which they were stored and, in order to create the impression that David was lying in bed, put the teraphim in the bed with its cover, in the shape of a cushion, at its head.[33] That the teraphim were kept in something similar to a cushion may be deduced from the fact that Rachel hid them in the cushion of a camel (Gen. 31:34): the cushion of the teraphim could be mistaken for the riding cushion of the camel.

6. The Burial Place of the Founder. According to the Jacobic cycle, Shechem was the foundation city where the ancestral gods were hidden and was also the location of Jacob's and Joseph's tombs (Gen. 50:5; cf. 33:19; Josh. 24:32). As has been first suggested by C. Bruston, and later elaborated by S. E. Loewenstamm, according to the old genuine tradition Jacob and Joseph were buried in Shechem, the cradle of the northern Patriarchal tradition (Gen. 50:5), while Abraham was buried in Hebron (Gen. 23).[34] It was the later priestly editor who transferred the burial places of all three patriarchs to Hebron, the former capital of Judah. Indeed, according to the Abrahamic cycle, in which Hebron plays a central role that was superimposed upon the Jacobic cycle, all three patriarchs

33. Compare 2 Kings 8:15: "he took the *mkbr* [quilt/cushion] and after dipping it in water, laid it over the king's face and so [Ben-Hadad] died," which means that he suffocated him with his pillow.

34. C. Bruston, "La Mort et la sépulture de Jacob," *ZAW* 7 (1887), p. 205; S. E. Loewenstamm, "The Death of the Patriarchs in Genesis," *From Babylon to Canaan: Studies in the Bible and Its Oriental Background* (Jerusalem, 1992), pp. 78–108.

were buried in Hebron; the old tradition about Jacob providing himself with a tomb in Shechem, however, is clearly attested in Gen. 50:5 (cf. 33:19).

The tomb of the hero played a very important role in the Greek world;[35] a *heroon,* in other words, a tomb of Aeneas, is mentioned by Dionysius of Halicarnassus (1:64:3) as existing in his own days in Lavinium.[36] Furthermore, as in Israel, where we find a rivalry between Shechem and Hebron concerning the tomb of Jacob, in Rome we are told by Dionysius of Halicarnassus that "though one place received the body of Aeneas, the tombs were many . . . ; he was honored with shrines in many places" (1:54:1). This emphasis on the place of burial explains the importance attached to the tombs of the Patriarchs in Shechem (Gen. 33:19; cf. Josh. 24:32) and in Hebron (Gen. 23).

The transfer of the bones of the hero from a foreign country, which is attested in connection with Jacob and Joseph (Gen. 47:30; 50:25; cf. Exod. 14:19; Josh. 24:32), was also an important matter with the Greek founders. As the bones of Joseph, the ancestor of Joshua, were brought from Egypt to Shechem, we read in Plutarch that the bones of Theseus, the national hero of Athens, were brought from the island of Skyros to Athens (Plutarch: *Theseus* 36). Similarly, we learn in Herodotus that the bones of Orestes, the son of Agamemnon, were sought by the Spartans and brought to Sparta (1:67–68).[37]

7. *Canaan versus Aram, Rome versus Carthage.* An important theme in the *Aeneid* is the tension between Rome and

35. Cf. Herodotus 6:38; Thucydides 5:2:1, and see below, pp. 32–34.

36. Cf. G. K. Galinsky, "The 'Tomb of Aeneas' at Lavinium" *Vergilius* 20 (1974), pp. 2–11; P. Sommela, "Das Heroon des Aeneas und die Topographie des antiken Lavinium," *Gymnasium* 81 (1974), pp. 273–97. On the various theories about the *heroon,* cf. Horsfall, "Enea" (n.9).

37. Cf. also Pausanias 3:3–7; and see A. J. Podlecki, "Cimon, Skyros and 'Theseus' Bones,'" *JHS* 19 (1971), pp. 141–43.

Carthage. There is a danger that Aeneas will marry Dido, the queen of Carthage, and thus that the message of Latium could fail; the gods of Aeneas, therefore, work to bring the hero back on track toward Rome. Mercury, the messenger of the gods, is sent by Jupiter to warn Aeneas not to forget the promise that his mother, Venus, had held out for him, and to urge him to sail at once to his destined land (4:219–37). After Aeneas's delay, Mercury is sent to him again, this time in a dream, and warns him once more to leave Carthage (4:554–70).

A similar situation may be discerned in the Jacob stories. There is the danger that Jacob will stay in Aram Naharaim, where he journeyed to flee from his brother Esau and to marry Laban's daughters. Had he stayed, he would have abandoned his mission to the promised land. Therefore, Jacob is called to return to his native land, and the call is made, as in the *Aeneid,* twice: the first time through direct revelation (v. 4) and the second time through revelation by dream (v. 11). Although in the final stage of Genesis (ch. 31) Jacob is said to leave Aram because of his quarrel with Laban, an older stratum (Elohistic?) in the chapter (vv. 10, 12a, 13) creates the impression that the affluence of Jacob (vv. 10, 12a; cf. 30:43) might have caused him to stay in Aram, necessitating the divine call to return to Canaan.[38]

How do we explain these common features in two works of literature created hundreds of years apart and reflecting two entirely different cultures? It should be clear, first of all, that the Aeneas legend and the stories associated with it are quite ancient and may be traced back—as the various paintings on archaeological artifacts show—to the seventh century B.C.E. That these stories actually belong to the genre of "foundation stories" about foundations of cities by single heroes has been noted by F. B. Schmid, who surveyed the foundation legends

38. For the complexity of the tradition in Gen. 31:1–16, cf. C. Westermann, *Genesis II* (Neukirchen-Vluyn, 1981), pp. 599 ff.

of the Greeks, and observed that the *Aeneid* epic was patterned after them.[39] The main problem we confront, however, when trying to compare the stories about the founder (*Ktistes*) of a Greek colony with the Patriarchal stories is that the Greek stories revolve around founding new cities, while the Patriarchal stories focus on founding a new nation in a new land.

When dealing with the Pentateuchal traditions, we must be aware of the stages in their development, such as the two cycles we have isolated in the Patriarchal Genesis stories, each of which revolves around a different city, Shechem in the northern Jacob cycle, and Hebron in the southern Abraham cycle. Another city in the north about which there is an important foundation legend (Gen. 28) is Bethel; indeed, the Jacob cycle reveals some tension between the cities of Shechem and Bethel, as suggested by the march from Shechem to Bethel after the battle in Shechem in Gen. 35:1–5.[40] Similarly, in Greek tradition, we find a rivalry between Lavinium and Alba Longa; the Penates were removed from Alba Longa but twice returned to their place of origin (Dion. Hal. 1:67:1–3). Furthermore, we find in the Greek foundation traditions disagreements between the settlers about the identity of the founder,[41] a phenomenon also attested in the Patriarchal traditions concerning Beer-sheba and Shechem. According to one tradition it was Abraham who founded the city of Beer-Sheba and gave it its name (Gen. 21:31); according to another, it was Isaac (26:23–33). Shechem was a site of similar controversy: according to Gen. 33:18–20, Jacob built an altar there and called it *El Elohey Israel* (El, the God of Israel), thus establishing for the first time an Israelite cult in a Canaanite city, but according

39. F. B. Schmid, *Studien griechischen Ktisissagen* (diss., Freiburg), 1947; F. Prinz, *Gründungsmythen und Sagenschronologie,* Zetemata 72 (Munich, 1981), is concerned with historical and not typological questions and therefore is less relevant for our purposes.

40. On a separate Bethel tradition concerning the death and burial of Jacob, cf. Loewenstamm, "Death of the Patriarchs" (n. 34).

41. Cf. Schmid, *Ktisissagen* (n. 39), pp. 58–59.

to 12:7, Abraham was the first to build an altar there.[42] These two traditions represent two different sources, which only strengthens the supposition that different circles within Israel claimed different ancestors for the foundation of various sites in the land of Canaan.

It should be noted that the Patriarchs built their altars outside the Canaanite cities,[43] a phenomenon also encountered in the Greek colonization tradition. According to Thuc. 6:3:7, the first Greek settlers in Sicily built an altar to Apollo that stood outside the city (see Chapter 2).

What was the motivation for the creation of these kinds of stories about the first ancestors? Apparently, at the end of the second millennium, the formation of petty states in the eastern Mediterranean area led to the development of the genre of foundation stories as we find them in the Greek sources. Amos 9:7 may serve as evidence: Amos compares the establishment of Israel with the establishment of Aram, originating in Kir, and the establishment of Philistines, coming from Kaphtor. As is well known, the Aramaeans—like the Israelites—formed a league of twelve tribes (Gen. 22:20–24), and as may be learned from Amos's prophecy, they also preserved memories of the native home they had left behind. The same pattern applies to the Philistines, though we do not have precise information about the formation of their league.

The psychology of "foundation" was so deeply rooted in the mind of the people of Israel that even Assyria and Babylonia were depicted as *founded* by one man, Nimrod (Gen. 10:8 ff.; cf. "the land of Nimrod" for Ashur in Mic. 5:5). Nimrod the hero-warrior (*gibbor*) is described as establishing

42. Compare Josh. 8:30: "At that time Joshua built an altar to Yahweh, the god of Israel, on Mount Ebal." For remnants of a cultic Israelite site on Mount Ebal of the twelfth century B.C.E., cf. A. Zertal, "An Early Iron Age Cultic Site on Mount Ebal: Excavation Seasons 1982–1987," *Tel-Aviv* 13–14 (1986–87), pp. 105–65.

43. Cf. Gen. 12:6: "he [Abraham] passed . . . as far as the site of Shechem," and Gen. 33:18: "he [Jacob] encamped before the city."

his kingdom in Babylon, Erek, and Akkad, and from there departing to *build,* as it were, the colonies in Ashur, and especially the large city of Ashur. The verb "to depart" (*yṣ*ʾ, *hlk*) from a certain place, coupled with "to build a city" (*bnh* ʿ*yr*) and the mention of its name, is characteristic of stories about founding a new settlement and is especially attested in connection with the Danites in Judg. 18:27–29 and with the cities founded in Transjordan (Num. 32:24–32).[44] Here, the formulation is very close to that of the Greek settlers, who speak about founding a city (not a land) and naming the city after the *oikist.* It is also reflected in Gen. 4:16 ff.: "Cain 'departed' (*yṣ*ʾ) . . . settled . . . and built a city . . . called the name of the city."

This psychology was evident as late as Josephus, who in his account about the beginning of Jerusalem (*Bellum* 6:438 ff.) relates that Malki-zedeq was the first to officiate as priest in Jerusalem (cf. Gen. 14:18), to build the temple there, and to call the city Jerusalem. In other words, Malki-zedeq was the founder of Jerusalem.[45]

The genre of foundation stories consists of two parts: the first part describes the migration of the ancestor, and the second describes the settlement. In contrast to Joshua, the settler, Abraham is a wanderer. The story about Aeneas reflects—as interpreted by Schmid—the legend about the hero-ancestor and not about the oikist who was the settler. In Israel as well as in Rome, the epic composers were aware—as indicated above—of the chronological-historical gap between these two stages. Just as Aeneas is the first ancestor of the nation, "the pater," and not the first settler, so is Abraham "the father"—and not, like Joshua, the conqueror and settler.

In contrast to the period of a wandering family, as repre-

44. Cf. Chapter 3.

45. Cf. remarks of B. Mazar, "Josephus Flavius, the Historian of Jerusalem," in U. Rappaport, ed., *Josephus Flavius—Collected Papers* (Jerusalem, 1982), p. 2 (Hebrew).

sented in the Patriarchal stories as well as in the *Aeneid,* the period of settlement involves the establishment of a policy of law and civil order. Therefore, after Romulus, the settler, comes Numa, the founder of the religious-cultic institutions. In Israel, these two figures correspond to Joshua and Moses, only in reverse order: first Moses, the legislator, and then Joshua, the settler. In one respect Romulus parallels Moses and not Joshua, and that is in the legend of exposure: like Romulus and Remus, who are cast into the Tiber and then rescued, Moses is cast into the Nile and rescued.[46]

Two stages in the tradition of colonization can also be discerned in other cultures of the eastern Mediterranean area, as, for example, in the history of the foundation of Carthage. Carthage was founded in 814 B.C.E., but tradition related its foundation to Azoros (= Zor) and Carchedon (= Carthage) of the late thirteenth century, as told by Philistos of Syracuse in the first half of the fourth century B.C.E.[47] The same pattern applies to Mopsos, the eponymous hero of "the house of Mpš" in Cilicia, whose heroic deeds belong to the second millennium B.C.E.; the actual ethnic existence, however, of Mopsos's people (= the Danunians in the Karatepe inscriptions) is attested in the first millennium.[48]

The two stages of the colonization tradition recognizable in ancient Israel, ancient Rome, Carthage, and the house of Mopsos may reflect a certain historical process. C. R. Whittaker has demonstrated in his elaborate study of the Western

46. For the various legends of exposure in the ancient world see Th. H. Gaster, *Myth, Legend and Custom in the Old Testament* 1 (New York, 1969), p. 78.

47. F. Jacoby, *Die Fragmente der griechischen Historiker* (Berlin-Leiden, 1923) 2 B, no. 556, F 47; cf. G. Bunnens, *L'expansion phenicienne en Mediterranee* (Brussels, Rome, 1979), pp. 127–28.

48. Cf. H. Donner and W. Röllig, eds., *Kanaanäische und aramäische Inschriften* (=*KAI*) (Wiesbaden, 1969), 26A, col. 1, 16; 2, 15; 3, 2. Cf. for discussion M. Astour, *Hellensoemitica* (Leiden, 1965), pp. 53 ff. See, recently, F. Bron, *Recherches sur les inscriptions pheniciennes de Karatepe* (Geneva, Paris, 1979), pp. 172 ff.

Phoenicians and their colonization that both the Greeks and the Phoenicians refer to two phases of Phoenician colonization.[49] The first phase comprises the beginning of a connection with the indigenous population (for purposes of trade), which is followed by a second phase involving a great influx of new settlers into the area and representing real colonization. These two stages are reflected in the traditions of both Roman and Israelite history; this chapter has examined the first stage, and in Chapter 2 we will look at the second stage, which also parallels the Greek colonization traditions.

Here I note that the pattern of three patriarchs embodied in the Patriarchal narratives of Genesis also has roots in the Greek world of colonization. The Greeks preserved the concept of *tritopateres* (= πρώτοιἀρχηγέται)[50] connected with the hero cult in the Greek settlements: special *heroons* were dedicated for the *tritopateres* and, as eponymous ancestors, they were the objects of special veneration, invoked in worship as the protectors of the colony, as will be discussed in Chapter 2. The three Israelite patriarchs were similarly invoked in time of crisis (cf. Exod. 32:13; Lev. 26:42; Deut. 9:22) and had a renowned tomb in Hebron (Gen. 23).

49. C. R. Whittaker, "The Western Phoenicians: Colonization and Assimilation," *Proceedings of the Cambridge Philological Society* (1974), pp. 58–79.

50. Cf. I. Malkin, *Religion and Colonization in Ancient Greece* (Leiden, 1987), pp. 206–12.

2

The Pattern of Israelite Settlement

A Comparison with the Pattern of Greek Colonization

As has been shown in the first chapter, in Israel as well as in the Aegean world there existed two stages in the crystallization of traditions related to the beginning of settlement in a new land. The first contains legendary stories of the first ancestor-hero who, with his family, arrives at the new settlement, while the second recounts the history of his descendants, who settle under the direction of a founder (*ktistēs*). In both the Hebrew and Greek cultures, we find that a gap of several centuries separates the first and second stages.

The discussion in this chapter concerns the second stage of the traditions: that of group settlement, for which an identical model can be found underlying both the Israelite and Greek traditions. This model is based on the assumption that all settlement is directed by the divine will and must comply with a series of sacred regulations. Thus, in both cultures, we find that priority was given to the erection of a temple on the site of the new settlement and to the division of the land among the tribes by means of divine lot. For example, in the *Laws* of Plato (745 b–c), we find a description of the founding of a settlement that shows surprising similarity to the account of the Israelite settlement and the division of the land by lot (before the Lord) in the book of Joshua. In Plato's *Laws* we read that "the lawgiver must found his city as nearly as possible in the center of the country . . ."; first, an acropolis (temple) must be established, and then, "starting from this [the acropolis] he must divide up both the city itself and all the country into twelve portions. . . . And he must divide the citizens also into twelve parts. . . . After this they must also appoint twelve allotments for the twelve gods, and name and consecrate the portion allotted to each god, giving it the name of 'phyle' [tribe]."[1] A similar procedure is reflected in the description of the division of the land in Josh. 18, where the tent of meeting is set up, after which the land is "written" (= delineated; see below) according to the inheritances of the tribes and divided up by lot before the Lord, at Shiloh (vv. 2–10).

This basic pattern of settlement, which includes the erection of a temple and the division of the land by lot, can be found earlier, in Homeric literature.[2] For example, we read in the *Odyssey,* book 6, lines 7 ff., that "Nausithous, the god-like man, brought the Phaeacians out from the enslavement to the Cyclopes,[3] led and settled them in Scheria, built a wall around their city . . . erected temples to the gods and divided the fields among them."

Also, we find in the *Laws* of Plato that the land was sacred to the gods and must remain the possession of the family to whom it had been allocated by lot, and "therefore the man who buys or sells the house-plot or land-plot allotted to him must suffer the penalty attached to this sin. The officials shall inscribe on tablets of cypress-wood written records for future

1. Loeb Classical Library.

2. On the reliability of Homer's descriptions in connection with the settlements, see H. Schaefer, *Probleme der Alten Geschichte, Gesammelte Abhandlungen und Vorträge* (Göttingen, 1963), pp. 362 ff.

3. Cf. the liberation of Israel from Egypt.

reference, and shall place them in the shrines" (741 c). This rule reminds us of the Israelite laws concerning the retaining of property within the tribe (Lev. 25:23; Num. 36).[4]

In both cultures, one must distinguish between events reflecting actual, historical processes in the development of settlement and the schematic descriptions of settlement as presented by narrators, editors and ideologues. For example, the description of Plato to which I have referred is undoubtedly idealistic-utopian in character,[5] as are the rest of his writings that are concerned with a program for establishing an ideal, reformed society. Nevertheless, the events he interweaves into his program, such as the erection of a temple in the new settlement and the distribution of the land by lot among the settlers, have their origin in the historical reality of Greek colonization. Evidence for this can be provided from the section quoted from Homer on Nausithous, who settled his men in Scheria, and from the various inscriptions relating to new settlements, to which I refer below.

The same distinction is true for Israel. For example, in Josh. 18:1–10 the priestly description of the setting up of the tent of meeting at Shiloh and of the casting of the lot before the Lord there, in order to allocate the land, is schematic-utopian in character, in keeping with the basic outline of the Priestly Code in the Pentateuch.[6] As will be indicated below, the description of the apportionment of the land underwent a process of nationalization and schematization. What originally constitutes a tribal area and a specific zone—the territory

4. In ancient Greece we also find the conception that the land was given to the tribes by the gods. Thus, we read the inscription from Colophon at Lydia: "It was decided by the people to include within the area of the city, in addition to the present city, the ancient city which the gods gave to our ancestors so that they might build altars and temples"; see B. D. Meritt, "Inscriptions of Colophon," *American Journal of Philology* 56 (1935), p. 361; see also below, p. 37.

5. Cf. G. R. Morrow, *Plato's Greek City* (Princeton, 1960), pp. 121 ff.

6. See M. Haran, "Behind the Scenes of History: Determining the Date of the Priestly Source," *JBL* 100 (1981), pp. 321–33.

around Shiloh on Mt. Ephraim—turned into the center of the whole tribal league of Israel.

This process of elaboration and schematization continued until the end of the monarchy. For example, in Ezekiel's program for Israel's restoration (40–48)[7] the land for the tribes in the future is apportioned not before the Tabernacle of Shiloh as in Josh. 18, but in Jerusalem, the central holy city in Ezekiel's time (45:1–8; 47:13–48:35). In place of the tabernacle placed in the midst of the "camp of Shiloh" (Josh. 18:1–9; cf. Judg. 21:12), we find in Ezekiel the house/temple in the midst of the city of Jerusalem (45:1–8; 48:8–22).[8] Further, a development occurred in Ezekiel concerning the extent of the land apportioned to the tribes. Cisjordan, in Ezekiel, contains not only the nine and a half tribes as in Num. 34:13–15 and Josh. 14:1–5, but all twelve. The basis for this interpretation lies in the priestly Shilonite delineation of the borders of the promised land, which does not include Transjordan (Num. 34:2–12; cf. Ezek. 47:13–23).[9] But whereas the old priestly literature accepts the fact of tribes settled in a part of the land that does not belong to the promised land proper,[10] Ezekiel's idealistic picture of the future incorporates all twelve tribes within the legitimate territory of Israel.

In spite of the elaboration and schematization of the original image of allotment of the land before the Lord in Shiloh, there is no reason to doubt the existence of a sacral center in Shiloh

7. For an analysis of these chapters, cf. M. Haran, "The Law Code of Ezekiel XL–XLVIII and its Relation to the Priestly School," *HUCA* 50 (1979), pp. 45–72; M. Greenberg, "The Design and Themes of Ezekiel's Program of Restoration," *Interpretation* 38 (1984), pp. 181–208.

8. This shift from "camp" (*maḥăneh*) to "city" (*ʿîr*) brought with it a new exegesis of the old priestly laws concerning purity and impurity in the area surrounding God's abode; cf. Y. Yadin, *The Temple Scroll* I (Jerusalem, 1977), pp. 215 ff. (English transl., 1983, pp. 277 ff.).

9. See B. Mazar, "Lebo-hamath and the Northern Border of Canaan," *The Early Biblical Period, Historical Studies* (Jerusalem, 1986), pp. 189–202.

10. See Chapter 3.

that served the settlers in Mt. Ephraim for the purposes of inquiring of God and casting the lot (see Judg. 21:19–23; 1 Sam. 1).

The basic elements of the settlement process in both the Israelite and Greek traditions can be enumerated as follows:

1. Inquiry at the Shrine. The new settlement had to be formed in accordance with a divine word mediated through prophecy.[11] Analogous to the typical Greek question posed by Dorieus at the oracle of Delphi, "if he should win the land whither he was preparing to go" (Herodotus, 5:43), are the questions posed by the Israelite settlers, such as:

> The Israelites inquired of the Lord, 'Which of us shall be the first to go up against the Canaanites and attack them?' The Lord replied, 'Let (the tribe of) Judah go up. I now deliver the land into their hands.'
>
> (Judg. 1:1–2)

> 'Please, inquire of God; we would like to know will the mission on which we are going be successful?' 'Go in peace,' the priest said to them, 'the Lord views with favor the mission on which you are going.'
>
> (Judg. 18:5–6)[12]

The place to which one came to inquire for advice concerning settlement was the prominent central shrine: in Greece the

11. E.g., Herodotus relates how Dorieus led a group of Spartans to a new settlement without inquiring at the Delphic Oracle or carrying out any of the usual customs (such as taking along the sacred fire and offering sacrifices) (5:42). On the use of prophecy for the purposes of settlement, see H. W. Parker and D. E. W. Wormell, *A History of the Delphic Oracle* (Oxford, 1956), pp. 71 ff.; J. Fontenrose, *The Delphic Oracle* (Berkeley, 1978), pp. 137 ff.

12. The question "whether the mission on which we are going will be successful" accords with the question to the Greek oracles "will I succeed in such and such a place [of settlement]?"; see Fontenrose, *Delphic Oracle* (n. 11), p. 441.

oracle at Delphi, and in Israel the shrine at Shiloh. As I. Finkelstein has shown,[13] Shiloh was the principal sacred place of Mt. Ephraim and had more than a hundred settlements around it. The most important part of Shiloh itself was the sacred site in which cultic tradition was perpetuated from the Middle Bronze Age onward.

2. Priestly Guidance. From these sacred places came divine instructions for the settlers through the priest or prophet who guided the founder. We find in Israel that Joshua was subject to divine law as mediated by Eleazar, the priest (Num. 27:19–22). Eleazar divided the land by lot before the Lord in Shiloh (Josh. 19:51; cf. 14:1, 14; Num. 26:1, 63; 32:2, 28; Josh. 18:1–10) and, together with Joshua, allocated the cities of refuge (Josh. 21:1). Phinehas, the son of Eleazar, also acted from Shiloh when he remonstrated against the erection of an altar east of the Jordan (Josh. 22:13, 30, 32).

Similarly, from the Greek inscriptions of Cyrene (see n. 16) we learn that Onymastos, the "seer," accompanied Battos, the founder of the settlement, and after his death was honored with a sacred grave, as was Battos.[14] This reminds us of the burial traditions of Joshua and Eleazar in Josh. 24:30–33. These accounts of cooperative activity in Shiloh are rooted in the priestly tradition, and there is no trace of them in the Deuteronomic tradition. While they underwent a process of elaboration in the course of the crystallization of the priestly literature, a process that went on for centuries,[15] it cannot be claimed that they are the invention of scribes. The parallel from ancient Greece could show us that cooperative activity of the "founder" and the priest, who came from the central shrine

13. I. Finkelstein, ed., "Excavations at Shiloh, 1981–1984: Preliminary Report," *Tel-Aviv* 12 (1985), pp. 123–80.

14. See W. Leschhorn, *Gründer der Stadt* (Stuttgart, 1984), pp. 67–68.

15. See M. Haran, "Shiloh and Jerusalem: The Origin of the Priestly Tradition in the Pentateuch," *Tarbiz* 31 (1962), pp. 317–25 (Hebrew) (= *JBL* 81 [1962], pp. 14–24, in English).

(at which the people inquired of the god), was a common phenomenon in the founding of settlements in the Eastern Mediterranean.

3. Divine Obligations. The compliance of the settlers with divine instructions, which stands out in the biblical traditions, is also reflected in the Greek settlement traditions. On a stele from Cyrene, which mentions the grave of Battos, the founder, alongside that of the "seer" from Delphi (see above), we find sacred laws,[16] whose contents have much in common with those of the Pentateuch. The laws on the Cyrene Stele open with a regulation concerning atonement sacrifice: a red goat is to be slaughtered for apotropaic purposes before the city gate (§ 1), which reminds us of the red heifer, slaughtered outside the camp (Num. 19).[17] This is followed by laws of impurity and purity in connection with a man having sexual intercourse with a woman and about a woman in childbirth (§ 3; cf. Lev. 15:16–18; 12:1–8). Juxtaposed is a law on the defilement of graves (§ 4, see below). The following paragraphs deal with the purification of the altar (§ 5; cf. Ex. 30:10; Lev. 16:18; Ezek. 43:18–27),[18] with matters of tithing and

16. U. v. Wilamowitz, "Heilige Gesetze, Eine Urkunde aus Kyrene," *Sitzungsberichte Akademie Berlin Phil.-hist. Klasse 1927,* pp. 155–76; K. Latte, "Ein Sakrales Gesetz aus Kyrene," *Archiv für Religionswissenschaft* 26 (1928), pp. 41–51; M. P. Nilsson, *Geschichte der griechischen Religion* 2[3] (Munich, 1974), pp. 73 ff.; R. Parker, *MIASMA, Pollution and Purification in Early Greek Religion* (Oxford, 1983), pp. 332–51. Although the inscription is from the fourth century, according to scholars, the laws themselves are ancient.

17. See the discussion by Latte, "Sakrales" (n. 16), pp. 41–42. There he comments on the parallel with Num. 19:1. The surprising fact that the ceremony is carried out not by Aaron but by Eleazar, who appears at the beginning of the section, can be explained with the help of the Greek stele where Onymastos from Delphi appears as the supervisor of matters of ritual, parallel with the figure of Eleazar, see above.

18. As in Ezek. 43:23 the ceremony of purification in the Cyrene stele is accompanied by a sacrifice without blemish (*βοτὸν τέλευν* = *par ben-bāqār tāmîm*).

consecration, connected with the value of a man (§§ 7–10; cf. Lev. 27) and with matters of refuge, including the refuge of a murderer[19] (§§ 17–19; cf. Num. 35; Deut. 19:1–13).[20] The laws open with the words of Apollo, who says that the regulations that he is issuing are for those coming to settle in the land of Libya. This recalls the opening found frequently in the biblical laws, "when you come into the land." The success of the settlers depends on their observance of the laws of Apollo,[21] which again recalls the warning in the priestly literature that the land will spew out those who settle on it if they do not fulfill the commandments of God (Lev. 18:28).

Apollo of Delphi was apparently of Eastern rather than Greek origin,[22] and in connection with the Amphictyonic

19. Here the murderer seeking refuge stays at the gate of the city, where he requests permission for refuge from three representatives of the city and three representatives of the tribes; cf. Josh. 20:4. Cf. my book *Justice and Righteousness in Israel and the Nations* (Hebrew) (Jerusalem, 1985), p. 73. The one seeking refuge (in Cyrene) sits at the threshold where he is washed and anointed (*νί*]*ζεν χαὶ χρῖσαι*); see Latte, "Sakrales" (n. 16), p. 49. Compare on this matter the house of Ekur in Sumer, which was some sort of refuge where clean clothes were laid on the altar in readiness for those whose sentence had yet to be decided. See references in my book *Justice and Righteousness*, pp. 58–59.

20. We find similar instructions in the inscription from the Island of Kos; see R. Herzog, *Heilige Gesetze von Kos* (Berlin, 1928). Here also we find instructions regulating various atonement and purification ceremonies, and warnings for priests against contact with dead bodies or graves and against entrance into a house where there is a corpse (§ 5). Likewise, there are laws of refuge regulating the shelter of the murderer, the runaway slave, and other types of exile (§ 13).

21. Cf. the oath of the founders from Cyrene: "According to the promise of success which Apollo made to Battos and the men of Thera who settled on Cyrene, as long as they fulfilled the covenants which their ancestors made"; see R. Meiggs and D. Lewis, *A Selection of Greek Historical Inscriptions* (Oxford, 1968), no. 5, lines 7–9; Wilamowitz, "Kyrene" (n. 16), p. 172: "Der Gott verspricht ihnen Libien zu behaupten, wenn sie die religiösen Pflichten nachkommen, auf die er Wert legt."

22. See U. v. Wilamowitz, "Apollon," *Hermes* 38 (1903), pp. 575 ff. Since then, more evidence on this matter can be adduced: (1) Apollo, like the Mesopotamian god Šamaš, is in charge of the oracles and signs of

oath, which was a kind of oath taken by devotees of Apollo of Delphi, we hear that the breaking of this oath would bring about a curse from the god, reminiscent of the biblical curse: "the land will not bear produce, the women will not give birth, and the cattle will not reproduce" (Aeschines 3:110–11). The same curses appear within the framework of the blessings and curses in the ceremony between Mt. Gerizim and Mt. Ebal (Deut. 27–28). There we read "Blessed shall be the issue of your womb, the produce of your soil and the offspring of your cattle" (28:4), and the diametrically opposite curse, "Cursed shall be the issue of your womb, the produce of your soil, the calving of your herd and the lambing of your flock" (28:18).[23]

In the foundation document at the Temple of Delphi, many details recall the customs of the Israelites upon their settlement in the land. For example, the members of the Amphictyonic League swore to punish anyone who violated the sanctity of the shrine at Delphi or was an accessory to such violation (Aeschines 2:115), and indeed Aeschines tells us of a city that was guilty of violating the shrine, and when the Pythia was asked about this matter she answered that they should make war against the city, ravage it, enslave its inhabitants, and

---

prophecy, and is identified with the sun. (2) Apollo is identical with the Mesopotamian god Nergal and the Canaanite god Rešeph; see my article, "Divine Intervention in War in Ancient Israel and in the Ancient Near East," in H. Tadmor and M. Weinfeld, eds., *History, Historiography and Interpretation* (Jerusalem, 1983), pp. 113–27. Like these gods, Apollo possessed a bow and arrows, and his arrows sent a plague on both man and beast. (3) The Muses sang of him in the choir alternately (= one voice answering the other, *Iliad* 1:603), as in the song of the angels in Israel and the ancient East. See my article "The Heavenly Praise in Unison," *Meqor Hajjim Festschrift für G. Mollin* (Graz, 1983), p. 427, and on the matter of the Muses, see p. 434.

23. For the place and significance of the set of blessings and curses in Deut. 27–28, see my article, "The Emergence of the Deuteronomic Movement: The Historical Antecedents," in N. Lohfink, ed., *Das Deuteronomium, Entstehung, Gestalt und Botschaft* (Leuven, 1985), pp. 78–80.

dedicate the land to Apollo, and that the land should never be cultivated again (Aeschines 3:107–09). At the time that this punishment was being inflicted, it was declared that any city that would not go to war against those who desecrated the holy place would be excommunicated from the shrine and cursed (3:122).

A parallel custom can be found in connection with the war against the inhabitants of Gibeah, who "committed an outrage in Israel" (Judg. 20–21). Like the tribes of Greece, who consulted the oracle before making war on those who violated the shrine, the Israelite tribes inquired of the Lord before going to war against Gibeah (Judg. 20:18, 27) and, as in Greece, the Israelites attacked the city, utterly destroyed it, and burned it down "completely" (vv. 40, 48).[24]

The Greek Amphictyons destroyed the treacherous city of Cirrha, executed its inhabitants, and denounced with a great oath any person who should rise and rebuild it (Aeschines 3:108), which recalls the oath of Joshua against Jericho (Josh. 6:26). In Israel as in Greece, condemnation (*ḥērem*) fell upon a city that refused to take part in the Holy War (Judg. 21:5–12). We hear of action taken against those transgressing against the assembly and its shrines in Israel, in the account of the erection of an altar east of the Jordan, which was considered an act of rebellion against the Lord (Josh. 22:19 ff.); the assembly of Israel gathered to make war on Gad and Reuben and to destroy their land (vv. 12, 33).[25]

I do not intend here to take up the analogy of the amphic-

24. Cf. Deut. 13:17 on the excommunicated city: "you shall burn the town . . . completely (*kālîl*) to the Lord your God, and it shall remain an everlasting ruin (*tēl ʿôlām*)," and Deut. 29:22: "it shall be devastated . . . beyond sowing and growing." Cf. the parallels with the ban of the Greek Amphictyony (a prohibition on plowing the land of a rebellious city). It appears that they did the same to Gibeah (cf. the ban on Jericho).

25. The expression *la ʿălôt laṣṣābāʾ . . . lᵉšaḥēt ʾet-hāʾāreṣ* is analogous to what we find in Aeschines in connection with the punishment of a treacherous city in the Amphictyonic covenant: *ἀναστήδειν*, "to wage war"; *στρατεύσειν*, "to raise an expedition" (Aeschines 2:115).

tyony as M. Noth has done in *Das System der zwölf Stämme Israels* (Stuttgart, 1930). Unlike Noth, I am interested not in analyzing the nature of the tribal federation of Israel, but rather in examining the regulations and procedure connected with the founding of a new society in a new settlement, and in showing the surprising analogy between the Israelite and Aegean worlds. As mentioned above, scholars have recognized the Greek practice associated with Apollo at Delphi as a foreign influence. If this is so, it is also possible that the practice was crystalized in the Orient and from there brought to Greece.[26] Elsewhere, I have discussed the dramatization of the curses, found in the oath of the founders of Cyrene, which accords with the enactment of the curses in the covenants of the ancient East. Especially instructive is the dissolving of the figurines of wax in the covenant ceremony, which has the purpose of illustrating the fate of someone who violates the covenant.[27]

4. The Founder's Tomb. The tomb of the "founder" was especially venerated in Greek culture,[28] as is evident in the

26. The institution of the Amphictyony and all that is connected with it, particularly as it crystalized in the shrine at Delphi, had its basis in the Orient. See, for example, F. R. Wüst, "Amphiktyonie, Eidgenossenschaft, Symmachie," *Historia* 3 (1954–55), p. 137. Wüst sees the source of the Amphictyony in a Greek league of tribes built according to a model that was accepted in Anatolia during the Hittite period. On the Amphictyony in the Hittite world see E. von Schuler, *Die Kaškäer* (Berlin, 1965), pp. 165–66.

27. Cf. my article "The Loyalty Oath in the Ancient Near East," *Ugarit-Forschungen* 8 (1976), pp. 400–401.

28. E.g., Herodotus 6:38 and Thucydides 5:11. The Greeks used to offer sacrifices to the souls of the founders and to pour oblations of blood on the tombs of the heroes. (See Leschhorn, *Gründer der Stadt* (n. 14), pp. 98 ff.) Also, competitions were organized in their memory. Importance was attached in this cult to the ceremony of the "memorial of the names" of the founders and their invitation to a cultic feast; cf. the Mesopotamian ritual of *kispu*. This ceremony is also known from the Hittites and perhaps passed from them to Greece. The Hittites called on

traditions of the founding of Cyrene. Battos, its founder, was venerated as a hero after his death, and therefore a grave was assigned to him in the center of the city.[29] Nearby were the graves of Onymastos, the "seer" from Delphi, and of the "three ancestors" (*tritopateres*),[30] as attested in the inscription of the sacred laws from Cyrene.[31]

---

the names of the Hittite kings who had died and invited them to the sacrifice. See L. Christman-Franck, "Le Rituel des Funerailles Royales Hittites," *Revue Hittite et Asianique* 29 (1971), pp. 61–111, and cf. the Aramaic inscriptions of Panamua, *KAI* 214, 15–17; J. C. Greenfield, "Un rite religieux araméen et ses parallèles," *RB* 80 (1973), pp. 46–52. This ritual can also be recognized in Babylonia in connection with the Hammurabi dynasty. See J. J. Finkelstein, "The Genealogy of the Hammurapi Dynasty," *Journal of Cuneiform Studies* 20 (1966), pp. 95–118. A ceremony for the memorial of names of the deceased kings of Ugarit can also be found. The kings were called *rpi arṣ* (RS.34.126). See P. Bordreuil and D. Pardee, "Le rituel funéraire ougaritique RS.34.126," *Syria* 59 (1982), pp. 123 ff. *rāpāʾ* is similar to the Greek ἥρως which has the meaning of both "hero" and "spirit of the dead."

When it was not clear who the real founder was, they used to invite the founder anonymously. In Zancle there was a tradition of various founders: "Let him who built our city come graciously to the feast [sc. of the founders]" (Callimachus, *Aitia* 2, fr. 43, 81–82), and see F. B. Schmid, *Studien zu griechischen Ktisissagen* (diss., Freiburg, Schweiz, 1947), pp. 58–59. In the memorial ceremony of the names of the Hammurabi dynasty, we find a similar form of address: "The dynasty which has been mentioned . . . and the dynasty which was not mentioned here . . . come, eat and bless the King"; J. J. Finkelstein, pp. 95–97, lines 29 ff.

29. The veneration of the grave of Battos is mentioned in Pindar: ἥρως . . . λαοσεβής (Pyth. 5, 49 f.); and there is also archaeological evidence for the existence of the hero-worship of Battos; see Leschhorn, *Gründer der Stadt* (n. 14), pp. 98 ff.

30. τριτοπατέρες were the first founders (πρώτοι ἀρχηγέται) of the ethnic group which is under discussion and they addressed them as the defenders of their descendants. See A. B. Cook, *Zeus* 3 (Cambridge, 1940), pp. 120 ff.; P. Kretschmer, "Zu *Glotta* 9, S. 208," 10 (1920), pp. 39 ff. For the correspondence between the τριτοπατέρες and the three patriarchs of Israel, see above, pp. 21.

31. See Leschhorn, *Gründer der Stadt* (n. 14), p. 67. These graves were distinguished from others there in that they did not defile the settlement. Cf. Tos. Baba Batra 1:11: "All the graves were cleared out, apart from

Similar traditions were preserved in Israel. According to one such tradition, preserved in the LXX, the flint knives used to circumcise the Israelites at Gilgal were placed in the grave of Joshua.[32] Juxtaposed to this we find brief notices of the transfer of the bones of Joseph to Shechem and of the grave of Eleazar, the priest, whose function was parallel to that of Onymastos, the "seer" from Delphi.

The transferring of the bones of the "founders" was an accepted custom in Greece. Analogous to the incident of the conveying of the bones of Joseph, the ancestor of Ephraim, from Egypt to Shechem (Josh. 24:32) is the account in Plutarch of the bones of Theseus, the hero from Athens, which were brought from Syracuse to Athens.[33] Also, Herodotus relates how the bones of Orestes, son of Agamemnon, king of Mycene, were brought to Sparta by the Spartans (1:67–68).

5. Naming the Land. Before embarking on a campaign of conquest, the Israelites would send spies to search out the land (Num. 13–14; Josh. 2; Judg. 18). After sending the spies and receiving divine counsel on how to control the area, they would begin to build the settlement and give the place a name. This typology is preserved in both Israel and Greece.[34] In biblical literature, one can discern a literary pattern in the

---

those of the king and the prophet . . . the graves of the house of David and of Huldah the prophetess were in Jerusalem and no one ever touched them." (See also Yerus Nazir 9:3, 57d; Aboth de-Rabbi Nathan 35 version A [ed. S. Schechter], p. 104.)

32. On the nature and reliability of this tradition, see A. Rofé, "The End of the Book of Joshua According to the Septuagint," *Shnaton* 2 (1977), pp. 217–27 (Hebrew).

33. Theseus 36, and see A. J. Podlecki, "Cimon, Skyros and 'Theseus' Bones,'" *Journal of Hellenic Studies* 19 (1917), pp. 141–43.

34. For this typology in the Israelite tradition in the light of the settlement of the tribe of Dan, see A. Malamat, "The Danite Migration and the Pan-Israelite Exodus-Conquest—A Biblical Narrative Pattern," *Biblica* 51 (1970), pp. 1–16. For the Greek tradition, see J. Graham, *CAH*² III 3 (1982), pp. 143–52.

stories of settlement in a new area, as is evident in the stories of the settlement of the tribe of Dan (Judg. 18:2, 5, 28–29; cf. Josh. 19:47). We find a similar pattern in connection with the settlement east of the Jordan, which, as will be demonstrated in chapter 3, had its origins in the migration of settlers from west of the Jordan (Num. 32:41–42).

The custom of naming a new settlement after the eponymous ancestor of the tribe, as in the settlement of Dan, or after the founder himself, as in Num. 32:41–42, is found in the area of Greek colonization,[35] as is the practice of changing the name of a settlement, as in Num. 32:38 (see Plato, *Laws* 704a; Herodotus, 4:147, 4).

6. Dividing the Land. In Israel as in Greece, the division of land among the settlers was by lot and each inheritance was of equal value.[36] Thus, an inferior property had to be larger in size than one of superior quality: "The city and all the land must be divided into twelve portions which are made equal by decreasing the size of the portions which contain good land and by increasing the size of those whose land is of an inferior quality" (Plato, *Laws* 745b). The division of the land of Canaan among the tribes of Israel was interpreted similarly: "the allotments should be fixed rather by valuation than by measurement" (*Ant.* 5:78); according to Rabbinic tradition, " 'Each portion shall be assigned by lot, whether for larger or smaller groups' (Num. 26:56)—this tells us that the Land of Israel was divided equally: according to evaluation (*šmywn*)" (Sifre Numbers 132).

Parallel procedures are found in measuring the land for the division. Joshua sent three men from each tribe to "write down" (= record) the land in order to divide it by lot (Josh. 18:4–10). A similar system was practiced by the Greeks. In the

35. I. Malkin, "What is a Name? The Eponymous Founders of Greek Colonies," *Athenaeum,* NS 63 (1985), pp. 114–30.

36. See Graham, *CAH*^{2} (n. 34), p. 151.

declaration of the settlement of Brea (445 B.C.E.), we read that ten men from each tribe (*phyle*) were chosen as *geonomoi* for the purpose of dividing the land.[37] Juxtaposed to the subject of land-division is a paragraph on the selection of a site for the shrine and its precincts,[38] which reminds us of the juxtaposition of the description of the erection of the tent of meeting with the account of the division in Josh. 18:1–10.

7. Divine Promise. The most surprising analogy is between the promise of land to the Greek settlers by Apollo and to the Israelite settlers by YHWH. Apollo not only directs the division of the land by means of the casting of the lot in his shrine, but also promises the land with an oath to the settlers. Thus Callimachus, a poet born in Cyrene, sings: "Apollo swore that he would establish the land of Cyrene, the oath of Apollo is valid forever" (Hymn to Apollo 5).

8. Setting Up Stones. In the Greek tradition of colonization, we find that the first settlers used to erect pillars of stone and monuments at the conclusion of their journey (e.g., Strabo 3:171, and cf. Herodotus 2:102–3),[39] a custom which is reflected in the setting up of stones at Gilgal by the people of Israel at the end of their migration (Josh. 3–4) and in the setting up of stones on Mt. Ebal (Deut. 27:1, 8; Josh. 8:30–35) on the day they passed over the Jordan (Deut. 27:2–3), which was "as soon as you come into the land which the YHWH your God is giving you" (v. 3).[40] This reminds us of the sacred laws on the stele at Cyrene which open with the words of

37. R. Meiggs and D. Lewis, *A Selection of Greek Historical Inscriptions to the End of the Fifth Century BC* (Oxford, 1969), no. 49.

38. I. Malkin, "What Were the Sacred Precincts of Brea?" *Chiron* (1984), pp. 43–48.

39. Cf. E. Norden, *Die germanische Urgeschichte in Tacitus Germania* (Leipzig, Berlin, 1922), pp. 183 ff.

40. See M. Haran, "Shechem Studies," *Zion* 38 (1973), pp. 8 ff. (Hebrew).

Apollo saying that the laws which he commanded were given so that they would be fulfilled in the new settlement of Libya (see section 3).

9. Building an Altar. The erection of an altar by Joshua on Mt. Ebal outside Shechem also belongs to the typology of "foundation of settlements" (*κτίσις*) as it is found among the Greeks. Thucydides relates that the first Greeks who arrived in Sicily settled at Naxos (eighth century B.C.E.) where they built an altar to Apollo, the founder, which stood outside the city (1:4:6) and which for centuries was visited by pilgrims (*θεωροί*) on their way to Greece (1:4:6). Similarly, we read in the inscription from Colophon, at Lydia, that the ancient city (which was outside the existing city of the day) was given by the gods to their ancestors, so that they might build altars there (see above, n. 4).

The altar on Mt. Ebal, the construction of which was connected with Joshua and which, in the opinion of A. Zertal, has now been discovered, must be understood in a similar manner.[41] The ancient altar ascribed to Joshua, was situated outside Shechem but for centuries was considered sacred to the Israelites and received special veneration during the period from Hezekiah to Josiah, a period of renaissance for the traditions of northern Israel (see the article cited in n. 23). Mt. Ebal is interwoven into an account of the offering of burnt-offerings and sacrifices of well-being (Deut. 27:6–7; Josh. 8:31). Similarly, in the Greek foundation traditions, we find the offering of sacrifices. For example, in connection with the establishment of Messene, it is related that Epaminondas and his men

41. Josh. 8:30, which begins with the words "Then (*'āz*) Joshua built," reflects an archival (ancient) formula. On the subject of these formulas, which open with the words "Then" (*'āz*) or "In his days" (*b^eyāmāw*), see J. A. Montgomery, "Archival Data in the Book of Kings," *JBL* 53 (1934), pp. 46–52. For a discussion of the discovery of the altar on Mt. Ebal, see A. Zertal, "An Early Iron Age Cultic Site on Mount Ebal: Excavation Seasons 1982–1987," *Tel-Aviv* 13–14 (1986–87), pp. 105 ff.

offered sacrifices to Dionysus and Apollo on the day the city was founded, and on the following days built walls around the city and houses and temples within it (Pausanias 4:27).

Also belonging to this context is the tradition of the writing of the Law on the stones on Mt. Ebal (Deut. 27:1–8).[42] As we have seen, in Cyrene, besides the stele of the founders, which concerned the obligations connected with settlement, there was another stele containing sacred laws, which the god Apollo commanded the settlers to observe on their arrival in the land of Libya (see above). In light of this, it seems that the divine laws written on the stones at the time of settlement were an integral part of the foundation ceremony and not an invention by the author of Deuteronomy. Certainly, "all the words of this law" (i.e., the entire book of Deuteronomy), written—as it were—on the stones, reflects the tendentiousness of the author of Deuteronomy, but the tradition itself of writing on stone monuments or on the stones of the altar on Mt. Ebal seems to have been ancient and already laid down before the author of Deuteronomy.[43]

The traditions of the setting up of stones at Gilgal to mark the beginning of the settlement (Josh. 3–4) and the erection of an altar on Mt. Ebal at the entrance into the inhabited land (Deut. 27:1–8) have their source, therefore, in the typology of the foundation ceremonies as preserved by the ancient Greek historians. The description of the ceremony at Gilgal seems to have had its source in the shrine of Gilgal in Benjamin, whereas the account of the Shechem ceremony originated at the sanctuary at Shechem on Mt. Ephraim, and we have a sort of competition between the shrines of the various tribes over the original site at which the foundation ceremony of the

42. On the Deuteronomic reworking of this tradition, see my *Deuteronomy and the Deuteronomic School* (Oxford, 1972), pp. 164–66.

43. See Haran, "Shechem" (n. 40). I therefore withdraw the claim I made in my book *Deuteronomic School* (n. 42), pp. 146–66, that the writing on the stones was an addition made by the author of Deuteronomy.

settlers in the land took place. The foundation ceremony at Gilgal is marked by the setting up of stones, circumcision, and celebration of the Passover (Josh. 5), while the ceremony at Shechem is marked by the setting up of stones and an altar, the making of a covenant (Josh. 24),[44] the reading of the words of the Law, and the declaration of the blessings and the curses (Deut. 27; Josh. 8:30–35). As we have seen, the Greek settlers at Cyrene were also obligated by their god to keep his commandments, and in another place we heard how failure to fulfill the covenant will invoke the curse of the deprivation of issue of the womb, seed of the earth, and offspring of cattle, as in the curse of Deut. 28:18.

The tradition of the sanctuary at Shiloh followed a different pattern. Although based on the typology of the founding of a new settlement, this tradition reflects the priestly aspect of the settlement: the relationship of the settlers with the central shrine, around which they dwell and from which they receive divine instructions. Among the settlers in Shiloh were priests who were concerned that the tabernacle of God should first be set up among the people as the place where they could receive divine confirmation concerning settlement and cast the lot to distribute the land among the tribes and families. The leader or founder was commanded to obey both the priest who officiated at this shrine and its sacred laws and to tend the graves of the founder and of the priest-prophet to whom the founder was subordinate (Josh. 24:30, 33). The elements laid down in the basic pattern of the founding of a settlement, such as inquiring as to the word of the Lord, casting lots for the land, erecting altars, and hewing stone monuments on the site of the settlement, all seem to reflect historical events, but they also underwent a process of nationalization and schematization, especially in the Israelite tradition. What had belonged for-

44. According to Josephus, the stones at Gilgal were used for building an altar like the ones on Mt. Ebal (Josh. 8:30–32), and as at Shechem sacrifices were offered on it (*Ant.* 5:20).

merly to the specific locality of Mt. Ephraim or of the tribe of Benjamin came to devolve upon Israel as a whole.

The Israelite traditions, which belong to a much earlier period than those of the Greeks, may help us arrive at a better understanding of the development of the Greek traditions of the foundation of settlements, which are known to us only from the beginning of the seventh century onward. It seems that, after the destruction of Troy and the collapse of the kingdoms of the eastern Mediterranean, the various ethnic groups followed a fixed procedure in their settlement, which included the following elements:

1. The obtaining of oracular confirmation for the settlement.

2. The erecting of monuments and altars and the offering of sacrifices on arrival at the new place of settlement.

3. The allocating of the land by means of divine lot.

4. The obligating of the settlers to observe the divine laws given to them.

5. The according of a prominent position to the leader-founder.[45]

6. The cooperation of the leader-founder and the priest of the central shrine, whose graves are to be especially revered by the settlers.

The question is not so much a matter of the influence of one culture upon another as of regulations for settlement in a new

45. Like Joshua, the founder in Greek colonization was divinely inspired and thus with both we find a combination of functions in their role as founder: (a) leadership of the people in war and settlement, (b) the building and establishment of the settlement, (c) responsibility for the legislation and administration. See Leschhorn, *Gründer der Stadt* (n. 14), p. 90. In the Greek tradition as in the Bible, these different stages are a result of the historical development of the figure of the leader.

place that were generally accepted throughout the Mediterranean area. This practice of settlement, which was based on empirical reality, was transmitted through folk legends and tales that were reworked in literary form and gradually developed into an epic of national creation. Such stories of the formation of settlements found acceptance among the people, a fact which is attested in Plato. When asked by Socrates what people love to hear more than anything else, Hippias replies, "They are very fond of hearing about the genealogies of heroes and men and the foundation of cities in ancient times" (Greater Hippias 4:285).[46]

Historical Facts behind the Israelite Settlement Pattern

In the previous section, I analyzed the typology of the conquest and presented a conventional pattern of settlement that was prevalent in Greece and in ancient Israel. I did not, however, investigate the possible historical reality behind this pattern, an inquiry that I shall undertake here as a continuation of the previous study, with reference to the events that shaped the settlement model.

The Camp Formation. A basic feature in the typology of the conquest is the movement of people in camps toward their destination. This is best exemplified in the story about the expedition of the Danites (Judg. 18). The Danites set out on their journey to Laish with their children, their cattle, and their household goods in front (Judg. 18:21). In a period parallel to that of the settlement of the Israelite tribes, the Sea Peoples used to travel in a similar manner as they migrated into the areas of Syria and Palestine in search of new lands in which to settle. In an inscription of Ramesses III (1194–1162 B.C.E.), it is

46. See also Strabo 10:3,5; Polybius 34 1:3.

related that the Sea Peoples, organized militarily, set up camp at Amurru,[47] and in some drawings on the wall of the Temple of Ramesses III in Medinet Habu these people are depicted as moving with women and children in wagons harnessed to oxen. From these illustrations we can learn that these Sea Peoples, like the Israelites, set out on expeditions for the purpose of settlement.[48] As A. Malamat has shown,[49] the Pentateuchal stories of the tribes of Israel in their encampments on their way toward the promised land in order to settle there parallel, from a typological point of view, the story of the migration of the tribe of Dan, and they are based on the model under discussion here: a wandering group of people, on their way to settle in a new land. Yet it seems that on their arrival in the promised land the migrating tribes intended to settle in unoccupied territory rather than in the cities that were already inhabited, and only after confrontation with the inhabitants of the cities were they forced to resort to warfare and military conquest. The same applies to the Sea Peoples, who also, as I have already suggested, had the goal of settlement, and it was only after they had been settled by Pharaoh of Egypt in the coastal cities that they became a prominent political force in the area.[50]

47. W. F. Edgerton and J. A. Wilson, *Historical Records of Ramses III, The Texts of Medinet Habu* (Chicago, 1936), pp. 49 ff.

48. For a discussion of this matter, see N. K. Sandars, *The Sea Peoples, Warriors of the Ancient Mediterranean 1250–1150 B.C.* (London, 1978), pp. 120–21, 169.

49. *Israel in Biblical Times* (Jerusalem, 1983), pp. 149 ff. (Hebrew); see also "The Danite Migration and the Pan-Israelite Exodus-Conquest—A Biblical Narrative Pattern," *Biblica* 51 (1970), pp. 1–16.

50. Sandars correctly observes in *Sea Peoples* (n. 48), pp. 169–70, that the Philistines did not intend to settle along the coast at all, but rather to take possession of the areas further inland; the Philistine cities were situated at some distance from the coast.

See papyrus Harris I from the period of Ramesses III: W. Ericksen, *Papyrus Harris I* (Brussels, 1933), = *ANET*², p. 262; cf. A. Alt, "Ägyptische Tempel in Palästina und die Landnahme der Philister," *Kleine Schriften* 1 (Munich, 1953), pp. 216–30.

In light of all this, one must consider seriously the various descriptions of the "camps" in the books of Joshua and Judges, for they can provide us with reliable information about the way in which the tribes of Israel settled during the period in which they established themselves in the land. In these books we read of the following camps: the camp of Gilgal (Josh. 2–10); the camp of Makkedah (Josh. 10:21); the camp of Shiloh (Josh. 18:1–10; Judg. 21:12) and the two camps of Dan (Judg. 13:25; 18:12).

It appears, from the description of the census of the people of Israel in the Wilderness (Num. 1–2; 10:11–29), that there were camps for the various tribes or groups of tribes. If we attempt to relate the camps enumerated above to the various tribes, it appears that the camp of Benjamin was at Gilgal (see below), the camp of Ephraim at Shiloh, the camp of Dan at Kiriath-jearim, and the camp of Judah at Makkedah (see Josh. 15:41), and it was only after the tribes achieved political unity that Gilgal and Shiloh were understood as the camps for all the tribes of Israel. The preeminence of the house of Eli, on the one hand, and the prominence of Ephraim, on the other, caused Shiloh on Mt. Ephraim to be viewed by tradition as the camp of (all) Israel (Josh. 18:9; Judg. 21:12), for it was there that the people of Israel erected the tent of meeting and began, under the leadership of Joshua and Eleazar the priest, the division of the land by lot before the Lord (Josh. 18:1–10; 19, 51; 21, 1–2).[51] Apparently, it was only after the enthronement of Saul at Gilgal that this camp, which belonged to Benjamin, of Saul's tribe, was understood to be the central Israelite camp.

After the enthronement of David, the tribe of Judah became the leading camp of Israel. In the description of the standards

51. Eli was the last judge (1 Sam. 4:18), whose sons were to have officiated after him in a priestly capacity. Thus there occurred a transition from spontaneous to institutionalized leadership by succession similar to that of the monarchy. Similarly, Samuel was the successor of Eli. See T. Ishida, *The Royal Dynasties in Ancient Israel* (Berlin, 1977), pp. 26–31.

of the people of Israel in the Wilderness, in Num. 1–2, we find that the standard of the camp of Judah is mentioned first, followed by the standards of Reuben, Ephraim, and finally, Dan. In this description, whose source is the priestly circles of Judah (P), the camp of Judah has priority (instead of the camp of Benjamin at Gilgal). The camps of Ephraim and Dan continue to hold a superior position,[52] as before, while the camp of Reuben represents the camp east of the Jordan (Reuben and Gad), to which Simeon in the south is attached.[53] A reference to the camp of the Israelites on the east bank of the Jordan is preserved for us in the biblical tradition of the encampment of Israel in the steppes of Moab: "They encamped by the Jordan from Beth-jeshimoth as far as Abel-Shittim, in the steppes of Moab" (Num. 33:49). According to a southern (Benjamite) tradition, the people of Israel set out from Shittim for Gilgal by way of the Jordan River (Josh. 3:1), which reminds us of a passage from the prophecy of Micah: "From Shittim to Gilgal" (6:5). Gilgal as a center from which Israelite tribes set out to conquer the west bank of the Jordan also appears in Judg. 2:1: "An angel of the Lord came up from Gilgal to Bochim." It seems, however, that the Israelite tribes were actually concentrated not in this area but in the Valley of Sukkoth, which is north of Shittim and Gilgal. This seems to be reflected in the Inscription of Merneptah: "Gezer has been taken, Yenoʿam has been made as that which does not exist. Israel has been laid waste, his seed is not."

52. Dan appears here together with the northern tribes, Asher and Naphtali, which shows us that, at the time of the composition of this list, Dan was already situated in the north, as in the list of Num. 13:4–15 and in contrast with that of Num. 34:21–23, where Dan appears between Benjamin and Joseph.

53. On the Mosaic league in Transjordan, see D. N. Freedman, "The Poetic Structure of Deuteronomy 33," in *The Bible World: Essays in Honor of C. H. Gordon* (New York, 1980), pp. 28–30. On the general view of Freedman concerning the pre-monarchic period, which reflects Albright's attitude, see the collection of Freedman's articles in *Pottery, Poetry, and Prophecy: Studies in Early Hebrew Poetry* (Eisenbrauns, Winona Lake, Ind., 1980).

Yenoʿam is identified with Tell El ʿAbeidiyeh, south of Chinnereth,[54] and the name "Israel," which appears after Yenoʿam, must therefore be east of the Jordan.[55] According to B. Mazar, the inscription refers to a settlement of Israelite tribes in the Valley of Sukkoth.[56] Penuel, which is near Sukkoth, is considered in folk tradition to be the place where the angel appeared to Jacob, changing his name to Israel (Gen. 32:29).[57] This may mean that the name "Israel" is anchored in the first tribal federation of Israel on the east bank of the Jordan. Mazar also connects to this area the settlement of Adam (= Tell ed-Dāmiyeh) in the Jordan region (Josh. 3:16; Ps. 78:60), where, in his opinion, the altar was erected by the tribes east of the Jordan, provoking the tribes west of the river to prepare for war against their brothers in the east (Josh. 22:9–34).

It is also possible that the story of Mahanaim in the Valley of Sukkoth, in which Jacob divides his people into two camps (Gen. 32:8), reflects the ancient reality of the existence of Israelite camps east of the Jordan analogous to those on the west bank. The existence of an Israelite camp in the area of Sukkoth may be reflected in Ps. 78:60: "he forsook the tabernacle of Shiloh, the tent he had set (*ʾhl škn*) *bʾdm* (= in Adam)."[58] Besides the tabernacle at Shiloh, there was a tent at Adam, i.e., the tent of the Israelite at the city of Adam, which paralleled the tabernacle of Shiloh at the Shilonite camp.

54. Cf. Y. Aharoni, *The Land of the Bible: A Historical Geography,* 2d ed., A. F. Rainey, ed. and transl. from Hebrew (London, 1979), p. 33. According to N. Na'aman, "Yenoʿam," *Tel-Aviv* 4 (1977), pp. 168–77, it is to be identified with Tell-Esh-Shihab, west of Edrei on the Yarmuk river.

55. Cf. Na'aman, ibid., p. 171.

56. B. Mazar, "Biblical Archaeology Today—The Historical Aspect," *Biblical Archaeology Today* (Jerusalem, 1985), pp. 16–20.

57. The LXX omitted the phrase "he called his name Israel" in Gen. 35:10 because it contradicts Gen. 32:29.

58. See S. D. Goitein, "The City of Adam in the Book of Psalms," *Bulletin of the Israel Exploration Society* (*Yediot*) 13 (1947), pp. 277–79 (Hebrew), and Mazar's comment on this article on pp. 17–18.

It would appear that a division of opinion existed among the Israelite tribes over the sanctity of the camp east of the Jordan, and that the Shilonite priests, who claimed exclusive sanctity for the camp of Shiloh, declared the area east of the river to be unclean (Josh. 22:19) and did not include Gilead within the framework of the borders of the promised land (see Num. 34:1–12).[59] This priestly circle, which stands behind the Priestly Code, did not accept the tradition of Penuel as the site of the revelation to Jacob in which his name was changed to Israel, and transferred this event to Bethel (Gen. 35:9–13).

In any event, the tradition of a "camp of Israel" in the periods of the wilderness wandering and settlement (Josh. 6:18, 23) reflects a historical situation in which the settlers organized themselves into camps as they set out to settle in a new land. However, whereas in the actual period of settlement there were separate camps for the various tribes, in later times the tribes described themselves as one camp of Israel (e.g., Gilgal), from which all Israel's allied tribes went forth to war and to which they returned (Josh. 4:19; 5:10; 9:6; 10:6, 15, 43).

This organization into camps was a military one for the purpose of forestalling enemy attack on the way, since the Israelite settlement was connected with warfare, as were many of the Greek settlements whose program involved warfare and the expulsion of the indigenous population.[60] For example, the tribe of Dan settled in the north after attacking the inhabitants of Laish with the sword and burning down the city (Judg. 18:27), and the people of Ephraim settled in Bethel only after they had razed it to the ground, smiting the inhabitants of the city with the sword (Judg. 1:24–26). It seems that other cities on Mt. Ephraim, such as Tappuah (Josh. 12:17), became the possession of the settlers by means of warfare.

However, these cases were essentially different in nature

59. On this matter, see Chapter 3.

60. On the military enterprises of the founder, see Leschhorn, *Gründer der Stadt* (n. 14), and the references there.

from the descriptions of the great conquest, as we have them in Josh. 1–11. As is well known, the conquests of Jericho and Ai are problematic from both the archaeological and the literary (etiological) points of view. On the other hand, the great wars of the south (Josh. 10), and at the Waters of Merom in the north (Josh 11:1–15), were fought after the settlement and as a consequence of its expansion. These wars took place after the tribes of Mt. Ephraim and the Galilean mountains had succeeded in gaining a foothold in the area and, as a result of this expansion, came into conflict with the Canaanite centers (see below).

The Development of the Tradition about the Founder. The Gilgal tradition linked Joshua to Gilgal and to the erecting of the stones there, whereas in the Shechem tradition Joshua was linked to Shechem, where stones were erected on Mt. Ebal and an altar was built. We are thus confronted with two competing traditions among the Israelite tribes—Ephraim (or rather, Joseph) and Benjamin—concerning the place where the act of foundation occurred. In fact, it seems that neither Gilgal nor Shechem was originally connected with Joshua; by the time Joshua was drawn to these two sites, they were already important places—one as the point of crossing of the Jordan and the other as the central city of Mt. Ephraim.

What, then, was the genuine place of Joshua's activity? How did it happen that Joshua turned into the founder and conqueror on a national scale?

In the Greek traditions of colonization we find three stages in the development of the image of the founder. In the first stage, he appears as leader of the expedition of a group of settlers; in the second stage, he is the builder of the city and its temple; and in the third stage, he appears as legislator and administrator concerned with the welfare of the settlement.[61]

61. B. Virgilio, "I Termini de Colonizzazione in Erodoti e Nella Tradizione Preerodotea," *Atti Della Academia Delle Scienze di Torino II,*

In fact, what we have here is the merging of various figures who were active in the foundation of the settlement over a considerable period of time into one central figure.

The same process may be discerned in the crystallization of the figure of Joshua in the Israelite traditions. In the original tradition, Joshua was the founder of a particular settlement, which he established and where he lived and was buried. In the course of time, on account of his particular success, his name became associated with the central city in the area and its shrine, and finally he became identified as the founder and legislator of the whole nation. Let me explain the process.

According to Josh. 19:50 Joshua built the city of Timnath-ḥeres/seraḥ in Mt. Ephraim and settled in it: "at the command of YHWH they gave him the town that he asked for, Timnath-seraḥ in the hill country of Ephraim; he built the town and settled in it"; and according to Josh. 24:30 he was buried in the same city (cf. Josh. 24:29–30; Judg. 2:9).

As will be shown in chapter 3, the phrase "he built . . . and settled" (*wybn wyšb*) is characteristic of the tradition of the foundation of new settlements, and the marking of the famous grave also belongs to the foundation typology. Timnath-ḥeres is related to the region of Mt. Ḥeres, which extended as far as the valley of Aijalon and Shaalbim, as may be learned from Judg. 1:35.[62] According to that verse, the Amorites who dwelt

---

Cl. de scienze mor., stor. e fil. 106 (1972), pp. 354 ff., 496 ff. This is exemplified by Battos, the founder of Cyrene, who was originally the ἀρχηγέτης or ἡγεμών i.e. the leader of the colonists, then became also the founder of the colony (οἰκιστής) and finally was seen as the king (βασιλεύς) of the polis; see Leschhorn *Gründer der Stadt* (n. 14), p. 70.

62. Cf. Z. Kallai, "The Settlement Traditions of Ephraim—A Historiographical Study," *ZDPV* 102 (1986), pp. 68–74; I. Finkelstein, S. Bunimowitz and Z. Lederman, "Excavations at Shiloh, 1981–1983" *Qadmoniot* 17, no. 1 [65] (1984), pp. 15–25 (Hebrew); I. Finkelstein and A. Brandl, "A Group of Metal Objects from Shiloh," *The Israel Museum Journal* 4 (1985), pp. 17–26.

in Mt. Ḥeres, Aijalon, and Shaalbim pushed the Danites into the hill country, but the Amorites were later dispossessed by the house of Joseph. Taking into account the tradition described in Josh. 10:10–14 about Joshua's pursuit of the Amorites from Gibeon along Beth-ḥoron as far as Aijalon, we may legitimately surmise that the victory of Joshua, the leader of the house of Joseph (cf. Josh. 17:14–18), is connected with the dispossession of the Amorites depicted in Judg. 1:35 (see Kallai [n. 61]).

The settlement of Timnath-ḥeres was made through oracular inquiry: "at the command of YHWH they gave him the town that he asked for" (Josh. 19:50); and similarly, we find in the tradition of Greek colonization that oracular responses from Delphi came mostly *post factum,* after the site for settlement was chosen, as was the case with Joshua. It is possible that at this early stage Joshua consulted the priests of the shrine of Shiloh, which served as a sacred site for the whole area from ancient times, as I. Finkelstein has recently suggested.[63]

The settlement of this area, which took place after a struggle with the Amorites, gave Joshua a reputation as a successful conqueror, thus bringing about his integration into the story of the fierce battle against the Amorite coalition led by the king of Jerusalem (Josh. 10:1–14), which resulted in a great victory for the Israelites. On account of this victory, Joshua was accorded the title of leader of the "house of Joseph" at Shechem, the central city of Mt. Ephraim, and in this capacity he came to be associated with the foundation ceremony at Mt. Ebal (Josh. 8:30–35) and the enactment of the covenant at the shrine of Shechem (Josh. 24). Later, the final victory at Hazor was ascribed to him (Josh. 11:1–15). In the course of time, during the days of Saul at the Gilgal shrine, it would seem that a cycle of traditions developed connecting Joshua with Gilgal, ascrib-

63. "Excavations at Shiloh 1981–1984: Preliminary Report," *Tel-Aviv* 12 (1985), pp. 159 ff.

ing to him the position of the supreme conqueror.[64] In these traditions he was also made the leading figure in the foundation ceremony at Gilgal, where the stones were erected, and the initiator of the ceremony of circumcision,[65] which was followed by the Passover offering (Josh. 5), two rituals basic to the religion of Israel. In the Gilgal cycle we also find the rigorous application of ban (*ḥērem*) of the Canaanites (Josh. 6:17), apparently influenced by the stringent policy of Saul toward the Amorites (1 Sam. 21:2).[66]

The Shilonite tradition, however, which stressed the priestly, oracular aspect of the settlement, is reflected—as indicated above—in the first stage of the tradition about the founder (Josh. 19:50) and therefore seems to be most ancient. One must bear in mind that the priestly Shilonite traditions were kept and fostered for hundreds of years in ancient Israel, and that therefore not all the details can be considered reliable. However, on the basis of comparison with the Greek procedure of colonization, the division of land according to divine lot and the resort to an oracle of a central shrine, so well preserved in the Shilonite tradition, appear to constitute genuine features of the settlement process in ancient Israel, save that they underwent schematization and nationalization as the priestly literature developed.

64. In the period of Saul, the central sanctuary was at Gilgal and, as shown below (Chap. 6), the upper limit for the formation of the traditions in Josh. 2–9 was the period of King Saul. Only with the political unification of the tribes of Israel into a kingdom could the idea of a national epic of the conquest of the land under one leader have been formed. The shift of the victorious figure from Ephraim to Benjamin may have been caused by the fact that Aijalon later became part of expanding Benjamin, as may be deduced from the comparison of 1 Chron. 7:21 with 1 Chron. 8:13; see Kallai, "Ephraim" (n. 62).

65. Circumcision is connected with the covenant in Gen. 17, and in Judaism it is called "covenant" to the present day.

66. This policy changed in the Davidic period; see S. Abramsky, "The Attitude towards the Amorites and Jebusites in the Book of Samuel: Historical Foundation and Ideological Significance," *Zion, Jubilee Volume* 50 (1985), pp. 27–58 (Hebrew).

I. Finkelstein concluded on the basis of his excavations (see nn. 62, 63) that the greatest concentration of early Israelite settlements were in the region of Shiloh because, in his opinion, Shiloh had been chosen as the first Israelite sacred center. My observations about Shiloh and its role in the settlement process may corroborate Finkelstein's conclusions.

3

The Borders of the Promised Land

Two Views

Although my topic in this chapter is *two* views of the extent of the land of Israel, in the Rabbinic literature we also find a third view concerning the borders of the holy land: the borders of those who came from Babylonia (*gbl ʿwly bbl*). According to this tradition, the holy land does not include the region of Samaria and the coast settled by foreigners; those who came from Babylonia considered their borders sanctified for eternity, unlike the borders of those who came from Egypt (*gbl ʿwly mṣrym*) (BT Arakhin 32b). But our discussion is mainly concerned with the borders of the pre-exilic period, as presented in the biblical sources, on which we shall concentrate here.

In the unbiased biblical sources, the borders of the Israelite settlement are indicated by the formula "from Dan until Beersheba."[1] However, in the texts crystalized in the priestly tradi-

1. Judg. 20:1; 1 Sam. 3:20; 2 Sam. 3:10; 17:11; 24:2, 15; 1 Kings 5:5; Amos 8:14. These borders are reflected in the book of Jeremiah (from the period of the expansion of Judah in the days of Josiah?): "Hark, one proclaims from Dan" (4:15); "The snorting of their horses was heard from Dan; [a]t the loud neighing of their steeds [t]he whole land quaked" (8:16). Compare as well 1 Kings 12:29–30 (the golden calves in Dan and in Bethel); Gen. 14:14 ("he pursued as far as Dan"); Deut. 34:1 ("and the Lord showed him the whole land . . . as far as Dan." The formula "from Dan until Beersheba" is not intended to encompass all the regions of the

tions and in texts relating to the period of national expansion, we find borders that extend beyond this area of Israelite settlement; in fact, these sources represent two ideal border-systems:

(1) The priestly delineation of the borders of the land of Canaan, "from Lebo-hamath until the wadi of Egypt"[2] is

---

land; rather, it indicates the largest cities at the northern and southern extremes of the land. When there is need of an exact delineation of the territories comprising the land of Israel according to its inhabitants in the area that is "from Dan until Beersheba," we find a topographic specification such as: "from Mount Halak, which ascends to Seir, all the way to Baal-gad in the Valley of the Lebanon at the foot of Mount Hermon" (Joshua 11:17; compare 12:7). These limits encompass the Israelite settlement extending from "the Large Crater" (Jebel Halak, southwest of wadi Hathirah; cf. A. Musil, *Arabia Petrae* 2: EDOM, 1 [Vienna, 1907], p. 170) as far as the territory at the foot of Mount Hermon, and to the Litani River in the north (cf. N. Na'aman, "The Inheritances of the Cis-Jordanian Tribes of Israel and the 'Land that yet remaineth,'" *Eretz-Israel* 16 [1982], pp. 152–58 [Hebrew] = *Borders and Districts in Biblical Historiography* [Jerusalem, 1986], pp. 36–73.) In the south, these border markings reflect the Israelite settlement in the flourishing period of the United Monarchy. Cf. Z. Kallai, "The Boundaries of the Land of Canaan and the Land of Israel in the Bible: Territorial Models in Biblical Historiography," *Eretz-Israel* 12 (1975), pp. 27–34 (Hebrew).

2. Lebo-hamat is Labweh, near the sources of the Orontes south of the city of Kadesh, which comprised a kind of natural border in the middle of the valley between the kingdom of the Hittites and the Egyptian empire. Also, in a later period the southern border of the province of Hamath extended there (cf. Ezek. 47:15; 48:1; Y. Aharoni, *The Land of the Bible: A Historical Geography,* rev. ed., A. F. Rainey, ed. [Jerusalem, 1979], pp. 67–77).

The Wadi of Egypt is generally identified with Wadi al-Arish; however, recently, N. Na'aman has suggested identifying it with the brook of Besor south of Gaza. Cf. N. Na'aman, "The Wadi of Egypt and the Assyrian Policy on the Egyptian Border," *Shnaton: An Annual for Biblical and Ancient Near Eastern Studies* 3 (1975), pp. 138–58 (Hebrew). We find support for this evidence of Gaza as a border in Gen. 10:19: "The Canaanite territory extended from Sidon . . . as far as Gaza"; also Josh. 10:41: "from Kadesh-Barne'a as far as Gaza" and 1 Kings 5:4: "For he controlled the whole region west of the Euphrates, from Tiphsah to Gaza." Nevertheless, there is no doubt that small settlements existed in the wilderness south and southwest of Gaza (the wildernesses of Sinai); therefore, we found in Num. 34, according to the precise description in this source, the promised land does not include the eastern side of the Jordan south of the Kinneret (map 1).[3] In the context of the first period of national expansion we find these border indications: "So Solomon and all Israel with him . . . from Lebo-hamath to the Wadi of Egypt observed the Feast" (1 Kings 8:65); similarly, in the period of expansion in the days of Jeroboam II (789–750 B.C.E.): "It was he who restored the territory of Israel from Lebo-hamath to the sea of the Arabah";[4] "Who will harass you from Lebo-hamath to the Wadi Arabah" (Amos 6:14). The territory of "the remaining land" (Josh. 13:2) that had not been conquered by Joshua was determined in accordance with these borders: all the land "from

---

agree with the Israelite and Assyrian historiographers that the borders included the territories south of Gaza. In these instances, natural features were utilized as border markers: a long wadi like Wadi al-Arish, or "the Shihor," which is the eastern branch of the Nile (Josh. 13:10; 1 Chron. 13:5). The Egyptians themselves did not view the Sinai wilderness as belonging to the land of Egypt, as N. Na'aman establishes, "Shihor of Egypt and Assyria Which is in Front of Egypt," *Biblical Studies: Y. M. Grintz Memorial Volume* (Tel Aviv, 1982), pp. 205–06 (Hebrew), and thus the Israelites could view regions of the wilderness in which they had settled as part of their land.

3. Cf. Num. 34:11–12: "the boundary shall continue downward and abut on the eastern slopes of the Sea of Kinneret. The boundary shall then descend along the Jordan and terminate at the Dead Sea." Vv. 13–15 in this chapter belong to a later framework that seeks to include the eastern side of the Jordan in the Promised Land, in contradiction to 34:2, according to which "the land of Canaan according to its borders" assigned to the Israelites does not include the eastern side of the Jordan. Thus, Ezekiel in his vision (47:13 ff.) uses an idiom identical to that in Num. 34:2—"the land fell as an inheritance"—in his words on the bequeathing of the western side of the Jordan to all twelve tribes of Israel. For the lateness of the framework passage discussed, cf.: A. G. Auld, *Joshua, Moses and the Land* (Edinburgh, 1980), pp. 75–78. Compare: Ezek. 47:13–48:29. On the basis of this text, all the tribes reside west of the Jordan, including Reuben and Gad, which in the biblical sources had settled east of the Jordan (Num. 32; 34:14–15).

4. 2 Kings 14:25, the border of northern Israel during the reign of Jeroboam II.

Baal-gad at the foot of Mount Hermon to Lebo-hamath" (Josh. 13:5; Judg. 3:3), i.e., the territory north of the springs of the Jordan as far as Lebo-hamath, as well as the land of Philistia (Josh. 13:2–3; Judg. 3:3). This system of borders includes territories that were inhabited by Israelites in the days of David, especially in the vicinity of Tyre and Sidon.[5]

(2) Another system of borders encompasses the territory "from the river Euphrates to the river of Egypt" (Gen. 15:19), or "from the wilderness to the Euphrates" (Exod. 23:31),[6] which includes the eastern side of the Jordan and all the land of Syria and Lebanon (map 2).

Let us explain these two idealistic systems in detail.

1. From Lebo-hamath to the Wadi of Egypt. As indicated, the border system of this type does not include Transjordan south of the lake of Kinneret, which seems difficult to understand because the Israelites inhabited Transjordan from the beginning of their settlement in the area (cf. Judg. 11:26). This problem was addressed by B. Mazar, and later by R. de Vaux, who observed that the border delineation of Canaan in Num. 34 corresponds to the region of the Egyptian province of Canaan in the period before the Israelite settlement.[7] The Egyp-

5. Josh. 19:28–30. Compare 2 Sam. 24:6–7. This area belongs, according to Z. Kallai, to the "remaining land" divided among the tribes, as opposed to other areas in the Lebanon that are part of the remaining land but were not divided among the tribes at all. Cf. Kallai, "Territorial" (n. 1). According to Na'aman, "Inheritances" (n. 1), Israelites did not settle in Tyre and Sidon, and these two cities were not divided among the tribes.

6. Compare Deut. 1:2, 11:14; Josh. 1:4.

7. B. Mazar, "Lebo-hamath—the Northern Border of Canaan," in S. Ahituv and B. Levine, eds., *The Early Biblical Period: Historical Studies* (Jerusalem, 1986), pp. 189–202, orig. pub. in *Bulletin of the Israel Exploration Society (Yediot)* 12 (1946), pp. 91–102 (Hebrew); and, later, R. de Vaux, "Le Pays de Canaan," *Journal of the American Oriental Society* 88 (1968), pp. 23–29. It may be that this extent of the province "Canaan" was accepted many hundreds of years prior to the entering of the Israelites into the land of Canaan, and that it does not necessarily reflect the limits of Canaan at the end of the period of Egyptian rule, as Mazar maintains. Cf. N. Na'aman, "Shihor of Egypt" (n. 2), p. 207.

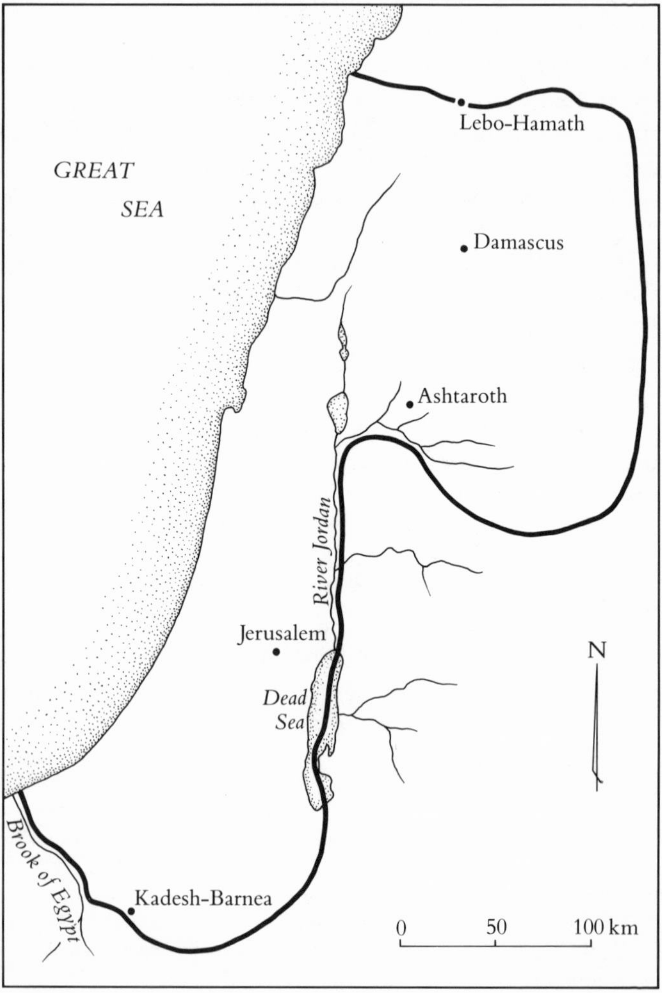

Map 1. Borders of the Promised Land, Numbers 34:3-12.

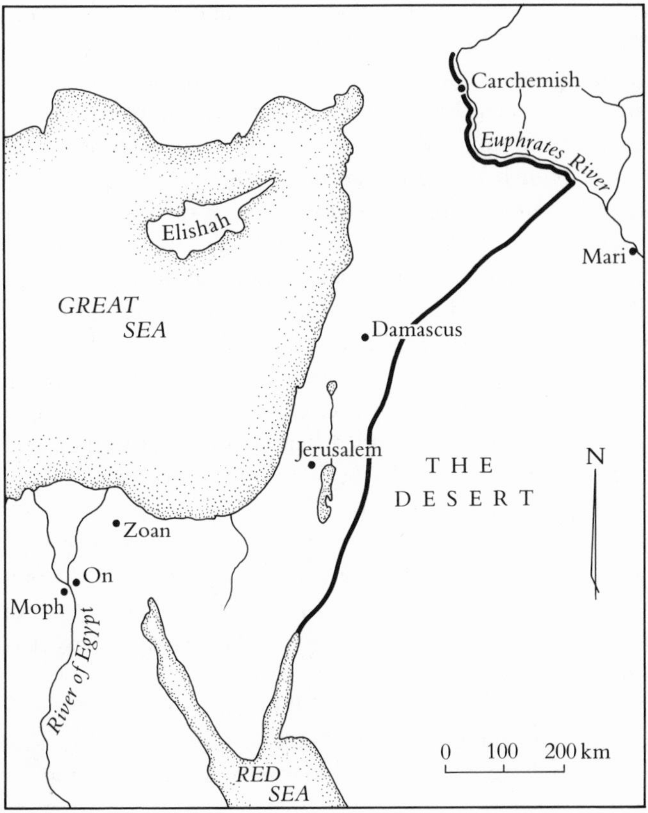

Map 2. Borders of the Promised Land, Genesis 15:18-21.

tian province of Canaan includes the land of Upe, the Damascene region, but excludes Transjordan just as in Num. 34.

This system conforms to the view accepted in most biblical sources in which the crossing of the Jordan marks the beginning of the conquest of the land of Canaan and also signals the point at which the commandments specific to the Land of Israel become binding.[8] The realization of the promise to the patriarchs came with the crossing of the Jordan, hence the dramatization of the event and the ceremony of the foundation at Gilgal, as expressed in the beginning of the stories of the conquest in Josh. 3–4.[9] In addition, it should be noted that the manna the Israelites ate in the desert stopped after the crossing of the Jordan[10] and that the circumcision of the Israelites upon their arrival in the Land of Canaan, shortly before they celebrated the first Passover in the Land, took place after crossing the Jordan to Gilgal to the west (Josh. 5:2–11). The setting up of the stones that the Israelites were commanded to erect on Mt. Ebal, and the ceremony accompanying this act, could only be fulfilled after the passage of the Jordan: "As soon as you have crossed the Jordan . . . you shall set up large stones . . . in order that you may come into the land that the Lord your God is giving you."[11] This is an ancient tradition, despite its appearance in a late book.

Furthermore, the angel who was supposed to bring the

8. Cf., for example, regarding the commandments of the dispossession in Num. 33:51–52: "When you cross the Jordan into the land of Canaan, you shall dispossess," etc.; and concerning the commandments of the cities of refuge in Num. 35:10: "When you cross the Jordan into the land of Canaan, you shall provide yourselves with places to serve you as cities of refuge," etc.

9. Cf. my article, "The Tradition of Inheritance of the Tribes of Israel in Canaan: the Model and Its Nature," Cathedra 44 (June/July 1987), pp. 12–13 (Hebrew).

10. Josh. 5:12; compare Exodus 16:35.

11. Deut. 27:2–3. Concerning the significance of this ceremony, cf. my article "Tradition of Inheritance" (n. 9), pp. 11–12.

Israelites to the Land and drive out before them the Canaanites, the Amorites, the Hittites, the Perizzites, the Hivites, and the Jebusites appears only after Joshua arrives at Gilgal and before the conquest of Jericho.[12] This angel, called "captain of the Lord's host," reveals himself to Joshua by saying "Now I have come" (Josh. 5:14), which means: now that I have arrived, the time of the conquest of the Land of Canaan has come. This same angel later goes up from Gilgal to the Bochim and admonishes Israel for not having destroyed the Canaanite altars (Judg. 2:1–4).

It is clear, then, that the realization of the promise of the Land of Canaan to the Israelites did not begin until Israel arrived at Gilgal. The territory of Transjordan was not included, at the outset, in the borders of the promise, and it was actually conquered only incidentally: because Sihon, the king of the Amorites, did not let the Israelites pass through his land on their way to the land of Canaan, they were obliged to fight him, and in this way his land was conquered and passed into the hands of Israel. With respect to the land of Og, king of the Bashan (Num. 21:33–35), it is evident that the relevant passage in the book of Numbers is an addition that was introduced under the influence of Deut. 3:1–3.[13] The chance nature of the

12. Exod. 23:20; 32:34; 33:2. Compare Exod. 14:19; Num. 20:16. The angel in its soteriological role is intentionally omitted from the book of Deuteronomy. Cf. my article, "The Emergence of the Deuteronomic Movement: The Historical Antecedents," in N. Lohfink, ed., *Das Deuteronomium, Entstehung, Gestalt und Botschaft* (Leuven, 1985), p. 84.

13. The Bashan is beyond the horizon of the traditions of the conquest in Num. 32 (for v. 42, cf. below). Moreover, the Bashan is included within the borders of the Promised Land according to Num. 34, which means that its conquest cannot be considered random, like the conquering of the land of Sihon. Cf. Z. Kallai, "Conquest and Settlement of Trans-Jordan: A Historiographical Study," *ZDPV* 99 (1983), pp. 110–18.

Concerning the influence of Deut. 3:1–3, cf. A. Dillmann, *Numeri*, Kurzgefasstes exegetisches Handbuch zum Alten Testament (Leipzig, 1886), pp. 133–34; S. R. Driver, *Deuteronomy* ICC (Edinburgh), 1902,

conquest of Transjordan is made clear in Num. 32: when the Reubenites and the Gadites ask to settle in Transjordan, their request is something of a surprise to Moses, who considers it a sin equal in weight to the sin of the spies (Num. 32:20–22).

In fact, the whole tradition about the settlement in Transjordan in Num. 32 is apologetic,[14] attempting to justify the settlement of the tribes on the eastern side of the Jordan by proving that the Gadites and the Reubenites actually fought with the rest of the tribes on the western side and were therefore allowed to settle on the eastern side. Only after they had committed themselves to go to war "before the Lord" (Num. 32:20–22)—in other words, at the place in which the tabernacle is located, on the western side of the Jordan—were they granted permission to build their cities in Gilead and to leave their families and herds there. Actually, Gilead was settled primarily by immigrants from the tribes of Manasseh (see below) and Ephraim,[15] and Num. 32 serves as a kind of legitimization of this settlement outside the borders of the Promised Land. Although the Gadites and the Reubenites did settle at a very early stage in the southern part of Transjordan,[16] the major settlement in Gilead, which is the heart of Transjordan,

---

pp. 46–47. The idioms in this passage are of a Deuteronomic character, especially "that no survivor was left," which is characteristic of Deuteronomic descriptions of the conquest. Cf. my book, *Deuteronomy and the Deuteronomic School* (Oxford 1972), p. 344.

14. Cf. in this matter S. E. Loewenstamm "The Settlement of Gad and Reuben as related in Num. 32:1–38—Background and Composition," *From Babylon to Canaan: Studies in the Bible and Its Oriental Background* (Jerusalem, 1992), pp. 109–30.

15. Num. 32:39–42. Cf. Judg. 12:4 ff.; 2 Sam. 18:6: "the forest of Ephraim."

16. The Reubenites were a nomadic tribe, as we learn from 1 Chron. 5:9–10: "He [Reuben] dwelt to the east as far as the fringe of the wilderness . . . and they occupied their tents throughout all the region east of Gilead." They maintained the institution of the *naśi'* until the days of their exile, in the days of Tiglath-pileser III (1 Chron. 5:6).

took place after the conquest of Cisjordan and was something of a new colony of the motherland in the west.[17]

The father-founder (*oikist*)[18] of the colony in Gilead, which in its broad sense included all the territory of the tribes settled in Transjordan,[19] was Machir, the son of Manasseh.[20] In the Song of Deborah, Machir appears in the region between Ephraim and Benjamin in the south and Zebulun and Issachar in the north (Judg. 5:14); this region corresponds to the territory of the tribe of Manasseh on the western side of the Jordan.

It is clear, then, that Machir migrated to the eastern side of the river not long before the period of Deborah in the middle of the twelfth century B.C.E.[21] There were Gileadites in Transjordan while Machir was still on the western side of the Jordan (Judg. 5:14, 17), but they became part of the federation of the twelve tribes only after affiliating with Machir-Manasseh. The tradition about the dwelling of the tribe of Gad in Gilead does not date as far back as this period; if it did, we would expect to find Gad, not Gilead, mentioned next to Reuben (Judg. 5:15–17). It should be noted that with the single exception of Gilead, all the ethnic groups in the Song of Deborah are designated by

17. On the relationship of Gad to Gilead and the settlement of Gad in Transjordan, with a discussion of "the land of Gad and Gilead" in 1 Sam. 13, cf. M. Noth, "Gilead and Gad," *ZDPV* 75 (1959), pp. 14–73.

18. On the colonization pattern in ancient Greece and in Israel, see above, Chapter 2.

19. Deut. 34:1; Josh. 22:9, 15; 2 Kings 10:33. For a discussion of Gilead in all its aspects, cf. N. Ottosson, *Gilead: Tradition and History* (Lund, 1969).

20. Num. 26:29; 27:1; 36:1; Josh. 17:1, et al.

21. In the opinion of Y. Aharoni, "Machir was the strongest family in the northern part of Mount Ephraim and only upon the migration of most of the family to Transjordan did the name of Manasseh ascend to the head of the western tribe. Machir became the patriarch of Gilead and due to its being the strongest family the rest of the families and clans of Gilead claimed descent from it over time." "The Settlement and the Inheritance," in B. Mazar, ed., *The History of the People of Israel* 2, *The Patriarchs and the Judges* (Jerusalem, 1967), p. 216 (Hebrew).

their tribal name: Ephraim, Zebulun, Issachar, Dan, Naftali, and Asher.

This situation is reflected in the story of Jephthah (Judg. 11), in which "the Gilead" designates both a land of origin and a people (Jephthah, the Gileadite), as well as a region.[22] Perhaps part of the Reubenite tribe also originated in Cisjordan, because Reubenite tribal names, such as Carmi, Hezron, and Bela, are found in the genealogical lists of Judah and Benjamin, while "the stone of Bohan, son of Reuben" is located not in the territory of the tribe of Reuben, as might be expected, but rather in the territory of Judah (Josh. 15:6, 18:17). In any case, there is ample evidence that Transjordan was settled by immigrants from Cisjordan;[23] in addition to Machir from the tribe of Manasseh, Ephraimite tribesmen also established colonies there.

Moreover, in the ancient accounts of the establishment of settlements in Transjordan by the Israelites,[24] a clear typology of colonization, as we have seen in the Greek tradition (see Chapter 1) reveals the following elements: (1)departing: "he went" (*hlk*); (2) conquering the territory: "he captured it" (*lkd*); (3) building a settlement: "he built a city" (*bnh*); (4) naming the place after the conqueror or settler (*qr' šm*): "The descendants of Machir . . . *went* to Gilead and *captured* it; "Jair, son of Manasseh, *went and captured* . . . and he *renamed* them Havvoth-jair"; "And Nobah *went and captured* Kenath and its dependencies, *renaming* it Nobah after himself"; "The Gadites . . . and the Reubenites *built* . . . and they *gave names* to towns they built" (Num. 32:34–42). The language of this story is similar

22. Note Mizpeh of Gilead (Judg. 11:29), as opposed to Josh. 13:26, where the name "Mizpeh" is associated with the tribe of Gad.

23. On the various traditions regarding Reuben, Gilead-Gad and Manasseh-Machir, cf. R. de Vaux, *The Early History of Israel* (London, 1978), pp. 551 ff.

24. On the antiquity of these lists and their similarity to the lists in Judg. 1, cf. G. B. Gray, *Numbers,* ICC, (Edinburgh, 1903), pp. 439 ff. Compare especially Judg. 1:26: "The man went . . . founded a city . . . and named it."

to that used to describe the settlement of the Danites in the north: "they built the city . . . settled in it and called its name Dan" (cf. above, pp. 34–35).

Settlement east of the Jordan, then, was considered secondary and therefore was not apportioned along with land on the western side by the casting of lots before the Lord at Shiloh (Josh. 14–19). Indeed, the eastern side of the Jordan is regarded in the ancient sources as an "impure land" that was not included in the inheritance of the Lord (Josh. 22:19). The Rabbis also saw in the conquest of Transjordan an act that had not received the a priori approval of God: with respect to the verse "you shall take some of every first fruit of the soil, which you harvest from the land that the Lord your God is giving you," Rabbi Simeon says, "Except Transjordan, which you took by yourself."[25]

The negation of the national-religious status of Transjordan finds expression in Josh. 22, a chapter of a priestly author, who delineates the borders of the Land without Transjordan (Num. 34:1–12). In Josh. 22:11–12, the Israelite tribes that are affiliated with the Tabernacle at Shiloh in Mt. Ephraim are appalled at the sight of the altar erected in Transjordan;[26] they condemn its builders as traitors and rebels, and they even invite the Transjordanian tribes to abandon their "impure" inheritance to cross over and acquire holdings "in the land of the Lord's own holding," wherein dwells the Tabernacle of the Lord (in Shiloh).[27]

25. Deuteronomy 26:2; Sifrei Deuteronomy 299.

26. In the opinion of B. Mazar, in his article "Biblical Archaeology Today: The Historical Aspect," *Biblical Archaeology Today: Proceedings of the International Congress of Biblical Archaeology: Jerusalem, April 1984* (Jerusalem, 1985), p. 17, the altar in question is the altar erected by the Transjordanian tribes in Adam the City (Tel ed-Dāmiyeh), which is at the fords of the Jordan; compare "the tent He set up at Adam" in Ps. 78:60, and cf. above, p. 45.

27. Cf. vv. 16–19. The passage in Ps. 78–60 says: "He forsook the tabernacle at Shiloh, the tent He had set up at Adam"; if that is the case, it means that the two centers in the north, the one east of the Jordan in Adam

The priests of Shiloh, in whose circles the Israelite Priestly Code originated,[28] conceived of the boundaries of the land of Canaan in accordance with boundaries accepted in the Egyptian empire on the eve of the Israelite conquest; in other words, the land of Canaan as given to Israel encompasses the same boundaries as the province of Canaan that had been delineated beforehand under the rule of Egypt. Just as God took the Israelites out of Egypt, so he took away the land of Canaan from the hand of Egypt and gave it to Israel.[29] Therefore, "the land of Canaan with its boundaries" (*ʾrṣ knʿn lgbltyh*) in Num. 34 corresponds to the land of Canaan as it was in the days of the Egyptian empire. This view, endorsed by the tribes of Israel, did not change after the two and a half tribes settled in Transjordan; the priests of Shiloh, who saw in the land of Canaan without Transjordan the portion cast by lot before the Lord at Shiloh,[30] were not willing to compromise in this matter, despite other, more popular views in which—as we shall see—Transjordan was considered an inseparable part of the original inheritance of Israel. Thus, in contrast to the tradition that identifies Penuel in Transjordan as the place where the God of Israel was revealed to Jacob and his name was changed to Israel (Gen. 32:25–33), the priestly tradition relates that the revelation to Jacob, as well as the changing of his name took place not in Penuel but in Beth-el, on the western side of the Jordan (Gen. 35:1–15; cf. above, p. 46).

2. From the River of Egypt to the River Euphrates. After

---

the City and the one west of the Jordan in Shiloh, were both abandoned by God.

28. Cf. M. Haran, "Shiloh and Jerusalem," *Tarbiz* 31 (1962), pp. 317–25 (Hebrew).

29. This outlook appears latent in the formula in Lev. 25:38: "I the Lord am your God, who brought you out of the land of Egypt, to give you the land of Canaan."

30. Josh. 18:8. On the importance and primacy of the tradition of Shiloh in the division of the land to the tribes, cf. above, pp. 39–40.

the wide-ranging conquests of David in Transjordan and the priestly ascendancy of the house of Zadok, which was no longer bound to the tradition of Shiloh that had originated in the house of Eli, the view of the borders of the Promised Land changed.[31] The Gilead and the valley of Sukkoth in Transjordan were recognized as belonging to the portion of the Lord, as we learn from a psalm attributed to David after his victories in Aram Naharaim and Aram Zobah:[32]

> God promised in His shrine: I would ascend Luz (= Beth-el),[33] divide up Shechem, and measure the valley of Sukkoth; Gilead and Manasseh would be mine, Ephraim my chief stronghold, Judah my scepter.
>
> Moab would be my washbasin. On Edom I would rest my shoe. Acclaim me, O Philistia. Would that I were brought to the fortress [of Tyre]. Would that I were led to Aram.

31. The tension between the priests of Jerusalem of the house of Zadok and the priests of Shiloh of the house of Eli appears to have been preserved in the story in 2 Sam. 15:23 ff., in which it is related that at the time of David's departure from Jerusalem, Zadok and the Levites carried the Ark of the Lord from the city. The next verse, 24, contains the expression *w-yʿl ʾbytr,* which must be interpreted as "Abiathar left the place" (compare *ʿlh* in the sense of "left the place" in Gen. 17:22; Num. 16:24; Jer. 34:21). Cf. also the medieval commentators and the rabbinic midrash on this matter: "Abiathar renounced the priesthood," *Seder Olam Rabbah* 14 (B. Ratner edition, pp. 30–31). In light of our assumption regarding the status of Transjordan in the eyes of the priests of the house of Eli in Shiloh, it becomes clear that Abiathar, who is a descendant of the house of Eli, opposed removing the Ark with the king to Transjordan, and therefore the king ordered that the Ark be returned to the city (v. 25). The presence of the Ark in Transjordan during the war with the Ammonites (2 Samuel 11:11) was apparently not according to the wishes of the priests of the house of Eli.

32. Ps. 60:8–9; 108:8–10. For a discussion of the background of this psalm, cf. Y. Aharoni, "The Conquests of David According to Psalms 60 and 108," in B. Uffenheimer, ed., *Bible and Jewish History: Dedicated to the Memory of J. Liver* (Tel Aviv, 1972), pp. 13–17 (Hebrew).

33. N. H. Tur-Sinai suggested reading here *ʾʿlh Lzh,* i.e., "I would ascend Luz," in *The Language and the Book,* vol. 2 (1952), p. 431. Z. Weisman also suggested such a reading and published his proposal, "Towards

Here, in the division of the Land ("I would divide [*'hlq*] . . . I will measure [*'mdd*]") according to the word of God (which was proclaimed in Beth-el and not in Shiloh), an equal place was reserved for Shechem and for Sukkoth, for the Hills of Ephraim and for the Hills of Gilead; in other words, there is no distinction between the eastern and western sides of the Jordan. That Transjordan territories were included in the Land of Israel of the United Monarchy may be learned from (1) the census of David (2 Sam. 24); (2) the list of Solomon's districts (1 Kings 4); (3) the delineation of tribal borders in Joshua 13–19; and (4) the list of Levitical cities in Joshua 21. The census of David starts from the southeast at Aroer in Transjordan, passes to northern Gilead, comes around Sidon to the fortress of Tyre, and then reaches the cities of the Hivites and the Canaanites in the west, along the coast. The census ends in the southernmost part of the country, Beer-sheba.

Solomon's districts (1 Kings 4) include Gilead and Bashan in Transjordan; the area of Asher, which extends in the north "unto great Sidon . . . till the fortress of Tyre" (Josh. 19:28–29); the Canaanite cities in the west; and the valley of Jereel (1 Kings 4:10–12) and Judah in the south.

The same situation is reflected in the tribal borders of Joshua 13–19 and in the Levitical cities (Joshua 21), as has been demonstrated by Z. Kallai in *Historical Geography of the Bible* (Jerusalem, 1986).

The view that the eastern side of the Jordan is included in the boundaries of the Promised Land, which was fostered in the days of the United Monarchy, stands at the foundation of the ideal model of borders in Gen. 15, "from the river Euphrates to the river of Egypt." Because this formula appears in the chapter of the "Covenant between the Pieces," which re-

---

an Explanation of "ʿlzh," *Beit Miqra* 34 (June/July 1968), pp. 49–52 (Hebrew), without knowing that Tur-Sinai had already suggested it.

flects the days of David,[34] it includes a promise that the progeny of Abraham will be given the land of the Ten Peoples (Gen. 15:19–21). The Ten Peoples include, in addition to those known to us from the lists of peoples in the land of Canaan, the Kenites, the Kenizzites, the Kadmonites, and the Rephaim, peoples who dwelled in the south of the land of Israel and in Transjordan.[35]

The same borders are reflected in Exod. 23:31: "I will set your borders from the Sea of Reeds to the Sea of Philistia, and from the wilderness to the River." The Sea of Reeds is at the southernmost point of the land (the Gulf of Aqabah); the Sea of Philistia (the Mediterranean) constitutes the western and southwestern border; "the wilderness" is the eastern and southern border; while "the River," the Euphrates, is the northern and northeastern border.[36] This maximal extent of the Land is also specified in the description of the kingdom of Solomon in 1 Kings 5:1: "Solomon's rule extended over all the kingdoms from the Euphrates to the land of the Philistines and the boundary of Egypt,"[37] and it finds expression even in the

34. Cf. B. Mazar, "The Historical Background of the Book of Genesis," in S. Ahituv and B. A. Levine, eds., *The Early Biblical Period: Historical Studies* (Jerusalem, 1986), pp. 49–62.

35. The "Kadmonites" apparently include the nomads in the eastern outskirts of the land of Israel, similar to the "Kedemites" (Judg. 6:3; 7:12; Jer. 49:28–29, 32; Ezek. 25:4 ff.). On the Rephaim on the eastern side of the Jordan, cf. Gen. 14:5: "the Rephaim at Ashteroth-karnaim;" Deut. 3:13: "all that part of Bashan which is called Rephaim country." Ammon was considered "Rephaim country" (Deut. 2:20–21), as was Moab: "they are counted as Rephaim" (Deut. 2:10–11).

36. Cf. Kallai, "Borders of Canaan" (n. 1), p. 29.

37. The parallel passage there (v. 4), "For he controlled the whole region beyond the river (*ʿbr hnhr*)—all the kings beyond the river, from Tiphsah to Gaza," should be attributed to the editor, because "beyond the river" as an indicator of Syria and the land of Israel is not known to us before the days of Esarhaddon, in the seventh century B.C.E., and the city Tiphsah, which is on the Euphrates (Tapsakos), is not known to us prior to the Persian period. Cf. "*ʿbr hnhr*," *Encyclopedia Miqra'it* 6, cols. 43–48; "*Tfsh*," ibid. 8, cols. 922–23.

psalms of an imperial nature,[38] as in the Psalm of Solomon: "Let him rule from sea to sea, from the river to the ends of the earth" (Ps. 72:8); and in Ps. 89:26: "I will set his hand upon the sea, his right hand upon the rivers."[39]

Delineations of borders using seas and rivers as boundaries are typical of imperial descriptions, but there is no support for the claims of some researchers that they represent a projection from the days of the Assyrian Empire.[40] Such borders appear in sources of several different types: for example, in the stories of the patriarchs (Gen. 15:18), in the epilogue of the law of the book of the covenant (Exod. 23:31), in a few psalms (72:8; 80:11; 89:26), and in various prophecies (Isa. 27:12; Mic. 7:12; Zech. 9:10). There is no reason to assume that all these do not precede the Assyrian period. Similarly, these borders match borders specified in other ancient passages that speak of the submission of peoples and nations in the regions of Syria and the Land of Israel: "Let peoples serve you, and nations bow to you" (Gen. 27:29), and "Let all kings bow to him, and all nations serve him" (Ps. 72:11), which can be comprehended only in light of the political reality of the time of David and the beginning of the period of Solomon. These writings on the submission of peoples and kings echo the description in 2 Samuel of the wars of David: "And the Moabites became tributary vassals of David"; "And the Arameans became tributary vassals of David"; "and all the Edomites became vassals of

38. Concerning the Israelite empire in the days of David and Solomon, cf. A. Malamat, "The Kingdom of David and Solomon and Its Relations with Egypt: A Superpower in the Making," in his book *Israel in the Biblical Period* (Jerusalem, 1983), pp. 167–94 (Hebrew). On the matter of the definition of the imperial borders, cf. my article "Zion and Jerusalem as Religious and Political Capital: Ideology and Utopia," in R. E. Friedman, ed., *The Poet and the Historian: Essays in Literary and Historical Biblical Criticism*, Harvard Semitic Studies 26 (Chico, Calif., 1983), pp. 97–99.

39. Compare Ps. 80:11.

40. E.g., Na'aman, "Shihor of Egypt" (n. 2), p. 208.

David"; "And when all the kings saw . . . they submitted to Israel and became their vassals."[41]

The Status of Transjordan According to Deuteronomy

The "imperial" boundaries described above were adopted by the Deuteronomic circle as the borders of the Promised Land. In contrast to the Priestly Code, the Deuteronomic circle sees the eastern side of the Jordan as an inseparable part of the land of Canaan. We shall enumerate the evidence for this:

1. Revelation to Moses. The description of the Promised Land that God showed Moses before his death (Deut. 34:1–4)[42] lists the Gilead as far as Dan, all of Naftali, the land of Ephraim and Manasseh, the whole land of Judah, the Negeb, and the plain and valley of Jericho: "This is the land of which I swore to Abraham, Isaac, and Jacob, 'I will assign it to your offspring.'" Unlike the ancient source discussed above, here the Promised Land includes the eastern side of the Jordan (the Gilead).

2. Beginning of the Conquest. In Deut. 1–3, the beginning of the conquest is not Joshua's crossing of the Jordan but rather Moses' crossing of the wadi of Arnon: "Up! Set out across the wadi Arnon! See, I give into your power Sihon the Amorite, king of Heshbon, and his land. Begin the occupation: engage him in battle. This day I begin to put the dread and fear of you

41. 2 Sam. 8:2, 6, 14; 10:19. Cf. my article "Zion and Jerusalem" (n. 38), pp. 91–93.

42. Here "viewing the land" has a juridical significance—the acceptance of ownership and right of possession—as does Abraham's "viewing of the land" and "walking about in it" in Gen. 13:14–17. Cf. D. Daube, *Studies in Biblical Law* (Oxford, 1949), pp. 24 ff.

upon the peoples everywhere under heaven, so that they shall tremble and quake because of you whenever they hear you mentioned" (Deut. 2:24–25).

These verses are reminiscent of Josh. 2:9–11; 4:24; and 5:1,[43] in which dread and fear fall upon the peoples before the great deeds performed by God for Israel at the time of their crossing of the Jordan.[44] The view according to which the conquest begins with the victory over Sihon, king of the Amorites, also appears in Deut. 2:31: "See, I begin by placing Sihon and his land at your disposal. Begin the occupation; take possession of his land."[45] These verses make it clear that the inheritance of the land actually began in the battle with Sihon,[46] in contrast to the assertion in Num. 21:21–25 that the Israelites were thrown unwillingly into battle because Sihon did not allow them to pass through his land. In Deuteronomy, the request for passage was only a pretext, whose entire aim was to provoke war; the Israelites knew that Sihon would refuse their request "because the Lord had stiffened his spirit" (Deut. 2:30), and in this war the Israelites were destined to gain a victory, following which they would occupy the land of Sihon.[47]

3. The Ban. Because the Deuteronomist regards Transjor-

43. Cf. F. Langlamet, "Gilgal et les Récites de la Traversée du Jourdain," Cahiers de la *Revue Biblique* 11 (Paris, 1969), pp. 72 ff.

44. For an analysis of the phenomenon and a comparison with Exod. 15:16, cf. W. L. Moran, "The End of the Unholy War and the Anti-Exodus," *Biblica* 44 (1963), pp. 333–42.

45. Compare Deut. 1:21.

46. The similarity in the beginning of the passage in Deut. 2:25—"This day I begin"—induced the rabbis to hypothesize that the conquest of the eastern side of the Jordan, like Joshua's conquest of the western side, had been accompanied by miracles and wonders: "The sun stood still for Moses like it had for Joshua" (BT Taʿanit 20 a; BT Abodah Zarah 25 a). Compare Targum Ps. Jonathan to Deut. 2:25.

47. For an explanation of the passage, cf. my commentary on Deut. 1–11, Anchor Bible (New York, 1991).

dan as an inseparable part of the Promised Land, the conquest of Transjordan necessitates application of the laws of proscription (*ḥerem*) that apply to the peoples of Canaan (Deut. 20:10 ff.): all inhabitants of the land of Sihon and Og, men, women, and children, must be banned (Deut. 2:34–35, 3:6–7), excepting only the cattle and spoils.[48] The parallel description of this battle, in Num. 21:21 ff., does not mention a ban in the conquered region in Transjordan.[49]

4. An Expanded Land. Deuteronomy not only conceived of Transjordan as an inseparable part of the Promised Land, in contrast to the tradition of Numbers, but it also outlined its territory as much more expansive than that in Numbers. Num. 21:24 describes the conquered territory of Sihon as extending "from the Arnon to the Jabbok," while in Deuteronomy it extends northward much farther than the Jabbok to include Gilead north of the Jabbok and the Arabah to the Kinneret (Deut. 3:16–17).[50]

A similar expansion appears in relation to Havvoth-jair. According to Num. 32:40–41, the villages conquered by Jair, son of Manasseh, belong to Gilead, as confirmed in Judg. 10:4: "Havvoth-jair . . . which are in the land of Gilead." But in Deut. 3:14 these villages are mentioned as located in the Bashan, north of Gilead. Moreover, the situating of Havvoth-jair in the district of Argob in the Bashan results in the curious identification of small villages with the large cities in Argob, "cities fortified with high walls, gates, and bars" (3:5), in contrast to the lists of the Solomonic districts (1 Kings 4:13), which clearly distinguish between Havvoth-jair in the Gilead

48. The ban on the inhabitants of the land of Canaan did not include spoils and cattle. Cf. Josh. 8:2, 27; 11:14.

49. Concerning the artificial attempts in medieval exegesis to learn from the ban of the land of Sihon and Og about the ban in the land of Canaan, cf. below, pp. 211–21.

50. Cf. also Josh. 12:2–5; 13:9 ff.

and the sixty cities fortified with "walls and bronze bars" in the Argob district: "he governed the villages of Jair, son of Manasseh, which are in Gilead," and "he also governed the district of Argob which is in Bashan, sixty large towns with walls and bronze bars." Instead of maintaining this distinction, the Deuteronomist expanded the meaning of Havvoth-jair by linking the villages to the region of the Bashan, and the Deuteronomic historiographer followed him and explicitly identified Havvoth-jair with the sixty cities in the Bashan: "and all of Havvoth-jair in Bashan, sixty towns" (Josh. 13:30).[51]

In fact, attestations indicating the expansion of Manasseh in the direction of the district of Bashan[52] are already found in Num. 32:42, in which Nobah conquers Kenath (southern Bashan);[53] this situation, however, does not closely parallel Deut. 3:10, in which large cities and spacious districts not even mentioned in Num. 32 are included in the boundaries of the Land: Ashtaroth, Edrei, Salchah, Argob, and the "sixty cities" of the kingdom of Og in Bashan. Although Num. 34 includes the Bashan in the borders of the Promised Land, the Deuteronomist nonetheless places it on the same level as the territory of Sihon, outside the normative borders of the Land of Canaan.[54]

5. Unconditional Gift. The special stance of Deuteronomy vis-à-vis Transjordan is also expressed in the description of the deliverance of Transjordan into the hands of the tribes of Gad

51. On the villages of Jair in the various sources, cf. Z. Kallai, *Historical Geography of the Bible* (Jerusalem-Leiden, 1986), pp. 253–57.

52. "The Kingdom of Og king of the Bashan" in Num. 32:33 is an addition following the interpolation in Num. 31:33–35. Cf. the commentaries.

53. Cf. B. Oded, "*qnt*," *Encyclopedia Miqra'it* 7, cols. 203–04. This expansion toward the Bashan might reflect a Judahite invasion, as we learn from 1 Chron. 2:21 ff., which tells us of marital ties between Hezron the Judahite and Machir the patriarch of Gilead.

54. Cf. Kallai, "Conquest and Settlement" (n. 13).

and Reuben.[55] According to Num. 32:16 ff., the territory is given to the Transjordanian tribes on the condition that they cross over the Jordan and fight together with their brethren before the Lord, but according to Deut. 3:15 ff. the territory is given to them unconditionally, reflecting the perspective of the author on this territory as part of the general portion of Israel. Moses says to them: "The Lord your God has given you this country to possess. You must go as shock-troops, warriors all, at the head of your Israelite kinsmen . . . until the Lord has granted your kinsmen a haven such as you have, and they too have taken possession of the land that the Lord your God is assigning them, beyond the Jordan" (Deut. 3:18–20).

In contrast to the source in Numbers, by which the rights of the Transjordanian tribes over their land are acquired through their participation in the war on the western side of the Jordan, scene of the true inheritance, in Deuteronomy they gain this land as part of the tribal inheritances given to them in the context of the division of the Promised Land. Because they have already arrived at their rest and inheritance (Deut. 3:20), these tribes are requested to help their brethren as well, who are still fighting to achieve it: "and they too have taken possession of the land that the Lord your God is assigning them, beyond the Jordan" (3:20).

Thus, what was in Numbers a settlement outside the borders of the Promised Land becomes in Deuteronomy a legitimate inheritance, which includes expansive territories. A similar pattern applies to the description by the Deuteronomic author in Josh. 13 of the division of the portions to the Transjordanian tribes.

When did this tradition of the application of "the Lord's portion" to Transjordan materialize? It appears possible to set its crystallization in the period of national expansion in the days

55. "the half-tribe of Manasseh son of Joseph" in Num. 32:33 is an addition. Cf. Loewenstamm, "Gad and Reuben" (n. 14), pp. 14 ff.

of Hezekiah or Josiah (with reference to the formation of the tradition from a literary-ideological perspective, as opposed to the underlying historical events). The expansion in the region of the eastern side of the Jordan actually commenced in the period of David and Solomon, as the list of Solomonic provinces in 1 Kings 4 attests; however, the ideologue of the period of Hezekiah and Josiah, the Deuteronomic author (or the Deuteronomic school), is the source who formulated this view of the extent of the Promised Land. Until this period, the sources adhered to the ancient view, according to which Transjordan is not part of the Promised Land, and only during the period of nationalist pride that characterized the time of Hezekiah and Josiah[56] was a new view elaborated. An ideology such as this one could not have been formed in the time of the great expansion—in the days of David and Solomon, or in the days of Jeroboam II—when the scribe would not have failed to distinguish between Havvoth-jair in the Gilead and the sixty fortified cities in the Bashan. Only a later scribe, who was writing when the Bashan was no longer in Israelite hands, might err in this way.

To which stage of the Deuteronomic school is it possible to attribute this ideology? We have based our evidence primarily on Deut. 2–3 and Deut. 34, chapters that apparently are part of a later edition of the book and may even belong to the editorial layer of the Deuteronomist who edited the historiography of the Former Prophets.[57] Indeed, in the code itself the old view still prevails that God's commandments are binding only after the crossing of the Jordan (11:31–32). Nevertheless, the reference to the imperial borders, which include the eastern side of the Jordan in the delineation of the Promised Land, is found in

56. Cf. my article, "The Awakening of National Consciousness in Israel in the Seventh Century B.C.E.," In *ʿOz le-David, Jubilee Volume: Biblical Essays in Honor of D. ben-Gurion* (Jerusalem, 1964), pp. 396–420 (Hebrew).

57. Cf. M. Noth, *Überlieferungsgeschichtliche Studien* (Halle, 1943), pp. 27–40.

Deuteronomy 11:24, a verse considered to be an original part of Deuteronomy: "from the desert to Lebanon and from the river Euphrates to the western sea will be your territory." In any case, this ideology is anchored in the Deuteronomic school and should be seen as an expression of the national consciousness characteristic of this school.

The View of the Second Temple Period

With the return of the exiles from Babylonia after the destruction of the Temple, the borders were altered to suit the new reality. In the Second Temple period, the area that was subject to the laws of purity and impurity, as well as the other laws that were binding upon the Land of Israel, was the region within "the borders of those who went up from the Babylonian exile" (*gblwt ʿwly bbl*), and no longer the previous "borders of those who came from Egypt" (*gblwt yṣʾy mṣrym*): "All territory settled by those who returned from the Babylonian exile" was "holy" (Sheviʿit Mishnah 6:1), but areas inhabited by Gentiles or Samaritans were not considered holy. We may observe a certain flexibility regarding territorial issues in a Rabbinic tradition that states: "many cities conquered by those who came from Egypt were not conquered by those who returned from Babylonia. . . . They left them so that the poor could rely upon them in the seventh year" (so that the poor could partake of the produce of these fields during the seventh year, as it was permissible to plow and sow them during the seventh year). The willingness to forgo areas of the Land of Israel in order to fulfill the commandment of giving gifts to the poor reflects an attitude that the land is a means to an end, and not an end in itself (BT Hagigah 3b; BT Hulin 7a).

4

Expulsion, Dispossession, and Extermination of the Pre-Israelite Population in the Biblical Sources

We have shown that there was a trend in biblical literature that tried to idealize, in a utopian manner, the borders of the promised land. Now we shall try to show that a similar utopian standard was applied to the problem of the dispossession of the Canaanite, pre-Israelite population.

Let us first analyze in detail the laws of dispossession. Laws regulating the relations of the Israelites to the inhabitants of the land of Canaan who preceded them are found in the three law codes of the Pentateuch:

1. in the so-called large Covenant code of Exod. 21–23, which is the most ancient code[1] (in the pericope of Exod.

1. The most important clue for the antiquity of the code is the law in Exod. 22:27: "You shall not curse/revile God nor put a curse upon a *chieftain* (*naśî'*) among your people." In the Biblical books referring to the monarchic period we hear about cursing/reviling *God* and *king* (1 Kings 21:10, 13; Isa. 8:21, and compare Prov. 24:21), and not about cursing God and *chieftain*. Chieftain (*naśî'*) occurs usually in the context of the wandering in the desert (the book of Numbers) and in the period of the settlement (Josh. 9:22), as well as in the genealogical lists of the tribes of nomadic character, such as Reuben (1 Chron. 5:1) and Simeon (1 Chron. 4:38). Cf. M. Weinfeld, "Chieftain," *Encycl. Judaica* 5, cols. 420–21.

23:23–33), and in the law of the small Covenant code in Exod. 34:11–17.

2. in the law of the priestly code in Num. 33:50–56.
3. in the Deuteronomic code: 7:1–5; 20:10–18.

The order of the laws—i.e., the Covenant code, the priestly code, and then Deuteronomy—seems to follow the actual chronological order of these scriptures, as we shall attempt to demonstrate.

Different attitudes toward the pre-Israelite population are represented in the aforementioned codes. The concept of "dispossession," however, is common to all three sources,[2] which are all based on the assumption that even though the dispossession is done or must be done by the Israelites, it is really done by the hand of God.[3] Thus, we find ambiguities in these chapters: on the one hand, God expels (*grš*), dispossesses (*hwryš*), sends away (*šlḥ*), annihilates (*klh*), thrusts out (*hdp*), drives out (*nšl*), destroys (*h'byd*), exterminates (*hšmyd*), and cuts off (*hkryt*) the Canaanites,[4] and on the other hand, the Israelites are commanded to do this.[5]

The point of view that the dispossession is accomplished by God is prominent not only in the law codes but also in the

2. In general we will use the term *dispossession*. When it is necessary to be more specific, we will use *expel* (*grš*), *exterminate* (*ḥrm*), etc.

3. For the combination of divine and human factors in Biblical historiography, see I. L. Seeligmann, "Menschliches Heldentum und Goettliche Hilfe," *Theologische Zeitschrift* 19 (1963), pp. 385 ff.

4. Exod. 23:29; 34:11, 24; Lev. 18:24; Deut. 4:38; 6:19; 7:1, 22, 23; 8:20; 9:3, 5; 11:23; 31:3, 4.

5. Exod. 23:31; Num. 33:52, 55; Deut. 7:22, 16; 20:17. Besides these references in the legal sources, we find the view about God's dispossession of the Canaanites in Deut. 33:27; Judg. 2:3; 6:9; 11:23–24; Amos 2:9; Ps. 78:55; 80:9; 1 Chron. 17:21; 2 Chron. 20:7. On the duty of the Israelites to dispossess the Canaanites in nonlegal sources, cf. Judg. 1:21, 27–28, 29, 30–31, 33. On the sin of not dispossessing the Canaanites in Judg. 1:1–2:5, cf. below, pp. 122–31, and see also Ps. 106:34–35.

literature that depends on them. An example is Josh. 24:12–13, which depends on pentateuchal sources (Exod. 23:28; Deut. 6:10–11): "I have sent the hornet before you and it drove them out before you . . . not by your sword or by your bow (*l' bḥrbk wl' bqštk*). And I have given you a land in which you have not labored and cities which you did not build and you have settled in them; vineyards and oliveyards which you did not plant, you are enjoying." The first clause in this passage—"I have sent the hornet before you and it drove them out before you"—draws on Exod. 23:28; what follows it—"not by your sword or by your bow"—is the development of Josh. 24:12.[6] Verse 13 of this passage—"the land in which you have not labored and cities which you did not build . . ."—is taken from Deut. 6:10–11.

A more radical statement that expresses this theological view is available in Ps. 44:3–7: "You [God] dispossessed nations by your hand and you planted them; you distressed them and drove them out (*wtšlḥm*);[7] it was not by their sword that they took the land; their arm did not save them but your right hand and your strength and the light of your face, because you liked them . . . so I will not trust in my bow nor will my sword save me."

In the law codes in the Pentateuch, God's intervention is expressed by the removal of the Canaanites in various forms: (1) God by himself expels the Canaanites (Exod. 23:29, 30; 34:11); (2) God sends his angel to expel the Canaanites and bring the Israelites into the land of Canaan (Exod. 23:20–23; 33:2); (3) God sends the hornet, which expels the Canaanites (Exod. 23:28; Deut. 7:20; cf. Josh. 24:12).[8] It must be emphasized that these texts belong to the rhetorical/homiletic frame-

6. This contrasts with Gen. 48:22: "which I took from the Amorites with my sword and bow"; for an apologetic view of this verse cf. the Targums.

7. For *šlḥ* (*pi ʿel*) in the sense of *expelling*, see below.

8. Cf. E. Neufeld, "Insects as Warfare Agents in the Ancient Near East," *Orientalia* 49 (1980), pp. 30–57.

work of the laws and not to the laws themselves. The laws of dispossession themselves, which we are examining, are formulated in terms of commandments and as such constitute instructions to be executed by the people. Let us now take up the evidence in the Pentateuch on the commandments connected to the "expulsion" by Israel of the pre-Israelite inhabitants:

1. Exodus 21–23. In the large Covenant code we read:

> When my angel goes before you and brings you to the Amorites and the Hittites and the Perizzites and the Canaanites, the Hivites and the Jebusites and I will annihilate them.[9] You shall not bow down to their gods; nor shall you serve them; nor shall you follow their practices, but you shall destroy them and smash their pillars. . . . I will deliver the inhabitants of the land into your hands and you will drive them out before you. You shall make no covenant with them and their gods. They shall not dwell in your land lest they cause you to sin against me, for serving their gods will prove a snare to you (Exod. 23:23–33).

The verb here for "dispossession" of the Canaanites, for both God (vv. 29, 30) and the Israelites (v. 31),[10] is *grš* = expel. This verb is used in the scriptures for "divorce" (*grš ʾšh,* Lev. 21:7, 14; 22:13), and it is parallel to the verb *šlḥ ʾšh* elsewhere in the scriptures (Deut. 24:1, 3; Jer. 3:1). Indeed, even with the expulsion of the Canaanites we find the expression (*šlḥ = piʿel*) in Lev. 18:24; 20:23 ("The nations which I sent away [*mšlḥ*] from before you"). And just as *grš* is accompanied by the

9. For the various lists of the Canaanite peoples and ethnic distinctions among these peoples, see T. Ishida, "The Structure and Historical Implication of the Lists of the Pre-Israelite Nations," *Biblica* 60 (1979), pp. 461–90.

10. The reading of the LXX and the Vulgate of this verse, *wegeraštimo* "and I will drive them out," is not anchored in the context that addresses Israel. See A. Dillmann, *Exodus und Leviticus,* Kurzgefasstes exegetisches Handbuch zum Alten Testament (Leipzig, 1877).

preposition *mpny: grš "mpnyk/mpnykm"* (Exod. 23:21, 29, 20, 31), *šlḥ* is accompanied by the same preposition in connection with the Canaanites (Lev. 18:24; 20:23).[11]

The argument for expulsion is religious: "lest they cause you to sin against me, . . . for [it] will prove a snare (trap = *lmwqš*) to you" (Exod. 23:33). The expressions "sin" (*ḥṭ'*) and "snare" (*mwqš*), as perpetuated in later sources, apparently draw from ancient traditions. In fact, all the laws concerning the dispossession of the Canaanites are combined with warnings against worshiping idols, and these warnings are even used as points of departure for the commandments for dispossession, as in the passage that we have analyzed here (Exod. 23:24–25) and in Exod. 34:12–13 (cf. Deut. 7:5; 20:18; Num. 33:52).

2. Exodus 34:11–16. A second source contains laws that treat relations with the pre-Israelite population:[12]

> I will drive out before you the Amorites, the Canaanites, the Hittites, the Perizzites, the Hivites, and the Jebusites. Guard yourself lest you make a covenant with the inhabitants of the land . . . lest it be a snare in your midst. But their altars you shall dismantle, and their monuments you shall smash and their sacred trees you shall cut down . . . lest you make a covenant with the inhabitants of the land and lust (*znh*) after their gods and sacrifice to their gods and he call you, and you eat his sacrifice; and you take his daughters for your sons, and your daughters

11. Compare Gen. 3:23 in connection with the expulsion of Adam from the garden of Eden, *wyšlḥhw,* with *wygrš* in v. 24. *hwryš,* which will be discussed later, is also accompanied by *mpny,* see Exod. 34:24; Num. 32:21; 33:52, 55. Although the command "they shall not dwell in your land" (v. 33) could be interpreted in various ways (including extermination), the phrase "and you will drive them out" in v. 31 certainly means expulsion and not extermination.

12. For a thorough analysis of this pericope, cf. J. Halbe, *Das Privilegrecht Jahwes Ex. 34:10–26, Gestalt und Wesen, Herkunft und Wirken in Vordeuteronomischer Zeit,* FRLANT 114 (Goettingen, 1975), pp. 119 ff.

> lust after their gods and they make your sons lust after their gods.

Here the emphasis is on a prohibition affecting social contact with the Canaanites—the making of covenants and marriage ties—and not a word is said about the expulsion or dispossession on the part of Israel; God alone will expel the Amorite and the Canaanite, etc., before Israel (v. 11). In the large Covenant code, expulsion is emphasized, so no mention is made of marriage ties. After the Canaanites are expelled and they are no longer living in the land of Israel ("they shall not dwell in your land" [Exod. 23:33]), there is no place for proscriptions concerning marriage with the Canaanites. But the present pericope, in which no mention is made of a commandment to expel the Canaanites, emphasizes the prohibition of marriage.[13] It seems that the source in Exod. 34 draws on Shechemite tradition such as Gen. 34, which is concerned with covenant bonds with the inhabitants of the land and marriage ties (*connubium et commercium*) in language similar to that of Exod. 34:16: "and we shall give our daughters to you and your daughters we shall take for ourselves" (Gen. 34:16; cf. 34:9, 21; see also Judg. 3:6). Like Exod. 23:20–33, Exod. 34:11–16 also combines warnings against relations with the Canaanites with warnings against idolatry: "lest it be a sin," "and they cause your sons to lust after their gods" (vv. 12, 16).

3. Numbers 33:50–55. Another series of laws bears on relations between the Israelites and the inhabitants of the land of Canaan:

> When you cross the Jordan into the land of Canaan, you shall dispossess (*hwryš*) all the inhabitants of the land, you shall destroy all their figured objects, you shall destroy all their molten images and all their high places you

13. Cf. J. Milgrom, "Profane Slaughter and a Formulaic Key to the Composition of Deuteronomy," *HUCA* 47 (1976), p. 6, n. 21.

> shall demolish. You shall inherit the land and take possession of it. And you shall apportion the land by lot among your families . . . clan by clan. And if you do not dispossess the inhabitants of the land, those whom you allow to remain shall be stings in your eyes and thorns in your side, and they shall harass you in the land in which you live.

Here is a passage of the priestly code, as we learn not only from the style,[14] but also from the fact that it incorporates a law of the division of the land by lot, which is the central concern of the priestly conquest tradition that originated in Shiloh (Josh. 18:1–10; cf. Num. 26:52–56; see Chapter 2). Another indication here of the priestly tradition is the mention of pagan cultic objects: in contrast to the other sources, which mention altars, pillars, and sacred trees or poles (*mzbḥwt, mṣbwt* and *'šrym*), that are generally found in open fields,[15] this source mentions cultic objects characteristic of temple enclosures. Here we find "figured objects" (*mśkyt*)[16] and molten images, which also appear in other priestly writings (Lev. 19:4, 26:1; cf. Lev. 26:30–31). Also appearing here are "high places" (*bmwt*), which in Lev. 26:30 are mentioned together with the "incense-stands" (*ḥmnym*) alongside sanctuaries, but which we do not find in other sources in the Pentateuch.

The verb utilized here concerning the dispossession of the pre-Israelite inhabitants of the land is not "expel" (*grš*) but "dispossess" (*hwryš*). Literally, this verb means to "cause to

14. Note the following phrases: *wydbr YHWH 'l Mšh* (v. 50); *'rṣ Kn'n* (v. 51); *mśkyt* (v. 12; compare Lev. 26:1); *ṣlmy* (v. 52; cf. Gen. 1:26–27; 5:3; 9:6); *whtnḥltm* (v. 54; compare Lev. 25:46; Num. 32:18; 34:13); *wṣrrw 'tkm* (v. 55; compare Num. 25:17–18).

15. Exod. 23:34, 34:13; Deut. 7:5; cf. Judg. 2:3. See Deut. 12:2–3; 1 Kings 14:23; 2 Kings 16:4, 17:10.

16. See Ezek. 8:12; Prov. 25:11 ("*mśkyt ksp*"); Lev. 26:1 ("*'bn mśkyt*," which means bas-reliefs). Cf. the Panamua inscription: "whqm lh mśky"; H. Donner and W. Röllig, *Kanaanäische und Aramäische Inschriften* 1, (Wiesbaden, 1962), no. 215, 1:8).

possess"/"inherit," and it shows a gradual transition to "exterminate" (Num. 14:12 [*ʾknw bdbr wʾwršnwʾ*]; Josh. 13:12; Zech. 9:14–15).[17] The use of this verb expresses an intermediate stage between expulsion (*grš*) in the ancient sources, and *hḥrym*, meaning extermination, in Deuteronomy, as will be discussed below. *Hwryš* can mean simultaneously both expulsion and extermination.[18]

The reason mentioned here for dispossession is not religious but political: "They shall harass you in the land in which you live" (Num. 33:55). In the historiographic source of the Deuteronomic school (Josh. 23:13)[19] the threat has a slightly different form: instead of "for stings (*lśkym*) in your eyes and thorns (*lṣnnm*) in your sides" (ibid.), there it appears as "and for stings (*lšṭṭ*) in your sides and thorns (*lṣnnm*) in your eyes," next to *mwqš* (= snare), which is attested in the earlier source above. *Mwqš* in the religious sense is coupled with national punishment in Judg. 2:3: "They shall become as traps (*lṣdm*) at their sides and their gods be a snare (*mwqš*) to them." These expressions—*śkym, ṣnynm, šṭṭ* (= *šwṭ*), and *ṣdym*—that are attested in Judg. 2:3[20] mean prickly thorns, the causes of pain and distress that these inhabitants would be to the Israelites. In this case, they suggest the harassment by the alien

17. Cf. N. Lohfink, "Die Bedeutung von hebr. *yrš* qal und hif.," *Biblische Zeitschrift* N.F. 26 (1982), pp. 14–33.

18. The ambiguity is reflected in the Targums: Onkelos and Ps. Jonathan translate *hwryš* "expel" (*trk*), while Targum Neophity translates "extermination" (*šyṣy*), as does the LXX (ἀπολλύειν, ἐξαίρειν, ἐξολετρεύειν). In Deuteronomy and in the Deuteronomic school, *hwryš* indicates extermination, as may be learned from 9:3, in which *hwryš* appears next to *hšmyd* and *hʾ byd*. Compare also 2 Kings 21:2 (*hwryš*) with v. 9 (*hšmyd*). *yrš* in Deuteronomy also implies extermination: see 2:12; compare 2:21, 22; 12:2, 29–30; 18:14; 19:1; 31:3.

19. For the nature of this farewell speech in the Deuteronomic school, see my book *Deuteronomy and the Deuteronomic School* (Oxford, 1972), pp. 10–14.

20. Unless we accept the reading of the LXX: *ṣrym* (συνοχάς), enemies; compare Targum: *lmʿyqyn*.

remnants of the settlers in the land of Israel (cf. Ezek. 2:6; 28:24: "Inflicting briars and painful thorns [*qwṣ*] from all about you who will despise [*hš'ṭym*] you"). This motif found in so many sources may allude to the existence of an ancient tradition on the topic of the relations of the Israelites with the native population.

In contrast to other sources that, in similar contexts, specify particular peoples (Exod. 23:23, 28; 34:11; Deut. 7:1; 20:17), here the lawgiver characteristically speaks about "all the inhabitants of the land" without identifying which inhabitants. This lack of specificity permits Nahmanides to interpret it as referring not necessarily to the seven peoples of the land of Canaan, but to all non-Israelite peoples. In addition, Nahmanides takes from this passage the message that the commandment was eternal: "That we were commanded to inherit the land which God gave . . . in every generation . . . to inherit the applicable forever, undertaken by every one of us, even after the exile" (*Criticisms on the Book of Commandments of Maimonides,* commandment 7). The interpretation of Nahmanides, which is not shared by others, stresses that the commandment to the Israelites in all generations is not only to inherit the land but also to dispossess its inhabitants.

However, this view is not the plain meaning of the scripture, which refers only to those who went out of Egypt and were about to enter the land of Canaan to divide it into inheritances; this is not an eternal statute (*ḥq ʿwlm*). The general expression "inhabitants of the land" (*ywšby h'rṣ*) is not unique to Num. 33 but may also be found in the sources of the book of Exodus (23:31; 34:12, 15) that refer to the expulsion of the Canaanites.[21]

4. Deuteronomy. The final source to be discussed here con-

21. See my book: *Deuteronomy and the Deuteronomic School* (n. 19), pp. 342–43.

cerning the ban of the Canaanites is Deut. 7:1–2; 20:10–18. In 7:1–2 we read:

> For (YHWH) shall bring you to the land whither you are going to inherit, and he shall make fall mighty nations before you, the Hittite and the Girgashite, and the Amorite, and the Canaanite, and the Perizzite, and the Hivite, and the Jebusite, seven mighty nations which are mightier than you. And YHWH your God will deliver them to you; and you shall smite them; you must annihilate them (*hḥrm tḥrymm*); you shall not make a covenant with them and you shall not spare them (*l' tkrt lhm bryt wl' tḥnm*). And you shall not marry them, you shall not let your daughter marry his son, and his daughter you shall not take as a wife for your son. For she will draw your son away from me and they shall serve other gods . . . but thus shall you do to them: their altars you shall dismantle and their steles you shall smash; and their sacred trees you shall chop down; and their idols you shall burn with fire.

On the topics of refraining from covenants with the Canaanites, the prohibition of contracting marriages with them, and the obligation to dismantle their altars, the author of the book of Deuteronomy depends on Exod. 23:20–34, but he adds a commandment unique to him, concerning the burning of idols (see Deut. 7:25).[22] The most important innovation by the author of Deuteronomy is the *ḥerem* of the seven peoples, which we shall discuss presently.

In a more legalistic passage, Deut. 20:16–18, we read:

> But in the towns of these peoples (the Canaanites) which

22. See Halbe, *Das Privilegrecht* (n. 12), pp. 119 ff. This commandment occurs for the first time in the book of Deuteronomy. In fact, David did not enforce this law; he just "carried them [the idols] off" (2 Sam. 5:21). The Chronicler who follows the Deuteronomic law has David giving an order "to burn the idols" (1 Chron. 14:12) instead of "carrying them off."

> YHWH your God has given to you for an inheritance, you shall not let a soul remain alive, for you must annihilate them (*hḥrm tḥrymm*): the Hittite, and the Amorite, and the Canaanite, and the Perizzite and the Hivite, and the Jebusite, as YHWH your God commanded you, so that they do not lead you to do all the abominations which they have done for their gods and sin against YHWH your God.[23]

In these two pericopes of Deuteronomy we find, for the first time, the use of the verb *hḥrym* concerning the Canaanites, in the sense of "annihilation."[24] We do not find this verb in the earlier sources, neither in connection with God who dis-

23. These verses constitute a reinterpretation of an older law pertaining to the imposition of corvée upon a Canaanite city that makes peace with the Israelites (vv. 10–14). The author of Deuteronomy, who demands absolute and unconditional *ḥerem* of the Canaanites, interpreted the old law of 20:10–14 as applying only to remote cities not belonging to Canaan (see A. Biram, "*mas ʿobed,*" *Tarbiz,* 23 (1944), pp. 137 ff.). Verse 15, which opens with the phrase "thus you shall deal with all the towns that lie very far from you," has the force of the Rabbinic casuistic term *bmh dbrym ʾmwrym* "in which case are these words said" = when does this apply; cf. A. Toeg, "Exodus XXII, 4: The Text and the Law in the Light of the Ancient Sources," *Tarbiz* 39 (1970), p. 229 (Hebrew); I. L. Seeligmann, "From Historic Reality to Historiosophic Conception in the Bible," in E. S. Rosenthal, ed., *P'raqim, Yearbook of the Schocken Institute for Jewish Research* 2 (Jerusalem, 1969–74), p. 294 (Hebrew).

24. The root *ḥrm* in the Semitic languages indicates both prohibition and sacredness; cf., e.g., Deut. 22:9: "You shall not sow your vineyards with another kind of seed, else the crop will become sacred (*tqdš*) (i.e., will be prohibited)"; compare Arabic *ḥrym*. *Ḥerem* in the context of war denotes dedication to God: if it is man or animal, it should be sacrificed to God, and if it is property, it should be devoted to him (Exod. 22:19; Lev. 27:29; Deut. 13:16; 1 Sam. 15:3, 33). The religious meaning of the root *ḥrm* is fully expressed in the Mesha inscription: "and I killed . . . seven thousand men . . . and women because I proclaimed them as *ḥerem* to Ištar-Kemos (*ky lʿštr kmš hḥrmth*); see Donner and Röllig, *KAI* (n. 16), no. 181:17. In the second temple period and in later periods, *ḥerem* acquired the meaning of expulsion and confiscation of property (Ezra 10:8). See W. Horbury, "Extirpation and Excommunication," *Vetus Testamentum* 35 (1985), pp. 19–38.

possesses nor in relation to the dispossessing accomplished by Israel. And in no other sources do we find such commands as "you shall not let a soul remain alive" (*l' tḥyh kl nšmh*) (Deut. 20:16; cf. Deut. 2:34; 3:3),[25] of which the Deuteronomistic historiographer makes frequent use (Josh. 10:28, 30, 33, 37, 39, 40; 11:11, 14). The book of Deuteronomy, which uses *hḥrym* concerning the Canaanites, consistently avoids the verb *grš* for "expel," in order to indicate that the seven nations are not to be expelled but exterminated. Alongside the verb *hḥrym* in Deuteronomy we find a series of other verbs connoting annihilation, such as *'kl* "devour" (Deut. 7:16), *klh* "put an end to" (Deut. 7:22), *hšmyd* "wipe out" (Deut. 7:24), and *h'byd* "cause to perish" (Deut. 7:24). When the author of Deuteronomy draws on earlier sources that do use the verb *grš,* he intentionally changes it to another verb in order to establish his own point of view. Entire phrases are transformed for this purpose; for example, Exod. 23:27, which says that God will panic the enemy so that he turns the nape of his neck to Israel (i.e., he flees), reads: "And I shall panic (*whmty*) all the people among whom you shall go and they shall turn tail and run (*ntn ʿrp*)." In the hands of the author of Deuteronomy, this passage becomes "And YHWH your God shall give them unto you, and he shall throw them into a great panic (*whmm mhmh gdwlh*) until they are wiped out (*ʿd hšmdm*)" (Deut. 7:23). Instead of "turning their back"—fleeing—the author of the book of Deuteronomy uses the term *hšmyd.* Moreover, he adds the phrase "nobody will be able to stand against you until he causes you to destroy them" (Deut. 7:22; cf. 11:25; Josh. 1:5).[26]

25. Compare Num. 21:35: "until no remnant was left" (*ʿd blty hš'yr lw śryd*), in a passage copied from Deut. 2:1–3. See commentaries and my article "The Extent of the Promised Land: The Status of Transjordan," in G. Strecker, ed., *Das Land Israel in Biblischer Zeit* (Goettingen, 1983), p. 70, n. 4.

26. For the military speech containing patriotic motives in the Deuteronomic work, see my book *Deuteronomy and the Deuteronomic School* (n. 18), pp. 45–51.

Another example of intentional change on the subject of the removal of the pre-Israelite population is Exod. 23:28. There we read that the hornet (*ṣrʿh*) is sent by God in order to drive out the Hivite, the Canaanite, and the Hittite from before the Israelites from his land. As a matter of ideological taste, the book of Deuteronomy completely drops the tradition of the angel (an objection to angelology),[27] but the hornet now acquires a function different from that in Exod. 23:28: God sends the hornet not to drive out the Canaanites, but to annihilate the remnants and the hidden enemies (*hnšʾrym whnstrym*) before the Israelites (7:20); the unhidden enemies the Israelites will destroy themselves.

What is the reason for these developments in the book of Deuteronomy, and how do we account for the adoption in this late book of a radical position concerning the pre-Israelite populations? *Ḥerem* in the sense of dedicating and offering to God is known to us from ancient periods in Israel and in other nations, as, for example, in the Mesha inscription.[28] Yet the ancient *ḥerem* was ostensibly a vow undertaken at the time of proclamation of outright war, as was the case at Jericho (Josh.

27. See my article "The Emergence of the Deuteronomic Movement: The Historical Antecedents," in N. Lohfink, ed., *Das Deuteronomium, Entstehung, Gestalt und Botschaft* (Leuven, 1985), p. 84.

28. Exod. 22:19; Lev. 27:29; 1 Sam. 15:3, 18, 33; 1 Kings 20:42; and compare Micah 4:13. Cf. n. 24, above.

For the connection between *ḥrm* and *qdš* (compared to the akkadian *asakku*) see A. Malamat, "The *Ḥerem* in Mari and in the Bible," *Y. Kaufman Jubilee Volume,* Jerusalem, 1961, pp. 149–58, (Hebrew). See also my article "The Royal and Sacred Aspects of the Tithe in the Old Testament," *Beer-Sheva* 1 (1973), p. 123, n. 6 (Hebrew), and also my article "*Ḥilul, kbisha* and *mirmas regel,*" *Meḥqĕrey Lašon, Hebrew Language Studies Presented to Zeev Ben-Hayyim* (Jerusalem, 1983), pp. 198–99, n. 20 (Hebrew).

Concerning the Mesha inscription, see n. 24 above. For cultic extermination carried out by other nations, see N. Lohfink, "*Ḥrm,*" in G. J. Botterweck and H. Ringgren, eds., *Theologisches Wörterbuch zum Alten Testament* 3 (Stuttgart, 1978), p. 204; S. E. Loewenstamm, "*Ḥerem,*" *Encycl. Miqraʾit* 3, cols. 290–92 (Hebrew).

6:17–18) and Arad (Num. 21:1–3).[29] Joshua proclaims in the siege of Jericho: "and the city shall be *ḥerem,* it and all which is in her, to the Lord" (Josh. 6:17). As a result of this dedication, everything in the city, "from man to animal" (Josh. 6:21), the silver and gold, and the brass and iron, are given to the temple treasury (Josh. 6:24). Were the *ḥerem* a custom that operated in accordance with the commands of the book of Deuteronomy—that all the population of the land of Canaan were subject to the law of the *ḥerem* (Deut. 7:2; 20:17)—there would be no reason to proclaim special status for the city of Jericho.[30] The case of the *ḥerem* of Arad in Num. 21:1–3 is similar: Israel vows (*ndr*) to the Lord that if God will give the Canaanites dwelling in the Negeb into their hands, then the Israelites will turn the cities and their inhabitants into *ḥerem*. A parallel tradition of the *ḥerem* in the Negeb district, at the hand of the tribe of Judah and Simeon, and of calling the place by the name *Ḥormah,* appears in Judg. 1:18.[31] According to the *ḥerem* law in Deuteronomy, the *ḥerem* applies, in any case, to all seven pre-Israelite peoples, thus rendering superfluous the Israelites' vow to put to *ḥerem* the Canaanites of Jericho and Arad.

It was the book of Deuteronomy that conceived the *ḥerem* as a commandment applying automatically to all the inhabitants of the land, whether or not they fought. This *ḥerem* is not conditional on any vow or dedication but is an *a priori* decree, which belongs more to utopian theory than to practice. In-

29. Compare Lev. 27:28–29, where *Ḥerem* executed against humans and beasts appears as part of a voluntary dedication, as a result of a vow; cf. v. 2: "when a man shall clearly utter a vow," *ky ypl' ndr,* 14 ff.; and compare to v. 21: "as a field devoted," *kśdh hḥrm*. See Seeligmann (above, n. 23), p. 295; M. Greenberg, "*Ḥerem,*" *Encycl. Judaica* 8, cols. 344–50.

30. Only by adopting the midrashic method can we claim that Joshua had executed in Jericho a more stringent extermination than that found in Deuteronomy; for that reason, a special kind of extermination must have been carried out (see BT Sanhed. 44a).

31. Of the relation between the tradition in Num. 21:1–3 and Jud. 1:17, see discussion below, pp. 130–31.

deed, in practice, the inhabitants of the Canaanite cities were not destroyed but rather placed under corvée labor, as we learn from 1 Kings 9:20–21: "All the remaining people of the Amorites, the Hittites, the Perizzites, the Hivites, and the Jebusites which were not from the Israelites themselves, among those which were left . . . which the Israelites could not destroy,[32] Solomon put them for corvée labor until this day." We also learn, from old traditions,[33] that the remaining Canaanites dwelt in their cities until the time of David and Solomon, and that these latter were placed under corvée labor (1 Kings 9:20–21; 2 Chron. 2:16). Furthermore, according to Judg. 1:32–33, some of these Canaanites even placed the Israelites in the north (on the coast and in Galilee) under corvée. As will be shown later, the imposition of corvée labor on the pre-Israelite inhabitants of the land *and not their dispossession*—as we find in Judg. 1—is represented as a sin. The angel of the Lord sent to bring the Israelites into the land (see above) reproves the Israelites about this matter, which he represents as a violation of the commandment not to make a covenant with the inhabitants of the land (Judg. 2:1–4).

Although in all the existing sources Israel is commanded to remove the Canaanites from the land, only in Deuteronomy is the removal interpreted as requiring complete annihilation. In the other sources, both expulsion and dispossession are commanded. According to the historical works, as we have indicated, the *ḥerem* on the Canaanites as commanded in Deut. 7:2; 20:16–17 was never carried out. The editor of the book of Joshua, who depends on Deuteronomy, tried to render an image of the conquest as proceeding according to command-

32. It seems that 2 Chron. 8:7–8 deliberately changed the phrase "Whom the children of Israel could not destroy," to "whom the children of Israel consumed not," (*l' kylwm*), and it views them as *gerim* (2 Chron. 2:16). See S. Japhet, *The Ideology of the Book of Chronicles and Its Place in Biblical Thought* (Frankfurt, 1989), pp. 334–47.

33. Judg. 1:21, 27–28, 29, 30, 31–33; and their parallels in Josh. 15:63; 16:10; 17:12–13, 14–18.

ments of the book of Deuteronomy; therefore, he speaks of total annihilation of all the inhabitants of the Canaanite cities of the land: "and Joshua smote all the land . . . and all their kings did not leave behind a survivor, and every single soul was destroyed as the Lord God of Israel commanded" (Josh. 10:40); "and all the cities of these kings and all their kings, Joshua seized and he smote them by the sword and annihilated them, as Moses the servant of the Lord commanded . . . every man they smote by the sword until they destroyed them and they did not leave any alive" (Josh. 11:12–14). According to this author, all the territory "from the Mount of Halaq in the south to Baal Gad in the valley of Lebanon" was seized by the Israelites in the days of Joshua, and not a single Canaanite was left behind in this area (Josh. 11:14–15, 16–17, 20; 12:7). Such a portrayal stands in complete contradiction to the core accounts of the tribal conquest in Judg. 1 and their parallels in the book of Joshua, according to which the Canaanite inhabitants persisted in the coastal cities and in the lowlands until Davidic times. In fact, the survivors of the Canaanites who were left in the land are the strangers (*gerim*) mentioned in most of the law codes in the Pentateuch.[34]

The law of *ḥerem* in Deuteronomy, then, is a utopian law that was written in retrospect. Deuteronomy adopted for itself the commandments of the old *ḥerem,* which was practiced in encounters with the enemies and which was intertwined with a vow and with dedication in proclaiming *ḥerem,* but Deuteronomy applied it in the manner of a theoretical *ḥerem* applying to all the pre-Israelite inhabitants. Furthermore, according to the author of Deuteronomy the *ḥerem* applied not only to the population west of the Jordan but also to the Transjordan population (Deut. 2:34; 3:10); Transjordan, in his view, as has been discussed in Chapter 3, is a part of the promised land.

The Rabbis could not accept this radical concept of total

34. See I. L. Seeligmann, "Ger," *Encycl. Miqraʾit* 2 (Jerusalem, 1954), p. 547.

ḥerem in Deuteronomy, and they circumvented the plain meaning of the scripture by introducing the accounts of Joshua's conquest as follows: "Joshua sent out three proclamations (*prostagmata*) to the Canaanites: 'Let him who would flee flee, let him who would make peace make peace, and let him who would make war do so.' "[35] Such an offer of options to the Canaanites stands in complete contradiction to the laws of *ḥerem* in Deuteronomy (7:2; 20:16–17), but it reflects the politics customary in dealings with other nations during Hasmonean times, when there was no inclination to annihilate strangers according to the commandments of the *ḥerem*. The purpose of the proclamations was to cleanse the land of idols and convert the inhabitants to Judaism insofar as possible, and anyone who opposed such measures was given the opportunity to leave the area.[36] Thus, for example, when the men of Gezer requested that Simeon the Hasmonean make a covenant with them ("he will give them the right hand"),[37] he consented; instead of annihilating them he expelled them from the city, purified their houses of idols, and settled in the city men who observed the Torah (1 Macc. 13:43–44). He treated the inhabitants of the Ḥaqra in Jerusalem similarly: "he gave them the right hand," made them leave the fortress, and cleansed it of idols (1 Macc. 13:49–50).

Thus we have seen that the total *ḥerem* of the pre-Israelite

35. Lev. Rabbah 17:6 (ed. Margaliot, pp. 386–87); Yerushalmi Shebiʿit 7:5, 36, d; Debarim Rabbah 5:14; and see below, pp. 152–53.

36. We therefore cannot accept E. Meyer's opinion, in *Ursprung und Anfaenge des Christentums* 2: *Die Entwicklung des Judentums und Jesus von Nazaret* (Berlin, 1925), pp. 281–82, that the Hasmoneans followed the extermination law as found in Deuteronomy. On the contrary, in their time the law was taken out of its context, in order to be adjusted to a new reality.

37. For this expression see M. Weinfeld and R. Meridor, "The Punishment of Zedekiah and That of Polymestor," in Y. Zakovitch and A. Rofé, eds., *I. L. Seeligmann Volume: Essays on the Bible and the Ancient World* 1 (Jerusalem, 1983), p. 229, n. 1 (Hebrew). For *qblt ymyn,* see S. Liebermann, "Notes," in E. S. Rosenthal, ed., *P'raqim, Yearbook of the Schocken Institute for Jewish Research* 1 (Jerusalem, 1967–68), pp. 98–101.

population, as described by the Deuteronomic writings, is unrealistic. What actually occurred was the expulsion and clearing out of the pre-Israelite inhabitants, and even that was not a one-time event but an ongoing process (cf. Exod. 23:29–30).[38] The *ḥerem* of Deuteronomy, then, is a wish originating in the eighth and seventh centuries B.C.E., the time of crystallization of the book of Deuteronomy.

We have discussed the background of the *ḥerem* of Deuteronomy and must now establish the background of the commandments concerning expulsion and dispossession that precede the utopian ideology of Deuteronomy. The laws of expulsion and dispossession of the pre-Israelite population crystalized in a period of tension with the inhabitants of Canaan, and unity among the tribes of Israel. The most suitable period for the crystallization of the laws of dispossession is that of King Saul, when there was a sense of tribal unification under one king. Furthermore, the most suitable place for the crystalization of these traditions is the shrine of Gilgal, which is commonly accepted as the place of the formation of the stories of conquest in Josh. 2–10.[39] The central place to which the stories are tied is Gilgal, where monumental stones are set up to commemorate the crossing of the Jordan (Josh. 3–4), and where the Israelites were circumcised (Josh. 5:2–8) and celebrated the Passover (Josh. 5:9–12); there, the captain of the Lord's Host (= an angel)[40] appears to Joshua before the con-

38. The verse in Deut. 7:22 is dependent on Exod. 23:29–30 and contradicts Deut. 9:3: "So shalt thou drive them out and make them to perish quickly," *whwrštm wh' bdtm mhr;* compare Josh. 10:42: "and all these kings and their land did Joshua take at one time," *lkd Yehosua pʿm 'ḥt,* with Josh. 11:18: "Joshua made war a long time with all those kings," *ymym rbym ʿšh Jehosua 't kl hmlkym h'lh mlḥmh*).

39. See A. Alt, "Josua," *Kleine Schriften* 1 (Munich, 1953), pp. 176 ff., and also M. Noth, *Josua,* HAT (Tübingen, 1953), p. 12; J. A. Soggin, *Joshua,* OTL (London, 1972), pp. 9–11.

40. The "Captain of the host of the Lord" is the angel sent by God to guide the children of Israel to the promised land (Exod. 23:20; 32:34; 33:2); see above, pp. 78 ff.

quest begins (Josh. 5:13–15), and thither the Israelites return after the wars (Josh. 10:15, 33).

Gilgal was the cultic center of the tribe of Benjamin, and the events of the conquest according to Joshua 2–10 occur in the district of Benjamin. These events begin in Jericho, move to Ay, to Gibeon, and to Beth-Horon, and conclude in the valley of Aijalon. All these cities are part of Benjamin's territory (Josh. 18:21–28),[41] and they delineate the main campaign of the conquest in Joshua 3:1–10:15. Saul, the first king of Israel, was originally from the tribe of Benjamin (1 Sam. 9:1), and the main sanctuary of this tribe was at Gilgal. Saul was bound to Gilgal: it is where he was crowned (1 Sam. 11:14–15), where he came to sacrifice before the battle with the Philistines (1 Sam. 13:7–15), and where he went to celebrate the victory over Amalek (1 Sam. 15:12 ff.). It seems reasonable that the main kernel of the laws of dispossession in Exod. 23:20–33 emerged in Gilgal,[42] in the times of Saul. The radical policy against the old inhabitants of the land is characteristic of those times, and Saul is portrayed as a man who plotted against the Gibeonites, "a remnant of the Amorites," whom he sought to destroy "in his zeal for the Israelites and Judah" (2 Sam. 21:2–3).

Against this background we can consider the story of the Israelites' illegitimate covenant with the Gibeonites in Josh. 9:6–7; 14–15.[43] The expressions used to describe this covenant

41. Aijalon became part of the tribe of Benjamin after its expansion toward the west, as we learn from 1 Chron. 8:13: "And Beriah and Shema, who were heads of fathers' houses of the inhabitants of Ayalon, who put to flight the inhabitants of Gath," (*hmh hbryḥw ʾt ywšby Gath*). The inhabitants of Gath who managed to kill the Ephraimites (1 Chron. 7:21) were driven off by the people of Benjamin. See Z. Kallai, "The Settlement Traditions of Ephraim: A Historiographical Study," *ZDPV* 102 (1986), pp. 72–73.

42. N. Lohfink, *Das Hauptgebot, Eine Untersuchung literarischer Einleitungsfragen zu Dtn. 5–11* (Rome, 1963), pp. 176 ff.; E. Otto, *Das Mazzotfest in Gilgal* (Stuttgart, 1975), pp. 203 ff.

43. Special attention should be drawn to verse 14: ". . . and they did not inquire of the mouth of the Lord," (*wʾt py JHWH lʾ šʾ lw*).

are the same as the language used in the law of dispossession in Exod. 23:20–33. The men of Israel say to the Hivite who is in Gibeon: "perhaps you dwell in my midst (*yšb bqrb*) and how shall I make a covenant with you? (Josh. 9:7). In Exod. 23:32–33 similar words are spoken against the inhabitants of Canaan: "You shall not make with them . . . any covenant. They shall not dwell in your land (*yšb bʾrs*) . . ." And, as scholars have suggested,[44] the story of the Gibeonites in Josh. 9 can be understood only by assuming that the law had been set up in the light of the prohibition to give the Canaanites the right to dwell among the Israelites, which is reflected in the desire of Saul not to allow the Gibeonites who dwelt in the land the right to settle in the mountains of the land of Israel.

Furthermore, even the institution of the *ḥerem* in its original form (see above) may be explained against the background of the time of Saul. The *ḥerem* of Jericho in Josh. 6:17–21 fits the hard line of Saul and seems to have originated at the sanctuary of Gilgal. The formulation of the *ḥerem* in Josh. 6:21, "And they destroyed everything in the city, man and woman, young and old, ox, and sheep, and ass by the sword," almost overlaps the formulation of the *ḥerem* that Saul cast over Nob, the city of the priests: "And Nob, the city of the priests, he killed by the sword, man and woman, child and infant, and ox, and ass, and sheep by the sword" (1 Sam. 22:19).[45] The same formulation appears in connection with the *ḥerem* of Amalek commanded by God to Saul: "Go and smite Amalek and destroy all therein and you shall not have pity on them, but shall kill

44. See M. Haran, "The Gibeonites, the Nethinim and the Sons of Solomon's Servants," *VT* 11 (1961), pp. 159–69; J. Halbe, "Gibeon und Israel," *VT* 25 (1975), pp. 613–41.

45. Of other Israelite cities, which were to be exterminated in a total manner, cf. what is said about "the rebellious city" (*ʿyr hnydḥt*) in Deut. 13:16: "Thou shalt surely smite the inhabitants of that city with the edge of the sword, destroying it utterly and all there is therein and the cattle thereof with the edge of the sword," and also the cities of Benjamin: ". . . and smote them by the edge of the sword, both the entire city and the cattle and all that they found" (Judg. 20:48).

man and woman, child and infant, ox and sheep, camel and ass" (1 Sam. 15:3).[46]

The period of Saul, then, is the most appropriate time for the crystallization of anti-Canaanite ideology, in contrast to the period of David and Solomon, who did not practice the *ḥerem* against the pre-Israelite inhabitants but rather placed them under corvée labor (1 Kings 9:20–21).[47] Moreover, from 2 Sam. 24, the account of David's census of his kingdom, we learn that "the cities of the Hivites and the Canaanites" are included in the census of the Israelite population (v. 7).[48] Indeed, the Gibeonites, to save their lives, turned to David to avenge them against the house of Saul, the king who had tried to annihilate them (2 Sam. 21:5, and see above), and David rescued them from annihilation. After the days of David and Solomon, there is no further mention of the destruction of Canaanite cities and their inhabitants. The author of the book of Deuteronomy thus revived the *ḥerem* from the times of Saul,[49] but whereas the old *ḥerem* had applied to specific encounters—with the Gibeonites, and at Nob, the city of the priests, and Amalek—the editor of the book of Deuteronomy

46. In the *Ḥerem* of Amaleq we find the camel along with the donkey; we have not found camels in other extermination formulas, because the enemy was not nomadic as here. Like the Midianites and the Išmaelites, the Amalekites, who dwelled in the desert, used camels. See Judg. 6:3–5: "The Midianites came up and the Amalekites and the children of the east . . . for they came up with their cattle . . . and their camels were without number." Compare Judg. 7:12; 1 Sam. 30:17.

47. Concerning the change in the matter of *Ḥerem* in the time of David and Solomon, see my article: "Zion and Jerusalem as Religious and Political Capital: Ideology and Utopia," in R. E. Friedman, ed., *The Poet and the Historian: Essays in Literary and Historical Biblical Criticism,* Harvard Semitic Studies 26, (Chico, Calif., 1983), pp. 81–85.

48. See S. Abramsky, "The Attitude Toward the Amorites and the Jebusites in the Book of Samuel: Historical Foundation and the Ideological Significance," *Zion* 50 (1985), pp. 27–58 (Hebrew).

49. Cf. J. Milgrom, "Profane Slaughter" (n. 13), pp. 6–8. However, (pace Milgrom) the campaign against the Gibeonites is not to be equated with the total ban of all the Canaanites, as Deuteronomy would have it.

depicted the *ḥerem* as originally applied to the seven peoples of the land of Canaan.

As we conclude our discussion, we should pose the question concerning why the Philistines were not banned. The Philistines, a bitter enemy of Israel, especially at the time of Saul, do not appear in the lists of nations to be banned. Why? The answer is that the Philistines, like the Israelites, were not natives in the Land of Canaan but intruders who appeared on the horizon in the middle of the twelfth century, after the Israelites had settled in the land. The definition of the native, pre-Israelite nations, like the delineation of the borders of Canaan, had already been fixed at the beginning of the settlement and could not be altered. This chronological issue may explain the tradition about the covenant of the Patriarchs with the Philistines (Gen. 21:22–34; 26:26–31), which stands in contrast to the tradition about the failed attempt at covenant-making with the Shechemites (Gen. 34) who belonged to the Hivites (Gen. 34:2).

All in all, in the biblical laws, the statutes relating to the pre-Israelite inhabitants show a developmental process: in the first version, reflected in Exod. 23:20–33; 34:11–16, the commandment prescribes "expelling (*grš*)" the Canaanites and avoiding any covenants with them—that is, refusing to allow them settlement in the land: "They shall not dwell in your land" (Exod. 23:33). In the second version, reflected in the priestly code in Num. 33:50–56, the commandment prescribes "dispossession (*hwryš*)" of the inhabitants of the land, which was interpreted as either expulsion or destruction. In the third version, reflected in Deut. 7:2; 20:16–17, the commandment prescribes the "ban (*ḥerem*)," which is interpreted as annihilation: "you shall not let any soul live" (Deut. 20:16). The *ḥerem,* the total destruction described in Deuteronomy, was never carried out (see 1 Kings 9:20–21), and this law must be seen as utopian.

As we move further from the historical situation, a more rigid picture appears, in which the laws gradually become idealized and unrealistic. The most extreme position crystalized during the period of national revival at the time of Hezekiah[50] and Josiah. In earlier days, complete destruction had been instituted as a vow and a dedication, on the occasion of a proclamation of war on a specific city or hostile group, even within Israel.[51] In contrast, the Deuteronomic *ḥerem* was conceived to apply a priori to all the inhabitants of the land of Canaan, regardless of whether they fought against the Israelites. Such total destruction must be understood as utopian, for it originated in a theoretical manner several centuries after the wars of Israel in Canaan.

50. Concerning the extermination of nomadic tribes in the time of Hezekiah, see: 1 Chron. 4:39–43: ". . . and destroyed them utterly, unto this day" (*wyḥrymwm ʿd hywm hzh*) (v. 41); "And they smote the remnant of the Amalekites" (*wykw ʾt šʾryt hplth l ʿmlq*) (v. 43). These verses could explain the background of the inclusion of the obligation to wipe out the memory of Amaleq in Deuteronomy (25:17–19). For discussion of the tradition of 1 Chron. 4:39–41 see N. Na'aman, "Pastoral Nomads in the Southwestern Periphery of the Kingdom of Judah in the 9th–8th Centuries B.C.E.," *Zion* 52 (1987), pp. 264–67 (Hebrew).

51. See above, n. 45.

5

The Conquest of the Land of Canaan

Reality and Ideology

The problem of the conquest of Canaan by the tribes of Israel is made extraordinarily complex by contradictions in the biblical sources. Some of these sources describe the conquest and settlement of the land as taking place without the participation of Joshua (Judg. 1, and see in particular 1:1b), and others, in which Joshua appears, exhibit differences among themselves regarding the methods of his war and conquests. For example, according to Josh. 10:40 ff.; 11:12 ff.; 12; and 21:41–43, Joshua smote all the kings of Canaan, captured their cities, and destroyed their inhabitants in the entire area of the land of Israel, from Baal Gad in the valley of Lebanon to Mt. Halak, which ascends toward Seir: "there was no city that made peace with the Israelites except the Hivites dwelling in Gibeon. They took all in war. For it was from YHWH . . . in order to exterminate them . . . in order to destroy them, just as YHWH commanded Moses" (11:19–20 and cf. 12:7; 21:41–43). In contrast, other sources say that Joshua did not succeed in driving out the Canaanites in Beth-shean and in the Jezreel Valley because of their iron chariotry (17:14–18). Thus, enclaves of the Canaanite peoples remained, and Canaanites continued to live in various cities in the land of Israel, such as Jerusalem, Gezer, Beth-shean, Megiddo, Acco, and other cities on the coast and in the valleys (Josh. 15:63; 16:10; 17:11–13; Judg. 1:21 ff.). We also learn from Judg. 4–5 that in the days of Deborah, after Joshua's generation, Canaanites still dwelt in the Jezreel Valley.

Factual contradictions are blatant in passages that recount the conquest of Hebron and Debir in Judah. According to Josh. 14:6–15; 15:13–19 (cf. Judg. 1:10–15, 20), Caleb the Kenizzite drove out the Anakim from the hill country of Hebron, and Othniel, the son of Kenaz, captured Debir; according to Josh. 10:36–39; 11:21–22, however, all of Israel conquered, under the leadership of Joshua, both Hebron and Debir, and the Israelites placed the Anakim from the hill country of Hebron under ban. Similarly, scholars have noted, on the one hand, the legendary character of the conquest stories related to Joshua (the stories about Jericho and Ai, Josh. 6–8), and, on the other hand, the artificiality and stereotypical character of the descriptions of the conquest in Josh. 10:28–39 (see below).

All of these difficulties have accounted for scholars' skepticism regarding the nature of Joshua's conquest. Three different schools of thought have emerged.[1] Although these schools conflict with one another, we will try to show below that one

1. Y. Kaufmann's approach (see especially his commentary on the book of Judges, 1959) has not found a niche in the scholarship on the subject because of its extremism and one-sidedness. Because of his eagerness to describe a unitary conquest of the land in the time of Joshua, he ignores the difficulties we have enumerated and tries to harmonize contradictions. He claims that the book of Joshua, which he believes was written close to the events, claims that the land was indeed conquered, although the Canaanites remained dwelling in its cities. But here he wholly ignores that layer in Joshua which says explicitly that Joshua took all of the land "from Mount Halak which goes up to Seir to Baal Gad in the Lebanon valley" and captured all of their kings, and that all was taken in war except for Gibeon (Josh. 11:15 ff.; cf. 10:40–42; 12:7–8; 21:41–43). He interprets these verses as an exaggerated formulation, with generalizing and overwrought language (see his commentary to Joshua, p. 36: "as if it had already been completed"; p. 155: "the exaggeration"; "this does not justify the conclusion that the book of Joshua tells of a complete conquest of all the land of Canaan"). Similarly, he ignores the passages that speak explicitly of a destruction of all the Canaanites and putting them under ban (11:20), which are related to the area from Baal Gad in the north to Mount Halak in the south—all this being done in agreement with the

approach does not necessarily preclude another; rather, each approach elaborates well a different aspect of the settlement process.

1. Albright's Archaeological School. The approach initiated by W. F. Albright attempts to discover in archaeological excavations confirmation of evidence in the Bible regarding the conquest of the land of Israel in the thirteenth century B.C.E. According to this approach, great Canaanite centers, such as Lachish, Debir, Eglon (Tell el-Hesi), and Bethel, were destroyed then.[2] In the 1950s, an important piece of evidence was added from Y. Yadin's excavations at Hazor,[3] which show that this city was destroyed at the end of the thirteenth century. The hypothesis prevalent among scholars of the Albright

---

commands of Deuteronomy (Josh. 11:15 ff.). We have in these verses a conception that runs like a red thread throughout the literary stratum (Deuteronomistic), and not simply a generalization found in an isolated verse (see below, pp. 149 ff.). In order to resolve the contradiction regarding the destruction of the Anakim (by Joshua, as opposed to Caleb), Kaufmann has to hypothesize that the Anakim returned to Hebron after Joshua's wars, and Caleb then drove them out. He admits that "the summary in 11:21–22 is really not exact," and thus claims that "there is no real contradiction between the stories" (p. 175).

The central weaknesses in his solution are his hypothesis about the relationship between Pentateuchal sources and the book of Joshua and his view that the book of Joshua came into being near the time of the events described in it. In order to maintain his thesis he needs to postulate that the Deuteronomistic stratum is ancient, which starkly contradicts his approach in his early writings (see M. Haran, "*Sugyot miqra*': Problems in the Composition of the Former Prophets, *Tarbiz* 37 [1968], pp. 1–14 [= *Likkutei Tarbiz* 1, pp. 155–68]; both Hebrew). We cannot go into detail here, but his hypothesis that all the traditions in the book of Joshua, including the lists of inheritances and cities, were already crystalized in the days of Joshua, is impossible from a historical and archaeological point of view. On the issue of the boundaries of inheritances and the lists of cities and their historical background, see Z. Kallai, *Historical Geography of the Bible* (Jerusalem: Leiden, 1986).

2. W. F. Albright, "The Israelite Conquest of Canaan in the Light of Archaeology," *BASOR* 74 (1939), pp. 11–23.

3. Y. Yadin, *Hazor* (Schweich Lectures: London, 1970).

school is that these cities were destroyed by the Israelite tribes at the time of their conquest. It must be noted, however, that these archaeological proofs are not unambiguous and that some of them have actually been revealed to be unreliable.[4]

It has become clear, for example, that Debir is identified not with Tell Beit Mirsim, as Albright suggested, but rather with Khirbet Rabud.[5] This adjustment weakens the archaeological line of explanation, because unlike Tell Beit Mirsim, which exhibits clear signs of destruction from the thirteenth century, Khirbet Rabud displays no sign of destruction in that century. Also, there is currently no proof that Lachish (Tell ed-Duweir) was destroyed in the thirteenth century;[6] in fact, evidence has been found of Egyptian rule at the site dating to the beginning of the twelfth century (the time of Rameses III).[7] Regarding Jericho and Ai, there are no signs that their walls were destroyed in the Late Bronze Age. As we will see, the stories of the conquest of these cities are etiological, a fact that lessens their historical validity.

Despite these difficulties, we cannot ignore the fact that a large number of Canaanite cities were destroyed in the thirteenth and twelfth centuries B.C.E. Even if we cannot relate this destruction to Joshua himself, it does testify to a war and conquest at the same time that the tribes of Israel began to take

4. It is to be noted here, that even if it were proven that a particular city was destroyed in the thirteenth century B.C.E., there would be no certainty that the destruction was the act of Israelites. The destruction might have come about by the Egyptian kingdom, by the Sea Peoples, or by Canaanites fighting among themselves.

5. M. Kochavi, "'Khirbet Rabûd' = Debir," *Tel-Aviv: Journal of the Tel-Aviv University Institute of Archaeology* 1 (1974), pp. 2–33.

6. See R. de Vaux, *The Early History of Israel to the Period of the Judges*, trans. D. Smith (London, orig. Paris, 1971), p. 506.

7. See O. Tufnell, *Lachish, The Bronze Age* 4 (London, 1958), pp. 37, 98; R. Giveon, "An Inscription of Rameses III from Lachish," *Tel-Aviv* 10 (1983), pp. 176–77; and also the discussion of D. Ussishkin, "Excavations at Tel Lachish, 1978–1983: Second Preliminary Report," *Tel-Aviv* 10 (1983), pp. 169–70.

possession of the land. Scholars have rightly noted that the methods of war that the tribes employed—ambushes (Josh. 7–8) and surprise attacks (Josh. 10:9; 11:7), i.e., various types of military strategies—accord with a tribal military response to the organized army of a fortified city. Only by stratagem could a tribal army avoid a head-on collision with a stronger enemy and rout it.[8] Hence, the conquest stories must be viewed as reflecting the reality of the period of Israelite tribal settlement, even though the stories were put in writing only at a later period. Moreover, we find in the descriptions of the settlement that the "camp" (*maḥănê*) served as a point of deployment for a tribe's military onslaughts: the warriors would go forth to battle from it and afterwards return to it (see Chapter 2). Gilgal is described as one such military base in the stories of Joshua (Josh. 5:10; 9:6; 10:6–9, 15, 46); it served as a bridgehead for invading the land of Canaan.[9] According to Josh. 10:21, there was also a "camp" in Makkedah in the lowland. As we will see, the story about Makkedah in Josh. 10:16 ff. belongs, from a literary point of view, to a separate unit, and it is tied, from a geographical point of view, to the lowland of Judah and not to the area of Benjamin to which the stories in Josh. 2:1–10:15 are tied. The geographical range of these stories is from Gilgal to Aijalon (*wĕ ʿad maqqēdâ* "and to Makkedah" in 10:10 is a later addition), whereas Makkedah belongs to Judah (see Josh. 15:41) and is far from the Aijalon Valley. The camp of Makkedah in Josh. 10:21 belongs, then, to the network of conquests in the south, along with Libnah, Lachish, and Eglon, and should thus be seen as a base distinct from Gilgal, though significant stories about military excursions from it have not been preserved.

In any case, the tradition about the "camp of Israel" in the period of wandering in the wilderness and in the period of

8. See, recently, A. Malamat, *Israel in Biblical Times* (Jerusalem, 1983), pp. 51 ff. (Hebrew).

9. See Malamat, *Israel* (n. 8), p. 62.

settlement (Josh. 6:18, 23) reflects a historical situation with tribes organized in camps prepared to go forth and fight. But while the different tribes, or groups of tribes, had separate camps in the actual period of settlement, in the later period when the conquest stories were written, only *one* camp of Israel was envisioned, such as Gilgal, from which all Israel launched their attacks and to which they returned, or the camp of Shiloh with its Tent of Meeting, where the conquered land was parceled out and from which men were dispatched to chart the land so it could be apportioned by lot to the tribes. Sending out people to chart the land is a practice paralleled in the descriptions of settlement in Greece (see Chapter 1).

2. The School of Alt and Noth. Scholars of this school claim that the settlement of the tribes of Israel in the land of Israel occurred largely without battle, in uninhabited areas of the hill country of the Galilee, Ephraim, and Judah.[10] Only after the Israelite tribes had become rooted in their settlements and were beginning to expand did they confront the inhabitants of Canaanite cities and become drawn into battle, as in the war with Sisera (Judg. 4–5). The stories of the conquest of Jericho and Ai, from this perspective, are simply legendary etiological stories that seek to explain, *ex eventu,* the existence of ruins of ancient cities in the area as evidence of a war with the Canaanites waged upon the entrance of the Israelite tribes into Canaan (see below, p. 149 ff.).

Many criticisms have been leveled against this type of explanation. Challengers have rightly claimed that the etiological nature of the story does not imply that the basic fact of conquering the cities is a fabrication. Yes, the storyteller was attracted to prominent and attention-commanding land-

10. In particular, see A. Alt, "Die Landnahme der Israeliten in Palästina," *Kleine Schriften* 1 (Munich, 1953), pp. 89–125; M. Noth, *Das Buch Josua,* HAT²; (Tübingen, 1953). And see the discussion of this approach in M. Weippert, *Die Landnahme der israelitischen Stämme in der neuren wissenschaftlichen Diskussion* (Göttingen, 1961), pp. 14–51.

marks, such as piles of stones or the ruined walls of a large tell, in order to embellish the Israelite wars of conquest, but this embellishment does not invalidate the fundamental existence of battles and conquest.[11]

Nevertheless, one must admit that the basic argument of this school—that settlement began quietly and peacefully—has some grounds. In Josh. 17:14–18 we find a report of a conversation that the descendants of Joseph (*bny ywsp*), or the house of Joseph (*byt ywsp*), had with Joshua.[12] Joshua admits here that the area of settlement must be expanded by cutting down forests, because the Canaanites living in the valley are strong and possess iron chariots that make them unassailable (see also Judg. 1:19). Archaeological evidence also lends support to this school's basic argument: abundant remains of dense Israelite (not Canaanite) residence from the period of the settlement have been discovered in the hill country of the Galilee, Ephraim and Manasseh, and Judah. Archaeological surveys have shown that during the twelfth century B.C.E. a great number of settlements suddenly appeared in the hill country of Ephraim and Manasseh, and of Judah, during an era when Canaanite settlements were flourishing in the land.[13] Similarly, archaeological surveys have revealed a system of fortified settlements on mountaintops in a strip of land between the Phoenician coast and the high mountains in east Galilee,[14] which strengthens de Vaux's hypothesis that what brought about the destruction of Hazor was the expansion of the tribes in the Galilee.[15]

11. Cf. below, p. 149 ff. See also de Vaux, *History* (n. 6), pp. 523 ff.

12. According to scholars, two traditions have been integrated in this passage, one about the *bĕnê yôsēp* and the other about the *bêt yôsēp*.

13. See Moshe Kochavi, "The Israelite Settlement in Canaan in the Light of Archaeological Survey," *Proceedings of the International Congress on Biblical Archaeology, 1–10 April 1984* (Jerusalem, 1985), pp. 54–60, and the recent work of I. Finkelstein, *The Archaeology of the Israelite Settlement* (Jerusalem, 1988).

14. Kochavi, "Israelite Settlement" (n. 13), p. 57.

15. R. de Vaux, *History* (n. 6), pp. 655 ff.

Moreover, as indicated in Chapter 2, the image of Joshua conquering the land by storm does not stand up to historical-critical scrutiny. Joshua succeeded in repelling the Amorites in the Aijalon Valley at the edge of the hill country of Ephraim, which made him a national hero, to whom in a later period all the acts of conquest were attributed (see Chapter 2). Judah and Simeon, furthermore, settled peacefully; as we will see, the stories about the conquests of Judah in Judg. 1 are not reliable. The conquest of Jerusalem by the Judahites, as described in Judg. 1:8, has no historical foundation, and neither do the rest of the conquests described later in that chapter. These conquest stories seek to glorify Judah's reputation and to attribute to the tribe heroic acts it did not perform: Hebron and Debir were conquered by the Calebites and Kenizzites; the city of Arad was not destroyed in the period of settlement and its ruins were actually settled by the Kenites; and the story about the conquest of Hormah has an etiological bent (*ḥormâ* = *ḥerem*) the historical basis of which is too distant to be clear (cf. Num. 21:1–3). The capture of Gaza, Ashkelon, and Ekron by Judah (Judg. 1:18) is bereft of historical foundation (on all this, see Chapter 6).

In contrast, the story in Gen. 38 indicates that Judah entered into marriage relationships with the Canaanites in the lowland of Judah, and in this way spread out across Timnah, Chezib, and Adullam in the lowland. As we will see, the greatness of the tribe of Judah lay in its ability to unite with various nomadic elements in the area of the Negev.

As we saw earlier in this chapter, the Israelite tribes operated in camps that were indeed set up to repel an attack in war, but which from the beginning were designed for a settlement campaign. It is necessary, therefore, to accept in principle the supposition that settlement was quiet, without war, at the beginning of this period. But we must also accept that there were military conflicts with the inhabitants of the area as the settlement progressed.

3. The Mendenhall-Gottwald School. G. Mendenhall, and following him, N. Gottwald, have suggested that a feudal rebellion occurred in the land of Canaan in the period of settlement.[16] They believe that this was not a massive invasion of nomadic tribes into the land of Canaan but rather a radical social change in the land. The inhabitants of Canaan in the period of settlement were prone to social agitation, and under the influence of a handful of Israelites who arrived from the desert, they rebelled against the kings of Canaan who were oppressing the farmers with heavy taxes. This rebellion found support in the religious ideology of Israel, which was founded on the covenant between God and his people, a covenant that precluded any possibility of entering into a vassal relationship with a mortal king.[17] The Mendenhall-Gottwald school has been criticized for disregarding the biblical evidence concerning the penetration of the Israelite tribes into Canaan. As we observed above, it is likely that, like the Sea Peoples, the Israelite tribes traveled in camps as they were spying out places for settlement and that there is no justification for denying the basic testimony about the migration of the population and its penetration into the land of Canaan.

Nonetheless, we are obliged to admit that the fundamental idea of the Mendenhall-Gottwald school—that an association between the Israelite and the old inhabitants of Canaan was formed at a particular historical stage—is reasonable and undoubtedly has constructive ramifications. We can learn about

16. G. Mendenhall, "The Hebrew Conquest of Palestine," *BA* 25 (1962), pp. 66–87; N. K. Gottwald, *The Tribes of Yahweh* (New York, 1979).

17. See G. Mendenhall, *The Tenth Generation: The Origins of Biblical Tradition* (Baltimore, 1973), pp. 1–31, 174 ff. M. Buber, *Kingship of God* (trans. from German; London, 1964) anticipated him in this matter, seeing in Gideon's utterance in Judg. 8:23 the principle that guided the tribes of Israel in the period of the judges. To our surprise, Mendenhall does not mention this.

the nature of the ferment and the insurgent spirit that prevailed in the area in the fourteenth century B.C.E. from the activity of the *Ḫabiru/ʿApiru* in the area as discussed in the El-Amarna letters. According to these documents ʿAbdi-Ashirta, the governor of the land of Amurru, apparently sent a message to the men of the city Ammiya with these words:[18]

> ʿAbdi-Ashirta has written to the host in the temple of Ninurta: "Muster yourselves, and let us attack Byblos—behold, th[ere is no] man who can rescue [i]t from ou[r] power—and let us drive the mayors from the midst of the lands, and let all the lands turn themselves over to the ʿAp[i]ru, and let an [al]liance[19] [be formed] for all the lands so that the sons and daughters may have peace forever. And even if the king comes out, as for all the lands there will be hostility toward him, so what can he do to us?"

A defiant action similar to this on the northern coast of Lebanon is found at Shechem, in the hill country of Ephraim. This city, which Joshua entered without battle and in which he made a treaty with the people (Josh. 24), aided rebel troops in the vicinity in the El-Amarna period, as did the land of Amurru under the leadership of ʿAbdi-Ashirta. Labʾayu from

18. Letter 74. Cf. R. F. Youngblood, "The Amarna Correspondence of Rib-Haddi, Prince of Byblos" (diss., Dropsie College, 1961). On the importance of this letter for understanding the relations between the population of the area and their rulers, see M. C. Astour, "The Amarna Age Forerunners of Biblical Anti-Royalism," in *For Max Weinreich on His Seventieth Birthday: Studies in Jewish Languages, Literature, and Society* (New York, 1964), *Leksikon fur der Nayer Yidisher Literatur* 3 (1960), pp. 6–17; P. Artzi, "'Vox Populi' in the El-Amarna Tablets," *Revue d'Assyriologie* 58 (1964), pp. 159–66; A. Altman, "The Revolutions in Byblos and Amurru during the Amarna Period and their Social Background," *Bar-Ilan Studies in History* (Ramat Gan, 1978), pp. 3–24.

19. The word "alliance" in line 36 here in the letter is *kittu* "truth." For "truth" in the sense of *treaty* or *covenant* in the Bible, see my article, "Bond and Grace: Covenantal Expression in the Bible and the Ancient Near East," *Leshonenu* 36 (1972), p. 87, n. 20.

Shechem and ʿAbdi-Ashirta of Amurru conspired together with the *Ḫabiru* (SA. GAZ), who were considered robbers and thus aroused the wrath of the leaders of Egypt and of the kings loyal to the pharaoh, such as Rib-Addi, king of Byblos, and ʿAbdi-Ḫeba, king of Jerusalem.[20] Like ʿAbdi-Ashirta, who made a treaty with the *Ḫabiṛu* against the king of Byblos, Labʾayu, king of Shechem, made a treaty with the nomads (the *Ḫabiru*) in the area,[21] in order to reduce the domain of the king of Jerusalem who was loyal to Egypt. It seems that in these circumstances the people of Shechem attempted to make a treaty with the sons of Jacob (Gen. 34), and under similar circumstances the Israelites entered Shechem and made a covenant there (Josh. 24). The associations of Abimelech with the people of Shechem (Judg. 9) must be viewed against a similar background.

Josh. 24 evidently deals with a treaty or covenant made by the inhabitants of a city who have encountered Israelite faith for the first time. Joshua's demand that the people put away the foreign gods they are serving (vv. 14, 23) is similar to the demands found in several stages of Israelite history (Gen. 35:4; after leaving Shechem; 1 Sam. 7:3–4; Judg. 10:16), but more decisive here is the fact that the relationship of the people of Shechem to the God of Israel is explicitly described as *incipient:* those entering into the covenant are placed in a position of choosing God, something that has no parallel in the rest of the Bible. In contrast to other passages, in which God is the one who chooses Israel, the people gathered in Josh. 24 are asked to

20. On these two kings and their complete loyalty to Egyptian rule, in contrast to ʿAbdi-Ashirta and Labʾayu, see P. Artzi, "*ʿAmarna: teʿudot ʾel ʿamarna,*" *Encyclopedia Miqraʾit* 6, pp. 250–51.

21. On Shechem's dependence on treaties with foreign powers that migrated through its locale, see H. Reviv, "Governmental Authority in Shechem in the Period of El Amarna and the Time of Abimelech," *Bulletin of the Israel Exploration Society* (*Yediot*) 27 (1963–64), pp. 270–75 (Hebrew). Also, *ʾēl bĕrît* and *baʿal bĕrît* in Shechem (Judg. 8:33; 9:4, 46) can tell us about the importance of treaties for this city.

decide which god(s) they will choose—the gods of their fathers or the God of Joshua: "But if it is bad to you to serve YHWH, choose today whom you will serve, whether it will be the gods whom your fathers served on the other side of the River, or whether it will be the gods of the Amorites in whose land you dwell. As for me and my household, we will serve YHWH" (v. 15). Furthermore, in contrast to Exod. 32:10, in which God wants to destroy the people of Israel and make a great nation of Moses, here, instead of God choosing Joshua, Joshua offers himself and his family for the service of YHWH.

Remarkably, it is no accident that the covenant that was made with the people of Israel at Sinai is not mentioned at all in Josh. 24; on the contrary, as M. J. Bin-Gorion has noted, the chapter here ignores the Sinai covenant.[22] The fact of the matter is, all the components found in the event at Sinai are found in the events at Shechem, to the extent that the covenant in Josh. 24 seems to substitute for the Sinai covenant. Note the following correspondences: (1) at Sinai, Moses and the people agree to express allegiance to the God of Israel (Exod. 19:7–8; 24:3), and in Shechem Joshua argues with the people and the people agree to serve YHWH (see below); (2) the declaration "We will do and will obey" in the Sinai covenant (Exod. 24:7) parallels the declaration "We will serve YHWH our God and we will obey his voice" in Josh. 24:24; (3) in the Sinai covenant, Moses sets up stone pillars as a sign of the covenant, and at Shechem, Joshua sets up a large stone as a witness of the covenant (Josh. 24:26–27); (4) with respect to the "statute and ordinance" (*ḥōq ûmišpāṭ*), Moses prescribed for Israel the words of YHWH and his statutes (*mišpāṭîm*) and wrote them in a book (Exod. 24:3–8), and Joshua laid down a statute and ordinance for Israel in Shechem and wrote the words "in a book of the instruction of God" (Josh. 24:25–26).

Though one cannot speak of a "conversion" of the residents

22. M. J. Bin Gorion (Berdichewski), *Sinai und Garizim* (Berlin, 1926).

of Canaan in the circumstances presented in Josh. 24,[23] the episode does bring to mind the procedures of proselytization found in later sources. Even after the people at Shechem express their readiness to serve YHWH (v. 19), Joshua tries to deter them from forming a covenant relationship: "You will not be able to serve YHWH because God is holy. He is a jealous God. He will not forgive your rebellious acts and your sins. When you abandon YHWH and serve foreign gods, he will again bring calamity on you and destroy you though he had done good to you" (vv. 19–20).

Only after the people remained firm without yielding ("No! We will certainly serve YHWH"; v. 21) did Joshua call them to witness that they had chosen to serve YHWH, and even with this call he stipulated that they remove the foreign gods that were among them (vv. 22–23). The people then responded: "We will serve YHWH our God and will obey his voice" (v. 24), and only then did Joshua enact the covenant for them.

These warnings and statements of deterrence bring to mind the halakhic rules by which converts were accepted in a much later period. Whoever sought conversion would be questioned to determine if his motive was fear (cf. the "converts [converting for fear] of lions" [*gērê ʿarāyôt*] in 2 Kings 17:24 ff.). Then, if no motive such as fear was evident, the person seeking to convert would be told how burdensome the yoke of the Torah would be and how much trouble he would have in observing it, advice intended to lead the prospective convert to withdraw. He would be discouraged in this way up to three times.[24] Although these halakhic rules were crystalized in a

23. See J. Milgrom, "Religious Conversion and the Revolt Model for the Formation of Israel," *JBL* 101 (1982), pp. 169–76.

24. See the entry "*gērût*" in the *Encyclopedia Talmudit* 6, pp. 426 ff., with references to rabbinic sources. In relation to receiving converts to Israel, there were certainly fluctuations in accord with the circumstances of a particular period (see E. E. Urbach, *The Sages: Their Concepts and Beliefs* [Jerusalem, 1975]), but it seems that regarding the issue we are speaking of here there was always agreement. A true convert was a *gēr*

later period, the basic test put to anyone who wanted to join the religion of Israel had existed from ancient times. Josh. 24 is the first example of this.

Gen. 34 tells us about attempts to develop an association between the Israelites and the people of Shechem. The establishment of an alliance with the sons of Jacob, through the council, by Hamor and his son Shechem reflects the two basic elements of a compact between different ethnic groups: marriage, and mutual business and trade (*connubium et commercium*). Note these verses: "These men are friendly to us (i.e., they have peaceful relations with us). Let them dwell in the land and let them travel around in it. . . . We will take their daughters as wives in marriage and we will give our daughters in marriage to them" (v. 21). But the sons of Jacob added another condition: the circumcision of every male (v. 22), which was a "sign" of a covenant (*ʾôt bĕrît*) in Israel (Gen. 17:10–11).

As many scholars have observed, at the foundation of Josh. 24 lies an ancient tradition,[25] to which a stereotypical tradition known from the Pentateuch was added later. According to the ancient tradition, Joshua put under covenant the inhabitants of Shechem, who did not belong to those leaving Egypt. Additionally, a tradition preserved in 1 Chron. 7:20 ff. indicates that Ephraim had resided in the land, and that Joshua, of the tenth generation from Ephraim, was never in Egypt and was a descendant of the original Hebrews (in contrast to the stories in the Pentateuch in to which Ephraim was born in Egypt and died there, and was only four generations distant from Joshua). In view of the older tradition, we can suppose that Joshua was originally an autochthonous figure[26] who, because of his vic-

---

ṣedeq "right and proper convert," who converted out of belief and not because of ulterior motives. This tendency already appears in the description of the Samaritans in 2 Kings 17:24 ff.

25. See, for example, Noth, *Josua* (ch. 4, n. 39).

26. S. Japhet sees in the tradition of Chronicles the fruit of a particular tendency. See her article "Conquest and Settlement in Chronicles," *JBL*

tories over the Amorites, was transformed into a national hero alleged to have come from Egypt with Moses, just as Caleb the Kenizzite was made into a Judean leader who came from Egypt with the Israelites. Joshua apparently represents the nomadic Hebrews, who were similar in character to the *Ḫabiru* in Shechem during the period of Labaya'. The religion of these Hebrews was founded not on the Sinai covenant, but rather on the "faith of the fathers," which was associated with trees of sacral significance, the terebinth, oak, and tamarisk. It may be that the "place of Shechem," the "oak of Shechem" (see Gen. 12:6), "the terebinth which is by Shechem" (Gen. 35:4), the "portion of the field" that Jacob acquired next to Shechem, and the altar he set up there (33:18–20) are places that were revered by these first Hebrews, who attempted to impart this form of worship to the Shechemites. In this way, the people of Shechem were brought into a covenant with the God of Israel, whom they served in the aforementioned places, and Joshua was not initially linked to Moses but to these first Hebrews in the land of Canaan. Joshua was made the successor of Moses only after the entire tradition was nationalized; he actually belonged to the generation before Moses, which recognized only the God of the patriarchs, and his name was Hoshea, without the element reflecting God's name that is incorporated into his name after Moses. The tradition connecting Joshua to Moses is that which ascribes to Moses the changing of the name Hoshea (bin Nun) to Joshua (Heb. *Yĕhôšuaʿ*; Num. 13:8–16). Notably, there is no element of the divine name in the names of other tribal leaders (see Num. 13:4–15; 34:19–29).

Dissociating Joshua from the exodus from Egypt solves many difficulties with the chronology of the settlement of the

---

98 (1979), pp. 205–18. It appears to me, however, that the tendency to see the settlement in the land of Israel as a continuous process from the period of the patriarchs—without the Exodus in between—is not solely ideological, but based on historical reality. Pentateuchal stories which contrast with this tendency were created on an ideological basis, with a blurring of reliable ethnic reality (and see above, Chapter 1).

Israelite tribes in the land of Israel. It means that we do not need to compress all the events into a period after the middle of the thirteenth century B.C.E., as has been the custom. Possibly, the Israelite tribes settled in the Galilee before the fall of Hazor in the last quarter of the thirteenth century B.C.E.,[27] and Shechem may have been in the hands of the Hebrews long before the end of the thirteenth century. This last possibility may be reflected in the tradition that Jacob took Shechem from the Amorites by sword and bow (Gen. 48:22). Recently, it has been revealed that the city Laish (= Dan) in the north was destroyed at the end of the thirteenth century B.C.E.,[28] which would suggest that the tribe of Dan settled in the coastal lowland before the twelfth century, the time generally acknowledged for this settlement.

The idea that the conquest of the land occurred after the tribes of Israel came from Egypt emerged in a later period. It appears that this perspective was born in a circle of some of those who had left Egypt, out of whom came the family of the house of Eli (1 Sam. 2:27). This priestly family, which based the cult of the tribes of Israel in the sanctuary at Shiloh, connected Joshua, the famous Ephraimite conqueror, to Shiloh and created the tradition about the division of the land at Shiloh under the supervision of Eleazar the priest and Joshua bin Nun (see Chapter 2).[29] Over the course of generations the received view that Joshua was the successor of Moses and served him in the wilderness of Sinai became established.

27. But see recently I. Finkelstein, *The Archaeology of the Israelite Settlement* (Jerusalem, 1988), who adduces evidence that in the Late Bronze Age the settlement in the upper Galilee was less dense than what Y. Aharoni determined in his archaeological survey, *The Settlement of the Israelite Tribes in the Upper Galilee* (Jerusalem, 1957) (Hebrew).

28. A. Biran, "Notes and News, Tel-Dan, 1984," *IEJ* 35 (1985), p. 187.

29. According to the original tradition, Joshua was associated with the cultic center at Shiloh and with the priest from Shiloh who directed him in dividing inheritances in the area (see above, pp. 50–51). This connection, however, predated the consolidation of the family of Eli there.

In any event, the view that settlement in the land of Canaan occurred only after the exodus from Egypt in the thirteenth century B.C.E. has no support. The families arriving from Egypt influenced unification of the Israelite tribes through their monotheistic faith, and as time passed, the coalition of the tribes of Israel adopted the tradition about a general exodus of all the tribes. But this tradition does not reflect the way events really materialized. The book of Chronicles preserves, paradoxically, amidst its dry lists, the original tradition that many tribes of Israel dwelt autochthonously in the land of Canaan without ever descending to Egypt (see note 26).

An important tribe whose consolidation occurred in the land of Canaan was the tribe of Judah, which began and grew by continually mixing with the indigenous inhabitants in the southern area. According to Gen. 38, Judah's sons were born of a Canaanite woman, a reflection of the assimilation of Judahite families with the local population, the inhabitants of Canaanite cities in the lowland of Judah: Timnah, Adullam, and Achzib. According to 1 Chron. 4:21–23, the family of Shelah, the son of Judah, includes Lecah (i.e., Lachish) and Mareshah, who both live in the lowland area. Other clans of Judah are also based in the local population. Caleb, who according to the tradition of Judah led the Israelites as they made their conquests (Judg. 1, and see above), is a Kenizzite (Num. 32:12; Josh. 14:6–7). In fact, the Kenizzites are numbered among the foreign peoples that Israel was to dispossess according to the covenant of Gen. 15 (see v. 19), and Kenaz was genealogically related to the Seirites (Gen. 36:9–11, 15, 42).

The major clans of Judah, according to the genealogical list in Chronicles,[30] Jerahmeel, Ram, and Caleb (1 Chron. 2:1, 8, 25, 27, 43), are foreign and were created by assimilation with

30. See recently G. Galil, "The Genealogies of the Tribe of Judah" (diss.; The Hebrew University, 1983). On the sparseness of the Israelite settlement in the area of Judah in the period of the settlement, see Finkelstein, *Archaeology* (n. 27).

various peoples in the south and in the Negeb: Edomites, Midianites, Horites, Ishmaelites, and others.

We learn about Judah's family ties with the Kenites in 1 Chron. 2:55, whereas we learn about their blood ties with the Midianites from Midianite names: Rekem (1 Chron. 2:43, 47; cf. Num. 31:8; Josh. 13:21), Jether and Epher (1 Chron. 2:17; cf. Gen. 25:4), and Ephah, Caleb's concubine (1 Chron. 2:46; cf. Gen. 25:4).

Furthermore, Horite elements are found in the genealogical list of Judah: for example: Onam and Oren (1 Chron. 2:25–26; cf. Gen. 36:23, 28), and Shobal and Menuhoth (1 Chron. 2:52; 4:1; cf. Gen. 36:20–23). Zerah from a family of Judah (Gen. 38:30; 1 Chron. 2:4, 6) is a recognized Edomite clan (Gen. 36:13), as is Korah (1 Chron. 2:43; cf. Gen. 36:16, 18).

In the territory of Simeon, which was incorporated into the middle of Judah's inheritance (see Josh. 19:1; 1 Chron. 4:24–33), we find the families of Mibsam and Mishma (1 Chron. 4:25), which are known from Gen. 25:13–14 as Ishmaelite families. Furthermore, in the Calebite and Jerahmeelite clans, which are listed as the main branches of the tribe of Judah, we find marriage ties with Egypt: Mared from the Calebites took Bithiah, the daughter of Pharaoh, as a wife (1 Chron. 4:18), and Sheshan of the Jerahmeelites gave his daughter to Jarha, an Egyptian servant (1 Chron. 2:34–35).

In northwest Judah, assimilation occurred with Horite and Hivite elements. Shobal, father of Kiriath-jearim, is known as belonging to a Horite family (cf. Gen. 36:20, 23) as well as to Menuhoth-Manahath, mentioned in 1 Chron. 2:52 (cf. Gen. 36:23). Kiriath-jearim itself is known as a Gibeonite town of the Hivites (Josh. 9:7, 17:11:19). It appears that Judah began to settle in Bethlehem and Giloh,[31] and only after some time did the tribe start to expand, while assimilating with the local

31. See Finkelstein, *Archaeology* (n. 27). On the excavations of Giloh, see A. Mazar, "Giloh, An Early Israelite Settlement Site near Jerusalem," *IEJ* 31 (1981), pp. 1–36.

population: the Canaanites and Hivites in the lowland of Judah, the Calebites in the mountain country of Hebron, the Kenites in the east Negeb, the Jerahmeelites in the west Negeb, Seir in the south, and Ishmael in the southwest.

In summary, it can be said that the settlement of the Israelite tribes in the land of Canaan resulted from a complex process covering a long period that began before the end of the thirteenth century B.C.E. It seems that the Hebrews (who came from the trans-Euphrates) who began to settle in the land belonged to a larger movement of landless *Ḫabiru,* who searched for land to acquire in the fourteenth and thirteenth centuries B.C.E. The name Asher is mentioned in Egyptian inscriptions of this period.[32] In a fourteenth-century letter from El-Amarna we read about "people put to forced labor" who were working in the area of Shunem (which belonged to the inheritance of Issachar). As A. Alt has observed, this document sheds light on the tribe of Issachar who became a "slave laborer" (*wyhy lms ʿbd*); Gen. 49:15).[33] Similarly, we learn from Gen. 34 that Simeon and Levi fought in Shechem, an event certainly belonging to the earliest period, before these tribes moved south; thus, the attempt of Simeon and Levi to settle in Shechem most likely fits in the period under discussion here. As noted above, because Ephraim and Joshua were native to the land of Canaan and did not come out of Egypt, Joshua's wars at Beth-Horon and the Aijalon Valley, which appear trustworthy, possibly occurred before the period of the Exodus in the middle of the thirteenth century.[34] We have also

32. See A. Gardiner, *Ancient Egyptian Onomastica* 1 (Oxford, 1947), pp. 192–93; cf. R. de Vaux, *History* (n. 6), pp. 664–65.

33. A. Alt, "Neues über Palästina aus dem Archiv Amenophis' IV," *KS* 3 (Munich, 1959), pp. 158–75.

34. See A. Alt, "Landnahme" (n. 10), pp. 176–92. The research of Z. Kallai and H. Tadmor on the state of Jerusalem in the El-Amarna period ("Bīt Ninurta = Beth Horon: On the History of the Kingdom of Jerusalem in the Amarna Period," *Eretz-Israel* 9 [*W. F. Albright Volume,* 1969–70], pp. 138–47 [Hebrew]) indicates that the hegemony of Jerusa-

seen that the tribe of Judah was consolidated mostly from native clans (the Calebites, Kenizzites, and Jerahmeelites) that were not associated with those who left Egypt. Thus, it is probable that the data in Chronicles about Israelites' settlement in the land continuously from the period of the patriarchs may have a basis in fact, as evidenced by detailed genealogical lists.

The faith of these tribes was that of the patriarchs: they believed in the "God of the fathers," a God not tied to a particular place, and in tutelary ancestral gods, i.e., the *tĕrāpîm* mentioned in Gen. 31:19, 34 (see above, pp. 11–13). More specifically, they believed in "El Shaddai," and also in *ʾēlîm* of various types linked to holy places near Canaanite cities, such as the Terebinth of Moreh, near Shechem, and the Terebinths of Mamre, near Hebron. The foundation of the tradition about Joshua's covenant with God for the people of Israel in Shechem (Josh. 24), which is independent of the Sinai covenant, may reflect this earlier stage of religious belief.

Another wave of Hebrews was active on the east side of the Jordan. These tribes also observed the religion of the patriarchs, associated with places such as Mahanaim, Sukkoth, and Penuel.

The concept of settlement accepted in the Bible was born when a group of Hebrews arrived in the land of Canaan from Egypt, a group connected with the Kenites and Midianites and with the tradition of a mountain of God at Sinai.[35] This group, or a significant part of it, apparently arrived in the heart of the mountain country of Ephraim and established its settlement at Shiloh, where the ark of the covenant that had wandered with the Israelites in the wilderness resided and where the Tent of Meeting was set up, which itself had been brought in from the

---

lem in the area, as reflected in Josh. 10, is close to the historical reality of the fourteenth century B.C.E.

35. See my articles, "The Tradition about Moses and Jethro at the Mountain of God," *Tarbiz* 56 (1987), pp. 449–60 (Hebrew); "The Tribal League at Sinai," in P. D. Miller and S. D. McBride, eds., *Ancient Israelite Religion: Essays in Honor of Frank Moore Cross* (Philadelphia, 1987), pp. 303–14.

wilderness. We find evidence of this in 1 Sam. 2:27: "Did I not reveal myself to the house of your father when they were in Egypt?" From this verse we learn that the family of Eli, which officiated before the ark of YHWH in Shiloh, traced its ancestry to an older priestly family in Egypt, which was tied in one form or another to Moses and Aaron. The names of Eli's sons, Hophni and Phinehas, are Egyptian, and another Phinehas, the son of Eleazar, the son of Aaron the priest, served at Shiloh (Josh. 22:12–13) and at Bethel (Judg. 20:27–28), whereas Jonathan, son of Gershom, son of Moses, served at Dan (Judg. 18:30). This priestly family at Shiloh created the association of Joshua with Moses (just as with Caleb and Moses in Judah) and represented Joshua as subservient to the instructions of Eleazar the priest, father of Phinehas (see Chapter 2).[36] Similarly, this priestly family connected Joshua with the Tent of Meeting in the wilderness and made him a servant of Moses (Exod. 33:7–11; Num. 11:28–29; Deut. 31:14–15).

One must suppose that this respected priestly family, which placed its settlement at Shiloh in the center of the hill country of Ephraim, is that which succeeded in imposing the religion of YHWH on all the tribes of Israel, and that the Tent of Meeting in Shiloh eventually came to be considered the place where the land of Canaan was parceled out to the tribes by lot before YHWH (see Chapter 2).

In this form, the tradition developed about an association of the tribes of Israel acting as a unified body. There was no longer a distinction between the tribes that dwelt in the land from the time of the patriarchs and those that arrived from the south, from the wilderness; all of them now shared in the heritage of the descent into Egypt, where they became a great people; all of them left Egypt under the direction of Moses and conquered the land of Canaan under the direction of Joshua. The truth, however, is that Hebrew tribes began to settle sporadically in the land in the middle of the second millennium

36. See n. 29.

B.C.E. and contended with the Canaanite cities in a few battles even before the arrival of those who had left Egypt. In the middle of the twelfth century, when the Sea Peoples came into the territories of Israel, the Hebrew tribes on both sides of the Jordan began to organize in preparation for settling in Canaan. We know of a camp at Shittim in the Plains of Moab (Num. 33:49; Josh. 3:1; Mic. 6:5), the camp of Gilgal (Josh. 3–4; Mic. 6:5; and see Chapter 2), the camp of Makkedah (Josh. 10:21), the camp of Shiloh (Josh. 18:9; Judg. 21:12), and the camp of Dan (Judg. 18:12). The camp of Shiloh, which was designated as the place of the ark in the Tent of Meeting, became a religious center of the tribes of Israel which preserved traditions of the exodus from Egypt. Shechem, which was also a religious center of the Israelite tribes, cultivated the ancient tradition of the Hebrews without any reference to the exodus from Egypt or the Sinai covenant. Only in a later period was this tradition amalgamated with the exodus tradition.

Joshua bin Nun, who was an Ephraimitic leader who did battle with Amorite kings in the Aijalon Valley (see Chapter 2), was transformed over time into a national hero to whom was ascribed the conquest of the land of Canaan when he went out to battle from Gilgal. He was seen as the leader who divided up the land by lot before YHWH in Shiloh. The summoning of the tribes of Israel to be gathered at Shechem was attributed to him. The reality, however, was that different local settlement traditions, initially independent of one another, each underwent separate development until, in a later period, they were united into one general national tradition.

6

The Conquest and Settlement According to the Different Accounts

The book of Joshua as we now know it is the product of a protracted process of literary composition and consolidation. Many scholars and exegetes have dealt with this process in detail. The book certainly preserves tribal and local traditions, but editing has transformed the traditions to present events as all-encompassing, and from a later historical perspective. The present form of Joshua has been shaped by a later editor, who was influenced in his language and ideology by the book of Deuteronomy.[1] This editor collected the fragmentary source material, arranged it, and provided summaries and a framework that agreed with his viewpoint, thereby creating a portrayal of a lightning conquest in the time of Joshua. As we will see below, this editor used cycles of several traditions available to him after passing through the hands of earlier collectors, such as the cycle of stories connected with the tribe of Benjamin (Josh. 2–9).

The collection of traditions and their arrangement in the book of Joshua parallels Judg. 1 to a certain extent, where we also find various traditions relating to the conquest of the land,

1. On the editorial style of the Former Prophets and its relationship to the book of Deuteronomy, see my book *Deuteronomy and the Deuteronomic School* (Oxford, 1972), pp. 320–59.

as gathered and arranged tendentiously by an editor. Because the editor of Judg. 1 worked in an earlier period, his product is shorter and less discursive than the book of Joshua. The antiquity of the tradition in Judg. 1:1–2:5 has tended to grant it extensive credibility among scholars, who have gone so far as to try to reconstruct from it the events of the settlement.[2] But there is no justification for this. As we will try to demonstrate, the tradition in Judg. 1:1–2:5 is no less tendentious than that in Joshua, though it is more reliable than that in the layer of Deuteronomistic editing in the book of Joshua. But the stories about the conquest themselves, as opposed to their framework, are no less reliable in Joshua than in Judg. 1. As for the short lists referring to the capture of cities and not driving out their inhabitants, the lists in Judg. 1, as we will see, below, are less reliable than their parallels in Joshua.

1. The Conquest Under the Leadership of the House of Judah (Judges 1:1–2:5). The introduction to this section

2. Recently, reservations have begun to be expressed about this matter. See A. G. Auld, "Judges I and History: A Reconsideration," *VT* 25 (1975), pp. 261 ff.; N. Rösel, "Judges 1 and the Problem of the Settlement of the 'Leah Tribes,'" *Proceedings of the Eighth World Congress for Jewish Studies* (Jerusalem, 1982), pp. 17–20 (Hebrew). The basic point of Rosel's claims is acceptable to me.

The theory of two waves of conquest, a first wave of tribes of the house of Joseph preceding a second wave of the tribe of Judah, is actually based on a comparison of Judg. 1 with the tradition in the book of Joshua. See, for example, Y. Aharoni, *The Land of the Bible: A Historical Geography* (2d ed.; ed. A. F. Rainey; London, 1979), pp. 209–20. In connection with the reliability of Judg. 1, see his words there: "There is no doubt that the brief notices collected in Judges 1 are among the most trustworthy and there is no reason to suspect their historicity, precisely because they do not always measure up to the later historical outlook which describes the conquest as one single campaign" (pp. 278–79, n. 76). For a criticism of the two-wave theory, see Rösel, "Problem" (n. 2). The different traditions in the Tetrateuch about the places where the Israelites wandered (Num. 20–21 vis-à-vis 33) have no connection with historical events but rather have to do with the issue of historiography, which arises out of different literary concerns.

(Judg. 1:1–4)—excluding the initial clause "After the death of Joshua," which belongs to a later author and which already presupposes the existence of the book of Joshua according to the received division of the books[3] (cf. "After the death of Moses" at the beginning of the book of Joshua)—serves as a heading for the conquest enterprise at the front of which marched the tribe of Judah. We learn in these verses that an ancient oracle of God commissioned this tribe with the task of initiating the war against the Canaanites: "The Israelites inquired of YHWH, saying: 'Who will go up for us first against the Canaanites to fight them?' YHWH said: 'Judah shall go up'" (vv. 1–2). This story contradicts the traditions in the books of Joshua, Numbers (27:15–23), and Deuteronomy (chaps. 1–3; 31:1–8), according to which Joshua initiated the war of conquest at God's command. Moreover, like the inquiry of YHWH in Judges before Judah goes forth to war,[4] the priestly tradition informs us in Num. 27:15–23 that after Joshua is appointed leader of the community, he will need to inquire of God, through the decision of the Urim by means of Eleazar the priest, with respect to

3. In the original edition of the Deuteronomistic history, the period of the conquest ends with Joshua's farewell speech (Josh. 23), whereas the period of the judges begins with the discourse in Judg. 2:11 ff. (see below on the farewell speech). The later writers, however, who divided the material into books (Joshua and Judges) found a place to insert between Josh. 23 and Judg. 2:11 the ancient tradition known to them regarding Joshua and the period of the judges. Josh. 24:1–28 and Judg. 1:1–2:5 are appendices of sorts that were added after the Deuteronomistic historiography had already been formed and in a period when the material was separated into books as we presently find them. Actually, these appendices contain glaring contradictions to the viewpoint of the Deuteronomistic editor: According to Josh. 24, Israel served foreign gods in the days of Joshua (v. 23), which contradicts the Deuteronomistic view (Judg. 2:7). Moreover, Judg. 1 presupposes Canaanite enclaves within the territory of the apportioned land of Israel, which contradicts the Deuteronomistic viewpoint about a total conquest in the days of Joshua. See below.

4. Inquiring of God before going forth to establish new settlements is found in the context of the settlement of the tribe of Dan (Judg. 18). This is a basic phenomenon found in the Greek colonization. See Chapter 2.

his "going out" and "coming in," i.e., concerning the wars he will fight (cf. Josh. 14:11: "As my strength was then, so it is now, to undertake battle and *to go out and to come in*").[5] According to this tradition, which is based in northern Israel (see below), the conquest of the land was begun by a leader from the house of Joseph who inquired of God through a priest associated with Shiloh in the hill country of Ephraim (see Chapter 2). In Judg. 1, however, the conquest was initiated not by a leader from the tribe of Ephraim but by the tribe of Judah.

A similar inclination to show the prominence of Judah over the other tribes is found in Judg. 20:18, in connection with the war against the Benjaminites: "They inquired of God . . . 'Who will go up for us first in battle against the Benjaminites.' YHWH said: 'Judah first.' " This language is identical to that in Judg. 1:1aβ, b.[6] Scholars have analyzed how Judg. 20:18 reflects the anti-Saul attitude of its Judean writer, who wanted to portray a prominent role for his tribe in the war against the Benjaminites at Gibeah, the city of Saul.[7] It appears, furthermore, that the passage in Judg. 1 was written with the desire to glorify the tribe of Judah against a background of disgrace

5. Y. Kaufmann, in his commentary to Judg. 1:1, claims that "we do not find in the time of Joshua or in the days of a judge that God was inquired of through a priest about going forth to war." He adds: "despite Num. 27:21." It seems to me, rather, that Num. 27:21 is an exemplary case for this matter. In ancient periods the kings and leaders inquired of YHWH before going out to war (see 1 Sam. 14:18, 36 ff.; 23:2 ff.; 2 Sam. 2:1; etc.). Num. 27:21 thus can constitute an ancient testimony for the matter of inquiring of YHWH by a leader. If we do not find this practice in the book of Joshua in regard to Joshua, this is apparently because it has been omitted by the Deuteronomistic editor, who had no need for the Urim and Thummim and inquiring of God by technical means. See what I have written in my book *Deuteronomy* (n. 1), pp. 233 ff.

6. I am not convinced that it is possible to prove that Judg. 20:18 precedes 1:1, unlike Auld in "Judges" (n. 2), p. 268.

7. See in particular M. Güdemann, "Tendenz und Abfassungszeit der letzten Capitel des Buches der Richter, *Monatschrift für die Geschrichte und Wissenschaft des Judentums* 18 (1869), pp. 357–68 and, recently, the entry "*šôpĕṭîm*" in the *Encyclopedia Miqra'it* 7, p. 594.

suffered by the other tribes especially the tribe of Benjamin (the tribe of Saul), which did not succeed in driving out the foreign inhabitants of Jerusalem, after the city had been conquered for Benjamin by the Judahites (see below).

According to the description in Judg. 1, Judah, together with Simeon his brother,[8] whose inheritance was integrated into the inheritance of Judah (cf. Josh. 19:1), went out against the Canaanites in battle, and smote them: "And YHWH delivered the Canaanites and Perizzites into their power" (Judg. 1:4). The "Canaanites and Perizzites" in the ancient biblical sources identify the early inhabitants of the land (see Gen. 13:7; 34:30; and the LXX of Josh. 16:10). There is a tendency to generalize from this expression and say that Judah actually smote all the inhabitants of the land of Canaan (cf. Gen. 34:30). The place of the battle, Bezek, perhaps as a reflection of the Judean editor's tendentiousness, locates the struggle in the place from which Saul went out to fight his first war against the Ammonites (1 Sam. 11:8). Against Bezek as the starting point for the first war of Saul, the Benjaminite, king of Israel, the editor of our chapter sets Bezek as the starting point for the wars of Judah against the Canaanites when the tribe begins to undertake settlement.

It might be argued that all the attempts to determine the actual geographic location of this Bezek are pursuits after wind: the writer has used here a well-known historical fact to advance a partisan goal, to denigrate Benjamin and praise Judah. One cannot identify Bezek here with Khirbet 'Ibziq, which is near Beth-Shean, and hypothesize that Judah went up into the passes of the hill country of Ephraim, because Judg. 1:1–2:5 is based on a tradition in which Israelite tribes ascended from across the Jordan around the area of Gilgal (2:1). In Judg. 1 we are dealing with literary motifs, as further

8. The cooperation between Judah and Simeon also appears in v. 17, and there is no justification for seeing this as a late motif, in contrast to Rösel, "Judges 1" (n. 2), p. 19.

evidenced by the anecdote that follows about the seventy kings whose thumbs and big toes were cut off and who gathered crumbs under Adoni-Bezek's table (in vv. 6–7). This little story serves the author by showing that Adoni-Bezek, king of Jerusalem, was punished measure for measure with the same cruelty he dealt out to the kings in subjugation to him. One wonders also if this story might invoke the Ammonite king Nahash who, before Saul went to war with him, was about to put out the right eye of all the people of Jabesh-Gilead (1 Sam. 11:2) for breach of treaty.[9] As a consequence, Saul went to war with him, but while no act to avenge the cruelty of Nahash the Ammonite is reported, the author in Judg. 1 was interested in emphasizing that when Adoni-Bezek behaved cruelly,[10] the Judahites meted out his just desserts.

According to all indications, Adoni-Bezek is a king of Jerusalem and is to be identified with Adoni-Zedek, king of Jerusalem (Josh. 10:1 ff.).[11] The story in Judg. 1 about the war with Adoni-Bezek and about bringing him to Jerusalem depends on an ancient tradition of an Israelite battle with a king of Jerusa-

9. According to the reading of the Qumran scroll, Nahash actually put out the right eye of each of them. See the text and the analysis in F. M. Cross, "The Ammonite Oppression of the Tribes of Gad and Reuben: Missing Verses from 1 Samuel 11 Found in 4Q Samuel[a]," in H. Tadmor and M. Weinfeld, eds., *History, Historiography, and Interpretation: Studies in Biblical and Cuneiform Literatures* (Jerusalem, 1983), pp. 148–58.

In light of the fact that the version from Qumran says that Nahash gouged out the eyes of the Gadites and Reubenites before deliberations with him, it is reasonable to posit that we have here a punishment for breaking a pact; see Cross, "Ammonite Oppression," p. 157, and n. 23 there. On piercing out the eyes of Zedekiah in connection with breaking his treaty with Nebuchadnezzar (2 Kings 25:7), see M. Weinfeld and R. Meridor, "The Punishment of Zedekiah and That of Polymestor," *Isaac Leo Seeligmann Volume* 1 (Jerusalem, 1983), pp. 223–29 (Hebrew).

10. Regarding cutting off hands and feet as a punishment for breach of covenant, see my article "Punishment" (n. 9). See also the Greek traditions on this matter in T. H. Gaster, *Myth, Legend, and Custom in the Old Testament* 2 (New York, 1969), pp. 416–17.

11. See Auld, "Judges I" (n. 2), pp. 268–69.

lem at the time of the conquest, a war that also stands behind the story in Josh. 10,[12] though the two stories differ geographically. The tradition in Josh. 10 is anchored in the cycle of stories of the tribe of Benjamin (Saul's tribe), whose scenes of battle are Gilgal, Jericho, Ai, and Gibeon—all in the inheritance of Benjamin (see above, pp. 94 ff.). Jerusalem was outside the area of war, and thus no attempts were made to capture it.[13] The editor of Judg. 1, in contrast, transferred the scene of battle to Jerusalem and even told of the city's capture.[14]

Actually, there is no hint of a capture of Jerusalem before the days of David. This account of such a capture in Judg. 1, the reliability of which is doubtful, has the aim of attributing to the tribe of Judah not only the conquest of the land but also the capture of the first capital of the Israelite kingdom. As we will see, the editor knew that the Jebusites lived in Jerusalem at that time, but he blames the Benjaminites for that (v. 21). Judah, therefore, is credited with the conquest of Jerusalem, while Benjamin is faulted for failing to expel the Jebusites—in explicit contradiction to Josh. 15:63 where the *Judahites* were the tribe incapable of driving out the Jebusites from Jerusalem.

From a perspective of historical trustworthiness, there is no difference between the events of conquest enumerated in the pre-Deuteronomistic portion of the book of Joshua (see below) and the events enumerated in Judg. 1. The two sources use popular folkloristic traditions and historical lists available

12. The description of this war seems to be a faithful representation of a real historical event in light of the condition of the Jerusalem kingdom just prior to the conquest. See Z. Kallai and H. Tadmor, "Bīt Ninurta = Beth Horon—On the History of the Kingdom of Jerusalem in the Amarna Period," *Eretz Israel* 9 (1969–70), pp. 138–47 (Hebrew).

13. In the battles after the war at Aijalon, the cities Makkedah, Libnah, Eglon, Hebron, and Debir were captured. Jerusalem was not captured. Even the Deuteronomistic editor who passed these stories on to us (see below) did not add Jerusalem to the list.

14. The idea that the Jebusites arrived at Jerusalem after the Canaanite city was destroyed by Judah (see Aharoni, *Land* [n. 2], p. 214) has no support and is pure conjecture.

to them in order to exalt their respective houses in whose names they speak. The narrator in Josh. 2–10 is interested in crediting the house of Joseph and Benjamin with the conquest, while the author of Judg. 1 wants to bestow the title of conqueror on Judah. The editor of the traditions in the (pre-Deuteronomistic) book of Joshua praises the roles of *Joseph* and *Benjamin* in the conquest: Joshua, through posterity of Ephraim, is the actor in the area of Benjamin, from Gilgal to Gibeon (Josh. 2–9), and in the Aijalon area he is the hero who subjugates the five Amorite kings (10:1–15), thereby becoming indeed the conqueror of Canaan. In contrast, the author of Judg. 1 praises Judah for its part in the conquest of Jerusalem and the entire southern district (Hebron and Debir; Arad and Hormah; Gaza, Ashkelon, and Ekron), thus making Judah the element responsible for taking possession of the "Canaanites and Perizzites" on behalf of all the Israelites. Therefore, the chapter begins with inquiring of YHWH regarding going up to battle against the Canaanites and concludes by marking off the southern boundary of the conquered land ("the territory . . . from the Scorpion Descent," v. 36; cf. Josh. 15:3 where this line appears as the southern boundary of Judah's inheritance; see also Num. 34:4). To be sure, the chapter leaves room for the activity of the house of Joseph in seizing Bethel (Judg. 1:22–26), but apart from this one achievement, which is actually accomplished by deceit and not by direct military confrontation such as the Judahites used in taking Jerusalem, the chapter does not ascribe anything to the merit of the house of Joseph and speaks disparagingly of him and the tribes associated with him, who did not drive out the Canaanites and the inhabitants of their cities and the cities' dependencies (vv. 27–28).

2. The Conquest of Hebron and Debir (verses 9–15). After recounting the conquest of Jerusalem, the editor of Judg. 1 describes Judah's success in war in the south: the Judahites fought there against the Canaanites dwelling in "the mountain country, in the Negev, and the lowland" (v. 9), an all-inclusive expression also used in the context of the conquests of Joshua in Josh. 10:40 (cf. Deut. 1:7: "in the mountain country, the lowland, and the Negev"). The list of Judah's conquests includes Hebron and Debir: Judah came to Hebron and smote the three kings of the Anakim there: Sheshai, Ahiman, and Talmai (Judg. 1:10).

This assertion stands in contradiction to what is reported in Josh. 14:6–15 and 15:13–17, where it is Caleb who conquers Hebron and expels the Anakim, and also contradicts what follows in Judg. 1 itself (see below). There is no doubt that the tradition concerning Caleb's conquest is ancient and more reliable, because the area of Hebron belonged to Caleb, a matter reflected also in the tradition of Num. 13–14. Indeed, only when the tribe of Judah became established in the south were the inheritances of Caleb and the Kenizzites swallowed up in the realm of Judah (as was the case with Simeon). At the end of the description of Judah's conquests in Judg. 1 we actually find mention, as we have already hinted, of the ancient tradition that Caleb expelled the "three Anakites" (v. 20). It is difficult to decide if the author of the chapter had reason to introduce this correction himself or if it was a corrective supplied by a later writer. It is clear, however, that at the beginning of his story about the conquest of the south, the writer was interested in showing that the Anakim were driven out by "Judah"; he used the ancient tradition that appears in Josh. 15:13 ff., but changed the subject: *Caleb* did not "go up" or "go,"[15] as in Josh. 15:15; rather, Judah did. Concerning Debir, the author leaves the episode as it is found in Josh. 15:16–19.

In the Deuteronomistic description of the national conquest under the leadership of Joshua, the conquest of Hebron and Debir, as is known, is attributed to Joshua in a campaign with

15. In Josh. 15:15 we find "he went up" (*wayyaʿal*), whereas in Judg. 1:11 we find "he went" (*wayyēlek*). The LXX text A has "they went" (*wayyēlĕkû*); text B has "they went up" (*wayyaʿălû*).

all of Israel (Josh. 10:29–37). Thus, we find three different traditions dealing with this conquest, which reflect three different eras. The most ancient and reliable attributes the victory at Hebron to Caleb (Josh. 14:6–15; 15:14). A later tradition, in Judg. 1 attributes the conquest of the city to the Judahites (v. 10), followed by a description of giving the city to Caleb (v. 20). The latest tradition, the Deuteronomist's, ascribes the conquest of Hebron to Joshua in his campaign with all the Israelites (Josh. 10:36–37).

3. Arad and Hormah (verses 16–17). After presenting the traditions of settling Hebron and Debir, the text in Judg. 1 offers traditions about settling the area of Arad and Hormah, south of the mountain country of Hebron. Just as the traditions about settling in Hebron and Debir are tied originally to autochthonous clans, i.e., the Calebites and Kenizzites, the tradition here concerning Arad and Hormah is connected originally to the Kenites and Jerahmeelites who lived in the south.[16]

Based on what we have learned from archaeological excavations, there were no Canaanite cities in the area of Arad and Hormah at the time of the conquest and settlement (the thirteenth century B.C.E.);[17] the tradition about a war with Israel by a Canaanite king of Arad, adduced in Num. 21:1, and the tradition about the defeat of the Israelites in a war with the Canaanites-Amorites at Hormah (Num. 14:44–45; 33:40; Deut. 1:44) must be considered anachronistic.[18] Actually, the

16. On this matter, see B. Mazar, "The Sanctuary at Arad and the Family of Ḥobab, Moses' Father-in-Law," *JNES* 24 (1965), pp. 297–303.

17. See, recently, A. Kempinski, O. Zimchoni, E. Gilboa, and N. Rösel, "Excavations at Tell Masos," *Eretz Israel* 15 (Y. Aharoni volume, 1981), pp. 154–80 (Hebrew).

18. Behind the traditions about the wars with the Canaanites in this area, apparently, are the fortified cities of the Canaanites from the Middle Bronze Age, which were obstacles to the nomads and were remembered for many years by those dwelling in the area. See Y. Aharoni, "Tel-Masos: Historical Considerations," *Tel-Aviv* 2 (1975), pp. 114–24.

Kenites and Jerahmeelites began settling there at the end of the thirteenth century B.C.E.[19] paralleling the settlement of the Calebites and Kenizzites in the hill country of Hebron; only later were the Judahites and Simeonites joined to them. As for Arad, Judg. 1:16 testifies that the Kenites went to settle there with the Judahites; as for Hormah, Judah again took for himself the conqueror's crown, telling us that he went with Simeon his brother and smote the Canaanites dwelling in the place (v. 17).

But we have noted that there were no Canaanite cities in this area at this period, only nomadic settlements of the Simeonites, Kenites, and Jerahmeelites (1 Sam. 30:29–30). If so, these passages, too, are anachronistic. The phenomenon here is actually similar to that in the case of Hebron: just as the author of Judg. 1 attributed to Judah the conquest really accomplished by the Calebites, so he attributed to Judah the capture of Hormah actually accomplished first by nomads in the area. With respect to Arad and Hormah, then, we see redactional development as with the stories of Hebron and Debir: just as the conquest of Hebron and Debir were attributed in the later stages of tradition to all the Israelites on a campaign led by Joshua (Josh. 10:36–37), the conquests of Arad and Hormah were attributed in the end to all the Israelites under the leadership of Moses (Num. 21:1–3).[20] As with Hebron, the author represents Judah as the tribe that stood at the head of the conquests in Arad and Hormah; in order to glorify the conquests of Judah, the author attributed to Judah and Simeon ancient traditions about the settlement of the Calebites, Kenizzites, and Kenites.

19. In the topographical list of Shishak, king of Egypt, we find *ʿrd yrḥm,* a phrase that shows the connection between Arad and the Jerahmeelite families. See Mazar, "Sanctuary at Arad" (n. 16), p. 124.

20. The fact that the national tradition is found in the book of Numbers does not mean it precedes the tradition in Judges. On this principle, see, recently, A. G. Auld, *Joshua, Moses and the Land* (Edinburgh, 1980).

4. The Conquest of Gaza, Ashkelon, and Ekron (verses 18–19). As a conclusion to the accounts of conquests of the south, we find a notice about the conquest of southern coastal cities: Gaza, Ashkelon, and Ekron (v. 18). This event has no historical basis.[21] The LXX reads: "And Judah did not capture Gaza . . ." instead of the language in the MT, "And Judah captured Gaza. . . ." The next phrase, "because the inhabitants of the valley were not expelled" (v. 19) was apparently understood to be in contradiction to v. 18 and led to the correction in the LXX.[22] Nevertheless, according to what appears in the MT, Judah did succeed in capturing the coastal cities but, as was the case with Jerusalem, was not able to expel their inhabitants. One must note that the verse does not directly say that Judah "did not expel" (*wĕlōʾ hôrîšʾ*), as is said of other tribes in what follows, but says, rather, *kî lōʾ lĕhôrîš,* a formulation using an infinitive without specifying the agent of the verb—because it was impossible to relate failure and lack of success explicitly to Judah.

5. Caleb Expels the Three Anakites (verse 20). Verse 20 is a sort of corrective footnote that darkens somewhat the bright picture at the beginning of Judg. 1 of the success of Judah's conquest. According to this verse it is Caleb, not Judah, who expels the three Anakites (see above, section 2). As we have noted, this verse represents a well-known fact that could not be contradicted and thus had to be brought in at the end as a miscellaneous note. The verse may be a later addition to the original text.

21. See Aharoni, *Land* (n. 2), p. 218. It seems that this piece of information is influenced by Judah's claim of dominion over the Philistine area. See Josh. 15:45–47; but there, the cities are Ekron, Ashdod, and Gaza. The source of the inclusion of these cities in this list (in Joshua) apparently reflects the period when Judah expanded in the days of Hezekiah (cf. 2 Kings 18:8) or Josiah. On this matter, see Z. Kallai, *Historical Geography of the Bible* (Jerusalem, 1986), pp. 372–77.

22. Ibid., p. 109.

6. The Benjaminites and the Jebusites who Dwelt at Jerusalem (verse 21). The Benjaminites did not expel the Jebusites that dwelt at Jerusalem, and the mention of Benjamin thereby calls to mind other northern tribes that did not drive out the Canaanites from their cities (vv. 27 ff.). As we remarked earlier, v. 21 contradicts Josh. 15:63, which says that the Judahites were not able to expel the Jebusites from Jerusalem, a discrepancy leading inescapably to the conclusion that Judg. 1:21 seeks tendentiously to glorify Judah at the expense of Benjamin.[23]

It is difficult to determine if this verse is attached as a conclusion to the preceding section about Judah's achievements, or if it is attached to the following list of failures of the house of Joseph to drive out the people of the land.[24] Admittedly, the episode in vv. 22–26 interrupts the report of failure by Benjamin and the other northern tribes, but if the author had followed a geographical order in his presentation[25] it would make sense to discuss Benjamin immediately after Judah. It is possible, too, that the author wanted to begin his listing with the most important failure, the failure to drive the Jebusites out of Jerusalem, which in the future would become "the chosen city."

7. The House of Joseph and Its Conquests (verses 22–26). Verses 22–26, which tell of the conquest of Bethel by the house of Joseph and which undoubtedly reflect an ancient tradition, may be considered an introduction to an account of the settlement of the northern tribes. The house of Joseph indeed con-

23. According to Auld, "Judges I" (n. 20), pp. 274–75, Josh. 15:63 is the original verse, and Judg. 1:21 is a tendentious reworking of the verse from Joshua.

24. It is possible to explain the unique expression *yšb ʾt* (*bny bnymyn*) instead of *yšb bqrb*, as found in what follows (vv. 29, 30, 32, 33), by saying the verse's language was derived from an ancient tradition (Josh. 15:63). See n. 23, above.

25. Z. Kallai, "Judah and Israel: A Study in Israelite Historiography," *IEJ* 28 (1978), pp. 254–55, n. 13.

quered Bethel, not, like Judah in its conquests, by methods of warfare, but by deceit: they penetrated the city through a secret entrance and then smote the inhabitants. But the tribes of the house of Joseph did not succeed in driving out the inhabitants of the other large cities that were Joseph's lot, such as Beth-Shean, Taanach, Dor, Ibleam, Megiddo, and Gezer (vv. 27–29). And even when the house of Joseph grew strong, instead of driving the inhabitants out, they put them under forced labor (v. 28).

The author drew these details about the tribes' failures to dispossess the people of the land from sources available to him.[26] We find the same details in the lists of inheritances in Josh. 14–19 (15:63; 16:10; 17:12–13). But the author of Judg. 1 gathered these details together to impress the reader with the failures of the northern tribes vis-à-vis the achievements of the Judahites, and he similarly adduced a list of failures related to the Galilean tribes: Zebulon did not drive out the inhabitants of Kitron and Nahalol (v. 30), and Asher not only did not succeed in driving out "the inhabitants of Akko, the inhabitants of Sidon, and Ahlab, Achzib, Helbah, Aphek, and Rehob," but even *dwelt in the midst of the Canaanites* (v. 32), who apparently prevailed over Asher in this region of strong Phoenician cities.[27] Naphtali, too, did not succeed in driving out the inhabitants of Beth-Shemesh and Beth-Anath (v. 33). And Issachar is not mentioned at all, because, as we learn from Gen. 49:14–15, he was himself enslaved by Canaanites in the area (whence, it seems, comes the name of Issachar: *ʾiš śākār:* "and he bent his shoulder to bear and became a slave laborer").[28]

26. But these lists do not precede the unified kingdom. See Kallai, *Geography* (n. 21).

27. See Y. Aharoni, "The Settlement and the Inheritance," in B. Mazar, ed., *The History of the People of Israel* 2, *The Patriarchs and the Judges* (Jerusalem, 1967), pp. 210 ff. (Hebrew).

28. On "people put to forced labor" (*ʾanšê mas*), who were accustomed to work in the Jezreel Valley in the period before the Israelite conquest, see the letter of Biridya, king of Megiddo, to the king of Egypt:

The Danites were also pushed into the hill country by the Amorites (v. 34), and, as we know from Josh. 19:47 and Judg. 18, they were finally forced to seek an inheritance in the north. Hence, they appear in Judg. 1 next to Naphtali in the north, which indicates that the author knew that Dan was now living in the north.

In comparison with the achievements of Judah in the south, the tribes of Israel in the north did not succeed in driving out the Canaanites, and even when they had the power to expel them they instead put the Canaanites under forced labor (v. 28). As we will see, they were considered to have sinned by doing this.

There is no doubt that the document in Judg. 1 serves to glorify the tribe of Judah and to lessen the stature of "Israel" in the north. This prejudice, which is interlocked, as we will see, with criticism of Benjamin, apparently derives from circles in the house of David who sought to show that not the tribes of the north but Judah, David's tribe, was that which stood behind the conquest of the land. The other tribes did not drive out the Canaanites from their cities, and only in the time of David did they prevail over them. Moreover, the tribes of the north sinned when they had it in their power to drive out the Canaanites from their cities but did not do so (v. 28), as is evident in the rebuke of the angel in Judg. 2:1–5. Because of this sin, the troubles of the period of the judges came about.

8. Joshua 2–11: The Conquest under the Leadership of the House of Joseph. Joshua does not appear in the description of the conquest in Judg. 1,[29] but in the block of stories in Josh. 2–11 he appears as the leader from the tribe of Ephraim[30] who is

---

"I am he who plows in the city of Shunem, and I am he who transports the men put under forced labor (to work)" (el-Amarna letter #365); see A. Alt, "Neues" (ch. 5, n. 33), pp. 169 ff.

29. On the introduction "After the death of Joshua" in Judg. 1:1, see section 1 of this chapter.

30. Num. 13:8; 1 Chron. 7:27; Josh. 19:49; 24:29–30; Judg. 2:9.

responsible for the entire conquest. Whereas the Judean tradition in Judg. 1 was interested in relating the entire conquest to Judah, the writer of Josh. 2–11 is interested in relating the conquest to the house of Joseph and to its leader Joshua. The house of Joseph, which dwelt in the center of the land of Israel, was numerous and powerful (see Deut. 33:17), so it is not surprising that their leader succeeded in being transformed into the central hero of the conquest, even though his actual sphere of activity is concentrated in the region of the Ephraimite hill country. In an early tribal tradition, Josh. 17:17–18, it is Joshua who acquired an inheritance for the house of Joseph and, through victory in the Aijalon Valley (Josh. 10:9–14), secured authority over the hill country of Ephraim as far as Azekah in the Elah Valley (see below). Moreover, Josh. 19:50 preserves a very ancient tradition about a personal act of Joshua that was tied to the hill country of Ephraim: the building of the city Timnath Seraḥ/Ḥeres in this region. As Y. Kaufmann perceived,[31] we have here a reliable historical event that may serve as evidence that Joshua actually founded a city in the hill country of Ephraim,[32] a city remembered because his grave was preserved there (Josh. 24:30; cf. Judg. 2:9), a suggestion of the great importance attached to graves of leaders who established settlements and headed cities.[33] Timnath Seraḥ/Ḥeres was a habitation apparently located in Mount Ḥeres,[34] where accord-

31. In his commentary to Joshua 19:50.

32. "He built the city and dwelt in it"; cf. the verse on the settlement of the Danites in Judg. 18:27–29, "They built the city and dwelt in it," and cf. Josh. 19:47. See also the term "build" (*bnh*) in connection with settlement in Judg. 1:26, and also in the passages in Num. 32:24 ff. See above, pp. 48 f., 62 f.

33. On this matter, see, recently, I. Malkin, *Religion and Colonization in Ancient Greece* (Leiden, 1988), pp. 189 ff.

34. See Z. Kallai, "Timnat-ḥeres," *Encyclopedia Miqra'it,* vol. 8, pp. 602–03. According to B. Mazar the reading Timnath-Seraḥ is preferable. He connects this with Serah the daughter of Asher, who like Beriah, son of Asher, settled in the hill country of Ephraim (1 Chron. 7:30 ff.). See

ing to Judg. 1:35 Amorites dwelt in early times; later, it was ruled by the house of Joseph. Joshua's expulsion of the Amorite kings from the Ephraimite hill country leads us to postulate that his victory is at the bottom of this notice of how the house of Joseph seized power in the area (and see Chapter 2).

Northern priestly traditions also connect Joshua to a particular holy place in the hill country of Ephraim, that is, Shiloh. According to these traditions, Joshua divided the land into inheritances for the tribes at Shiloh, in partnership with Eleazar the priest.[35] Similarly, he sought Eleazar's counsel before going forth to battle (Num. 27:19–23; and see Chapter 2). Joshua, the leader from the house of Joseph, received prophetic legitimation for his activities at the Shiloh sanctuary in the hill country of Ephraim. It is worth noting that alongside the tradition about the tomb of Joshua in Timnath Seraḥ/Ḥeres (Josh. 19:50; 24:30; Judg. 2:9), we find another tradition concerning a grave in the Ephraimite hill country, that of Eleazar, son of Aaron, the priest, in Gibeah of Phinehas. (Josh. 24:33). Interestingly, we also find a tradition in Greece about the grave of a founder that is near the grave of the prophetic priest who aided him (see Chapter 2). The Israelite traditions apparently can be traced to Shiloh, because the tabernacle of Shiloh was understood in the priestly tradition as the place where Joshua and Eleazar the priest divided up the land by lot "before YHWH" (Josh. 18:1–10; 19:51); According to these traditions, Phinehas, son of Eleazar, continued to serve as priest in the Shiloh sanctuary after the death of Joshua (Josh. 22:9–34)

B. Mazar, *Canaan and Israel: Historical Essays* (Jerusalem, 1976), p. 112, n. 56.

35. Num. 34:17; Josh. 14:1; 17:4; 19:51; 21:1. One should note that these verses were attached to the traditions at a later stage (see Auld, *Joshua* (n. 20), 53 ff.) and reflect additions from priestly sources. Yet this does not indicate the time of the basic tradition about Joshua and Eleazar at Shiloh. This tradition was certainly not invented after the destruction, even if it was added to the verses in a late period.

and served before the ark of the covenant at Bethel (Judg. 20:28), which was also in the Ephraimite hill country.[36]

These priestly traditions, which are interested not in descriptions of war but rather in description of parceling out and dividing the land, constitute an important link in the history of the tribes' settlement in the land of Israel. They recount matters that are not reported at all in the other traditions about the conquest, such as the role of prophecy in the settlement, the determination of the central sacral site, and the division of the land by lot for the various tribes. These matters are also known from the world of Greek colonization (see Chapter 2).

The Greek parallels indicate that the priestly traditions about the settlement in the Pentateuch and book of Joshua are not late theological speculations but are anchored in and bound to the reality of the actual process of making new settlements in antiquity, particularly in the eastern basin of the Mediterranean after the collapse of the kingdoms at the end of the thirteenth century B.C.E. As we saw above, (Chapter 2), the Sea peoples who sought to settle in the area operated by methods similar to those employed by the Israelite tribes in their settlement of the land of Canaan.

Other traditions in the book of Joshua connect the tribe of Ephraim, and its leader Joshua, to Shechem in the Ephraimite hill country (Josh. 21:21).[37] According to Josh. 24:25, Joshua made a covenant with the people in Shechem and set for them "statutes and ordinances" (*ḥōq ûmišpāṭ*), and according to the tradition of the Deuteronomistic stratum in Josh. 8:30–35 Joshua built an altar to YHWH there (on Mt. Ebal) and conducted the ceremony of blessing and cursing. It should be noted that Shechem controlled all the mountain area from the

36. On the attempt to find traces of this tradition in the addition in the LXX to Josh. 24:28–33, see A. Rofé, "The End of the Book of Joshua According to the Septuagint," *Shnaton* 2 (1977), pp. 217–27 (Hebrew).

37. "The Mount of Ephraim" includes the entire central area of the land of Israel and thus encompasses Manasseh, Ephraim, and Benjamin. See Kallai, *Geography* (n. 21), 47.

Jezreel Valley to the lowland of Judah in the period before the settlement of the Israelites.[38] Thus, if Joshua seized power over the hill country of Ephraim, it is possible that he entered Shechem, too, though it should be admitted that we do not know when or how the Israelites penetrated Shechem because the Bible does not preserve a tradition about a battle in this city.[39] It seems that the Israelites succeeded in making a treaty with the inhabitants of the place,[40] similar to the treaty they made with the Gibeonites. As we have indicated above (Chapter 2), the tradition about the penetration of the Hebrews into Shechem appears to be ancient.

Next to Shechem was an ancient sacred site at which the tribes of Israel would gather for religious ceremonies. Joshua, who achieved such great victories in the hill country of Ephraim, conducted these assemblies, according to the tradition, a role that made him like a "judge," who acquired a central position after his victory in battle (Judg. 8:27 ff.; 11:6). In any event, it seems that the descriptions of Joshua's activity at Shechem in Josh. 8:30–35; 24 are motivated by the late national tradition about Shechem's place in the history of Israel (cf., for example, Gen. 12:6–7; 33:18–20), and that their origin is in a desire to connect Joshua to an important city that was, in the words of A. Alt, "the uncrowned queen of the land of Israel."[41] The Deuteronomist attributed to Joshua the setting up of an altar at Mt. Ebal and the writing of a "copy of the instruction of Moses" on stones there, in agreement with Deut. 27:1–8, whereas the tradition in Josh. 24:1–28, presupposing that he stood at the head of a federation of twelve

38. See recently on this matter, N. Na'aman, "Society and Culture in the Late Bronze Age," in I. Eph'al, ed., *The History of Eretz Israel* 1 (Jerusalem, 1982), p. 216 (Hebrew).

39. There is no description of the conquest of Shechem, and the name of the king of Shechem is lacking in the list of thirty-one kings in Josh. 12.

40. See H. Reviv, "Governmental Authority in Shechem in the Period of El Amarna and the Time of Abimelech," *Bulletin of the Israel Exploration Society* (*Yediot*) 27 (1963–64), pp. 270–75.

41. "Jerusalems Aufstieg," *KS* 3, p. 246.

tribes, attributed to him the making of a covenant with the people of Shechem. Actually, the covenant at Shechem and the setting up of an altar and stones there represent the entrance to the promised land, analogous to the setting up of the stone at Gilgal in Josh. 3–4. The erection of stones at Gilgal by Joshua is actually a tradition that rivals that of setting up an altar of stones at Mt. Ebal.[42]

From a typological perspective, the traditions of Shechem and Gilgal are foundation legends (Greek *ktisis*),[43] which recount the establishment of Israel in its land as accompanied by impressive religious ceremonies.[44] The Pentateuchal literature deals with the establishment of the people before they came to the land of Israel, at Sinai and the Plain of Moab, so we find similar accompanying ceremonies there.[45] However, as Bin-Gorion recognized in his book,[46] the Sinai covenant and that of Shechem traditions compete with one another. The tradition in Josh. 24 is totally ignorant of the Sinai covenant made by Moses (Exod. 24), and sets up in its place the covenant at Shechem made by Joshua (v. 25). Joshua established "statutes and ordinances" in Shechem and wrote down a "book of God's instruction" (*spr twrt 'lhym;* v. 26), much as Moses did at Sinai (Exod. 24:3–7; and see above, p. 110).

42. According to M. Haran, the story about Gilgal belongs to the Yahwist source, while the story about Mt. Ebal belongs to the Elohist source; in both of the stories, altars of stone were erected. See his article "Shechem Studies," *Zion* 38 (1973), pp. 13 ff. (Hebrew).

43. J. Licht dealt with this matter in "The Biblical Claim about the Foundation," *Shnaton* 4 (1980), pp. 98 ff. (Hebrew), but he is referring to the establishment of Israel in the Plains of Moab (Deut. 26:16; 27:9–10).

44. See Chapter 2.

45. The foundation ceremony in the Plains of Moab, in which it is proclaimed "this day you have become a people to YHWH your God" (Deut. 27:9), is tied there actually with the ceremony at mounts Gerizim and Ebal. The covenant at the Plains of Moab, in my opinion, mixes "foundation" in the wilderness with a "foundation" in the land. Compare the erection of the twelve pillars at Sinai (Exod. 24:4) to the erection of the twelve stones at Gilgal.

46. *Sinai und Garizim* (Berlin, 1926).

The block of chapters 2–10 in the book of Joshua tells us about the tradition of the sanctuary at Gilgal and its connection with Joshua. The scene of the wars in this section is the inheritance of Benjamin (Gilgal, Jericho, Ai, and Gibeon). The place that served there as the deployment site for war was Gilgal (9:6; 10:6, 15, 43; cf. 14:6). Scholars have assumed that the sanctuary at Gilgal is the place where the stories in this group of chapters were created,[47] a reasonable assumption. The upper boundary chronologically for the formation of this sort of string of stories is the period of King Saul, and we might note a number of indications that link this block of stories with Saul or the time of Saul. (1) Saul, of Benjaminite origin, was made a king in the sanctuary of Gilgal (1 Sam. 11:14–15) and operated mainly at this sanctuary (13:12–18; 15:12). (2) Only when the Israelite tribes were unified politically for royal rule was it likely that a desire arose to concretize in written tradition the national epic of the conquest of the land by one leader. (3) The zeal of king Saul, who, "by his zeal for the Israelites and Judah" (2 Sam. 21:2 ff.), plotted against the Amorites inhabiting the land, corresponds to the idea of *ḥerem* ("ban") expressed vigorously in the story about the conquest of Jericho and the deed of Achan. The type of *ḥerem* used against Jericho in Josh.—"men and women, young and old, and cattle, flock animals, asses, by the sword" (v. 21)—brings to mind the *ḥerem* that Saul was commanded to carry out in 1 Sam. 15:3 and in Saul's ban against Nob, the priestly city, in 1 Sam. 22:19: "men and women, children and infants, cattle, asses, and flock animals, by the sword" (see Chapter 4). (4) The description of presenting the tribes in order to determine the guilty party by lot (Urim and Thummin) is congruent with the description of inquiring of YHWH in 1 Sam. 14:40 ff. in connection with Saul and Jonathan. (5) The central place of the ark of the covenant in Josh. 3, 4, and 6 indicates that these stories were

47. M. Noth, *Josua*, HAT^2 (Tübingen, 1953), pp. 12 ff.; cf. also J. A. Soggin, *Joshua*, OTL (London, 1972), pp. 10 ff.

crystalized in a period when the ark of the covenant of YHWH was used to accompany warriors to battle. (6) Is it possible to suppose that the description of the Gibeonites, who tricked Israel by their request to make a treaty (Josh. 9:3–18), has its source in the house of Saul and seeks to justify Saul's breach of the treaty (2 Sam. 21)?

Even if the consolidation of these stories in Joshua cannot be attributed to the period of Saul, the events described therein clearly occurred in the region of the land of Benjamin and have a special connection with Gilgal. If so, their place of creation is likely in the land of Benjamin. The fact that Achan, the troubler of Israel, is from the tribe of Judah probably testifies to the antagonism toward Judah in these stories (Josh. 7:1, 18).

We will try now to track traditions of the conquest in Josh. 2–11. Chapter 2, which opens with the description of Joshua sending out spies, probably reflects a reliable historical event. Sending out men for reconnaissance was a widespread phenomenon in the east.[48] Moreover, a prostitute's or innkeeper's house was the accustomed place for meeting with spies, conspirators, and the like. Thus, for example, we read in Hammurabi Code: "If scoundrels plot together [in conspiratorial relationships][49] in an innkeeper's house, and she does not seize them and bring them to the palace, that innkeeper shall be put to death" (law § 109). In a Mari letter we read about two men who sow fear and panic and cause rebellion in an army.[50] Also, the pattern of a three-day stay in an area when pursuing escapees has support in ancient eastern sources; for example, the

48. The spies at Mari are called "men of tongue," *awīlē šă lišānim*. We also find in the descriptions of an Egyptian battle on the walls of a sanctuary two spies who are beaten to make them reveal the place of the "vanquished leader of the Hittites"; see H. J. Breasted, *Ancient Records of Egypt* 3 (New York, 1906), pp. 329–30.

49. *ittarkasu* is from the root *rakāsu* = "bind." Like the Hebrew *qšr,* it has a sense of physical binding and another sense of treacherous conspiracy; cf. Ps. 31:21.

50. See J. M. Sasson, *The Military Establishments at Mari* (Rome, 1969), pp. 39 ff.

instructions to the Hittite tower commanders specify that if an enemy invades a place he must be pursued for three days. In the same collection of instructions we find that it is forbidden to build an inn (*arzana*)[51] in which prostitutes live near the fortress wall, apparently because of the kind of danger described in Josh. 2. Rahab's method of hiding the spies has a parallel in the story of hiding Jonathan and Ahimaaz in 2 Sam. 17:19–20. Moreover, we find that letting down an endangered person through a window, in the story about David and Michal in 1 Sam. 19:12, is similar to the story in Joshua 2. In ancient Greek literature we read about a whore in whose memory a sanctuary of Aphrodite was dedicated, after she helped an enemy escape outside a wall.[52] All these bits of evidence indicate that the story about Rahab has a firm foundation in reality, that the city was conquered by stratagem,[53] much as in Judg. 1:22–26, and that the continuation of the story about the real conquest of Jericho was cut short, to make room for a miraculous and supernatural story (Josh. 6). There is some tension between the story in chapter 2 and the legendary description of the conquest of Jericho in chapter 6. According to 2:15, Rahab is dwelling in the wall structure, whereas 6:20 says that despite the wall having fallen, Rahab was removed from her house (v. 22 ff.). Similarly, it is difficult to understand the reason for sending the spies to Jericho if the

51. See E. von Schuler, *Hethistiche Dienstanweisungen* (Osnabrück, 1957), p. 42, col. 1:15–16; p. 44, col. 2:27–28. For an explanation of the term *arzana,* see H. Hoffner, "The Arzana House" *Anatolian Studies Presented to H. G. Güterbock* (Istanbul: Nederlands Historisch-Archaeologisch Institut in Het Nabije Oosten, 1974), pp. 113–21.

52. On this story and similar stories in Greek and Roman literature, see H. Windisch, "Zur Rahabgeschichte (Zwei Parallelen aus der Klassischen Literatur)," *ZAW* 37 (1917–18), pp. 188 ff.; G. Hölscher, "Zum Ursprung der Rahabsage," *ZAW* 38 (1919–20), pp. 54 ff.; S. Wagner, "Die Kundschaftergeschichten in Alten Testament," *ZAW* 76 (1964), pp. 255 ff.

53. Also see, recently, A. Malamat, Israel in Biblical Times (Jerusalem, 1983), pp. 69–72 (Hebrew).

walls were simply going to fall down miraculously anyway. And Josh. 24:11 says that the nobles of Jericho fought with Israel, a datum that does not fit with the story in chapter 6.

In light of all this, it is reasonable to think that at one time the story about the spies at Jericho existed by itself, like the story about the reconnaissance mission of the Josephites at Bethel (Judg. 1:22–26), and that only later the spy story was tied to Joshua and all of Israel, and the tradition about the miraculous conquest of the city came into being. Encircling the city with the ark of the Covenant accompanied by horn blasts came from a liturgical ceremony that was customary at Gilgal.[54]

The conquest of Ai and the story about the *ḥerem* of Achan (chaps. 7–8) have some basis in reality, but archaeological discoveries make clear that in the period of the Israelite conquest there was no Canaanite settlement in Ai and that it remained desolate for hundreds of years before the period of the conquest. The Israelite settlement began only in the second half of the twelfth century B.C.E. It is possible, then, that the story reflects a local battle of Israelites with a weak Canaanite settlement (cf. Josh. 7:3), and that later the battle was attached to the wars of conquest.[55]

The story about the pact with the Gibeonites and the war with the five Amorite kings (chaps. 9–10) reflects one of the important events in the period of the conquest. The area north of Jerusalem as far as Beth-Horon belonged to the land of Jerusalem, as we learn from letter #290 from el-Amarna, which says that Bit Ninurta = Beth-Horon, "the city of the land of Jerusalem," joined with the *Ḫabiru* people, that is, it

54. The celebration of the Passover at Gilgal in Josh. 5 is also anchored in a ceremony in which the event of the exodus from Egypt is dramatized in the sanctuary of Gilgal. See on this matter Soggin, *Joshua* (n. 47), pp. 54 ff. and bibliography.

55. See J. A. Callaway, "New Evidence on the Conquest of ʿAi," *JBL* 87 (1968), pp. 312 ff.

rebelled against Jerusalem.[56] In view of this, the Gibeonite treaty with the Israelites, which was formed later in the period of the conquest, must have further endangered the position of the king of Jerusalem; he therefore organized a coalition of five Amorite kings and went out to fight against the Gibeonites and the Israelites. The battle in the Aijalon Valley brought a crushing defeat for the king of Jerusalem and those who had made a pact with him (Josh. 10:8–14). Through this battle, dominion over the hill country of Ephraim was assured by the Israelites. We can imagine that over the years, the victory in the Aijalon Valley magnified Joshua's reputation among the Israelite tribes and transformed him into the conqueror of the land of Canaan (see above).

The pericope about the covenant with the Gibeonites undoubtedly reflects a real event, as we learn from the story in 2 Sam. 21:1–6, but whether Joshua actually participated in making this treaty is in doubt. A priestly tradition inserted in Josh. 9 says that the chieftains of the congregation (*nśy*ʾ*y h*ʿ*dh*), not Joshua, made the treaty.[57] (vv. 15, 21). Also, we need to remember that Gibeon belonged to the tribe of Benjamin, not Ephraim.

In contrast to the story about the battle in the Aijalon Valley, which reflects an actual event, the story about the conquest of Makkedah, Libnah, Lachish, Eglon, Hebron, and Debir (Josh. 10:28–39) belongs to a later editorial stratum; its description is stereotypical[58] and full of Deuteronomistic for-

56. See Z. Kallai and H. Tadmor, "Bīt Ninurta" (ch. 5, n. 34), pp. 138 ff.

57. See what I have written on this issue in "Review Article on *Gibeon and Israel,* by J. Blenkinsopp," *IEJ* 26 (1976), pp. 62–63.

58. It is not a description of a real event, but rather a schema built on (1) capture, (2) smiting by the sword, and (3) putting under ban and not leaving a remnant (which is formulated in the style of Deuteronomy): "and they captured it . . . smote it . . . and all living creatures . . . he did not leave anyone alive."

mulas, and it contradicts the early traditions about the conquest of Hebron and Debir by Caleb and Othniel ben-Kenaz (see above, p. 128 f.). If authentic information has been preserved in the story,[59] it reflects later battles of the tribe of Judah with the cities of the region,[60] and not Joshua's campaign at Aijalon. Needless to say, Josh. 10:40–43 is an editorial summary, which extrapolated from the battle in the Aijalon Valley the conquest of the entire south.

As for the story about the war at the Waters of Merom and the conquest of Hazor in Josh. 11, one must note that archaeological excavations at Hazor lead to the unambiguous conclusion that the city was destroyed at the end of the thirteenth century B.C.E., the period of the Israelite settlement.[61] Nevertheless when the passage about the war at the Waters of Merom is compared to the story of the war of Deborah and Barak (Judg. 4–5), many difficulties are apparent. Some scholars claim that the war with Sisera preceded that of the Waters of Merom,[62] and that Hazor fell only after the break-

59. The verse "then Horam the king of Gezer went up to help Lachish" (v. 33) is taken apparently from an earlier source, since archival material generally begins by "then" (*'āz*), as in Akkadian introductions (*ina ūmē*). See J. A. Montgomery, "Archival Data in the Book of Kings," *JBL* 53 (1934), pp. 49–52, and recently, M. Cogan and H. Tadmor, "Ahaz and Tiglath-Pileser in the Book of Kings: Historiographic Considerations," *Eretz-Israel* 14 (1978), p. 56.

60. Lachish was destroyed in the twelfth and not the thirteenth century B.C.E.; see D. Ussishkin, "Excavations at Tel Lachish 1978–1983: Second Preliminary Report," *Tel-Aviv* 10 (1983), pp. 92–175. According to N. Na'aman the basic description in Josh. 10 about the king of Jerusalem who stands at the head of a pact of southern kingdoms "is not consistent with what we know from the documents. It is not possible to suppose that Jerusalem had the power to lead cities like Lachish and Eglon"; "Society and Culture" (n. 38), p. 220. But this view can be contested.

61. See Y. Yadin, *Hazor* (Oxford, 1972), pp. 9 ff., 131 ff.

62. See B. Mazar, "The Exodus from Egypt and the Conquest of the Land," *The History of the People of Israel* 2, *The Patriarchs and the Judges*, pp. 198–99; and Malamat, *Israel* (n. 53), pp. 221–22; also see Aharoni, *Land* (n. 2), pp. 220 ff.

down of the Canaanite military order in the Jezreel Valley. The association of Hazor's destruction with Joshua is then a tendentious creation of the writer of chapters 2–11 in the book of Joshua.[63]

In light of all this, it would appear that the settlement of the tribes in the land of Israel took quite a long time, and that only after they became numerous and powerful did they succeed in exercising dominion over most of the area. The Canaanite cities on the coast and in the valleys maintained their status as independent cities until the time of David. The block of traditions in Josh. 2–11 came into being, then, out of a desire to ascribe to Joshua all the wars of conquest, even though in terms of actual historical development these wars occurred over the period of many generations.

As we already hinted, the aim of these stories was to immortalize the impressive national experience of the conquest of the land of Canaan under Joshua's leadership, which in actuality had constituted the beginnings of the establishment of Israel in its land. The wonders and miracles adduced here echo the events of the exodus from Egypt: crossing the Jordan on dry ground (chaps. 3–4); the revelation of the chief of YHWH's army to Joshua (5:13–15); and the victory when Joshua stretches out the javelin in his hand toward the city and does not draw his hand back, which brings to mind the victory when Moses holds up his hands (8:18, 26; cf. Exod. 17:11). Like Moses, Joshua sends out spies, performs a Passover (Josh.

63. The description of the battle as it appears before us, the Canaanite pursuit "to Sidon the Great up to Misrephoth on the west, and to the Valley of Mizpah on the east" (Josh. 11:8), does not predate the united kingdom because the geographic scope here fits the territorial scope of the united kingdom. See Z. Kallai, "The Boundaries of Canaan and the Land of Israel in the Bible: Territorial Models in Biblical Historiography," *Eretz-Israel* 12 (N. Glueck volume, 1975), pp. 27–34 (Hebrew); also N. Na'aman, "The Inheritances of the Cis-Jordanian Tribes of Israel and the 'Land That Yet Remaineth,'" *Eretz-Israel* 16 (H. M. Orlinsky volume, 1982), pp. 154 ff. (Hebrew).

5:2–12), organizes covenant ceremonies (8:30–35; cf. 24:26, where Joshua writes in a book of God's Torah), and more. The ark of the covenant plays an honored part in these stories: it passes before the Israelites when they cross the Jordan (chaps. 3–4) and accompanies them when they encircle the walls of Jericho (chap. 7). These data show that the entrance of the Israelites into the promised land was performed according to all the rules of holiness, and that God was with them in their battles (10:14). As we suggested above, it seems that in the days of Saul all these events were identified with the sanctuary at Gilgal, with the liturgical ceremonies that appear in these chapters serving to tie the exodus from Egypt to the conquest of the promised land.

The stories, religio-educational in character, were made concrete in the eyes of the reader by an etiological motif that accompanied each of them. The stories at Gilgal are put forth "for a memorial to the Israelites forever" (Josh. 4:7), since it was here that the Israelites crossed the Jordan. The circumcision that enabled the people to celebrate the passover (cf. Exod. 12:43–48) explains the name Gilgal (Josh. 5:9); the conquest of Jericho is immortalized by the sight of destroyed walls, and the breach of *ḥerem,* by the pile of stones in the valley of Achor (7:24–26). The treaty with the Gibeonites is rendered concrete by the existence of hewers of wood and drawers of water at the sanctuary (9:27), and the cave at Makkedah and the trees near it bring to mind the war with the Amorite kings (10:26–28). This invocation of etiology does not imply that the stories were invented for the purpose of etiological explanation, as a few scholars have claimed, because it is merely secondary, used only to add extra power to a tradition that already exists.[64] The goal of the stories was to

64. See the articles of I. L. Seeligmann, "Aetiological Elements in Biblical Historiography," *Zion* 26 (1960–61), pp. 141–61 (Hebrew), and B. S. Childs, "A Study of the Formula 'Until this Day,'" *JBL* 82 (1963), pp. 279–92. Also see J. Bright, *Early Israel in Recent History Writing* (London, 1956), pp. 79 ff.

make the religious experience tangible and real, and to make it a didactic tool of great power, as is expressed clearly in the "children's question" ("and when your children ask") in Josh. 4:6–7, 21–24. Indeed, the "children's question" appears in a similar form in stories of the exodus from Egypt in the Torah (Exod. 12:26;[65] 13:14), the goal of which is to impart national education by means of the Passover ceremony. The exodus from Egypt and the entrance to the promised land were, then, a basis for educating the younger generation, and the two events together were actualized in rites: the first by the Passover offering and the second by the procession of the ark at Gilgal.

9. The Last Editor of the Conquest Stories. The Deuteronomistic editor who gathered the traditions in Josh. 2–12 and gave them a framework was more interested in the historiosophic perspective than in supernatural events, social institutions, and cultic customs.[66] The principal feature of his orientation was the fulfillment in tangible terms of YHWH's word to the patriarchs giving the promised land to Israel. This orientation is clear in the discourse at the beginning of the book of Joshua in which God promises the leader that he will be with him in conquering the land in its ideal boundaries: "from the wilderness . . . to the large river, the Euphrates river" (1:4); it is also evident in the summary words of the editor, in Josh. 21:41–43: "And YHWH gave Israel all the land that he swore to give their fathers . . ."; and it is expressed in the farewell speech put in the mouth of Joshua in chapter 23.

65. Compare "What are these stones for you?" with "What is this ritual for you?" in Exod. 12:26, and see my commentary to Deuteronomy in Anchor Bible (New York, 1991), pp. 328 f., regarding the change that occurred in the educational concept of the issue of "the child's question" in Deut. 6:20–25.

66. On the cold attitude of the writer of Deuteronomy toward the cultic institutions like the ark of the covenant, sacrifices, and so forth, see my book *Deuteronomy and the Deuteronomic School* (n. 1), pp. 191 ff., and my commentary to Deuteronomy (n. 65), pp. 37 ff.

The editor was familiar with the fact that Joshua did not conquer the land in its promised boundaries, i.e., to the Euphrates; therefore, he put in Joshua's mouth the promise that "the remaining land" would be conquered by the coming generations as long as they walk in YHWH's paths and observe his commandments. Nevertheless, according to the editor's description, all the land was captured in its real borders, "from Mt. Halak that ascends to Seir, to Baal Gad in the Lebanon Valley," by Joshua (11:17; 12:7), and it was given to the Israelites and they settled it (21:41).

The historical traditions that the editor adduced, however, present an entirely imperfect picture of the conquest. The specific wars discussed in these traditions are few and quite sporadic: the conquest of Jericho and Ai, the war with the five Amorite kings in the south (10:1–27), and the war at the Waters of Merom in the north (11:1–10). We find nothing in these traditions about battles and wars in the great political centers in Canaan, such as Megiddo, Taanach, Jokneam, Tirzah, Bethel, Shechem, Beth-Shean, Jerusalem, Gezer, and so forth. In order to describe an all-inclusive and one-time conquest of the land of Canaan, the editor of the material in Josh. 1–12 used several separate conquest traditions that were available to him, as well as a schematic list of Canaanite cities and their kings (Josh. 12).[67] If he had had access to traditions about the conquest of great Canaanite centers his work would have been easier, but because such traditions were unavailable to help him, he was forced to arrange such traditions as he had in a way that would leave the impression of the conquest as a systematic national operation: a battle in the central region (Jericho, Ai, and the Aijalon Valley), a campaign to the south and a battle in the north (Hazor).

Thus the battle against all the land of Canaan was made to

67. The list was composed, it seems, in the time of Solomon. See V. Fritz, "Die Sogennante Liste der Besiegten Könige in Josua 12," *ZDPV* 85 (1969), pp. 136 ff.

appear decisive. But the truth of the matter is, as we have emphasized, that these wars do not describe the conquest of the land. The battle in the center was not directed at conquering the Canaanite cities—in fact, Jerusalem, which stood at the head of the Amorite coalition, did not fall. The goal of this engagement was to fend off the attack against the Ephraimites, Benjaminites, and Gibeonites, who had made a treaty with the others. The southern campaign is unaccompanied by descriptions of wars, though the editor did include a list of conquered cities (Josh. 10:28 ff.). It is an artificial list, the details of which contradict what we know from the book of Joshua (see above with regard to Hebron and Debir). The story of the battle in the north, also, describes only the destruction of Hazor, not the conquest of the cities in the Galilee.

In order to portray a general conquest, the editor used, as we have said, a literary strategy: he represented the battles in the Aijalon Valley and at the Waters of Merom as decisive encounters resulting in the conquest of the whole land. His summary of what followed from the battle at Aijalon is merely a generalization: "And Joshua smote all the hill country, the Negev, the lowland and the foothills, and all their kings. He did not leave anyone alive and every living thing he put under ban. Joshua smote them from Kadesh-Barnea to Gaza, and all the land of Goshen to Gibeon" (Josh. 10:40–41).[68] His summary after the battle in the north is similar: "Joshua took all this land, the hill country, the whole Negev, all the land of Goshen, the lowland and the Arabah, and the hill country of Israel and its lowland. From Mount Halak which ascends to Seir, and to Baal-Gad in the valley of the Lebanon" (11:16–17).

68. Professor B. Mazar indicated to me (oral communication) that the borders mentioned in v. 41 exactly matched the borders of Judah in the Josianic period: Kadesh Barnea in the south, Gaza in the southwest, and Gibeon in the north. Kadesh Barnea was fortified by Josiah; see R. Cohen, "The Excavation at Kadesh Barnea," *Biblical Archaeologist* 44 (1981), pp. 93–107.

The available traditions about these events provided no details about these total conquests.

The generalizing and inclusive manner of the Deuteronomistic editor's presentation is also expressed in the matter of the ban on the Canaanites. According to Judg. 1 and parallel verses in Josh. 15:63; 16:10; 17:11–13, the Israelites did not succeed in driving out the Canaanites from most parts of the land. Canaanites remained in Jerusalem, Beth-Shean, Taanach, Dor, Ibleam, Megiddo, Gezer, Beth-Shemesh, Aijalon, Shaalbim, Akko, Sidon, and other places, in the midst of the tribes who are held accountable for the continuing Canaanite presence. But this description conflicts with the all-inclusive presentation of the editor, as reflected in Josh. 1–12, in which Joshua conquered all the land of Canaan, captured the Canaanite cities and their kings (chap. 12), and put all the land's inhabitants under ban (10:40; 11:14–15, 20). In his description of total *ḥerem,* the Deuteronomist relies on the *ḥerem* law in Deuteronomy (Deut. 20:10–18), according to which it is forbidden to keep any Canaanite alive. Because Joshua was responsible, in the opinion of the editor, for the conquest operation, it was impossible for him not to act in accordance with the commandments given to Moses, his master; indeed, the editor makes this point explicitly: "They smote every human with the sword until they were destroyed. They did not spare any soul. What YHWH commanded Moses his servant, so Moses commanded Joshua, and thus Joshua did. He did not deviate at all from all that which YHWH commanded Moses" (Josh. 11:14–15). The Deuteronomic conception of *ḥerem* as a decree that applied automatically to all the inhabitants of the land of Canaan, whether a war was being waged or not, has a utopian character that made it unacceptable even to the Sages.[69] In reality, *ḥerem* was the result of a vow declared at the

69. "R. Ishmael b. Nahmani said . . . Joshua bin-Nun sent three orders to them: The one who wants to turn away may turn away, (the one who wants) to make peace may make peace, and (the one who wants) to

time of war, as we find in the cases of Arad (Num. 21:1–3) and Jericho (Josh. 6:17), and not an automatic decree (see above, Chapter 4). *Ḥerem* was also decreed when going out to war against non-Canaanite peoples, such as Amalek (1 Sam. 15:3). We know that the Canaanites, however, remained in the land, and that the Israelites were not able to put them under ban. Only Solomon put them to forced labor (1 Kings 9:21).

If we summarize the transformations of traditions in the Bible in relation to the conquest of the land, we arrive at an overall picture. An all-inclusive war of the Israelite tribes with the Canaanites could have occurred only at the end of the settlement period, not at the beginning, and indeed we find such a national war in the days of Deborah, which was directed against central cities, such as Megiddo and Taanach. Tribes from the Galilee (Naphtali, Zebulun), from the Jezreel Valley (Issachar), and from the hills (Ephraim, Machir, and Benjamin) participated in this war. In contrast, earlier wars were defensive in character and restricted to particular areas. Joshua's greatness is rooted not in the conquest of Canaanite cities, but in his success in withstanding the pressure of the king of Jerusalem in the south and the Amorites in the lowland. As we have seen, the description in Josh. 10:28 ff. about cities such as Lachish, Hebron, and Debir is artificial and not reliable, and the ascription of the destruction of Hazor to Joshua is also doubtful. Joshua himself confessed that he was not capable of competing with the Canaanites in the valleys, who had iron chariots (Josh. 17:14–18).

Against this background, Joshua acquired fame in the war at Aijalon (Josh. 10:12–14) and following his victory there became the leading figure in the conquest of the land.[70] When the epic about the national Israelite conquest began to be formed

---

make war may do so" (Lev. Rabbah 17:6, M. Margaliot, pp. 386–87; cf. the Jerusalem Talmud, *Shebiʿit* 6:1, 36c; also Deuteronomy Rabbah 5:14) and see above, pp. 92–93.

70. See A. Alt, "Josua," *KS* 1 (Munich, 1953), pp. 176–92.

(not before the period of Saul), Joshua was cast as the warrior who conquered the land of Israel for the people of Israel. According to the traditions that apparently began at the Gilgal sanctuary, Joshua's battle sorties from his base at Gilgal conquered all the area of Benjamin. Thus, he was considered a distinguished spiritual leader who performed wonders and miracles like Moses and performed impressive religious ceremonies. In priestly traditions that came together, it seems, at Shiloh, the figure of Joshua became defined as a religious leader who would ask the counsel of YHWH by means of Eleazar the priest and who, along with this priest, divided the land among the tribes before YHWH at Shiloh (Josh. 18:1–10).

The north Israelite traditions from the period of the monarchy connect Joshua to the capital city, Shechem. According to these traditions, Joshua built an altar with inscribed stones in Shechem, a tradition that parallels the setting up of stones at Gilgal. Also, according to another early tradition he made a covenant with the people of Shechem and placed "statutes and ordinances" there (Josh. 24:25–26).

These traditions, which set Joshua at the head of the conquest, were created at the sanctuaries of Gilgal, Shiloh, and Shechem—in other words, at centers in the north. In Judah, a contrasting picture of the conquest of the land was formed during the united monarchy, in which Joshua is missing altogether. Judg. 1, which in geographical background reflects the period of the unified kingdom,[71] does not attribute any conquest to Joshua but rather sets up Caleb (vv. 12–15, 20), the chieftain of the tribe of Judah (Num. 13:6; 34:19), as the leader in the area of Hebron and Debir. As discussed above, Judg. 1 is characterized by a strong polemical prejudice against the northern tribes. Yet, just as Judg. 1 tendentiously omits Joshua from the conquest operation, the northern traditions in Josh. 2–11 omit Caleb from the campaign. In fact, not only is Caleb not mentioned in these traditions, but his conquests of cities in Judah, which are credited to him by the tribal tradi-

71. See Kallai, *Geography* (n. 21), pp. 235 ff.

tions in Josh. 14–19, are attributed instead, in Josh. 10:28 ff., to Joshua.

In the Pentateuchal literature we find Joshua mentioned alongside Caleb, though according to the evidence the two figures were joined at a later stage (Num. 14:6, 30, 38; 32:12; Deut. 1:36–38).[72]

The version in Judg. 1 was not taken up by the Deuteronomistic editor of the Former Prophets but was inserted later as an appendix. The Deuteronomist, like the book of Deuteronomy that functions as a source for him, constructs his composition on northern foundations[73] and ignores the Judean version of things. He gives Shechem a place of honor and attributes to Joshua the performance of a rite at Mt. Gerizim and Mt. Ebal, a rite that functions as a sort of *inclusio* to the book of Deuteronomy (Deut. 11:26–30; 27:11–13). Writers from the period of Josiah, in whose time this Deuteronomic school began to function, paradoxically ignored the tendentious Judean tradition in order to make way for a north Israelite legacy about Joshua as the conqueror of the land. By this time, there was no longer need to compete with the northern tribes, and Judah saw itself as an inheritor of Israel's position; in Joshua, Judah claimed a warrior who belonged to them no less than to the Josephites, who saw in him a great warrior belonging to them before the destruction of Samaria. Moreover, Shechem was rehabilitated, whether in the tradition of Deuteronomy (chapter 27) or the later Deuteronomistic tradition (Josh. 8:30–35). According to the Deuteronomistic school, Jerusalem assumed the role of Shechem after the building of the temple in the days of Solomon, but in the days of Joshua, Shechem had been the chosen place.

72. See S. E. Loewenstamm, "Settlement of Gad and Reuben" (chap. 3, n. 14).

73. On the northern foundations of the book of Deuteronomy, see my commentary on Deuteronomy (n. 65), pp. 44 ff.

7

Two Introductions to the Period of Judges

Judg. 1, with Judg. 2:1–5, constitutes a sort of prologue to the period of the judges, and, in light of this role it parallels the prologue to the period of the judges in Judg. 2:6 ff.[1] Both introductions attempt to explain and justify the troubles that continually befell Israel in the days of the judges, but Judg. 2:6 ff., as a product of the pragmatic historiosophic (Deuteronomistic) school (see below), is formulated as a continuous discourse. The prologue in Judg. 1:1–2:5, however, which belongs to an earlier and less pragmatic stratum, was handed down in the form of a list of historico-geographical facts (Judg. 1), which speak for themselves, as we will see below, with an additional rebuke from a divine messenger (2:1–5).

Researchers have long observed the parallel between the two introductions, but the relationship between them has not been examined adequately because of a lack of consensus about their character and composition. In our discussion here we will approach the problem anew by employing an ideological criterion in addition to a literary-stylistic criterion in order to clarify the perspectives of each of these introductions; through this inquiry, the conquest and the period of the judges, as conceived in the earlier sources, on the one hand, and in the

1. On this matter, see E. O'Doherty, "The Literary Problem of Judges 1:1–3:6," *CBQ* 18 (1956), pp. 1–7.

later (Deuteronomistic) sources, on the other, will become clear.

The prologue in Judg. 1:1–2:5 seeks to tell us that the Israelites did not drive out the Canaanites who dwelt among them, and that therefore the Canaanites and their gods were "as adversaries and a snare" (2:3) to them. This perspective is made evident by the particular way the historical facts are presented. The original form of the historico-geographical list, which the author of the prologue adduces, spoke of the *inability* to drive out the Canaanites (cf. Judg. 1:21 with Josh. 15:63; and Judg. 1:27 with Josh. 17:12), whereas the editor asserted an *unwillingness* to drive them out. He changed the passage in which it is said that "they *were not able* to drive [them] out" so that it reads, in the verses before us, "they *did not* drive [them] out" (Judg. 1:21, 27), which emphasizes the Israelites' sin of failing to expel the Canaanites.[2] Even when Israel grew strong and subdued its enemies, and therefore had the opportunity to drive them out, it did not drive them out but rather put them to forced labor (Judg. 1:28, 33, 35), which was a sin. After presenting the historical facts, the editor adduced the words of the angel of YHWH, in which the sin of not driving out the Canaanites is denounced and explained as "making a covenant with the inhabitants of the land" (2:2).

The angel of YHWH is the angel that, according to Pentateuchal tradition, was sent by God to bring the Israelites to their land (Exod. 23:20–23; cf. Exod. 32:34; 33:2; Num. 20:16). There, God tells the Israelites to obey the angel (Exod. 23:21), and here, the angel says in his rebuke: "but you did not

2. Unlike most scholars, Y. Kaufmann in his commentary (1956) adduces contrary evidence from v. 19, in which it is said that "they were not able to expel (*kî lo ʾlĕhôrîš*) the inhabitants of the valley because they had iron chariots": i.e., "the question is not a question of willingness" (p. 67). But from this verse, which speaks about Judah, one cannot adduce evidence. The whole chapter is edited out of a clear Judean bias, and the sin of not expelling the Canaanites is attributed in it mainly to Israel and not to Judah. See Chapter 6.

obey me" (Judg. 2:2). The angel's rebuke and its language reflect the JE and P Pentateuchal traditions associated with the conquest of the land (Exod. 23:20–33; 34:10–16; Num. 33:50–56).[3] Every term in vv. 1–3 derives from one of these traditions, and all of them refer to the sin of not driving out the Canaanites. But even though the Israelites are commanded to drive out the Canaanites, this was accomplished with the help of God and thus appears to be the act of God.[4] Hence, in Exod. 23:20 ff., in addition to the warning not to make a covenant with the Canaanites and not to allow them to dwell in the Israelites' land ("you shall not make a covenant with them or their gods. They shall not dwell in your land lest they cause you to sin against me . . . for they [the Canaanites] shall be a snare to you" [vv. 32–33]), it is said there: "*I shall send my* terror before you. . . . *I will send* hornets before you and they will expel the Hivites . . . from before you. . . . little by little *I will expel* them from before you . . . for *I will give* the inhabitants of the land into your power and you shall expel them from before you" (vv. 27–31). The expulsion is thus performed here by God as well as by the Israelites (see Chapter 6).

It should be noted that at the beginning of this passage the expulsion is credited to God, but toward the end it is attributed to the Israelites: "and *you shall expel* them from before you,"[5] which indicates that God's participation in the deeds of the Israelites in driving out the Canaanites was present in all stages

3. K. Budde, *Das Buch der Richter* (Tübingen, 1897), p. 17. Budde adduces these verses with the addition of other passages (Exod. 3:17; Deut. 31:16, 20) as being "alle aus JE," but he erred in regard to Num. 33, which is from P. I tend to accept the opinion of Y. Kaufmann about the antiquity of P, although I believe it was parallel with D, not prior to D. See my book *Deuteronomy and the Deuteronomic School* (Oxford, 1972), pp. 179–89.

4. Cf. Deut. 33:27; Josh. 24:8–12; Ps. 44:3–4; 105:44; etc. (see above, pp. 77 ff.).

5. It seems to me now, in contrast to my previous supposition (*Deuteronomy* (n. 3), p. 47, n. 1), that one should not accept the reading of the LXX and Vulgate, "and I will expel them from before you" (*wĕgērastîmô*).

of the biblical tradition, permitting no distinction between expulsion by the Israelites and that performed by God.

Similarly, Exod. 34:11 ff. opens with the promise that God will drive out before Israel all the Canaanites, etc. (v. 11), but immediately thereafter it warns not to make a covenant with the inhabitants of the land "for fear that they become a snare in your midst" (v. 12). There is no doubt that this prohibition against making a covenant is to be explained both here and in Exod. 23:22–33 in the sense that one is not to allow the Canaanites to dwell in the land (cf. Deut. 7:2).

Y. Kaufmann claims that not expelling the Canaanites does not figure as a sin in the Bible.[6] The expulsion is the duty of God, and non-expulsion is understood as a punishment from God, not as the sin of the Israelites. He draws this inference from Josh. 23 and Judg. 2:21, where it is said that God will no longer expel the remaining nations, as a punishment for association with the Canaanites. But these passages belong to the Deuteronomistic stratum, which, as we will see, has a special conception concerning the matter of the expulsion that must not be used to interpret the other passages. The command to expel the Canaanites is implicit in the verses we adduced from Exod. 23 and 34, and it appears explicitly in Num. 33:50–55: "You shall drive out all the inhabitants of the land from before you . . . but if you do not drive out the inhabitants of the land from before you,[7] then those of them whom you allow to remain shall be as barbs in your eyes and thorns in your sides (*lśkym bʿynykm wlṣnynm bṣdykm*)." The expression "they shall be adversaries for you (*whyw lkm lṣdym*)," found in the angel's words in Judg. 2:3, indicates a connection with the conception in Num. 33, as Kaufmann himself concedes.[8] The threat in

6. In his commentary to Judges, p. 68.

7. Kaufmann, on Judges, p. 68, n. 9, interprets "And if you do not drive (them) out" as meaning "if you make peace with them." But this is not the plain meaning of the biblical text.

8. See his commentary on this verse.

Josh. 23, which is clearly a Deuteronomistic chapter, has no connection with Judg. 2:2–3, the style of which is altogether devoid of Deuteronomistic terminology;[9] Therefore, there is no support for Kaufmann's claim that the threat in Josh. 23 has been changed into a prophecy.[10]

In contrast to the passage we are dealing with and the other pre-Deuteronomistic passages that speak of the expulsion (*grš*) of the Canaanites,[11] the book of Deuteronomy and the Deuteronomic school completely avoid the term *grš* with reference to the Canaanites. Instead, they employ the verb *hôrîš* and other verbs that express the notion of annihilation, ban, destruction, and ruin, by both God and Israel together, so as to give no quarter to the erroneous idea that expelling the Canaanites from the land is enough.[12]

But there is more. In contrast to Judg. 2:2, and in contrast to other pre-Deuteronomistic sources that warn against making a covenant with the *inhabitants of the land* (*yšby h'rṣ*) and prescribe expelling them and driving them out,[13] the Deuteronomistic sources speak about driving out "these/those nations" (*hgwym h'lh/hhm*),[14] a phrase alluding to "the nations that remain" (*hgwym hnšʾrym*), those outside Israel's area of settlement (Josh. 23:4, 12, 13; Judg. 2:23; 3:1). Judg. 2:1–5, then, which

9. In regard to this terminology, see my book *Deuteronomy* (n. 3), pp. 320 ff. On the other hand, expressions appear here that do not appear in the Deuteronomistic literature, such as *he ʿĕlā mimmiṣrayim* "bring up from Egypt" (and not *hôṣîʾ*, as in the Deuteronomic literature), *hēpēr bĕrît* "violate the covenant" (v. 1), *yōšĕbê hā ʾāreṣ* "inhabitants of the land" (v. 2), *gērēš* "expel" (v. 3). On the last two terms, see my book *Deuteronomy*, p. 342, no. 5; *hēpēr bĕrît* in Deut. 31:16 is not evidence, because Deut. 31:15–22 is an Elohist passage and does not pertain to the body of the book of Deuteronomy; see my book, p. 10.

10. See his commentary on Judges, p. 59.

11. Exod. 23:28–30; 32:2; 34:11; Josh. 24:12, 18; Judg. 6:9.

12. See, e.g., Deut. 7:2, 16, 22–23; 9:3, 5; 20; 16–17; etc., and see above, pp. 77 ff.

13. Exod. 23:31, 34:12, 15; Josh. 24:18; Num. 33:52, 55. See F. Langlamet, "Israël et l'habitant du pays," *RB* 76 (1969), pp. 330 f.

14. See my book *Deuteronomy* (n. 3), pp. 342–43.

speaks about expulsion (*grš*) in regard to the inhabitants of the land (*yšby h'rṣ;* see below), belongs to the pre-Deuteronomic level, which deals with expulsion of the inhabitants of the land of Canaan itself, in contrast to the Deuteronomic stratum, which speaks about the expulsion of the remaining nations.

Although in Josh. 23 we find terminology from JE, P, and D together,[15] in Judg. 2:1–3 (as we have seen) we find terminology only from JE and P, which indicates that the passage in Judg. 2 is prior to Josh. 23. In Judg. 2:1–5, then, we have an ancient introduction that is based on the pure tradition of the first four books of the Pentateuch. The parallel introduction in Judg. 2:11 ff.,[16] however, except for the ancient interpolation in Judg. 3:1b–2a.,[17] which certainly interrupts the continuity, constitutes a clear Deuteronomistic discourse.[18]

15. This combination likely indicates that (see n. 3) the Deuteronomist had before him the Priestly traditions, and not the reverse.

16. It is true that Judg. 2:6–10 belongs to the same (= Deuteronomistic) section as Judg. 2:11 ff. (cf. v. 7 with Deut. 11:1; v. 10 with Deut. 11:2), but it also contains ancient information. On the relationship between Judg. 2:6–10 and Josh. 24:25–31, see A. Rofé, "The Composition of the Introduction of the Book of Judges," *Tarbiz* 35 (1967), pp. 206–07 (Hebrew).

17. In this interpolation, the original meaning of *lnswt bm i't yśr'l* (i.e., to train or instruct Israel by means of them) is retained. Cf. 1 Sam. 17:39, and see the comments of A. Ehrlich on Judg. 3:1–2, *Randglossen zur hebräischen Bibel* (Leipzig, 1908–14), and also O. Eissfeldt, "Zwei verkannte militärtechnische Termini," *VT* 5 (1955), p. 237. The Deuteronomist in his discourse has removed the phrase from its original meaning and has given it a theological sense. On this matter, see, recently, I. L. Seeligmann, "Indications of Editorial Alteration and Adaptation in the Massoretic Text and Septuagint," *VT* 11 (1961), pp. 213–15 (in a Hebrew version: M. Weinfeld, ed., *Likkutei Tarbiz* 1 [Jerusalem, 1979], pp. 290–91).

18. Kaufmann (in his commentary to Judges, pp. 30–31) concedes a linguistic affinity between Deuteronomy and the framework of the book of Judges. He claims, however, that linguistic affinity with Deuteronomy does not necessitate a late dating. According to him, only where one finds the idea of cultic centralization may one assume influence from the time of Josiah. But the dating of Deuteronomy should not be determined by this criterion alone. Stylistic peculiarities have more to bear on this question

Both Judg. 2:11–19 and its sequel, Judg. 2:20–3:4 are typical of Deuteronomic style.[19] The expressions "transgress the covenant of YHWH which he commanded their fathers" (2:20); "to walk in the path of YHWH" or "in the paths of YHWH" (2:22; note "to walk in *them,*" *bām*); "to hearken unto the commandments of YHWH" (3:4; cf. 2:17); "to prove . . . to know" (3:4),[20] and also "to drive out quickly" (2:23)[21] are

---

than allusions to the centralization of the cult. It remains a fact that a style of this sort, which is found in Deuteronomy, is not found in biblical literature prior to the seventh century. See J. Bright, *Early Israel in Recent History Writing* (n. 64), p. 68 ff. For a penetrating argument with Kaufmann on the matter of the editing of the Former Prophets, see M. Haran, "*Sugyot miqra*ʾ*:* Problems in the Composition of the Former Prophets," *Tarbiz* 37 (1967), pp. 1–4 (= *Likkutei Tarbiz* 1, pp. 155–68); both Hebrew. Cf. also above, pp. 100–101 n. 1.

19. W. Beyerlin, "Gattung und Herkunft des Rahmens im Richterbuch," in *Tradition and Situation, Festschrift A. Weiser* (Göttingen, 1963), pp. 1–29, who does not regard the pragmatic framework of the book of Judges as having a Deuteronomistic character (see below), still cannot ignore the fact that Judg. 2:11–19 contains phrases found exclusively in Deuteronomic literature. Yet he maintains that Judg. 2:11–19 is a post-Deuteronomic supplement, without attempting to prove this contention. He emphasizes that this passage at least is not pre-Deuteronomistic ("jedenfalls nicht in der vordeuteronomischen Epoche entstanden ist"). But no one has challenged this. What Beyerlin has to do in order to bear out his surmise is to prove that the passage in question is not the work of the Deuteronomist, which he did not do.

20. In regard to "the covenant of YHWH which he commanded (*bĕrît YHWH ʾăšer ṣiwwâ*)," cf. Deut. 4:13; 28:69; Josh. 23:17; Jer. 11:3–4 (a Deuteronomistic prose discourse). In regard to the expression "to prove . . . to know (*lĕnassôt . . . lādaʿat*)" cf. Deut. 8:2; 13:4. For the other expressions, see my book *Deuteronomy* (n. 3), pp. 320 ff.

21. A quick conquest fits the Deuteronomistic descriptions of conquest, particularly Josh. 10:40–42 (in v. 42: "at one time"). Deut. 7:22 is dependent on Exod. 23:29–30, but in this quotation the tendentiousness is evident. The phrase "until you have multiplied to take possession of the land" (*ʿd ʾšr tprh wnḥlt ʾt hʾrṣ;* Exod. 23:30b) is dropped from Deuteronomy, and not for nothing. Josh. 11:18 does not contradict the idea of a quick conquest, because the fact that the conquest was achieved by Joshua, though it continued "many days," is interpreted as a quick conquest, relative to the difficulty and immensity of the task. Cf. the settle-

clearly Deuteronomic. In contrast, the verses in Judg. 3:5–6 belong to another, pre-Deuteronomic stratum. They lack Deuteronomistic terminology and even contradict what is said in the Deuteronomistic discourse that precedes them; they do not deal only with the nations that remain in the region of the coast and the Lebanon (v. 3), but with all of the nations in the land of Canaan.[22] Moreover, the settlement among the peoples of Canaan in v. 5 does not agree with the perspective reflected in the Deuteronomistic discourse, according to which, as we will see later, the nations had remained only in those areas of the ideal land specified in v. 3 and in Josh. 13:2–5. Influence from the JE source in Exod. 34:11 is certainly evident in Judg. 3:5–6. The verse from Exodus, like the Judges passage, lists six nations, not the seven we find in the reworking of this source in Deut. 7:1.[23]

The discourse in Judg. 2:11–3:4 is homogeneous not only in style but also in structure. One should not discern in it, as many do, a combination of sources and layers.[24] While it is not impossible that the Deuteronomist used earlier material that was available to him, the discourse as it has come from him is characterized by uniformity and logical sequence. As Y. Kaufmann has shown, the speech intends to answer several questions connected with the period of the Judges,[25] not, as some claim, to provide several answers to the same question. The first question is: Why was Israel delivered into the hands of pillagers and oppressors in the time of the Judges? The text

---

ment at Kadesh "for many days" in Deut. 1:46, though it refers to many months and not many years, because the Israelites walked in the wilderness for thirty-eight years after this (Deut. 2:14).

22. See also O. Eissfeldt, *Die Quellen des Richterbuches* (Leipzig, 1925), pp. 3–4 and S. R. Driver, *Introduction to the Literature of the Old Testament* (New York, 1956), p. 165.

23. See N. Lohfink, *Das Hauptgebot* (Rome, 1963), pp. 74 ff.

24. See the various commentaries to the book of Judges, and see esp. J. A. Soggin, *Judges,* Old Testament Library (London, 1981), pp. 25–27, and also A. Rofé, "Composition" (n. 16), pp. 201–13 (Hebrew).

25. In his commentary on Judges, pp. 88 ff.

gives the answer in Judg. 2:11–15. The second question is: Why did the Israelites not drive out the remaining nations? The answer to this comes in vv. 16–21. The third question is: Why did Joshua not conquer these nations? The answer to this, according to Kaufmann, is in Judg. 2:22–23; 3:1–4. But because the third answer according to this delineation would not fall in sequence, it seems to me that Judg. 2:22–23 alone responds to this question, whereas Judg. 3:1 ff. (excluding vv. 1b–2a; see above) answers an additional, fourth question: Who are these nations?

It is customary to see in v. 20 the beginning of a new topic, unconnected to the previous verses. But this topic, and the subjects presented after it, actually develop out of what comes before. The discourse opens with the sin of idolatry, which stirs the wrath of God and leads to God's selling the transgressing Israelites into the hands of the surrounding enemies (2:11–15). But, full of compassion for his afflicted people, God raises up judges who deliver the Israelites from their distress. Instead of repenting as a result of these acts of deliverance, the Israelites become more corrupt than "their fathers" and serve other gods, thereby more severely arousing God's anger. He decides to put into effect the threat already announced in the Deuteronomistic farewell oration placed in the mouth of Joshua (Josh. 23:12–13), that the nations that Joshua left would not be driven out (Judg. 2:16–21). But the question then arises: why did Joshua leave them and not drive them out? The answer comes in vv. 22–23:[26] Joshua's sparing the rest of the nations

26. Y. Kaufmann disperses the obscurity around vv. 22–23. Still, in his book *The History of the Israelite Religion* 2 (Tel Aviv, 1947), pp. 374–75 (Hebrew), he rightly saw (relying upon the commentary of G. L. Studer, *Das Buch der Richter* [Bern, 1835], which for some reason did not gain the attention of other scholars) that "in order to prove (*lĕma ʿan nassôt*)" correlates with "which Joshua left (*ʾăšer ʿāzab yĕhôšuaʿ*)," and not with "I will no longer expel (*lōʾ ʾôsîp lĕhôrîš*)." The meaning of the passage is, then, that Joshua left the nations in order to prove Israel thereby, as opposed to the customary interpretation, that God swore he would not

was "for the purpose of proving Israel by them." Since the Israelites did not pass this test, the fate of the remaining land, whose extent we read about in 3:1 ff., was decreed.[27]

What we have, then, in Judg. 2:11–3:4 (or more fully, 2:6–3:4; see note 16) is a continuous, unbroken discourse, the Deuteronomist's introduction to the period of the judges, which is different from the preceding introduction in Judg. 1:1–2:5. The pre-Deuteronomistic prologue—and, as we will see, the pre-Deuteronomistic pragmatism that is in Judges generally[28]—explains the troubles in the period of the judges as deriving from the sin of not driving out the Canaanites. Moreover, as can be gathered from the historico-geographical list in Judg. 1, from the words of the divine messenger in Judg. 2:1–5, and from Judg. 3:5–6 (as we have seen above), the editor of these passages is thinking of the non-expulsion of the Canaanites that are within the borders of the actual land, i.e., in the Canaanite enclaves that are found amidst the Israelite area of settlement.

This conception does not accord with the spirit of the Deu-

---

expel the nations in order to thereby prove the Israelites. According to the usual interpretation, v. 22 contradicts vv. 20–21, because in the latter verses God did not expel the nations because the Israelites sinned, whereas in v. 22 God did not expel the nations with the prior intention to provide a test for the Israelites. This perceived contradiction is what obliges scholars to discover different layers in this passage.

27. V. 4 brings us back to the idea of putting the Israelites to the test, which was broken off by the list of nations in Judg. 3:1–3; see S. R. Driver, *Introduction* (n. 22), p. 166.

28. If there are difficulties in the Pentateuch in distinguishing between J and E (see, for example, P. Volz and W. Rudolph, *Der Elohist als Erzähler—ein Irrweg der Pentateuchkritik* [Berlin, 1933]; W. Rudolph, *Der 'Elohist' von Exodus bis Josua* [Berlin, 1938], then making this distinction is even more difficult in the literature of the Former Prophets. R. Kittel even rejects, in a more than convincing way, the existence of the Pentateuchal sources in this literature (R. Kittel, "Die pentateuchischen Urkunden in den Büchern Richter und Samuel," *ThStKr* 65 [1892], pp. 41–47). We do not need to speak, then, about the J and E sources in this context, but only about a pre-Deuteronomistic stratum.

teronomist. According to his scheme, the Canaanites dwelling in the land in the days of Joshua were put *totally* under ban, following the law of the ban in Deut. 20:16–17 (Josh. 10–12;[29] 21:41–43), and thus no Canaanites remained in the areas settled by the Israelites. There is therefore no sense in accusing Israel of not driving out the Canaanites dwelling among them. On the other hand, the Deuteronomist did admit that Canaanites remained in the areas *bordering* the Israelite settlement,[30] i.e., in the area of the "remaining land" (the seacoast and the area from Baal-Gad to Lebo-Hamath) that had not actually been conquered.[31] The survival of these Canaanites within the area of the "remaining land" was not considered a sin in the eyes of the Deuteronomist, because Joshua had driven out the Canaanite peoples according to God's command. The expulsion of these remaining, bordering nations was understood as a conditional promise, a promise that appears only with the Deuteronomic school (Deut. 11:22–25;[32] Josh. 23; Judg. 2:20–

29. The descriptions of putting peoples under ban in Josh. 10:28–43 and 11:12–20 are based on the law of ban in Deut. 20:10 ff. and are formulated in a clear Deuteronomistic style (cf. Deut. 2:34–35; 3:3, 6–7; 7:2; 13:16–17; 20:14–17). Also, taking down the bodies of kings from the gibbets in Josh. 10:27 is a Deuteronomistic addition, in the spirit of Deut. 21:23 (cf. Josh. 8:29). On this subject, see I. L. Seeligmann, "Aetiological Elements in Biblical Historiography," *Zion* 26 (1961) p. 154 (Hebrew).

30. "And all the Canaanites (*wĕkol-hakkĕnaʿănî*)" in Judg. 3:3 and "all the land of the Canaanites (*kol-ʾereṣ hakkĕnaʿănî*)" in Josh. 13:4 refer, respectively, to the Phoenicians and to the coast of Phoenicia, according to B. Maisler (*Untersuchungen zur alten Geschichte und Ethnographie Syriens und Palästinas* [Giessen, 1930], pp. 59 ff.), but not according to Noth (in his commentary on Joshua, HAT², p. 75). Maisler's view that "the Sidonians (*haṣṣidônîm*)" in Judg. 3:3 is only a gloss added to "and all the Canaanites (*wĕkol-hakkĕnaʿănî*)" is reasonable, because in Josh. 13:6 we find Sidonians ("all the Sidonians [*kol-ṣidônîm*]") in the general sense of Canaanites and the inhabitants of the coast (= Phoenicians). See Y. Kaufmann in his commentary to Josh. 13:6 and also Z. Kallai, "The Boundaries" (ch. 6, n. 63), *Eretz Israel* 12 (N. Glueck volume; 1975), p. 30 and n. 16.

31. In relation to this area and its borders, see Chapter 3.

32. It is possible that Deut. 19:8 ("and if YHWH your God expands your territory, as he has sworn to your fathers, and gives to you all the land") belongs here as well.

23). God promises the expulsion of the remaining nations on the condition that the Israelites not cleave to them and not adopt their ways. Failing to expel the Canaanites, which in the pre-Deuteronomic sources was considered a *sin,* was converted into a *punishment* for sin; and while the earlier sources ascribed not driving out the Canaanites to Israel, the Deuteronomist ascribed it to God, as a punishment for the sin of the Israelites (Judg. 2).

The pre-Deuteronomic sources see the tribes responsible both for the settlement and for failure to drive the Canaanites out of the tribal territory (Josh. 14:6–17:18; 18:11–19:48; and also Judg. 1). Driving out the Canaanites is a command given to the tribes, and not driving out the Canaanites is therefore their sin. The Deuteronomic source, in contrast, views the settlement and the failure to drive out the Canaanites as a national affair: Joshua is responsible for the conquest of the land by the command of God, with the participation of the whole nation. What was not conquered was considered the failure of the nation. But according to this conception, as opposed to the earlier view, not driving out the Canaanites was not the fault of Joshua and those of his generation: it was God who allowed these nations to remain, in order to put Israel to the test. If they would not follow the customs of the nations around them, they would be worthy of conquering the remaining land, but if they followed the foreign practices, they would not conquer it. Because the ensuing generations did not pass the test, the remaining land was forfeited forever.

This decisive decree is indeed typical of the Deuteronomistic outlook regarding the realization of God's word in the history of Israel, as described by von Rad.[33] The idea of the realization of God's word by itself—in other words, the conception of the prophetic word as "an acting force begetting future events"[34]—is already found in the early strata in the

33. See G. von Rad, *Studies in Deuteronomy,* (London, 1953), pp. 78 ff.

34. As phrased by I. L. Seeligmann, "Aetiological Elements" (n. 29), p. 167.

Pentateuchal literature; for example, the promise to the fathers in Genesis regarding giving the land to their posterity is actually the prophetic word of God, as realized in the conquest by the Israelites.[35] But the innovation of the Deuteronomist was to convert the prophetic word of God into a guiding historiographic principle, by which every event of religio-political significance must have occurred by the power of the divine word that preceded the event. And what is more, the historical reality needed to agree exactly with this divine word; in the words of the Deuteronomist himself: "Not one word of YHWH will fall to the ground" (Josh. 21:45; 23:14; 2 Kings 10:10). If the divine word is not realized, or not realized fully, then the Deuteronomist reconstructed the divine word or altered it, so as to ensure that the original prophecy would not be proved wrong. Kaufmann, who dealt with the "negative prophetic cycle" in the prophetic sections of the former prophets, defines this phenomenon: "When an original word of God fails to be realized or is not entirely realized, a second word of God appears after it which destroys and annuls the former or circumscribes it so that it is the second word of God which is fulfilled."[36] This phenomenon actually is characteristic only of the Deuteronomistic historiography. The Chronicler's historiosophy stands in contrast; he leaves out the negative prophetic cycles and builds his historical work only on a positive cycle. The historiosophic principle of the Deuteronomist is given its clearest expression in the prophetic promise about conquering the land, but this was a promise that was not completely realized. The fathers had been promised the land from the River of Egypt to the Euphrates (Gen. 15:18; Exod. 23:31), as reaffirmed in God's words in the Deuteronomic literature (Deut. 1:7; 11:24; Josh. 1:1–9), but in historical reality, as expressed by the Deuteronomist (Josh. 10–11), this promise was only partially realized: Joshua conquered the land

35. Ibid., p. 166.
36. *Toledot* (n. 26), vol. 4 (1956), p. 458.

"from Mount Halak that rises up to Seir, and to Baal-Gad in the Lebanon valley" (Josh. 11:17). He commanded the remaining areas be conquered after his death (Josh. 23), something that was never achieved.[37] In order that the first promise not be found unfulfilled, the Deuteronomist found a second divine word that canceled the first promise: "YHWH became angry at Israel and said: Because this nation has transgressed my covenant which I commanded their fathers, and (because) they did not obey me, I will not further drive out from before them any of the nations which Joshua left when he died" (Judg. 2:20–21).

The difference between the pre-Deuteronomistic and Deuteronomistic sources with respect to not driving out the peoples of Canaan entails a further difference in the conception of the Israelite sin. The offense of which the pre-Deuteronomistic editor speaks in his introduction to the book of Judges, and also in his pragmatic passages, is the sin of worshipping the gods of the inhabitants of the land that the Israelites had actually conquered. In the pre-Deuteronomistic stratum of Judges we find exhortations concerning the destruction of altars and the cutting down of Asheroth (Judg. 2:2; 6:25–32), which accord with the injunctions in earlier sources of the Pentateuch (Exod. 23:23–24; 34:12–13).[38] Needless to say, the altars that were destroyed and Asheroth that were cut down during the period of the judges must have been located within the area of Israelite settlement, for it is quite improbable that altars would be destroyed in areas remote from the Israelite settlement and inhabited only by foreigners. Indeed one may learn from the pre-Deuteronomistic sources both about the Canaanites' dwelling among the Israelites (Josh. 16:10; 17:12;

37. The deficiency in the conquest has to do with the old borders consecrated at Shiloh by the Priestly source ("from Lebo-Hamath to the Brook of Egypt"; see Chapter 3), and not with the imperialistic borders characterized by stereotypical boundary lines that lack concrete markers.

38. Similar commands in Deuteronomy (7:5; 12:3) are drawn in fact from these sources (= the large and small Book of the Covenant).

Judg. 1:27, 30) and about the Israelites' dwelling among the Canaanites (Judg. 1:32, 33; 3:5), which, according to these sources, led to a physical and cultural amalgamation of the Israelites with the Canaanite inhabitants of the land (Judg. 2:2; 3:6). The gods worshipped by the Israelites, according to this view, were the gods of the Amorites, among whom and in whose land the tribes of Israel were dwelling (Josh. 24:15; Judg. 2:2; 6:10).

The Deuteronomistic oration, on the other hand, which opens the period of the judges (Judg. 2:11 ff.), speaks of Israelite worship of "other gods from among the gods of the peoples who were round about them" (v. 12; cf. Deut. 6:14; 13:7–8) and not of the gods of the peoples *in whose land* Israel dwelt. This point of view is especially evident in the Deuteronomistic farewell address in Joshua (chap. 23), in which Joshua warns the people not to adhere to the rest of the nations who remained, who were the inhabitants of the remaining land,[39] yet has nothing to say against contact with the Canaanites who inhabit the conquered land. The Canaanites who inhabited the land had already been destroyed by Joshua in the national wars of conquest; the only remaining threat to the Israelites was the nations remaining on the periphery and their gods.

In contrast to the earlier sources, which were written when the danger still existed of assimilation with those Canaanites "inhabiting the land," in the period when the Deuteronomistic work came into being, the imminent danger confronting Israel was that posed by the Canaanites who were in the remaining land, i.e., the inhabitants of the seacoast and the Lebanon (the Phoenicians).

The sin of the Israelites according to the pre-Deuteronomistic tradition, therefore, was not driving out the Canaanites dwelling within the area of Israelite settlement and yearning

39. See the commentary of Y. Kaufmann on the book of *Joshua* (Jerusalem, 1963) (Hebrew).

after their gods. This historiosophic view does not fit the conception of the Deuteronomistic editor, who, not surprisingly, ignored the historical prologue (Judg. 1:1–2:5) expressing this view and wrote his own prologue consistent with his ideological principles.

The Deuteronomistic conception of the conquest brought with it a clear distinction between the period of total conquest achieved by the initiative of Joshua, the great military leader, and the period of pressure after Joshua's death from the "enemies that were round about" (Judg. 2:14). The corvée labor of the conquered peoples, of which Judg. 1 speaks, stands in direct contradiction to the law of the ban in Deut. 20 (compare Deut. 7:1–5) and the Deuteronomistic descriptions in Josh. 10–11, according to which Joshua did not leave a single soul alive within the boundaries of the land of Canaan (Josh. 10:40, 11:14). In Deut. 20:10–15, only remote cities that were not of the peoples of Canaan and that accepted a peaceful solution were allowed to be put to forced labor. The Deuteronomistic scheme does not admit of the possibility that Joshua, who did all as Moses had commanded, did not put to the ban those Canaanites who dwelled among the Israelites, who are described in Judg. 1:27 ff. and the parallel passages in Josh. 15–19. Indeed, in the Deuteronomistic strand of Joshua-Judges, the period of Joshua is depicted as a golden age in which the Israelites worshipped only YHWH (Judg. 2:7, 10), and only with the passing of Joshua's generation did the Israelites begin to do evil in the sight of God.

But in the pre-Deuteronomistic substrata of the books of Joshua and Judges up to 1 Sam. 12, we hear of one sin, the sin of worshipping "the foreign gods (*'ĕlōhê nēkār*) of the land," a sin about which God speaks to Moses in the Elohist passage Deut. 31:16 and which first appears in the Elohist tradition in the patriarchal narratives (Gen. 35:2). Great and minor prophets all warn against this sin. Joshua, when establishing a covenant with the people, commanded them to remove the foreign gods from their midst (Josh. 24:23). The anonymous prophet in Judg. 10:11 ff.[40] admonished the people for worshipping other gods, and in response the Israelites removed the foreign gods (Judg. 10:15); Samuel acted in a similar manner (according to 1 Sam. 7:2–4). Thus, Moses, Joshua, Samuel, and other anonymous prophets reproved the Israelites for this sin, and following such admonition the people confessed their sins, removed the foreign gods from their midst and repented (Josh. 24:21 ff.; Judg. 10:10–16; 1 Sam. 7:3 ff.).[41] From the religio-historiosophical point of view there is no difference at all between the period of Joshua and the period of the judges; in both periods, the Israelites worship foreign gods. This perspective is not found in the Deuteronomistic stratum, which clearly distinguishes between the two periods.

Kaufmann and, independently, W. Beyerlin, have examined the two distinct historical perspectives in the book of Judges concerning the nature of the period of the judges.[42] According to the conception expressed in the introductory address in Judg. 2:11–19, the whole era was marked by unrelieved sinfulness; however, according to the view that these scholars believe is expressed in the passages constituting the framework of the book of Judges, the era was marked by the alternation of periods of sin and punishment with periods of

40. This is certainly not a Deuteronomistic passage (contra M. Noth, *Überlieferungsgeschichtliche Studien,* [Halle, 1943], p. 51). See W. Beyerlin, "Geschichte und heilsgeschichtliches Traditionsbildung im A. T. (Richter VI–VIII)," *VT* 13 (1963), pp. 10–11. See also M. Haran, "Shechem Studies," *Zion* 38 (1973), p. 3, n. 6 (on the matter of the foreign gods).

41. Y. Kaufmann in his commentary on the book of *Judges* (Jerusalem, 1959), p. 49 (Hebrew), rightly speaks about the admonishing prophets in the period of the judges, who include: YHWH's angel (Judg. 2:1–5), a prophet (6:7–10), a spokesman (= prophet) for YHWH (10:11–15), along with prophets of deliverance. All of these belong, in my opinion, to the pre-Deuteronomistic (Elohistic?) stratum. The Deuteronomistic editing recognizes only judges of deliverance in this period, not angels or prophets of deliverance.

42. Kaufmann, commentary on Judges, pp. 51–53; Beyerlin, "Geschichte" (n. 40).

repentance and deliverance. Although these scholars correctly perceive a distinction between two perspectives, the conception of alternating sin and repentance does not exist in *all* the passages of the editorial framework outside Judg. 2:11–19. We find repentance accompanied by putting away foreign gods only in 10:10b–16, whereas in the other editorial passages we find mention only of the Israelites' crying to YHWH (3:9, 15; 4:3; 6:6, 7). Kaufmann and Beyerlin both interpret "crying to YHWH" as repentance. But crying to YHWH *by itself*, unaccompanied by explicit language on the subject, does not necessarily suggest repentance; it may express a condition of distress, rather than a state of repentance to God.[43] In Judg. 4:3—"then the Israelites cried to YHWH (*wyṣʿqw bny yśrʾl ʾl YHWH*), for he [Sisera] had nine hundred chariots of iron and oppressed the Israelites cruelly for twenty years"—it is obvious that the cry is forced from the people by suffering and oppression, and that it is in fact an appeal for help and not a cry for repentance. Furthermore, the verse: "Go and cry to the gods whom you have chosen" (10:14; cf. Jer. 11:12), certainly does not intend to urge the Israelites to return to the foreign gods, but rather serves as an ironically mocking exhortation to ask *them*, and not the true God, for aid. Thus the sequence composed of (a) sin, (b) punishment, (c) crying out and repentance, and (d) sending of a deliverer is not found in the usual (Deuteronomistic) passages of the editorial framework of

43. As in Judg. 10:10 and 1 Sam. 12:10. In Judg. 10:10, the cry does not have such an unambiguous meaning. According to Budde (*Das Buch der Richter* [n. 3], 79) Judg. 10:10a belongs to the Deuteronomistic editorial framework, while 10b belongs to the earlier stratum. See also R. Kittel, *Geschichte des Volkes Israel* (1.2; Gotha, 1917) 5.A2. If we accept the prevailing opinion that at the end of Judg. 2:15 the text "they cried out to YHWH" dropped out (and according to Budde in *Richter*, the phrase *wyzʿqw ʾl yhwh* was omitted because of the similarity to *wyṣr*, which follows), we find an identity in wording in Judg. 10:9b–10a and Judg. 2:15: "And Israel was in sore straits and they cried . . . (*wtṣr lyśrʾl mʾd wyzʿqw*)" (Judg. 10:9–10), "and they were in sore straits (and they cried) . . . (*wyṣr lhm mʾd [wyzʿqw]*)" (Judg. 2:15).

Judges, but only in 10:12–16, a passage long recognized as exceptional in contrast to the rest of the pragmatic framework of Judges and as similar in character to Josh. 24; Judg. 2:1b–5; 6:7–10; 1 Sam. 7:3–6; 10:18–19; 12:10–11—all of which appear Elohistic. These latter passages, as we have seen, mention prophets who reproach the people about worshipping the foreign gods of the land in which they live, whereas the other passages of the pragmatic framework, make no reference whatsoever to any prophet or rebuking angel, or even to any act of repentance. Indeed, only in the pre-Deuteronomistic elements embedded in Judges (2:1b–5; 6:7–10; 10:11–16) do we find the *Bundesbruch-rîb* noted by Beyerlin and others,[44] whereas in the rest of the pragmatic editorial framework we do not find a single *rîb* scene, only pragmatic outlines related to past events. These pragmatic outlines presuppose the idea of a breach of covenant but no longer incorporate the *rîb,* which, as Beyerlin concedes, has been transformed in these framework passages into narrative-didactic material. Although Beyerlin argues that this editing is not necessarily late, we might propose instead that the *Bundesbruch-rîb* in its narrative-didactic form underlies the whole Deuteronomistic theodicy. Are we then to say that this also took shape in the time of the early kingdom?

Beyerlin tries to disprove the Deuteronomistic character of the pragmatic framework of Judges on stylistic grounds, too. He finds that, of the seven regularly recurring formulas in these framework passages, only two (*ʿśh hrʿ bʿny YHWH* "did what was evil in the sight of YHWH" and *ḥrh ʾp YHWH* "the anger of YHWH was kindled") commonly appear in the Deuteronomic part of the Old Testament, while the other five (*ʿbd ʾt hbʿl* "serve the Baal"; *mkr,* in the sense of "gave them into the power of"; *ṣʿq/zʿq lYHWH* "cry out to YHWH"; *knʿ* "be

44. Beyerlin, "Geschichte," n. 40; H. B. Huffmon, "The Covenant Lawsuit in the Prophets," *JBL* 78 (1959), pp. 285 ff.; G. E. Wright, "The Lawsuit of God," *Israel's Prophetic Heritage: Essays in Honor of J. Muilenburg* (London, 1962), pp. 45 ff.; J. Harvey, "Le 'Rib-pattern': Requisitoire prophetique sur la rupture de l'alliance," *Biblica* 43 (1962), pp. 172 ff.

subdued/subdue"; *šqṭ h'rṣ* "the land was quiet") are not at all characteristic of this literature.[45] But this assertion is not precisely correct. The expression *ʿbd 't hbʿl* ("worship the Baal") appears frequently from the hand of the Deuteronomist in Kings, as Beyerlin admits, though he maintains that a distinction must be made between the phrase *ʿbd 't hbʿlym* ("worship the Baals") in the framework of Judges and in Hosea and the phrase *ʿbd 't hbʿl* ("worship the Baal") in the Deuteronomist in the book of Kings.[46] It is doubtful, however, whether such a distinction has any real foundation. In the prophetic narratives, side by side with the usual expression *ʿbd 't hbʿl* and *ʿbdy hbʿl* (2 Kings 10:19 ff.), we find mention of worship of *the bʿlym* (1 Kings 18:18). Hosea uses both the plural and the singular as well: "and silver . . . and gold which they used for Baal" (2:10); "but he incurred guilt through Baal and died" (13:1), which Beyerlin did not note. (For the plural see 2:15, 19.)

Jeremiah, too, uses both singular and plural without distinction (2:8; 23:13, 27; as against 2:23; 9:13). *mkr,* in the sense of "gave into the power of," occurs (in the *hitpaʿel*) in Deut. 28:68 and in the Deuteronomist in Kings (1 Kings 21:20, 25; 2 Kings 17:17). *zʿq 'l yhwh* is found in a prose (= Deuteronomistic) sermon in Jeremiah (11:11–13). *knʿ lpny (mpny)* or *knʿ tḥt yd* is found, outside Judges, only in Deuteronomistic (1 Kings 21:29; 22:19) and post-Deuteronomistic (Ps. 106:42; 2 Chron. 33:12; Neh. 9:24) literature, whereas *šqṭ h'rṣ* is a set phrase (cf. Josh. 11:23b; 14:15b) that even Beyerlin concedes to be of late date. Nonetheless, even if all these expressions are actually early, this fact in itself would not warrant our denying the passages in which they occur from the Deuteronomistic stratum. Neither the author of Deuteronomy nor the Deuteronomist were working in a vacuum; they derived their ideas and idioms from the early heritage of Israel, especially that in the north. What was novel in their work was not simply that they

45. "Geschichte" (n. 40), pp. 10–13.
46. Ibid., p. 10, n. 31.

used these ideas and idioms, but that they worked them into a pragmatic context.[47]

The Deuteronomistic character of the editorial passages in Judges can also be deduced from the manner in which they were being inserted into the book, which is the same as in the book of Kings. In both these books, the editorial comments and criticism appear whenever there is a change of leadership: in Judges, between one judge and the next; in Kings, between one king and the next. The only difference is that in the pragmatic passages in Kings, praise alternates with censure, while in the passages in Judges, there is only censure ("and they did what was evil in the sight of YHWH," never, "and they did what was right in the sight of YHWH").

Thus, the extremely unfavorable verdict on the period of the judges is the verdict of the Deuteronomist alone. In his view, God sent judges to deliver Israel, not as a consequence of their calling out to him and their repentance, but because "he was moved to pity by their groaning" (2:18), in other words, out of pity for them in their affliction;[48] in the pre-Deuteronomistic pragmatic strand embedded in Judges, however, the deliverance is preceded by the people's cry of confession of sin,[49] a conception also expressed in the pre-Deuteronomistic general introduction to Judges. There, in response to the angel's rebuke in 2:1–3, the people lift up their voices, weep, and sacrifice to YHWH (Judg. 2:4–5; cf. Judg. 20:26; 21:1–4). Indeed, according to the conception of the pre-Deuteronomistic editor, this episode from the pre-Deuteronomistic general prologue characterizes the period of the judges, a period in which sin and repentance alternate with

47. See my book, *Deuteronomy and the Deuteronomic School* (n. 3), pp. 1–9.

48. On *nḥm* with the meaning of *rḥm* "have compassion on," see Judg. 21:6, 15; Jer. 20:16; Ezek. 24:14; Ps. 90:13; see also Kaufmann in his commentary on 2:18.

49. Judg. 10:15; 1 Sam. 7:3; 1 Sam. 12:10; see also Kaufmann in his commentary on Judges, p. 52.

one another. But in contrast to this perspective, the opening Deuteronomistic speech (2:6 ff.) clearly implies that not only did the Israelites show no sign of repentance, they did not even obey their judges (2:15) throughout the period of the judges.

The Deuteronomist, then, impresses on each age its own historiosophical stamp: the period of Joshua is the period of pure worship of YHWH, while the period of the judges is one of sin. Even when YHWH does raise up judges to deliver the Israelites, these judges are incapable of leading the people back to what would benefit them. All this is in contrast to the earlier editor, who regards the period of Moses and Joshua and the period of the judges as sharing a uniform character: the Israelites commit sin in all periods but when they cry out to YHWH and repent, then YHWH sends them deliverers (*môšîʿîm*), these being Moses, Aaron, Joshua, Gideon, Jephtah, and Samuel (Josh. 24:5; 1 Sam. 12:11). Moses is the deliverer par excellence. In the Elohist strand of the Pentateuch he, too, appears, as do the judges, after the Israelites cry out to God and call for help before him (Exod. 2:23–25; 3:7 ff.). Joshua also constitutes a judge-deliverer type,[50] according to the ancient traditions.[51] He miraculously delivered Israel in many wars (Josh. 10:9–14, cf. chaps. 7–8) and as an official "judge" in times of peace,[52] he also took care of the routine religious and so-

50. See R. Smend, *Jahwekrieg und Stammesbund* (FRLANT; Göttingen, 1963), pp. 40 ff.

51. According to Alt (A. Alt, "Josua," *KS* 1 [Munich, 1959], pp. 187 ff.) the traditions in Josh. 10:1–14; 17:14–18 and ch. 24 reflect the original image of Joshua. See the discussion above, pp. 133 ff.

52. On this function of judges (and not of minor judges only), see A. Alt, "Die Ursprünge des Israelitischen Rechts," *KS* 1 (n. 50), pp. 300 ff., and also see R. Smend, *Jahwekrieg* (n. 51), pp. 34 ff. Smend's view is reasonable, that some of the judges (and especially Jephthah) were the fixed leaders of the congregation after they proved their ability in war, as we have found in the rule of the cities of Sumer. On this, see T. Jacobsen, "Early Political Development in Mesopotamia," *Zeitschrift für Assyriologie* 52 (1957), pp. 91–140. See, recently, A. Altman, "The Development of the Office of 'Judge' in Pre-Monarchic Israel," *Proceedings of the Seventh World Congress of Jewish Studies: Studies in Bible and the Ancient Near East*

cioeconomic course of life in the tribes of Israel (Josh. 24; 17:14–18). In Deuteronomistic literature, however, Joshua figures as a national army leader and conqueror, not as a savior and judge; accordingly, the period of Joshua is one of offensive and aggressive wars, while that of the judges is one of defensive wars and repelling acts of oppression.

This distinction between the period of Joshua and the period of judges is a late distinction, not to be found in the early traditions.[53] In early traditions, conquests and defense in the face of oppression are commingled (Judg. 1:1–26 along with 27–36; esp. v. 34). The times of Joshua, according to these traditions, did not involve conquest alone, and the subsequent period was not marked only by oppression. Thus, we hear of Canaanites with iron chariots oppressing Israel in Joshua's lifetime (Josh. 17:14–18), and we hear of conquests without his presence (Judg. 1:1–26). Only the Deuteronomist draws a line between Joshua and the period of the judges.

The period of the judges is portrayed by the Deuteronomist as an age of political and religious anarchy, an extremely negative assessment resulting from the positive light in which the Deuteronomistic authors regarded the monarchy.[54] Kaufmann

---

(Jerusalem, 1981), pp. 11 ff. (Hebrew). This possibility exists also in regard to Joshua (see Smend, *Jahwekrieg* in his book, pp. 40–41).

53. Kaufmann, in his commentary on Judges, pp. 1–14, claims that the distinction of three periods in the history of Israel is an ancient distinction, which is expressed in the accounts of the wars between Num. 21 and 2 Sam. 23. He finds three types of wars in these stories: (a) offensive wars of conquest; (b) defensive wars of liberation; and (c) imperial wars. Although we must admit that before the Deuteronomist historiographer ancient Israel knew of wars of conquest, on the one hand, and wars of liberation aimed at preserving the status quo, on the other, however, in the ancient tradition this was a typological distinction and not just a literary-chronological one; in the Deuteronomistic literature this distinction was also a literary-chronological division.

54. It must be said, in contrast to the idea commonly accepted, that the Deuteronomistic circle did not at all adopt a negative stance vis-à-vis the monarchy. It is implied in Deut. 17:20 ff. that the author was actually

is therefore correct in stating that the author of the general introduction "has darkened the colors and depicted the period black on black . . . *in order to exalt the monarchy!*" (emphasis added).[55] This dimming of colors also finds expression in the recurring refrain in chapters 17–21: "In those days there was no king in Israel; every man did what was right in his own eyes" (17:6; 18:1; 19:1; 21:25).

M. Buber sees in this refrain the work of authors/editors with promonarchic biases,[56] and it does appear that they were Deuteronomistic.[57] The view expressed in this refrain under-

---

interested in the welfare of the monarchy and the continuation of the dynasty, "so that he may live long in his kingdom, he and his children, in the midst of Israel." With respect to the Deuteronomist, it should be noted that an author at the heart of whose ideology stands the chosen king David and his city Jerusalem can in no way hold an antimonarchic bias. The antimonarchic traditions in 1 Sam. 8–12 are not Deuteronomistic. See A. Weiser, *Samuel 7–12* (FRLANT 81; Göttingen, 1962); F. Crüsemann, *Der Widerstand gegen das Königtum* (WMANT 49; Neukirchen, 1978).

55. In his commentary on Judges.

56. Buber, *Königtum Gottes* 41 (Berlin, 1932), (= *Malkhut shamayīm* [trans. Y. Amir] [Jerusalem, 1965] p. 67). M. Noth, "The Background of Judges 17–18," *Israel's Prophetic Heritage: Essays in Honour of J. Muilenburg* (n. 44), pp. 68 ff., maintains that these verses in 17–18 form an integral part of the story, while those in 19–21 have been interpolated by an editor. This does not seem plausible. The dictum "In those days there was no king etc." in chs. 17–21 serves a common purpose: that of finding fault with the period of the judges and thereby proving the vital need for the monarchy, whose growth is described in the following chapters (the narratives describing the times of the judges continue until 1 Sam. 12; see above). It therefore does not stand to reason that this same dictum previously served another purpose (in chapters 17–18), as Noth would have it. His assumption as to the aim of the story in Judg. 17–18 is similarly lacking in conclusive evidence.

57. It might be that the Deuteronomistic scribes had intentionally arranged these chapters at the end of Judges to point out that the monarchy was an unavoidable outcome of the anarchic state of affairs prevailing in those times. There is no need to regard these chapters as a post-Deuteronomistic supplement. This is rather ancient material of which the Deuteronomistic scribes availed themselves. The fact that these chapters

lies the law concerning the centralization of the cult of Deuteronomy: "You shall not act according to all the things that we do here this day, *each one doing what is right in his own eyes* (emphasis added) (*kl hyšr bʿynyw*). For you have not yet come to the rest and to the inheritance" (Deut. 12:8, 9). The "rest" and "inheritance" (*mnwḥh* and *wnḥlh*) were attained after the monarchy was established (2 Sam. 7:1, 11; 1 Kings 5:18; 8:56).[58] It was only then that the law of cultic centralization had relevance (1 Kings 3:2). The period in which "each one did that which was right in his own eyes" is, according to the Deuteronomistic circle, the pre-monarchic one, as evidenced in the recurring refrain in Judg. 17–21. Perhaps some significance might also be attached to the fact that the refrain in full ("in those days there was no king in Israel but each one did that which was right in his own eyes") occurs only in the context of private and provincial sanctuaries (the sanctuary of Micah in 17:1–5; those of Bethel, Mizpah, and Shiloh in 21:1–24), whereas in regard to social and ethical disorder (18:1 ff.; 19:1 ff.) only the shortened refrain occurs, which speaks only of the absence of a king ("in those days there was no king in Israel").

Additionally, it seems that the Deuteronomist was not able to explain the observance of commandments included in the "Book of the Torah" without a king-like leader, represented by the figure of Joshua (Josh. 1:7–8; 8:30–35; 22:5; 23:6).

---

are not set in the usual pragmatic framework ("and they did what was evil in the eyes of the Lord" etc.), but rather are accompanied by short refrains, can be duly accounted for. We are dealing here with the corrupt ways of families or tribes, not the entire nation. This does not render these chapters as suitable to the wider national scope evident in chapters 2–16.

58. The Israelites in the days of Joshua had succeeded in gaining rest when they had been made secure from their enemies (Josh. 21:42; 23:1), but this rest was only temporary. After the death of Joshua they were again subject to enemy oppression (cf. "and he sold them into the hand of their enemies all around; they were no longer able to stand before their enemies" [Judg. 2:14], with "and he gave them security all around . . . and not one of their enemies could withstand them" [Josh. 21:42]). This oppression continued until the days of David (2 Sam. 7:11).

According to his perspective, the Torah was an ideal constitution for the royal rule (1 Kings 2:3),[59] and the greatness of David obtains its orientation when, after Joshua, David establishes the rule of the Book of Torah and observes it (1 Kings 3:14; 9:4; 11:33, 35; 14:8; etc.). The fact that the Deuteronomist cannot explain implementation of the Torah in a non-monarchic system accounts for the difference between representations of the period of the judges and the monarchic period. In Judges, sin is attributed to Israel ("and *they* did what was evil . . .") whereas in Kings, sin is attributed to the king alone ("and *he* did what was evil").

This difference has appeared to some scholars, incorrectly, as inconsistency in the Deuteronomistic work.[60] Actually, according to the Deuteronomist's conception, only the king is capable of enforcing the laws of the Book of Torah; therefore, it is the king's responsibility to see that the people observe the Torah. In the period of the judges, when there was no king, there was no chance to put these laws into effect, so the period was conceptualized as an era in which "each one did what was right in his own eyes."

The Deuteronomistic authors illuminated every period with a particular historiosophical light, thereby imparting to it a specific religious image. The period of Joshua was a golden epoch in which the Israelites worshipped YHWH and therefore won brilliant victories in the area of the conquest. The period of the judges constitutes *the* period of apostasy, during which Israelites worshipped the gods of the surrounding peoples and were therefore "sold" into their hands to be oppressed. The period of the monarchy also opened with glim-

59. Compare the law in Deuteronomy, in which the institutions of judgeship, kingship, priesthood, and prophecy are surveyed one after another (Deut. 16:18–18:22). The institutions are characteristic of ancient royal rule.

60. See, for example, G. von Rad, *Theologie des Alten Testaments* 1 (Munich, 1957), pp. 343–44.

mering rays: David did that which is righteous in the sight of God with all his heart and soul (cf., e.g., 1 Kings 11:4) and won sweeping political success. In the Solomonic period, however, religious deterioration set in, as expressed in idolatry (from this perspective, the period of Solomon continues the period of the judges), while in the kingship of Judah the sin was mainly the "high places." Each epoch, therefore, was stamped by the Deuteronomist with its own particular imprint. Consequently, the question of why problems stemming from one historical period find no mention in the narration of later periods—as Kaufmann asks with respect to the problem of not expelling the people in the land[61]—is not valid.

61. In his book *The Biblical Account of the Conquest of Palestine* (Jerusalem, 1953), and also in his commentaries on Joshua and Judges.

8

The Inheritance of the Land

Privilege versus Obligation

No other people in the history of mankind was as preoccupied as the people of Israel with the land in which they lived. The whole biblical historiography revolves around the Land. The pivot of the patriarchal stories is the promise of the land for the Patriarchs and their descendants. The stories of the Exodus and the wanderings in the desert are a kind of preparation for the entrance into the Land; the stories of the conquest describe the struggle with the Canaanites over the Land; and the whole survey of the periods of the judges and the monarchy is concerned with the gradual loss of the Land. Because of the sins of the period of the judges, the Israelites did not manage to conquer the "remaining land" (Josh. 13:1–2) and the "remaining nations" (Josh. 23:4–16; Judg. 3:1–4) on the coast and in the Lebanon. The great loss of land occurred during the monarchy: first came the loss of the northern kingdom (the ten tribes) because of the sins of Jeroboam and Ahab, and then came the fall of Jerusalem and the exile of Judah because of the sin of Manasseh (2 Kings 21). The writing of the historiography was actually motivated by the effort to explain why Israel and Judah went into exile (2 Kings 17:1–23; 21:11–16).

Israel's preoccupation with the Land can be explained by its unique history. Unlike the Mesopotamians, Egyptians, and Hittites, who did not preserve any history from before their entrance into their land, Israel kept in memory its existence before the settlement in the Land of Canaan. According to the tradition, Israel's ancestors came from Aram Naharaim, then went down to Egypt, and only after the Exodus from Egypt did they settle in the Land. Their dwelling in the Land of Canaan, therefore, was not self-explanatory; it was considered an act of grace, a gift of God, a privilege accorded them as a result of the loyalty of the patriarchs to God (Gen. 22:17–18; 26:5; Deut. 7:8; 9:5b; 11:15).

The divine promise of land to an ethnic group or tribe who goes to settle in a new territory is not unique to Israel. It is a phenomenon also found among other peoples, particularly in the Greek world, when the colonization of the Mediterranean shores first began (see Chapter 2).

What is unique about Israel's relationship to the land is neither the divine promise nor the permanence of the patrimony, but rather the religious and moral ramifications of the promise: the belief that, in order to dwell safely in the land, it was necessary to fulfill the will of the God who gave the land. The land was thus transformed into a kind of mirror, reflecting the religious and ethical behavior of the people; if the people were in possession of the land, it was a sign that they were fulfilling God's will and observing his commandments; if they lost the land, it was an indication that they had violated God's covenant and neglected his commandments. All of biblical historiography is based upon this criterion: the right to possess the land.

As early as the covenant with Abraham (Gen. 15), the conditionality of the promise of the land is implied. The sin of the Canaanites is the cause of their expulsion from the land: "For the sin of the Amorites is not yet complete" (v. 16),[1] which by allusion suggests that if the Israelites sin, they too might lose the land. A similar outlook is found in Gen. 18:19, in the words of God concerning Abraham: "For I have singled

1. We do not find Deuteronomic expressions here, and therefore there is no warrant for a late dating of the chapter (exilic or post-exilic).

him out, that he may instruct his children and his posterity to keep the way of the Lord by doing justice and righteousness[2] in order that the Lord may bring about for Abraham what He has promised him." Dwelling in the land was contingent on keeping the commandments; if the Israelites did not keep the commandments, the land would spew them out, as it did to the nations who lived there before them (Lev. 18:28). This view achieves fullest expression in Deuteronomy and the Deuteronomic literature.[3]

One has to admit that the conditionality of the inheritance of the Land, which is attested primarily in Deuteronomy and the Deuteronomic school, in editorial layers of JE (Gen. 15:16; 18:19), and in the priestly code (Lev. 18:26–28; 20:23–24; chap. 26), is not explicit in the old traditions themselves. Indeed, it seems that the fall of Samaria and the northern exile triggered the development of the idea of conditionality. Although the idea itself might be old, albeit not expressed explicitly, the prevailing notion before the fall of Samaria was that the Land was given to the Israelites forever (Gen. 13:15; 17:8; Exod. 32:13). Only after the loss of the northern territories was the covenant of God with the Patriarchs interpreted as based on condition.

The same pattern developed with the Davidic covenant. The covenant of God with David, which contained an unconditional promise of eternal dynasty for David (2 Sam. 7:13, 16; Ps. 89:29–38), was interpreted after the disruption of the Davidic dynasty as originally given on condition (1 Kings 2:4; 8:25; 9:4–9).[4]

In the eighth century B.C.E., when the Assyrians began mass deportations of peoples, the problem of exile turned into

2. For the meaning of "justice and righteousness" (*mšpṭ wṣdqh*) see my book *Justice and Righteousness in Israel and the Nations* (Jerusalem, 1985), (Hebrew).

3. Deut. 4:26; 6:15; 11:17; 28:21, 63; 29:27; Josh. 23:13, 15, 16; 1 Kings 9:7; 13:34; 14:15.

4. See Chapter 9.

a central problem in the national consciousness of Israel. The disaster was explained by the breach of covenant with God. The two separate covenants—the one with the patriarchs, which constituted a promise, and the other, which constituted a pledge, an obligation to observe the law—were joined. The promise of land for the patriarchs was understood as conditioned on the observance of the law, and the promise of the Davidic dynasty was understood after the fall of Judah as conditioned on the realization of the Sinaitic pledge to keep the law.[5]

Indeed, the period of the Assyrian conquest and mass deportation was a period of the awakening of national guilt feelings, as may be learned from the prophecies of Hosea, which are permeated with the idea of repentance.[6] In Hosea, we find that Israel will return to its God after abandoning foreign worship (2:16–18; 3:5; 6:1; 14:2–9), and verses that correspond, significantly, to the passages about repentance in Deuteronomy[7] and Jeremiah. We read in Hosea: "I will return to my place until in their trouble they seek me, in their distress they will search for me (*bṣr lhm yšḥrnny*): Come, let us return to YHWH for he has torn us and will heal us" (5:15–6:1). The same phraseology is found in Deut. 4:29–30: "You will seek there YHWH your God . . . when you are in distress (*bṣr lk*) . . . and you will return to YHWH your God," which may

5. On the Davidic Covenant see my article "Covenant Davidic," in *Interpreter's Dictionary of the Bible, Supplementary Volume* (Nashville, Tenn., 1976), pp. 188–92.

6. Cf. A. Biram, "Hosea 2:16–25," in *E. Urbach Volume* (Jerusalem, 1955), pp. 116–39 (Hebrew). See M. Buber's definition of Hosea's prophecy: "die grosse Hoseanische Abrechnung" (the great Hoseanic settlement account), *Königtum Gottes* (Heidelberg, 1932), pp. 103–16.

7. On the guilt feelings of the northern tribes who went down to Judah after the fall of Samaria, see my article: "The Emergence of the Deuteronomic Movement," in N. Lohfink, ed., *Das Deuteronomium, Entstehung, Gestalt und Botschaft* (Leuven, 1985), pp. 87–89.

be compared with Jer. 29:13–14: "you will seek me . . . and I will restore you" and with 1 Kings 8:47–48.

The idea of return to the land after return to God is actually expressed in the priestly source of the Pentateuch, as well as in the book of Deuteronomy. In the priestly source we read:

> and you shall perish among the nations . . . and those of you who service shall be headsick over their iniquity . . . and their uncircumcised heart shall humble itself . . . then I will remember my covenant with Jacob . . . Isaac . . . and Abraham . . . and I will remember the land. (Lev. 26:38–42; compare also vv. 44–45)

Similarly we read in Deut. 4:27–31:

> YHWH will scatter you among the nations . . . but if you search for YHWH your God you will find him . . . when you are in distress . . . and in the end you shall return to YHWH your God and obey him. . . . he will not forget the covenant which he made with your fathers.

As in Lev. 26:38 ff. we find exile and repentance here, following which God will remember the Covenant with the patriarchs.

The same themes are evident in Deut. 30, which corresponds nicely to Deut. 4:27 ff. Both passages form a kind of inclusio for the core of Deuteronomy.[8]

> When all these things befall you . . . amidst the various nations to which YHWH your God has banished you and you return to YHWH your God . . . then the Lord your God shall restore your fortunes (*šb šbwtk*) and will bring you together again. (30:1–5)

These words were not spoken in vain; the exiled recognized

8. Cf. my commentary to Deuteronomy in the Anchor Bible series (New York, 1991), pp. 214–21.

their sins and believed that if they truly repented they would return to their land. This is attested in the letter of Jeremiah to the exiled:[9]

> You will search for me and you will find me . . . and I will restore your fortunes and gather you from all the nations (Jer. 29:13–14).

The formulation is similar to that of Deut. 4:24 ff., perhaps because it is a quotation from Deut. 4 or perhaps because the style is prevalent in the exilic period. Identical formulas are found in the Deuteronomistic liturgy in 1 Kings 8:48–51.

All these passages reflect the consciousness of guilt among the Israelites of the exilic period, along with the will to return to God wholeheartedly, and indeed, this is the time in which idolatry was permanently eliminated in Israel. After the exile we hear no more about pagan worship, either in the Land of Judah or in the diaspora.[10] This deep guilt-consciousness motivated the writing of the Deuteronomistic historiography. The books of Kings were written to demonstrate that the sins of the northern Israelites caused the fall of the northern kingdom and the sins of Judah brought about the destruction of the southern kingdom; the conclusion to be deduced is that if Israel would return to its God, then the grace would be renewed.[11] From the prayer of Nehemiah (Neh. 1:8–11) we learn that the threats of Lev. 26 and Deut. 28 were deeply incised on the heart of the people who returned to Judah and that the promise of the renewal of God's grace as found in the Pentateuch had encouraged them to return and to rebuild the ruins of Jerusalem and Judah.

9. For our purpose here, which is the unraveling of the motif of repentance, it does not matter whether these are the words of Jeremiah himself or an elaboration by the editor of the book of Jeremiah. In either case, they reflect the spirit of the period of decline and destruction.

10. Cf. Kaufmann, *The History of the Israelite Religion* 4 (Jerusalem, 1956), p. 18 (Hebrew).

11. Ibid., pp. 40–41.

Sins that Forfeit the Right to the Promised Land

In all the biblical sources, the assertion is repeated that Israel will be expelled from the land for the violation of its religious and spiritual obligations—in other words, for breaking the covenant. We have seen above that the reduction of the territory of the promised land was explained as a punishment for making a covenant with the Canaanites and worshipping their gods. The priestly source, which emphasizes God's presence in the land of Israel and therefore obligates the observance of the laws of holiness and purity, speaks of fornication and incest as those acts which defile the land (Lev. 18:24 ff.). When defiled, the land "spews out" its inhabitants: ". . . thus the land became defiled; and I called it to account for its iniquity, and the land spewed out its inhabitants" (Lev. 18:25).

Blood that is shed in the land in which God abides also pollutes the land and defiles it:

> You shall not pollute the land in which you live; for blood pollutes the land, and the land can have no expiation for blood that is shed on it, except by the blood of him who shed it. You shall not defile the land in which you live, in which I Myself abide, for I, the Lord, abide among the Israelite people." (Num. 35:33–34)

This view, which holds that bloodshed defiles the lands and leads to its desolation and the expulsion of its inhabitants, dates back to ancient times. We read, for example, in Gen. 4:11–12 that because of the blood of Abel the land is cursed and will not yield its produce: "Therefore you shall be banished from the ground, which opened its mouth to receive your brother's blood from your hand. If you till the soil, it shall no longer yield its strength to you."[12] Similarly, we read in 2 Sam.

12. Compare Deut. 21:4 in connection with the unknown murder and the "heifer" that is to be executed at a flowing wadi, a place "which is not worked or sown," that is, an uncultivated place. This symbolizes

21:1–14 that the land suffered a three-year famine because of the bloodguilt of Saul's killing of the Gibeonites.

The Gilboa mountains were also cursed by the blood that had been shed upon them; they received neither dew nor rain (2 Sam. 1:21–22). This example recalls Danel's curse concerning his son's murder in the Ugaritic epic *Aqhat:* "No dew, no rain, no upsurge of the deep."[13] In a Hittite source, too, the king declares that the gods have avenged the murdered king's blood, in that the murderer's land no longer yielded its produce,[14] and Greek literature provides the example of the land of Thebes, cursed because Oedipus had murdered his father.[15]

In Israel, the concept develops that land may be cursed and turned into a wasteland not only by bloodshed but also by adultery, theft, taking a false oath, and other sins. This concept is most fully expressed in the words of the prophets. Hosea states, "[False] swearing, dishonesty, and murder and theft are rife. . . . For that the earth is withered (*t'bl h'rṣ*), everything that dwells on it languished" (Hos. 4:2–3). The meaning of the Hebrew word *'bl* in this context is not "sorrow and mourn-

---

the unproductive land caused by the pollution of bloodshed; see D. P. Wright, "Deuteronomy 21:1–9 as a Rite of Elimination," *Catholic Biblical Quarterly* 49 (1987), pp. 394–95.

13. A. Herdner, *Corpus des tablettes en cunéiformes alphabétiques* (= *CTA*) (Paris, 1963), no. 19, 1, 44–45: *bl ṭl bl rbb bl šrʿ thmt*. On the basis of this text H. L. Ginsberg proposed to read in 2 Sam. 1:21 *šrʿ thmt* instead of *śdy trwmt* ("An Ugaritic Parallel to 2 Sam. 1:21," *JBL* 57 [1938], pp. 209–13), and to translate it as "the upsurge of the deep." T. L. Fenton defended this reading convincingly, in "Comparative Evidence in Textual Study: M. Dahood on 2 Sam. 1:21 and *CTA* no. 19 (1 Aqht), 1, 44–45," *VT* 29 (1979), pp. 162–70. See however the discussion of K. McCarter, *2 Sam.* 1:21, Anchor Bible (New York, 1986), pp. 70–71, where he proposes to read, with Gordis, *šdy thmt,* based on the Aramaic verb *šdy* "pour, flow."

14. H. E. Sturtevant and C. Bechtel, *A Hittite Chrestomathy* (Philadelphia, 1935), pp. 183–93 (1:69–71); cf., W. Eisele, "Der Telepinus-Erlass," diss. (Munich, 1970), p. 27.

15. Sophocles, *Oedipus* 22–25: "for as you see yourself our ship of state . . . foundered beneath a weltering surge of blood, a blight is on our harvest."

ing," but rather, "dryness."[16] Desolation of the land (= dryness) is due to breaking the covenant. This is uniquely expressed in Isa. 24:4 ff.:

> The earth dries up and withers, the whole world withers and grows sick . . . because they have broken the laws, and violated the eternal covenant. For this a curse has devoured the earth and its inhabitants stand aghast. . . . The new vine dries up, the vines sicken and all the revelers turn to sorrow. Silent the merry beat of tambourines . . . the merry harp is silent.

In these verses, descriptions of desolation and drought appear in conjunction with the cessation of joy. We find the combination of these two motifs in political contracts regarding the violation of a covenant. For example, in the treaty from Sefire between the king of Katak and the king of Arpad (eighth century B.C.E.), we read that if the king of Arpad should break the covenant, locusts and worms will consume the produce of the land, no grass or vegetation will be seen, the sound of the lyre will not be heard, and the land will become a wasteland, overrun by wild animals.[17]

We actually find a similar pattern in the list of curses appearing in Lev. 26. There, it is stated that if Israel violates the covenant with God, the land will not yield its produce, will

16. *abālu* in Akkadian means to be dry, and hence *tabalu* "dry land" in Akkadian and *tbl* in Hebrew, which is equivalent to *yabašah* (dryland); cf. *'bl,* which parallels *ybš* in Amos 1:2; Jer. 12:4; 23:10, and see G. R. Driver, "Confused Hebrew Roots," in *M. Gaster Anniversary Volume* (London, 1936), pp. 73–83. One has to take in account the double entendre of *'bl:* "to mourn," on the one hand and "be dry," on the other.

17. See J. A. Fitzmyer, *The Aramaic Inscriptions of Sefire* (Rome, 1967), 1 A 27f (p. 14): "For seven years may the locust devour (Arpad), and for seven years may the worms eat . . . may the grass not come forth so that no green may be seen . . . nor may the sound of the lyre be heard in Arpad . . . may the mouth of Scorpion, the mouth of a bear . . . eat . . . may its vegetation be destroyed unto desolation"; cf. my book *Deuteronomy and the Deuteronomic School* (Oxford, 1972), pp. 123–26, 140–41.

become overrun by wild animals, and will turn into a wasteland (Lev. 26:20–22). Similar forms of retribution for breaking the covenant can be found in Isa. 33:8 ff.: "Highways are desolate, wayfarers have ceased, a covenant has been renounced. . . . the land is wilted and withered . . ." In Jeremiah, perhaps through the influence of Hosea, we also find that adultery and taking a false oath cause the land to dry up: "For the land is full of adulterers, the earth lies parched because of a curse, the pastures of the wilderness are dried up" (Jer. 23:10).[18] It appears, therefore, that the expression "to dry up" (*'blh h'rṣ*) is a fixed motif in Israelite prophecy, which describes the punishment for the terrible sins that the land cannot bear, such as murder, adultery, taking a false oath, and breaking the covenant. The land does not respond to those who commit such sins; it becomes a wasteland.

The idea that exile and desolation are the punishment for failing to observe God's commandments is based, therefore, in the typology of violating a covenant. One who violates a covenant with his sovereign can anticipate exile and the desolation of his land.[19] This is the case with Israel, the vassal, who breaks the covenant with its sovereign, the God of Israel. The same pattern can also be seen in the Assyrian treaty between Esarhaddon and his vassals:[20]

> [If you break the covenant] . . . may Zarpanitu . . . destroy your name and your seed from off the land

18. Cf. Jer. 3:1 in connection with adultery: "would not such a land be defiled" (*ḥnp tḥnp*); 3:2: "you defiled (*wtḥnypy*) the land with your fornication"; cf. v. 9. It seems that Jeremiah is influenced here by priestly literature, i.e., Num. 35:33. For other priestly expressions in Jeremiah see *'or,* as opposed to *thw wbhw* (4:23) (as in Gen. 1:2–3); *qr' drwr* ("proclaim freedom") in Jer. 34:8, 15 compared with Lev. 25:10; *kbš* ("subdue") in Jer. 34:16 compared with Gen. 1:28.

19. Cf. my book *Deuteronomy and the Deuteronomic School* (n. 17), pp. 109 ff.

20. Cf., recently, S. Parpola and K. Watanabe, *Neo Assyrian Treaties and Loyalty Oaths* (Helsinki, 1988), p. 46.

> (ll.435–36). May Adad . . . deprive your fields of [grain], may he [submerge] your land with a great flood, may the locust . . . devour your harvest; may the sound of mill and oven be lacking from your houses. (ll.440–44)[21]

However, besides elaborating the violation of covenant as an all-inclusive sin, the biblical sources differ in their characterization of and emphasis on specific sins.

1. Transgressing the Laws of the Sabbatical and Jubilee Years. The priestly source, which connects the laws of the Sabbatical and Jubilee years with the covenant at Sinai and the declaration of freedom therein ("for all Israelites are My servants . . ."),[22] views the transgression of these laws as the primary reason for the exile of Israel from its land. There is a direct correlation between the crime and its punishment: the nation that does not allow the land to rest in the Sabbatical and Jubilee years will be cast out, leaving the land to lie fallow so as to compensate for those years in which the laws of the Sabbatical years had not been observed: "Then shall the land make up for its Sabbath years throughout the time that it is desolate . . . it shall observe the rest that it did not observe in your Sabbath years while you were dwelling upon it" (Lev. 26:34–35). Thus, the seventy years of Babylonian exile are explained in the book of Chronicles as punishment for seventy years in which the land should have lain fallow while the Israelites were dwelling in it (2 Chron. 36:21). Observing the laws of resting the land is, according to the priestly sources, a necessary condition for dwelling in the land.

2. Idolatry. According to the Deuteronomic sources, the

21. For the latter curse, cf. Jer. 25:10, and see my book *Deuteronomy and the Deuteronomic School* (n. 17), pp. 141–42.

22. For the freedom declaration (*derôr*) at Sinai, cf. my book *Justice and Righteousness* (Jerusalem, 1985), pp. 138–42.

sin of idol worship is the determining factor which will cause Israel to perish from its land. Such is the case in Deut. 11:16–17:

> Take care not to be lured away to serve other gods and bow to them. For YHWH's anger will flare up against you, and He will shut up the skies so that there will be no rain and the ground will not yield its produce, and you will soon perish from the good land which YHWH is giving you.

Traces of the land-oriented view found in the priestly source are also preserved here. Exile appears in conjunction with the description of a land which, because of the sin of idolatry, withholds its produce. But in the Deuteronomic source, the image of exile is generally free of references to desolation and barrenness, and there is no evidence of the kind of personification that describes the land as "spewing forth its inhabitants" or "resting."[23]

The expression "perish from the land" (*'bd mn h'rṣ*), which is used to denote exile, is also found in Hittite and Assyrian covenant texts.[24] In Deut. 28:63, we find the verb "*nsḥ,*" which is the Assyrian verb par excellence for "exile" (*nasāḥu*). The expressions "to perish" (*'bd*) or "to be wiped out" (*hšmd*) from the land also appear in Deut. 4:25–27, 6:14–15, 28:63, 30:18. Sections of Former Prophets, which are dependent on Deuter-

23. According to the view of the priestly source the land fulfills its duty, as it were, toward God every seventh year ("and the land shall observe a Sabbath to the Lord"; Lev. 25:2), as the Israelite does every seventh day, cf. my *Deuteronomy and the Deuteronomic School* (n. 17), p. 223. For the demythologization of the law in Deuteronomy, see ibid., pp. 190 ff.

24. Cf., e.g., *ištu erṣeti zêrka liḫalliqu* = "they will make perish your seed from the earth," E. F. Weidněr, *Politische Dokumente aus Kleinasien,* (Leipzig, 1923), p. 34 ll. 65–66; cf. also VTE ll. 537–39 (= Parpola and Watanabe, *Neo Assyrian Treaties* [n. 20], p. 51): "may your name, your seed and the seed of your sons and your daughters disappear from the earth" (cf. ll. 542–44).

onomy, speak of "perishing from" (*'bd mn*), "cutting off from" (*hkrt mn*), and "uprooting from" (*ntṣ mn*) the good land (Josh. 23:15, 16; 1 Kings 9:7; 14:15; cf. Jer. 12:14).[25]

3. Intermarriage. Because the pursuit of idolatry was linked to contact with pagans who worshipped idols, we find that in Deuteronomistic literature the threat of exile appears not only in the context of idolatry but also in conjunction with marriage to the non-Israelites who had remained in the land:

> For should you turn away and attach yourself to the remnant of those nations . . . and intermarry with them . . . know for certain that your God will not continue to drive them out before you; they shall become a snare and a trap for you . . . until you perish from the good land . . . (Josh. 23:12)

The view that intermarriage will lead to annihilation is most clearly expressed in the words of Ezra, who quotes from the prophets:

> Which you commanded us through Your servants the prophets when You said, the land which you are about to possess is unclean through the uncleanness of the people of the land,[26] like the uncleanness of a menstruous woman, through their abhorrent practices with which they, in their impurity, have filled it from one end to the other. Now then do not give your daughters in marriage to their sons or let their daughters marry your sons . . . you shall not seek their welfare or their good forever, then you will be strong and enjoy the bounty of the land and bequeath it to your children forever.[27] (Ezra 9:11–12)

25. Cf. my *Deuteronomy* (n. 17), pp. 346–47.

26. Read with H. L. Ginsberg, *The Israelian Heritage of Judaism* (New York, 1982), p. 16: *ʿmy h'rṣ*.

27. We find here a jigsaw of scriptures from Pentateuchal and prophetic texts, e.g.: "the land which you are about to possess" is a Deuteronomic stock phrase (Deut. 4:5; 7:1; 11:10, 29; 23:21); "the uncleanness

Later, Ezra explicitly states that marriage to daughters of the idolatrous nations is a great sin, which will bring about the annihilation of the people:

> Shall we once again violate Your commandments by intermarrying with these peoples who follow such abhorrent practices? Will you not rage against us till we are destroyed without remnant or survivor? (Ezra 9:14)

It is obvious that Ezra's decision to establish the prohibition of intermarriage as the first and foremost condition for national existence was in keeping with his lifework: the expulsion of foreign wives from the society and the separation of the community of the Israelites from foreign nations (cf. Neh. 9:2).[28]

4. Justice and Righteousness. The notion that the promise made to Abraham was contingent upon the pursuit of justice and righteousness appears in the Pentateuch:[29]

> For I have singled him out, that he may instruct his children and his posterity to keep the way of the Lord by establishing righteousness and justice, in order that the

---

of the people of land like the uncleanness of a menstruous woman" (*kndt ʿmy hʾ rṣ*) is taken from Ezek. 36:17: "their land . . . as the uncleanness of a menstruous woman"; "from end to end" (*mph ʾl ph,* literally "from mouth to mouth") taken from 2 Kings 21:16; "do not give your daughters in marriage . . ." taken from Deut. 7:3 (cf. Exod. 34:16); "you shall not seek their welfare or their good forever" (*lʾ tdrš šlmm wṭwbtm ʿd ʿwlm*) is taken from Deut. 23:4; "then you will be strong" (*lmʿn tḥzqw*) taken from Deut. 11:8; "and eat/enjoy the bounty of the land" (*wʾkltm ʾt ṭūb hʾrṣ*) is taken from Isa. 1:19. The words of Moses and the scriptures in the former and latter Prophets are all ascribed to "the words of your servants the prophets" (*dbry ʿbdyk hnbyʾym*).

28. For Ezra's expulsion of the foreign wives, in the light of a similar phenomenon in the Greek *poleis,* cf. M. Heltzer, "A New Approach to the Question of the 'Alien Wives' in the Books of Ezra and Nehemiah," *Shnaton* 10 (1986–89), pp. 83–92.

29. For the concrete and real meaning of *mšpṭ wṣdqh,* cf. my book *Justice* (n. 22).

> Lord may bring about for Abraham what He has promised him. (Gen. 18:19)

Sodom and Gomorrah, cities that did not practice justice and righteousness and "did not support the poor and the needy" (Ezek. 16:49), were destroyed by divine decree, and the descendants of Abraham were commanded to follow the path of justice and righteousness, so that God could fulfill his promises.

However, it is in the words of the classical prophets that this outlook is fully crystalized. The classical prophets, reacting to the exile and liquidation of nations, a practice the Assyrian empire introduced, predict that oppression and violations of justice will lead to destruction and exile. As. Y. Kaufmann has demonstrated, the classical prophets put special emphasis on this idea.[30] According to Amos and Isaiah, the punishment for violation of social justice is exile: "But let justice well up like water and righteousness like an unfailing stream . . . , I will drive you into exile (*whglyty*) beyond Damascus" (Amos 5:24–27);[31] "They drink [straight] from the wine-bowls. . . . Assuredly, right soon they shall head the column of exiles (*yglw br*ʾ*š gwlym*) . . ." (Amos 6:6–7); "Who at their banquets have lyre and lute . . . and wine . . . therefore my people will suffer exile for not giving heed . . ." (Isa. 5:12–13). Other prophets predict barrenness and destruction for violation of social justice:

30. Cf. Y. Kaufmann, *The History of the Israelite Religion* 3 (Tel Aviv, 1948), pp. 76 ff. But we cannot agree with Kaufmann that the classical Israelite prophets were the first to raise the idea of social morality as a condition for national survival; see my remarks, "Recent Publications," *Shnaton* 5–6 (1981–82), pp. 233–34.

31. It should be noted that Amos was the first to use the term *glh* for exile; in the Pentateuch this term does not occur. Indeed, Amos prophesied during the period when the Assyrians started to exile peoples. Cf. B. Oded, *Mass Deportations and Deportees in the Neo-Assyrian Empire* (Wiesbaden, 1979).

> Listen to this . . . who detest justice and make crooked all that is straight. . . . Her rulers judge for gifts. . . . Assuredly because of you Zion shall be plowed as a field, and Jerusalem shall become heaps of ruins, and the Temple Mount a shrine in the woods. (Mic. 3:9–12)

Jeremiah states the terms explicitly:

> No, if you really mend your ways . . . if you execute justice between one man and another . . . then only will I let you dwell in this place, in the land which I gave to your fathers. . . . And now because you do all these things . . . I will cast you out of my presence as I cast out your brothers and the whole brood of Ephraim. (Jer. 7:5–15)

> Render just verdicts morning by morning; rescue him who is robbed from him who defrauded him. Else my wrath will break forth like fire and burn with none to quench it. . . . I shall set fire to its forest; it shall consume all that is around it. (Jer. 21:12–14)

> Do what is just and right; rescue the robbed from his oppressors; do not wrong the stranger, the fatherless, and the widow; commit no lawless act. . . . But if you do not heed these commands . . . this house shall become a ruin. (Jer. 22:3–5)

It should be noted that although these prophets emphasize justice and righteousness, they do not ignore other heinous sins. Thus, in a prophecy in which Jeremiah warns that the breach of social justice will lead to destruction, he also mentions the sins of murder, adultery, and idolatry (Jer. 7:9; cf. 22:3). What is unique about classical prophecy is that it elevated social morality to the level of one of the basic conditions for the survival of the nation in its land, contrary to the popular view, which held that what God most required was cultic worship (cf. Jer. 7:21–22).

5. Sabbath Observance. During the time of the destruction

and exile, there was apparently a slackening in Sabbath observance; consequently, in this period Sabbath observance was held up as a central factor in Israel's existence. We learn from Amos that, during the days of the First Temple, even unscrupulous merchants had refrained from selling grain and wheat on the Sabbath (Amos 8:5);[32] it appears, therefore, that only in the period of the exile did the nation become negligent about observing this commandment.[33]

In Jer. 17:21–27, we read that if the people of Judea observe the Sabbath, Jerusalem will remain forever; if they do not, the city will be destroyed:

> If you obey Me—declares YHWH—and do not bring in burdens through the gates of the city on the Sabbath day, but hallow the Sabbath day . . . this city shall be inhabited for all time . . . but if you do not obey my commandment to hallow the Sabbath day and carry in burdens through the gates of Jerusalem on the Sabbath day, then I will set fire to its gates; it shall consume the fortress of Jerusalem and it shall not be extinguished.

We do not know if this prophecy, in its present form, constitutes the *ipsisimma verba* of Jeremiah or, as many believe, reflects editing undertaken during the exile.[34] In any event, it is a product of the exilic prophets, who view Sabbath observance as a condition for Israel's existence. Ezekiel, too, views

32. Cf. my "God the Creator in Gen. 1 and in the Prophecy of Second Isaiah," *Tarbiz* 37 (1968), pp. 127–28 (Hebrew).

33. See M. Greenberg, "*Pršt hšbt* in Jeremiah," in B. Z. Luria, ed., *Studies in the Book of Jeremiah* 2 (Jerusalem, n. d.), pp. 23–52 (Hebrew). According to Greenberg, the slackening in Sabbath observance started at the time of Manasseh, king of Judah.

34. Cf. my article "Jeremiah and the Spiritual Metamorphosis of Israel," *ZAW* 88 (1976), pp. 17 ff. The stress on "the city" in this pericope may allude to the time of restoration because, as we will see below, after the destruction the focus shifted from the *land* to the *city*. Indeed, Nehemiah, when speaking of the sin of desecration of the Sabbath refers to the city (13:18) rather than to the land.

the desecration of the Sabbath as a decisive factor in the people's history (Ezek. 20:12–13, 20–21), while the anonymous prophet of the exilic period encourages the people, especially those non-Jews who "attached themselves to YHWH," to observe the Sabbath (Isa. 56:1–8). In another instance he conditions the new settlement of the nation on observing the Sabbath:

> If you refrain from trampling the Sabbath, from pursuing your affairs on My holy day, if you call the Sabbath 'delight,' YHWH's holy day 'honored,' and if you honor it and go not on expeditions [commercial enterprise], nor look to your affairs nor strike bargains (*dbr dbr*), then you can seek favor in the sight of the Lord. I will set you astride the heights of the earth, and let you enjoy the heritage of your father Jacob—for the mouth of YHWH has spoken. (Isa. 58:13–14)

As I have indicated elsewhere, the expressions "doing business" (*ʿśwt ḥpṣ, mṣʾ ḥpṣ*), "bargaining" (*dbr dbr*), and "undertaking a business journey" (*ʿśwt drk*) are all acts pertaining to trade.[35] These verses, therefore, refer to the same type of Sabbath violation that is found in Jer. 17:21, "Don't carry burdens on the Sabbath day, bringing them through the gates of Jerusalem," and in Neh. 10:32, "The people of the land who bring their wares and all sorts of foodstuffs for sale on the Sabbath day." Nehemiah goes even further, and places the blame for the first destruction of Jerusalem on Sabbath viola-

35. See my "The Counsel of the 'Elders' to Rehoboam and Its Implications," *Maʿarav, A Journal for the Study of the Northwest Semitic Languages and Literatures* 3:1 (1982), pp. 43 ff., nn. 81–82. Although we followed here the translation of the Jewish Publication Society, "trampling in the Sabbath" (compare NEB translation: "to tread the Sabbath underfoot"), which goes well with my observations about the semantics of "desecration" (cf. my: "ḥlwl, kbyšh wmrms rgl," in *Hebrew Language Studies Presented to Zeev Ben Hayyim*, [Jerusalem, 1983], pp. 195–200), the interpretation of *hšbt rgl* as abstaining from commercial expedition should not be excluded.

tion: "What evil thing is this that you are doing, profaning the Sabbath day. This is just what your ancestors did, and for it God brought all this misfortune on the city . . ." (Neh. 13:17–18). These verses recall the words of the Rabbis, based on Isa. 56:1–8: "If Israel would observe two Sabbaths as prescribed, they would immediately be redeemed" (BT Sabbath 118b).

As we have seen, it is clear that in each generation, the Israelites have attempted careful examination of their ways and deeds in order to discover which sin had caused or would cause exile and destruction. So, too, each generation defined the essence of the sin according to its own beliefs, values and historical circumstances.

The Land in the First Temple Period and Jerusalem in the Second Temple Period: The Shift from Land to City

After the fall of the kingdoms of Israel and Judea, the returning Israelites concentrated around the Temple and the city of Jerusalem. Due to the concentration, the religious and national emphasis, as reflected in Second Temple period sources, shifted from "the land" to "the city" and "the Temple." National destruction is expressed not in terms of "loss of the land" or "exile,"[36] as in the First Temple period sources, but rather through the concept of the destruction of the Temple (*ḥurban beŷt hammiqdash*). The expression, "the destruction of the First Temple" (*ḥurban habbayit harishôn*), in the sense of loss of independence, is actually anachronistic; it is an analogy based on the expression "the destruction of the Temple" (*ḥurban habbayit*) that appears in Rabbinic literature, referring primarily to the destruction of the Second Temple. The usage of the word "Temple" (*bayit*) to refer to the entire nation

36. See above, pp. 184 ff. Cf., e.g., Amos 7:11, 17; 2 in Kings 17:23; 25:21.

originated in the Second Temple period, during which Jerusalem became a temple city; the surrounding settlements were subordinate to Jerusalem, and the entire life of the nation became dependent on the existence of the city and its Temple.

A similar phenomenon can be found with respect to the temple cities of Mesopotamia and Asia Minor.[37] We know of entire territories, especially in Anatolia, which were inhabited by thousands of people who lived around the area of the temple.[38] The temple and its surrounding areas enjoyed an autonomous status—a gift granted by the king to the inhabitants; it is in this light that we should understand the Edict of Cyrus.

That the population inhabiting such a settlement was totally dependent on the temple can be seen in writings of Libanius, a renowned Antiochian orator of the fourth century C.E., who describes the effect of the temple's destruction upon the eastern settlements: "A settlement whose temple has been destroyed is as if struck with blindness, and no longer exists; the temples are the soul of the settlement, and the basis for its social life."[39] Indeed, in the days of the return to Zion, the center of life in the renewed settlement, was "the holy city" (*ʿir haqodesh*), an expression which first appears during this period (Isa. 48:2; 52:1; Neh. 1:18; Dan. 9:24), when Jerusalem received the status of a temple city and all that that entailed.[40]

We can also learn from the words of the prophet Zechariah that during the days of the return to Zion, Jerusalem was regarded as the soul of the nation:

37. On Mesopotamia, cf. H. Tadmor, "Royal City and Holy City in Assyria and Babylonia," *Town and Community* (Lectures delivered at the twelfth convention of the Historical Society of Israel, December 1966) (Jerusalem, 1967), pp. 179–206 (Hebrew). On Asia Minor, see A. Archi, "Città Sacre d'Asia Minore," *La Parola del Passato* 20 (1975), pp. 329–44.

38. See T. Zawadzki, "Quelques remarques sur l'etendue et l'accroissement des domaines des grands temples en Asia Mineure," *Eos* 46 (1952–53), pp. 83–96.

39. Libanius, *Pro Templis* 9.

40. Cf. my *Justice and Righteousness* (n. 2), pp. 57–78.

> Shout for joy, Fair Zion! for lo, I come; and I will dwell in your midst . . . And YHWH will take Judah to himself as his portion in the holy territory, and he will choose Jerusalem once more." (Zech. 2:14–15)

In these verses, the expression "the holy territory" (*'admat haqodesh*) is parallel to that for Jerusalem, "the holy city." The actual meaning of this expression is *the territory/earth of the holy*—in other words, the ground belonging to the holy area (the Temple and Temple city); it does not mean "holy land," since such a concept does not appear in the Old Testament.[41] Even the Rabbis, when speaking of the holiness of the land, are referring not to some concept of holiness inherent in the land itself, but rather to laws of holiness that are binding upon anything that has to do with the land of Israel (see below). The expression *'admat haqodesh* in Zech. 2:15 should therefore be understood as referring to the area surrounding the Temple, namely, Jerusalem.

The shift from land to city is even clearer in Nehemiah. Deut. 30:5 states "And YHWH your God will bring you to the land which your forefathers occupied," which is paraphrased in Nehemiah, "and YHWH will bring them to the place that I have chosen [Jerusalem] to cause My name to dwell there" (Neh. 1:9). Nehemiah asks the Persian king to rebuild the "city of my fathers' tomb" (Neh. 2:5). According to Nehemiah, Israel's "shame" (*ḥrph*) is not based on the fact that the land of Israel lies in the hands of strangers, as in the book of Lamentations, "Behold, and see our shame. Our inheritance is turned unto strangers, our house unto aliens" (Lam. 5:1–2). Rather, the "shame" lies in the fact that the walls of Jerusalem are in ruins (Neh. 2:17).

Just as Nehemiah reinterpreted Deut. 30:5 to refer to Jeru-

41. The term "Holy Land" appears in the Apocrypha and in Philo; cf. 2 Macc. 1:7; Wisd. of Sol. 12:3; The Testament of Job 33:5; 2 Baruch 63:10, 84:8; Sybilline Oracles 3:267; Philo, *The Heir* 293; *Special Laws* 4, 215 (ἱερὰ χῶρα); *On Dreams* 2, 75.

salem, the author of 2 Maccabees, in his letter to the Jews of Egypt, re-interprets the promise of redemption in Deut. 30:3–5. These verses speak of God who in his mercy will gather all Israel from the ends of the earth and bring them to the land in which their forefathers lived: "As He has promised in the Torah . . .[42] that soon He will have mercy on us and gather us from all the earth under the heavens to the holy place" (2 Macc. 2:18). In this verse we find the same elements as in Deut. 30—mercy and the gathering of the people from all ends of the earth—but here the people will be gathered not in *the land* but rather at *the holy place*.[43] Post-exilic discussions of defense stress the nation, not the territory; in the days of Nehemiah, the Jews fought their enemies not to defend the cities of the land, as in 2 Sam. 10:12, "for the sake of our people and the cities of our God," but rather to defend "your brothers, sons, daughters, wives and homes" (Neh. 4:8).

During the period of the Hasmonean war, as well, we hear of war for the sake of the people, the city, and the Temple, and not for the sake of the land:

> So they said to one another, "Let us restore the shattered fortunes of our nation, let us fight for our nation and for the temple." (1 Macc. 3:43)

> Better die than look on while calamity overwhelms our people and the temple. (1 Macc. 3:59)

> They made up their minds to fight . . . because Jerusalem, their Temple and the holy objects were in danger. (1 Macc. 15:17)

42. It is possible that the promise alludes also to Exod. 19:6, "a Kingdom of priests and a holy nation," which is appropriate following the previous verse about kingdom, priesthood, and the temple, but there is no doubt that the main kernel of verse 18 is based on Deut. 30:1, 5, as has been shown by F. M. Abel, *Les livres des Maccabées,* (Paris, 1949).

43. *εἵς τον ἅγιον τόπον*. When he refers to the land he uses the term *γῆ*: *ἅυια γῆς* (1:7); see n. 41, above.

Their fear was first and foremost for the sacred shrine.

In addition to fighting for the sake of the people and the Temple, they also fought on behalf of the *Torah,* in other words, for values. Mattathias called for a struggle against the Greek enemy in the name of zealous devotion to the Torah:

> Every one of you who is zealous for the Torah and strives to maintain the covenant follow me! (1 Macc. 2:27)
>
> But now my sons, be zealous for the Torah and give your lives for the covenant of your fathers. (1 Macc. 2:49)
>
> And Simon said, "I need not remind you of all that my brothers and I and my father's house have done for the laws and the holy place, what battles we have fought, what hardships we have endured." (1 Macc. 13:3)
>
> Simon and his brothers risked their lives in resisting the enemies of their people, in order that the Temple and the law might be preserved. (1 Macc. 14:29)

Even though in the course of the Hasmonean wars, vast areas were recaptured from within the territory of Israel, the Hasmonean leaders do speak of war not for the sake of the land, but rather for the sake of the people, the Temple, and the Torah.[44]

In the Temple Scroll from Qumran we also sense this shift from the land to the city and its holy areas. The Pentateuch contains many verses which speak of the impurity of the land: "You shall not defile the land . . . in which I myself abide, for I, YHWH, abide among the Israelite people" (Num. 35:34); ". . . so that they do not defile the camp in whose midst I dwell" (Num. 5:3); ". . . you shall not defile the land which YHWH is giving you to possess" (Deut. 21:23). The Temple Scroll, however, refers to the *impurity of the city,* and, when quoting from the Pentateuch, intentionally rewrites the verses and substi-

44. Cf. W. D. Davies, *The Gospel and the Land,* (London, 1974), p. 91.

tutes the concept of the city for that of the land. For example, "You shall not defile *the city* in which I Myself abide, for I YHWH shall abide among the Israelites forever" (Temple Scroll 45: ll. 13–14). This verse is actually a quotation from Num. 35:34 cited above, except that the term *the city* replaces that of *the land*. Only where reference to the land is unavoidable, such as with respect to graves within the borders of the land, does the scroll state, "You shall not defile your land" (Temple Scroll 48: ll. 10–11). But even in this case, we do not find the expected "You shall not defile the land (*hʾrṣ*)," as in Num. 35:34, but "*your* land (*ʾrṣkmh*)," which could be interpreted as "those areas in your possession," as opposed to the entire land as a whole. Also compare: "You shall not defile the city in which I cause My name and My Sanctuary to dwell" (Temple Scroll 47: ll. 10–11), and cf. also: "You shall not defile my sanctuary and my city with skins" (Temple Scroll 47, l. 17).

Expressions regarding concepts of purity and impurity in the Temple Scroll limit the holiness of the entire land to the holiness of one city alone, a concept that is actually the basis for the halakhic rules in Rabbinic literature. Prohibitions which, according to the Pentateuch, pertain to the entire camp (*mḥnh*) of Israel, here pertain to the Temple city alone.[45]

This shift from the land to Temple city must be understood in the light of historical circumstances. During the Second Temple period, a large percentage of Jews lived in Babylonia and Egypt;[46] the Jews of the land of Israel shared with them a sense of national identity, a relationship expressed through consanguinity, observance of the Torah, and loyalty to Jerusalem and the Temple. The "land," in the territorial sense, could

45. Cf. Y. Yadin, *The Temple Scroll* 1 (Jerusalem, 1983), ch. 5.

46. The diaspora as a characteristic feature of the Jewish people is already attested in the book of Esther: "there is a certain people, scattered and dispersed among the other peoples in all the provinces of your kingdom, whose laws are different from those of any other people. . . ." (3:8). The land of Israel is not mentioned here at all.

not express the essence of the nation, and because the land was inhabited by Samaritans and other non-Jews, it could not be viewed as the true unifying factor. In addition, all hope of ever reconquering the northern areas of Israel, which comprised the greater part of the promised land, had been abandoned; not even the territorial expansion during Hasmonean times was viewed as fulfillment of the goal of reconquering the land.

During the Hasmonean period, it is not the *conquest of land* that is referred to but rather *holding on to inherited territory.*[47] Thus, for example, Simon the Hasmonean states:

> We have neither taken other men's land nor have we possession of that which belongs to others, but of the inheritance of our fathers; howbeit, it was held in possession of our enemies wrongfully for a certain time. But we, having taken the opportunity, hold fast to the inheritance of our fathers.[48] (1 Macc. 15:33–34)

During this period, even the settlement of Jerusalem is described as the inheritance of a desolate hill, so as to avoid providing a pretext for accusations that the Jews conquered Jerusalem by force:[49]

47. This view prevails in the book of Chronicles which seems to evade the topic of conquest; see S. Japhet, *The Ideology of the Book of Chronicles and Its Place in Biblical Thought* (Frankfurt, 1989), pp. 363–65. The phrase "inheritance of land" (*yrš h' rṣ*) in this book signifies holding of the land rather than conquest. Thus, "so that you inherit the land" (*lmʿn tyršw 't h' rṣ*) in 1 Chron. 28:8 means "that you possess the land," not that you conquer it; see also H. G. M. Williamson, *1 and 2 Chronicles,* The New Century Bible Commentary (London, 1982), p. 181. The observance of the laws will bring constant possession of the land and no more abandonment of it.

48. *κλῆρονομια τῶν πατὲρων* means the inheritance of paternal estate in general, as in 1 Kings 21:3: *nḥlt 'bwty* "the inheritance of my fathers," and does not refer to the territory of the *promised land*. The verb *αντέχειν* here translates Hebrew *hḥzq;* cf. Isa. 56:2, 4, 6; Prov. 3:18; Neh. 4:10.

49. On the complaints of the gentiles concerning the possession of the land by the Jews and the endeavor of the Jews to legitimize their settle-

> And now they have returned to their God, and have come up from the dispersion where they are dispersed, and have taken possession of Jerusalem where their sanctuary is, and have settled in the hill country for it was desolate.[50] (Jth. 5:19)

Although there was a strong awareness of the land and its extension during the Second Temple period, especially in Hasmonean times, it was based on unrealistic utopian concepts. The promised land was seen as comprising almost the whole territory of the Near East (1Q Gen. Apoc. 21, 15–19; cf. Jubilees 8:20–21), a view influenced in part by contemporaneous Greek geographic models.[51] These broad delineations of the borders of the land of Israel legitimized the dispossession of the Canaanites by the old Israelites but did not guide the Hasmoneans in their war campaigns: through all their conquest activities, the Hasmoneans never relied on the ancient laws of the Pentateuch concerning the dispossession of the Canaanites and the inheritance of the promised land. The old Genesis traditions were rewritten in the light of contemporary events, but as a matter of practice the Hasmoneans neither mentioned nor implemented the ancient laws concerning the conquest of the land.[52]

---

ment in Eretz Israel, see J. H. Lewy, *Studies in Jewish Hellenism* (Jerusalem, 1969), pp. 60–78 (Hebrew). Especially significant are the attestations in the Rabbinic sources about the claims of the gentiles that Joshua was a brigand (ληϭτὴς).

50. Cf. Y. M. Grintz, *Judith* (Jerusalem, 1957), p. 114.

51. See F. Schmidt, "Jewish Descriptions of the Settled Land during the Hellenistic and Roman Periods, " in A. Kasher, G. Fuks, and U. Rappaport, eds., *Greece and Rome in Eretz Israel: Collected Essays* (Jerusalem 1989), pp. 85–97 (Hebrew).

52. Cf. D. Mendels, *The Land of Israel as a Political Concept in Hasmonean Literature,* Texte und Studien zum Antiken Judentum 15 (Tübingen, 1987), pp. 63 f., 129 f. On E. Meyer's view concerning this matter and its refutation, see Chapter 4, n. 36.

Conception of the Conquest of the Land during the Second Temple Period

Second Temple literature transformed older views of the conquest of the land in the days of Joshua: on the one hand, this literature asserted that the nations were not dispossessed, because the land was legally inherited from the ancestors, and on the other, the concept prevailed that the land was desolate before its occupation.[53] According to the book of Jubilees (chap. 8), Shem, the son of Noah, inherited the entire ideal land of Israel (from the Euphrates to the Red Sea), while the Genesis Apocryphon describes how Abraham established a claim to this area by encircling it (Gen. Apoc. 21:15–19).[54] Later, the Canaanites took the land by force and were therefore cursed (Jubilees 10:29–34). The book of Jubilees thus deviates from what appears in the list of nations in Gen. 10, in which the land of Canaan was allotted to Ham's son, Canaan (Gen. 10:15–19).

The claim that the land of Canaan had actually been a part of Shem's inheritance that was then stolen by the Canaanites also appears in Rabbinic sources. We read, for example, in the Midrash Aggadah on Gen. 12:6:

> "The Canaanites were then in the land"—for the land of

53. Thus, for example, we find in the description of Hecataeus of Abdera (Diodorus 40.3) that the Judeans entered a deserted land (ἐρῆμος, a term found in Jth 5:19; see M. Stern, *Greek and Latin Authors on Jews and Judaism* 1 (Jerusalem, 1976), pp. 20–24. According to D. Mendels, "Hecataeus of Abdera and a 'Jewish Patrios politeia' of the Persian Period (Diodorus Siculus 40, 3)," *ZAW* 95 (1983), pp. 96–100, Hecataeus' description draws from Jewish traditions prevalent in the Persian period; cf. the view of the Chronicler mentioned above, n. 47.

54. See J. A. Fitzmyer, *The Genesis Apocryphon of Qumran Cave 1,* 2nd rev. ed., (Rome, 1971), col. 21, 8–19 (p. 68); see F. Schmidt, "Jewish Descriptions" (n. 51). "Encircling the land," like "walking about the land" (Gen. 13:17), has a juridical connotation; cf. Yerus. Kiddushin 1:3, 60c; BT B. Batra 100a.

> Israel was cast in the lot of Shem, as it is written, "and Malchizedek, the king of Shalem," etc. (Gen. 14:18). When God divided the land between Noah's three sons, Noah prohibited his sons from entering the boundaries of each other's territory. The seven nations entered the land of Canaan and transgressed his prohibition. Therefore God commanded, "You must annihilate them" (Deut. 20:17).[55]

In this, the Rabbis provide a justification for the expulsion of the Canaanites.

Also, the Rabbis commonly held that Israel did not conquer the land by force, because the Canaanites and Amorites willingly abandoned the land to make way for Israel:

> The Canaanites merited having the land named after them. What had they done to merit this? When they heard that Israel was entering the land, they made way for them. God said to them: "Since you made way for my children, I will name the land after you, and give you a land as lovely as this one." Which land was it? Africa.[56]

Similarly, we read in Tosefta Shabbat 7:25 (Lieberman, p. 29):

> Rabban Shimon ben Gamliel said: There is no nation as reasonable as the Amorites, for we find that they believed in God, and settled in Africa, and God gave them a land as beautiful as their own, and the land of Israel was named after them.[57]

This view is also suggested in the writings of Philo: "[The Israelites] were not men of war . . . but rather few in num-

55. Midrash Agaddah, Buber 1, p. 27; see V. Aptowitzer, "Les premiers possesseurs de Canaan, légends apologétiques et exégétiques," *RÉJ* 82 (1926), pp. 282 ff.

56. Mekhilta Pascha, sec. 18 (ed. Horowitz, pp. 69–70).

57. S. Lieberman, *Tosefta Ki-Fshuṭah* 3 (New York, 1962), p. 105.

ber . . . who received their land [from the Syrians and Phoenicians] of their own free will" (*Hypothetica* 6.5).[58] Even the expulsion of the Canaanites from the land is described as a passive act, quite unlike the description in the book of Joshua. In the Wisd. of Sol. 12:8 we read: "You even spared them [the Canaanites] as people, and you sent the hornet as a fleet is sent out against the camp to destroy them slowly." In several Rabbinic sources we find a version of events that clearly contradicts the literal meaning of the biblical account: Joshua gave the Canaanites a choice, according to these sources, of either evacuating the area to make way for the Israelites, or making peace with them:

> Joshua sent three proclamations [*prostaqmata*] to the Canaanites: He who wishes to leave shall leave, he who wishes to make peace shall make peace, and he who wishes to fight shall do so.[59]

The laws of warfare appearing in Deut. 20:10–28 are in clear contradiction to this midrash. According to these laws, peace may only be offered to the "distant cities" (v. 15), whereas the nations of Canaan must be utterly annihilated: "You shall not let a soul remain alive" (v. 16). To justify the offer of peace to the Canaanites, the midrash in Deuteronomy Rabbah (S. Lieberman, pp. 29–30) invokes the precedent of Moses, who offered peace to the Amorite king, Sihon (Deut. 2:26).[60] This allusion does not draw on the literal meaning of the passage, for in the case of Moses, the context of the peace offer was a request to pass through Sihon's land; it should not be confused with the laws of war in Deut. 20, which pertain to wars of conquest. In any event, this offer of peace ultimately served as a

58. F. M. Colson, Philo 9, Loeb Classical Library, pp. 419–21.

59. Lev. Rabbah 17, 6 (ed. Margaliot, pp. 386–87); Yerus. Sheb 6:5, 36c; Debarim Rabbah 5, 14; compare Chapter 4 above.

60. Cf. Sifrei Deuteronomy, Sec. 199, (ed. Finkelstein, p. 237, ll. 7–8).

provocation, since God had originally commanded the Israelites to fight the Amorites and inherit their land (Deut. 2:24).[61]

The midrash concerning the proclamations sent by Joshua to the Canaanites reflects the tendency of Second Temple Judaism to depict Israelite settlement as a process that was perfectly legal according to Second Temple period concepts of legality, avoiding both the laws of annihilation found in the Pentateuch, which reflect the realities of the ancient world, and the wars of annihilation so characteristic of ancient times (cf. Mesha Inscription).[62]

A similar tendency is reflected in a Rabbinic source concerning the acceptance of Canaanites who repent, an idea which self-evidently contradicts the biblical injunction to wipe out the Canaanites. In Sifrei Deuteronomy sec. 202 (Finkelstein, p. 238) we read: " 'Lest they lead you into doing all the abhorrent things'—this teaches that if they repent, they shall not be killed." Also, in Tosefta Sotah 8:7 (Lieberman, p. 205), it is stated in regards to the inscriptions on the stone on Mt. Ebal, "And they inscribed at the bottom: 'Lest they lead you'—if you repent we shall accept you . . ."; and in the Geniza fragment of Mechilta Deuteronomy we find, "At the bottom of the stones it was written: 'whoever wants to accept *his right hand* let him come and accept.' "[63]

The belief that it is possible to accept the Canaanites if they repent, makes its way into Hellenistic sources of the Second Temple period. Thus, we read in the Wisd. of Sol. 12:8–12

61. The Rabbis felt the difficulty in offering peace here: "The holy said to him: 'I told you to fight with him but you offered him peace' " (Debarim Rabbah 5, 13).

62. *KAI* 1, no. 181:6–7. On the ban of Deuteronomy (7:1, 20:16–18), see above, Chapter 4.

63. For the reference and its interpretation, see S. Lieberman, *Sotah Tosefta ki-pheshutah*, Part 8, Order Nashim (New York, 1973), pp. 700–701. On "accepting the right hand" as "making a covenant," see S. Lieberman, "Notes," in E. S. Rosenthal, ed., *P'raqim—Yearbook of the Schocken Institute for Jewish Research of the Jewish Theological Seminary of America*, 1 (Jerusalem, 1967–68), pp. 98–101 (Hebrew).

that the "hornet" was sent to the Canaanites in order to bring about their repentance (*topon metanoias*).[64] Philo is even more specific: "If the enemies [Canaanites] are willing to repent . . . and show an inclination to peace, they will gladly accept the covenant with them,"[65] an expression quite similar to the two Rabbinic sources cited above, particularly in the striking resemblance of "accepting the right," in the Mechilta, to the *acceptance* of Canaanites who repent, in order to establish a peace treaty, in Philo's writings.

Thus, biblical concepts of conquest and annihilation underwent a transformation in Second Temple period literature.[66] The concept of totally annihilating the Canaanite population was viewed with great reservation, and there was a desire to depict relations with the Canaanites in terms of peaceful negotiations. Even more, the emphasis on the territorial essence of the land of Israel and the Jewish people was replaced by new spiritual, non-territorial definitions.

The Promised Land: Spiritualization of the Territorial Concept. In the eyes of Jewish writers from the Hellenistic period, such as Eupolemus, the son of Yohanan, Joshua's greatness lay not so much in his conquest of the land as in his establishment of the Tent of Meeting in Shiloh. Similarly, David's fame lay in those deeds that ultimately enabled Solomon to build the Temple. The prophets, the sanctuary in

64. On *topos* as Hebrew *maqom* with the late Hebrew connotation "possibility/chance," see L. Ginzberg, *The Legends of the Jews* 4, pp. 120–21, n. 701.

65. *On the special Laws* 4, 221.

66. In this case there are clear overlappings between the Rabbinic literature and the Jewish-Hellenistic writings of the Second Temple period. One should therefore view the Rabbinic traditions as rooted in the ideological reality of the first century C.E. On the Christian understanding of the conquest, see G. Stroumsa, "Old Wine and New Bottles: On Patristic Soteriology and Rabbinic Judaism," in S. N. Eisenstadt, ed., *The Origins and Diversity of Axial Ages Civilizations* (Albany, N.Y., 1986), pp. 259–60.

Shiloh, and the Temple in Jerusalem—and not the conquest of the land in battle—are the central topics in Eupolemus' survey of Jewish history.[67]

Josephus and Philo express similar views. Josephus cites Agatharchides, who had ridiculed the Jews, saying that during the days of Ptolemy the Jews caused their city to fall into the hands of enemies because of "a folly" (the laws of the Sabbath). In response, Josephus writes:

> Agatharchides mocks these things, but others, who may examine these things without prejudice, will find that it is worthy and important that there are people whose laws and fear of God are more important to them than their own safety and their land.[68]

The concept of the promised land actually undergoes a transformation in the writings of Josephus.[69] It is no longer just the area of Canaan that lies open to the Jewish people, but the entire world. Instead of the promise of the land of Canaan, we find the vision and destiny of a people who will fill the entire earth.

Thus, the promise to Jacob in Gen. 28:13–14:

> The ground on which you are lying I will give to you and your offspring. Your descendants shall be as the dust of

67. Mendels, in *The Land of Israel* (n. 52), p. 30, n. 5 argues that I do not consider the importance of the Land in Eupolemus. I discuss Eupolemus, albeit briefly, in my article, "The Inheritance of the Land," *Zion* 49 (1984) p. 133. Mendels states that Eupolemus expresses a sentimental contact with the land (on p. 30), but evidence for this is not presented. On Eupolemus, see Y. Gutman, *The Beginnings of Jewish-Hellenistic Literature* 2 (Jerusalem, 1963), pp. 73–94, 155–58; B. Z. Wacholder, *Eupolemus, A Study of Judeo-Greek Literature,* (Cincinnati, 1974).

68. *Against Apion* 1 209–10. Here, Josephus ignores the changes that had been introduced concerning waging war on the Sabbath; cf. 1 Macc. 2:39–42; Antiq. 12 274–76.

69. Cf. B. Halperin-Amaru, "Land Theology in Josephus' *Jewish Antiquities,*" *JQR* 71 (1981), pp. 202–29.

> the earth; you shall spread out to the west and to the east, to the north and to the south.

is paraphrased by Josephus: "To your children . . . I hereby give rule over this earth, and they shall fill all the earth and all the sea under the sun" (*Antiquities* 1:282).

This vision is reflected in the book of Jubilees, where, in the words of God to Jacob in Bethel, we find:

> I am YHWH who created the heaven and the earth, I will increase you and multiply you exceedingly and kings shall come forth from you and they shall judge everywhere wherever the foot of the sons of man has trodden. I will give to your seed all the earth under heaven and they shall judge all the nations according to their desires, and after that they shall get possession of the whole earth and inherit it forever. (32:18–19)

It seems that Josephus has drawn from such sources. Similarly, with respect to Balaam's prophecy about the fate of Israel, "Who can count the dust of Jacob . . . ?" (Num. 23:10), he writes:

> For there is not a race on earth which you shall not, through your virtue . . . be accounted to excel. God having regard for none among men but you . . . that land, then to which he himself has sent you, you shall surely occupy: it shall be subject forever to your children and with their fame shall all earth and sea be filled and you shall suffice for the world, to furnish every land with inhabitants sprung from your race. (Ant. 4:114–16)

This view even influences the way in which Josephus relates the prophecy of the return to the land. Instead of describing the return as it appears in the Bible, Josephus writes of the rebuilding of cities and the Temple (Ant. 4:314).

A similar approach can be found in Jewish liturgy of Rabbinic origin, such as "May the temple be speedily rebuilt in our days" and other prayers.[70] The festive Musaf prayer, for example, which opens "And because of our sins we were exiled from our land," closes with, "And bring us to Your city Zion . . . there we will offer our obligatory sacrifices."[71] We thus see that the purpose of the return to the land was to enable the worship of God in the Temple.

Philo goes even further, when, through the use of allegory, he interprets the concept of "inheriting the land" as "inheriting wisdom."[72] In this conception of Jews as constituting a nation that transcends race and citizenship, Philo formulates a new conception of nationality, one expressed in terms not of race or territory, but of religion and culture. Palestine, symbolized by its capital city Jerusalem, was looked upon as the mother country of all the Jews.[73]

Obviously, such views would correspond to those of the Hellenistic Jews who were living in the diaspora.[74] These ideas were shaped by the political reality of the times, in particular by the absence of an independent political government, for even Agrippas was appointed by Rome. But we must acknowledge that this political reality had the effect of providing for the spiritualization of physical territorial concepts.[75]

70. Cf. Abot 5:23: "May it be your will . . . that the Temple be speedily rebuilt in our days." This is actually the genuine conclusion of the Tractate Abot. See J. N. Epstein, *Introduction to the Text of the Mishnah*, pt. 2 (Jerusalem-Tel Aviv, 1964), p. 978 (Hebrew).

71. Rev. S. Singer, ed., *The Standard Prayer Book* (New York, 1943), p. 339.

72. See, e.g., *The Heir* 4 96–99, Loeb Classical Library, transl. F. H. Colson. Cf. also Philo, *Supplement I, Questions and Answers on Genesis* (ed. R. Marcus) 3, 16. In his view, the Euphrates in Gen. 15:18 symbolizes the joy: *εὐφράτης = εὐφροσύνη*.

73. H. A. Wolfson, *Philo* 2 (Cambridge, Mass., 1947), p. 401.

74. See A. Shalit, *Antiquities of the Jews by Josephus* 2 (Jerusalem-Tel Aviv, 1955), p. 43, no. 295a (Hebrew).

75. However, one should not ascribe to Philo a total negation of the physical aspect of the land of Israel; cf. B. Schaller, "Philon von Alexandria und das 'Heilige Land,'" in G. Strecker, ed., *Das Land Israel in biblischer Zeit*, Jerusalem Symposium, 1981 (Göttingen, 1983), pp. 172–87.

It is in Rabbinic literature that the land begins to take on eschatological significance.[76] The verse, "Your nation is all righteous, they will inherit the land forever" (Isa. 60:21) is understood in Mishnah Sanhedrin 11:1 as referring to inheritance of a part of the world to come.[77] Another verse, "But he who takes refuge in Me shall possess the land and inherit My holy mountain" (Isa. 57:13), is explained by commentator D. Kimchi, as follows: "The world to come is called the land of the living and the holy mountain," an interpretation that clearly corresponds to the Rabbis' approach. And the expression "holy mountain," in "And in that day a great ram's horn shall be sounded, and the strayed . . . shall come and worship the Lord on the holy mountain, in Jerusalem" (Isa. 27:13), is interpreted as the world to come in BT Sanhedrin 110b. In Mishnah Sanhedrin 10:3, Rabbi Akiva explains that the people cast in "the other land" (Deut. 29:27) are not in "the real land," namely, the world to come, but rather "the netherworld," from which no one ever returns. "Just as the day passes and never returns, so too they go and never return."[78]

Inheriting the land was understood by the Rabbis as being granted a place in the eternal world, as, for example, in Mish-

---

Schaller justifiably emphasizes the importance of Philo's words about the ceremony of the waving of the first sheaf, where he praises the Land of Israel (*Special Laws* 2 162–70), though even here he sees the offering of the sheaf "both of the nation's own land as well as of the whole earth" (2, 171).

76. See E. E. Urbach, "Inheritance Laws and After-Life," *Proceedings of the Fourth World Congress of Jewish Studies* 1 (Jerusalem, 1967), pp. 139–40 (Hebrew; English abstract, p. 263).

77. Cf. the Testament of Job 33:2–9 where the "holy land" (ἁγία γῆ) is identified with the "world to come" (literally, "the unchangeable world," ἀπαραλλάκτου); see, for the text, S. P. Brock, *Pseudoepigrapha Veteris Testamenti Graece* 2 (Leiden, 1967), and the discussions: B. Schaller, *Das Testament Hiobs* (Gütersloh, 1979), p. 353; R. Hanhart, "Das Land in der spätnachexilischen Prophetie," in G. Strecker, ed., *Das Land Israel in biblischer Zeit* (Göttingen, 1983), p. 136.

78. Compare the Mesopotamian expression for the netherworld: *māt la târi* "the land of no return."

nah Kidushin 1:10: "He who observes even one commandment is rewarded, will be granted a long life, and will inherit the land."[79]

Rashi and Maimonides both correctly interpret this "inheriting" as inheriting the world to come.[80] The eschatological interpretation of the phrase "inheriting the land" was exceedingly popular among the early Christians, and was rooted in the common wisdom of Jewish belief of the times as well.[81] Thus, the Rabbis' eschatological interpretation of the phrase "inheriting the land" can be said to have preceded the days of the destruction.

In this period a spiritualistic approach to the land of Israel began to develop. Just as Jerusalem took on a double meaning, as both the celestial and terrestrial Jerusalem,[82] the land of Israel also became understood in both the realistic and metaphysical sense.

Following the Bar Cochba revolt, a period in which there was danger that Jewish settlement in Israel would be diminished, we detect a kind of propaganda in favor of Israel and settlement in the land. Until this time, it had seemed quite natural to dwell in Israel; there had been no need to encourage settlement.[83]

79. Cf. Urbach, "Inheritance Laws" (n. 76).

80. There is no justification for the interpretation by J. N. Epstein, *Introduction to the Tanaaitic Literature* (Jerusalem, 1957), p. 53, that the author has in mind the real, physical land; see S. Safrai, "And all is According to the Majority of Deeds," *Tarbiz* 53 (1983–84), pp. 36–37 (Hebrew).

81. Cf. W. D. Davies, *The Gospel and the Land* (London, 1974), pp. 161 ff. For some corrections of Davies's views, see G. Strecker, "Das Land Israel in früh Christlicher Zeit," in Strecker, ed., *Das Land Israel in biblischer Zeit* (n. 75), pp. 188–200. On common Jewish belief, see D. Flusser, *Jewish Sources in Early Christianity: Studies and Essays* (Jerusalem, 1979), pp. 188–200.

82. Cf. S. Safrai, "The Land of Israel in Tannaitic Halacha," in Strecker, ed., *Das Land Israel in biblischer Zeit* (n. 75), pp. 201–15.

83. Cf. I. Gafni, "The Status of Eretz Israel in Reality and in Jewish Consciousness Following the Bar-Kokhva Uprising," in A. Oppen-

Holy Land. *Holiness of the Land* involves purity which all the inhabitants of the land were commanded to observe, based on the belief that the entire land belongs to the God of Israel: "Where the Tabernacle of the Lord abides" (Josh. 22:19). He who lived outside the land lived on unclean soil (Amos 7:17). In reference to exile, Hosea said, "They shall not be able to remain in the land of YHWH . . . and shall eat unclean food in the land of Assyria"; "They will offer no libations of wine to the Lord . . . all who partake of which are defiled . . . What will you do about the feast days, about the festivals of the Lord?" (Hos. 9:3–5). Hosea could not envision celebrating the holidays in exile. The Rabbis referred to the land outside of Israel as "the land of the nations" (*ʾrṣ hʿmym*), permeated with impurity ("impurity of the land of the nations").[84] It was difficult to imagine a life of holiness and purity outside the borders of Israel.

Although the entire land of Israel enjoyed an equal status in regard to the laws of purity and impurity, Jerusalem, the city of God's sanctuary, was considered particularly holy. In Mishnah Kelim 1:6–9, different areas of the land and the Temple are ranked according to specific aspects of holiness:

> The Land of Israel is holier than any other land. Wherein lies its holiness? In that from it they may bring the *ʿOmer,* the first fruits, and the two loaves, which they may not bring from any other land. The walled cities are even holier, in that they must send forth the lepers from their midst. . . . Within the wall is even holier, for they may eat the lesser holy things and the second tithe. The Temple Mount is even holier, for no man or woman that has a flux, no menstruant, and no woman after childbirth may enter therein. The *ḥyl* [rampart] is even holier, for no non-Jew and no one who has been near a corpse may enter therein. The court of the women is even holier, for

heimer and U. Rappaport, eds., *The Bar-Kokhva Revolt: A New Approach* (Jerusalem, 1984), pp. 224–32 (Hebrew).

84. Cf. Safrai, "Land," in Strecher, ed. (n. 75), p. 206.

> no one that had immersed himself that day may enter therein. . . . The court of the Israelites is even holier, for no one whose atonement is yet incomplete may enter therein. . . . The court of the priests is even holier, for the Israelites may not enter therein. . . . Between the porch and the altar is even holier, for no one may enter therein with hands and feet unwashed. The holy of holies is the holiest of all, for no one may enter therein except the High Priest on the Day of Atonement.

We have before us a system of concentric circles: the innermost and most important circle was the holy of holies. The source of holiness was God's presence in the holy of holies, and not the site itself.

In conclusion, we find that the land of Israel was originally conceived as a gift given by God to his people, thus accounting for the significance of the promise of the Land in Israel's religion. The Israelites had always believed that they were privileged to have received the land, but that they had to merit this gift, or it would be taken from them as it had been taken from the Canaanites before them. Biblical historiography essentially revolves around this issue of the promised land and the right to keep it.

While Israel's history from Abraham to Joshua essentially deals with preparations to enter the promised land, the period between Joshua and the exile is nothing but the story of constant struggle to hold onto the land and live within its borders. Faced with the threat of exile in the eighth century B.C.E., the Israelites were forced to scrutinize all their deeds and acknowledge that in order to live in the land, they must fulfill God's will and observe His commandments. This understanding triggered the development of the historiography and theodicy of the Former Prophets, in which the exiles from the northern and southern kingdoms were explained as the direct result of Israel's sins.

The burden of sin had a powerful effect upon the exiled in

Babylonia, who reacted by returning wholeheartedly to their God. But the Restoration was marked not by the desire to reconquer the land, but rather by the goal of resettling the land and rebuilding the religious-spiritual center in Jerusalem. The Temple and the commandments became the focal point of life in the renewed community, and the land thus became a means towards an end, not an end in itself. Even when the nation was roused to battle in Hasmonean times, they fought not to reconquer parts of the promised land, but for the sake of the Temple, God, and the commandments.

Towards the end of the Second Temple period the concept of the land underwent a process of spiritualization, as did Jerusalem. Jerusalem was interpreted in the ideal sense as "the kingdom of heaven" and "the celestial Jerusalem," and inheriting the land was similarly interpreted as receiving a place in the world to come. Nevertheless, the observance of the commandments remained linked to settlement in the land itself, observance of laws pertaining to the land, and, above all, worship of God in the Temple. Judaism has never described the nation's redemption apart from return to the physical land. Unlike Christianity, which in certain periods attempted to strip Jerusalem and the land of all realistic meaning and view them as symbols alone,[85] in Judaism, the physical land and physical Jerusalem continually served as a base for spiritual symbols.

85. See J. Prawer, "Jerusalem in Jewish and Christian Thought of the early Middle Ages," *Cathedra* 17 (1980), pp. 40–72 (Hebrew).

9

The Covenantal Aspect of the Promise of the Land to Israel

Two types of covenants are found in the Old Testament: the obligatory type reflected in the covenant of God with Israel and the promissory type reflected in the Abrahamic and Davidic covenants.[1] The nature of the covenant of God with Israel has been thoroughly investigated and recently clarified by a comparison with the treaty formulations in the ancient Near East.[2] The nature of the Abrahamic-Davidic covenants, however, is still vague and needs clarification. This chapter suggests a new way of understanding the character of the Abrahamic-Davidic covenants by means of a typological and functional comparison with the grant formulae in the ancient Near East.[3]

1. See, e.g., D. N. Freedman, "Divine Commitment and Human Obligation," *Interpretation* 18 (1964), pp. 419–31, and R. E. Clements, *Abraham and David,* Studies in Biblical Theology, Sec. series 5 (London, 1967). Cf. also N. Lohfink, *Die Landverheissung als Eid,* Stuttgarter Bibelstudien 28 (Stuttgart, 1967) and F. C. Fensham, "Covenant, Promise and Expectation in the Bible," *Theolgische Zeitschrift* 23 (1967), pp. 305–22.

2. Cf. G. E. Mendenhall, "Covenant Forms in Israelite Tradition," *Biblical Archaeologist* 17 (1954), pp. 50 ff.; K. Baltzer, *Das Bundesformular,* 2d ed., Wissenschaftliche Monographien zum Alten und Neuen Testament 4 (Neukirchen, 1964); D. J. McCarthy, *Treaty and Covenant,* 2d ed., Analecta Biblica 21a (Rome, 1978); M. Weinfeld, *Deuteronomy and the Deuteronomic School* (Oxford, 1972).

3. A. Poebel, *Das Appositionell Bestimmte Pronomen der 1 Pers. Sing. in den westsemitschen Inschriften und im A.T.,* Assyriological Studies 3, Orien-

Two types of official judicial documents had been diffused in the Mesopotamian cultural sphere from the middle of the second millennium onward: the political treaty, which is well known to us from the Hittite empire,[4] and the royal grant, the classical form of which is found in the Babylonian *kudurru* documents (boundary stones)[5] but which also occurs among the Hittites[6] in the Syro-Palestine area[7] and in the neo-Assyrian

---

tal Institute (Chicago, 1932). Poebel suggested that the promise to the Patriarchs bears the character of an oral "Belehnungsurkunde." His suggestion was based on the syntactical function of the phrase "I am the Lord" preceding the promise of the land. According to his view, the phrase "I am the Lord" is a typical opening phrase of royal documents in the ancient Near East, which has to be connected with and understood as the following: "I am the one who did so and so, etc.," and not "I am the Lord" as an independent phrase of self-introduction. This assumption, which seems to be correct, is not sufficient to bear out the thesis about the identity of the Abrahamic-Davidic covenant with the grant. We must, however, give credit to Poebel for his penetrating glance into the nature of the covenant in Israel, which, although expressed in one sentence, antedated Mendenhall (see n. 2) by twenty-two years. Cf. his summation of the syntactical discussion, "Wir sahen auch, dass in jedem einzelnen Fall die Anwendung der dem Herrscher und Urkundenstil entlehnten Formell durchaus der Situation angemessen war, weil die Verheissung, den Nachkommen der Erzväter das Land Kanaans zu verleihen, gewissermassen eine mündliche Belehnungsurkunde ist und auch die Bundesschliessung Gottes mit Israel nach der Absicht der Erzähler ahnlich wie der Abschluss eines Bundnisses zwischen politischen Staaten oder Herrschern unter dem Gesichtspunkt eines rechtlichen Staatsaktes betrachtet werden soll" (p. 72).

4. Cf. E. Weidner, *Politische Dokumente aus Kleinasien: Die Staatsverträge in akkadischer Sprache aus dem Archiv von Boghazköi, Boghazköi Studien* 8 (Leipzig, 1923); J. Friedrich, *Staatsverträge des Hatti Reiches in hethitischer Sprache, MVAeG* 31 (1926); 34 (1934).

5. L. W. King, *Babylonian Boundary Stones and Memorial Tablets,* (London, 1912). Cf. also F. X. Steinmetzer, *Die babylonischen Kudurru (Grenzsteine) als Urkundenform,* Studien zur Geschichte und Kultur des Altertums 11 (Paderborn, 1922).

6. Cf. H. Güterbock, *Siegel aus Bogazköy, AfO,* Beiheft 5 (1940), especially pp. 47–55, which deal with the "Landschenkungsurkunden"; K. Riemschneider, *Die hethitischen Landschenkungsurkunden,* Mitteilungen des Instituts für Orient-forschung 6 (Berlin, 1958), pp. 321–81.

7. Cf. the gift-deed of Abban to Yarimlim in D. J. Wiseman, *The*

period.[8] The structure of both of these types of documents is similar. Both preserve the same elements: a historical introduction, border delineations, stipulations, witnesses, blessings, and curses.[9] Functionally, however, there is a vast difference between these two types of documents. While the "treaty" constitutes an obligation of the vassal to his master, the suzerain, the "grant" constitutes an obligation of the master to his servant. In the "grant," the curse is directed toward anyone who violates the rights of the king's vassal,[10] while in the treaty the curse is directed toward the vassal who violates the rights of his king. In other words, the "grant" serves mainly to protect the rights of the *servant,* while the treaty protects the rights of the *master.* In addition, while the grant is a reward for loyalty and good deeds already performed, the treaty is an inducement to future loyalty.

Alalah Tablets, no. 1* (London, 1954), complemented by the tablet ATT/ 39/84 published by Wiseman in "Abban and Alalah," *JCS* 12 (1958), pp. 124 ff., for which see also: A. Draffkorn, "Was King Abba-AN of Yamḫad a Vizier for the King of Ḫattuša?" *JCS* 13 (1959), pp. 94 ff., and the Ugaritic donation texts in *PRU* 2 and 3.

8. Cf. J. Kohler and A. Ungnad, *Assyrische Rechtsurkunden,* no. 1–30 (Leipzig, 1913); J. N. Postgate, *Neo-Assyrian Royal Grants and Decrees* (Rome: Pontifical Institute, 1969).

9. For the structure of the Hittite treaties, cf. V. Korošec, *Hethitische Staatsverträge* (Leipzig, 1931), and for the structure of the *kudurru* documents, cf. F. X. Steinmetzer, *Kudurru* (n. 5).

10. Cf. the kudurru inscriptions in L. W. King, *BBSt* (n. 5) and the neo-Assyrian grants in Kohler-Ungnad, *ARu* no. 1–30 (n. 8); J. N. Postgate, *Royal Grants* (n. 8), no. 1–52. A peculiar threat occurs in an Old Babylonian grant from Hana, *bāqir ibaqqaru . . . kupram ammam qaqqassu ikkappar* ("whoever challenges the gift, his head will be covered with hot pitch"), in M. Schorr, *Urkunden des altbabylonischen Zivil-und Prozessrechts,* VAB 5, no. 219 (Leipzig, 1913), pp. 17–24. At times the donor takes upon himself a conditional self-curse as, for instance, in the grant of Abban, where Abban takes the following oath: *šumma ša addinukummi eleqqû* = "[may I be cursed] if I take back what I gave you" (Wiseman, *AT* [n. 7] 1*, pp. 16–20). For the conditional oath sentences, see W. von Soden, *Grundriss der akkadischen Grammatik,* Analecta Orientalia 33 (Rome, 1952), 185g,i.

The covenant with Abraham and the covenant with David indeed belong to the grant type and not to the vassal type of document. Like the royal grants in the ancient Near East, the covenants with Abraham and David were gifts bestowed upon individuals who excelled in loyally serving their masters. Abraham is promised the land because he obeyed God and followed his mandate (Gen. 26:5; cf. 22:16, 18), and David is given the grace of dynasty because he served God with truth, righteousness, and loyalty (1 Kings 3, 6; cf. 9:4; 11:4, 6; 14:8; 15:3). The terminology used in this context is indeed very close to that used in the Assyrian grants. For example, in the grant of Aššurbanipal to his servant Balṭaya we read:

> I am Aššurbanipal . . . who does good (*ēpiš ṭābti*) . . . who always responds graciously[11] to all the officials who serve him and returns kindness to the servant (*pālihi*) who keeps his royal command, whose heart is devoted [lit., is whole] to his master, served me [lit., stood before me] with truthfulness, acted perfectly [lit., walked in perfection] in my palace, grew up with a good name and kept the charge of my kingship. I took thought of his kindness and I have established his gift . . .[12] Any future prince from among the kings my sons . . . do good and kindness to them and their seed. They are friends and allies (*bēl ṭābti, bēl dēqti*) of the king their master.[13]

11. *it-ta-nap-pa-lu ina damqāti*. The reading *apālu* ("to answer") and not *abālu* ("lead, direct") is supported by the vassal treaties of Esarhaddon, lines 98, 236 (D. J. Wiseman, *The Vassal Treaties of Esarhaddon,* Iraq 20 (London, 1958), where R. Borger ("Zu den Asarhaddon—Verträgen aus Nimrud," *ZA* 20 (1961), pp. 177, 182) reads correctly: *ina kināte tarṣāti lā ta-ta-nap-pal-šu-ú-ni* ("if you do not respond with truth"). In a similar context we read in 1 Kings 12:7: *wʿnytm wdbrt ʾlyhm dbrym ṭwbym,* which means: "you will respond graciously"; in other words, "comply with their requests." See my article "The Council of the 'Elders' to Rehoboam and Its Implications," *Maʿarav, A Journal for the Study of the NorthWest Semitic Languages and Literatures* 3 (1982), pp. 25–54 (ch. 8, n. 35).

12. For this reading cf. my article "Covenant Terminology in the Ancient Near East and its Influence on the West," *JAOS* 93 (1973), p. 195, n. 77.

13. Postgate, *Grants* (n. 8) no. 11, pp. 1–13, 42–45.

The gift comes as a reward for the "good and kindness" shown by the official to his master, the king, and is considered itself as "good and kindness (*ṭābtu damiqtu*)."[14]

This is very similar in concept to the gifts bestowed upon Abraham and David, the faithful servants.[15] Like the Assyrian king who, prompted by the kindness of his servant, promises "good and kindness" (*ṭābtu damiqtu*) to his descendants, so does YHWH to the offspring of Abraham.

> Know, therefore, that . . . your God . . . keeps his gracious covenant (*šmr hbryt whḥsd*) to the thousandth generation of those *who love him and keep his commandments.* (Deut. 7:9)[16]

Although this verse is taken from Deuteronomy, which was written relatively late, its basic formula goes back to the more ancient sources, such as Exodus 20:6 (cf. Deut. 5:10):

> The God who does kindness (*ʿśh ḥsd;* cf. *ēpiš ṭābti,* above) to the thousandth generation of those *who love me and keep my commandments,*

and also,

> Who keeps kindness (*nṣr ḥsd*) to the thousandth generation." (Exod. 34:7)

The kindness (*ḥsd*) of God to David is likewise extended to

14. *ṭābtu damiqtu* is a hendiadys, which denotes covenantal relationship; see my article "Covenant Terminology" (n. 12), *JAOS* 93 (1973), pp. 191 ff.

15. For Abraham and David as Yahweh's servants see Gen. 26:24; Ps. 105:6, 42; 2 Sam. 3:18, 7:5, etc.

16. "Who love him and keep his commandments" refers to the Patriarchs (like most of the Commentaries, cf. M. Weiss, "Some Problems of the Biblical 'Doctrine of Retribution,'" *Tarbiz* 32 [1963–64], pp. 4 ff. [Hebrew]) and thus parallels the phrase in the Aššurbanipal grant, "returns kindness to the reverent who keeps his royal command."

the future generations as may be seen from 2 Samuel 7:15 and 22:51; 1 Kings 3:6 and 8:23; and Psalms 89:34 f. Furthermore, as the official of Aššurbanipal is called *bēl ṭābti bēl damiqti* "friend and ally" (lit., "man of kindness and favor") so are Abraham and David "the lovers" and "friends of God."[17]

The phrase found in the grant of Aššurbanipal, "who returns kindness to the reverent (lit., "the one who fears") who keeps his royal command," which is parallel to "keeps/does kindness to those who love me/him and keep my/his commandments" in the quoted verses, is also found in reference to God's followers in general. Thus we read in Psalms 103:17–18,

> But the kindness of YHWH is from everlasting to everlasting upon them that revere (lit., fear) him (*yr'yw*) and his righteousness to children's children to those who keep his covenant (*lšmry brytw*) and remember his commandments (*wlzkry pkdyw*) to do them.[18]

The phrase *ṭābtašu ahsusma* "I took thought of his kindness" in Aššurbanipal's address to his loyal servant reminds us of God's words to Israel in Jeremiah's prophecy. "I took thought of (*zkrty lk*) the kindness (*ḥsd*) of your youth . . . following

17. Ibid., and see also Isa. 41:8: *'brhm 'whby*. David is called *ḥsyd* in Ps. 89:20. (Read *lḥsydk* with manuscripts and versions; the reading *lbḥyrk* in 4Q Ps. 89 [J. T. Milik, "Fragment d'une source du Psautir (4Q Ps. 89) et fragments des Jubilés, de Document de Damas, d'un phylactère dans la grotte 4 de Qumran," *RB* 73 (1966), p. 99; cf. also E. Lipinski, *Le Poème royal du Ps. 89, 1–5, 2–38* (Paris, 1967), pp. 70 ff.] is not original and was influenced—in my opinion—by verse 4a.) Compare also *tmyk w'ryk l'yš ḥsydk* (should perhaps be read as: *l'yš ḥsdk*) in Deut. 33:8. Here the term is ascribed to Levi who, like David, was devoted to God and therefore was granted priesthood (see below, pp. 262–64). The phrase *bēl ṭābti bēl damiqti* equals the Hebrew *ḥsyd/'yš ḥsd;* compare, e.g., *bēl dami* with *'yš dmym* in Hebrew. As is the Akkadian *bēl ṭābti/damiqti,* so the Hebrew *ḥsyd/'yš ḥsd* is not a man who is shown kindness but the one who shows kindness, i.e., practices *ḥesed* and fulfills the demands of loyalty. Cf. N. Glueck, *Ḥesed in the Bible* (Cincinnati, 1967), pp. 66–69.

18. Compare Ps. 119:63: *lkl 'šr yr'wk wlšmry pqwdk,* which exactly parallels the Assyrian phrase dealt with.

me[19] in the desert" (Jer. 2:2). The "kindness" referred to is the one that Israel did with her God for which she was granted the land (cf. v. 7 and Jer. 31:1 f.). However, unlike the promise to David, where the imagery is taken from the royal sphere, in Jeremiah the imagery is borrowed from the familial sphere. A similar typology is actually found in legal documents of a marital nature. For example, in a gift deed from Elephantine we read, "I took thought of you . . . (*ʿštt lky*) . . . and have given it to . . . in affection (*brḥmn*)[20] since she took care of me . . ."[21] The gift by the father is then motivated as in Jeremiah by the devotion of the donee, his daughter (see below, pp. 233 f.).

God's promises to Abraham and David and their descendants are motivated by loyal service and are typologically parallel to the "royal covenantal grants" of the Hittites and Assyrians. Also, as will be shown, the analogy goes even further. Hittite and Assyrian grants are similar to God's covenants with Abraham and David even in their formulation of the commitment *to keep the promise to the descendants* of the loyal servants.

A Hittite grant typologically similar to the grant of dynasty to David is the decree of Hattušili concerning Middannamuwa, his chief scribe.

> Middannamuwa was a man of grace (*kaniššanza* UKÙ-*aš*)[22] to my father . . . and my brother Muwatalli was kindly) disposed to him, promoted him (*kanešta . . . para*

19. *hlk ʾḥry* in Hebrew and *alāku arki* in Akkadian are legal formulae of the marital and political spheres; cf. my "Covenant Terminology," no. 12, *JAOS* 93 (1973), p. 196, n. 83.

20. Cf. the discussion of the term in Y. Muffs, *Studies in the Aramaic Legal Papyri from Elephantine* (Leiden, 1969), pp. 40 ff., 132 f.

21. E. Kraeling, *The Brooklyn Museum Aramaic Papyri,* no. 9 (New Haven, 1953), pp. 16–17.

22. For clarification of this term, cf. A. Goetze, *Hattušiliš* (*MVAeG* 29/3, 1924; Leipzig, 1925) pp. 64–65.

> *huittiiat*)[23] and gave him Hattuša. My grace (*aššul*) was also shown to him . . . I committed myself for (*šer memiiahhat*) the sons of Middannamuwa . . . and you will keep (*pahhašdumat*) . . . and so shall the sons of my son and the grandsons of my son keep. And as my son, Hattušili, and Puduhepa, the great queen, were kindly disposed (*kanešta*) towards the sons of Middannamuwa so shall be my sons and grandsons . . . And they shall not abandon the grace (*aššulan anda lē daliianzi*) of my son. The grace and their positions shall not be removed (*ueh-*).[24]

Like Hebrew *ṭwbh/ḥsd,* Akkadian *ṭābtu/damiqtu,* and the Aramaic *ṭbt,* the Hittite *aššul* and *kannešuuar* connote kindness and covenantal relationship.[25] As in the case of David, in the Hittite grant the promise is to be "kept"[26] to the future generations of the devoted servant, i.e., "the man of grace."[27] The most striking parallel to the promise to David is the last sentence: "they shall not abandon the grace . . . their position shall not be removed." The language (*anda*) *daliia,* equivalent to the Akkadian *ezēbu* and the Hebrew *ʿzb,* which is often employed

23. The verbs in question correspond to *nṭh* and *mšk* in Hebrew (*kaniniia* = Akk. *kanāšu* = Hebr. *nṭh,* and *huittiia* = Akk. *šadādu* = Hebr. *mšk*), both employed with *ḥsd: nṭh ḥsd* (Gen. 39:21), *mšk ḥsd* (Jer. 31:3, Ps. 36:11; 109:12). Goetze (ibid.) related *kaneššuuar* to *rēma rašû* in Akkadian and correctly remarked that the object corresponding to *rēmu* in Hittite gradually became superfluous since it had been implied in the verb itself. The same equation has to be made, in my opinion, in regard to the Hebrew *nṭh ḥsd/mšk ḥsd* and also *mṣʾ* = *rāšû.*

24. A. Goetze, *Hattušiliš* (*MVAeG* 29/3; Leipzig, 1925), pp. 40–44; (*KBo* 4, 12).

25. *aššul* = SILIM -*ul* (SILIM = *salīmum*). *kaneššuuar* is synonymous with *aššul;* see Goetze, *Hattušiliš,* (n. 24), pp. 64–65.

26. *pahš* = Akk. *naṣāru* = Hebr. *šmr/nṣr,* verbs employed in connection with keeping the promise.

27. It occurs to me that *kaneiššanza* UKU-*aš* is equivalent to the Hebrew *ʾyš ḥsyd* and the Akkadian *bēl ṭābti/damiqti* appearing frequently in the context of grants.

in connection with *ḥsd/ḥsd w'mt,* and *ueh* ("turn away," remove) is equivalent to the Hebrew *swr,* which appears in 2 Sam. 7 in a phrase similar to that of the Hittite grant *wḥsdy l'yswr mmnw*—"and my grace shall not turn away from him" (v. 15).

The formulations concerning the promises to Abraham and David are overlapping. Thus we read in Gen. 26:4–5, "I will give to your descendants all these lands . . . inasmuch as Abraham obeyed me (*šmʿ bqly*)[28] and kept my charge (*wyšmr mšmrty*), my commandments, my rules and my teachings,"[29] a verse preserving verbally the notion of keeping guard or charge (*iṣṣur maṣṣarti*) found in the Assyrian text. The notion of "serving perfectly" found in the Assyrian grants is also verbally paralleled in the Patriarchal and the Davidic traditions. Thus, the faithfulness of the Patriarchs is expressed by "walk(ed) before me" (*hthlk lpny*—Gen. 24:40; 48:15 = JE; 17:1 = P), which is equivalent to the expression *ina mahriya ittalak/izziz* in the Assyrian grant. The P source adds to *hthlk lpny* the phrase *whyh tmym* (Gen. 17:1), which conveys the idea of perfect or loyal service expressed in the Assyrian document by (*ittalak*) *šalmiš*.[30] According to P, not only Abraham but also

28. Cf., in the Amarna letters, *amur arda ša išme ana šarri bēlišu* (behold, the servant who obeys the king, his Lord) (*EA* 147, 48 f.).

29. This verse is not necessarily Deuteronomic; *šmʿ bqwl,* along with other terms expressing obedience, is very frequent in the Deuteronomic literature, which stresses loyalty to the covenant, but this does not mean that the terms were coined by the Deuteronomic school. The combination of *ḥqym wtwrwt* ("laws and teachings") is never found in the Deuteronomic literature. Deuteronomy always uses Torah in the singular and usually with the definite article *htwra* ("the law"). On the other hand, this combination is attested to in JE (Exod. 18:16, 20). The origin of *šmr mšmrt* is not Deuteronomic; see my *Deuteronomy and the Deuteronomic School* (n. 2), Appendix A.

30. Cf. Mal. 2:6—*bšlwm wbmyšwr hlk 'ty*—which means "he served me with integrity and equity"; see Y. Muffs, *Aramaic Papyri* (n. 20), pp. 203–04 (following H. L. Ginsberg). This phrase occurs in connection with the grant of priesthood to Levi (see below). For the interpretation of *ittalaku šalmiš* as "served with integrity" and not as Kohler-Ungnad trans-

Noah was rewarded by God (Gen. 9:1–17) for his loyalty, which is expressed by the very phrase used to describe Abraham's devotion: *hthlk ʾt ʾlhym, hyh tmym* (6:6, 9).[31]

David's loyalty to God is couched in phrases that are closer to the neo-Assyrian grant terminology. Thus, the terms "who walked before you in truth, loyalty[32] and uprightness of heart" *hlk lpnyk bʾmt wbṣdqh wbyšrt lbb* (1 Kings 3:3, 6); "walked after me with all his heart" *hlk ʾḥry bkl lbbw* (14:8); and "a whole heart (like the heart of David)" *lb šlm (klbb dwd)* (15:3)[33] are the counterparts of the Assyrian terms "with his whole heart" *libbašu gummuru;* "stood before me in truth" *ina mahriya ina kināti izizuma;*[34] and "walked with loyalty (perfection)" *ittalaku šalmiš,* which come to describe the loyal service as a reward for which the gift was bestowed.[35]

---

lates—"in good or peaceful condition (wohlbehalten)"—see Y. Muffs, ibid., p. 203. *alāku/atalluku šalmiš* is equivalent to *hlk btm* ("walk with integrity") (Prov. 10:9) and to *hthlk btm lbb,* which in Ps. 101:2 is connected with *bqrb byty* (within my house/palace).

31. However, in contradistinction to the JE source, where the loyalty of the Patriarchs is a matter of the past, in the priestly source it is anticipated.

32. *ṣdqh* here means loyalty and faithfulness, as does *ṣdq* in a similar context in the Panamuwa inscriptions (*KAI* 215:19, 216:4–7, 218:4), where *bṣdq ʾby wbṣdqy hwšbny mrʾy . . . ʿl krsʾ ʾby* has to be understood as: "because of my father's and my own loyalty, the king has established me on the throne of my father." Virtually the same idea is expressed in 1 Kings 3:6: "You have done grace with your servant David my father as he walked before you in truth, loyalty and uprightness of heart and you kept your grace (promise) and gave him a son to sit upon his throne as at present."

33. Cf. also 2 Kings 20:3.

34. As in Hebrew *hthlk/hlk lpny,* so also in Akkadian *ina pāni alāku/atalluku* is similar in connotation to *ʿmd lpny=ina pāni uzzuzu,* but the latter seems to have a more concrete meaning—praying, interceding, worshiping and serving—whereas the former is more abstract. Cf. Jer. 18:20. For discussion of these terms, cf. F. Noetscher, *'Das Angesicht Gottes schauen,' nach biblischer und babylonischer Auffassung* (Würzburg, 1924), pp. 83 ff., 112 f. A phrase identical with *hlk lpny DN bṣdqh* may be found in the Hittite *A-NA PA-NI DINGIR, MEŠ para handandatar i̯i̯a-* (cf.

In the grants from Ugarit the loyalty of the donee is expressed by terms such as "he exerts himself very, very much for the king his lord."[36] Similarly, in a deed from Susa convey-

---

A. Goetze, *Hattušiliš* (n. 22) 1:48, *MVAeG* 29/3 (1924) 10, and his note on pp. 52–55 there), which means, "to walk before the gods with righteousness/loyalty," *handai* is equivalent to the Akkadian *kunnû*, and *handandatar* is rendered by NÍG.SI.SÁ-*tar* (NÍG.SI.SÁ = *mīšarum*), which also supports our analogy. Instances of *para handandatar* in which the gods show *para handandatar* in distress, war, etc. (cf. Goetze, *Hattušiliš* (n. 22) 1:45, 2:15, 45, 3:18, 23) might be put in the proper light by the biblical *ṣdqh*, which also connotes salvation. For the saving acts of God by means of *ṣdqh*, see, e.g., Ps. 31:2, 71:2, 143:11; *para handandatar* is revealed by the gods (A. Goetze, *Die Annalen des Muršiliš*, MVAeG 38 [Leipzig, 1933], 46:15), and the same is said about God in Israel in Isa. 56:1 and Ps. 98:2. Even the phrase in the introduction to the Apology of Hattušili, *ŠA dIŠTAR para handandatar memahhi* (l. 5), may be better understood on the basis of biblical parallels. Reciting or telling God's *ṣdqh* is very common in the Old Testament and is clearly attested in the ancient poem of Judg. 5 (v. 11).

As in the Assyrian documents, in Hittite the idiom "to walk in righteousness/loyalty before RN," in the sense of serving loyally, is attested in the treaties (cf. A. Kempinski and S. Košak, "The Išmeriga-Vertrag," *Die Welt des Orients* 5 [1970], 192:13). The idiom seems to have been rooted in the royal sphere and then projected onto the divine realm.

35. The close affinities to the neo-Assyrian phraseology in these verses may be understood in light of an identical chronological and cultural background. All of these verses appear in a Deuteronomic context, which means that they were styled in the seventh century, a period in which the above-mentioned documents were written. On the affinities of the Deuteronomic literature to the neo-Assyrian literary tradition, see my *Deuteronomy and the Deuteronomic School* (n. 2), 1972.

36. *ana šarri bēlišu anih danniš dannišma, PRU* 3, 140:27–30; cf. *ana šarri anih/ītanah, PRU* 3, 84:24, 141:29, 108:16, 110:7. Cf. the Barrakib inscription, *wbyt ʾby [ʿ]ml mn kl* ("and my father's house exerted itself more than anybody else," *KAI* 216:7–8), which occurs in a passage expressing the loyalty of Barrakib to Tiglath-Pileser (see above, n. 32). Two different interpretations have been given to the phrase *wbyt ʾby [ʿ]ml mn kl*, but neither of these is satisfactory. F. Rosenthal (*ANET*, 2d. ed., p. 501), following H. L. Ginsberg (*Studies in Koheleth* [New York, 1950], p. 3, n. 2a) translates, "the house of my father has profited more than anybody else," but this does not fit the immediate context, which is concerned with loyalty to Tiglath-Pileser. The same argument applies to B. Lands-

ing a gift from a husband to his wife we read, "it is given her as a gift because she took care of him and worked hard for him."[37] The same motivation occurs in a deed from Elephantine quoted above: "I took thought of you (*ʿštt lky*) during my lifetime and have given you part of my house . . . I Anani have given it to Yehojišma my daughter in affection since she took care of me (supported me) (*lqbl zy sbltny*) when I was old in years and unable to take care of myself."[38] The verb *anāhu,* expressing the exertion of the vassal to his lord and the wife to her husband, actually means to toil, to suffer, but in our context they denote exertion and devotion. The notion of exertion is sometimes completed by the verb *marāṣu* ("to be sick"), as, for instance, in a letter from El-Amarna where the vassal says, "Behold I exerted myself to guard the land of the king (*ētanhu ana nāṣar māt šarri*) and I am very sick" (*marṣaku danniš*).[39] In fact, the verb *marāṣu* in Akkadian has also the meaning of "to care for," as does the Hebrew *ḥlh.*[40] Held

---

berger's translation, "the house of my father was more miserable than any body else" (*Sam'al, Studien zur Entdeckung der Ruinenstätte Karatepe* [Ankara, 1948], p. 71), which is diametrically opposed to Rosenthal's translations. Besides, Landsberger's translation is contradicted by the Panammuwa inscription (*KAI* 214:9), a fact of which Landsberger was aware (ibid., n. 187). Donner's translation, which we have adopted, is the most satisfactory and is now supported by the Akkadian parallels. It seems that *ʿml* is the semantic equivalent of *anāhu.* Similarly *manahātu* means "results of toil," as does the Hebrew noun *ʿml;* for the Hebrew *ʿml* in this sense, cf. H. L. Ginsberg, *Qohelet* (Tel-Aviv, 1961), pp. 13–15 (Hebrew).

37. *aššum ittišu īnahu̯ dulla ill[iku] nadišši qiš[ti], MDP* 24, 379:7 f.; for an analysis of this document see J. Klima, "Untersuchungen zum elamischen Erbrecht," *Archiv Orientální* 28 (1960), p. 39.

38. E. Kraeling, *The Brooklyn Museum Aramaic Papyri* (n. 21), 1953, 9:16–17.

39. EA 306:19–21.

40. Cf. especially 1 Samuel 22:8—*w'yn ḥlh mkm ʿly* ("and nobody cares about me")—in the context of loyalty to the king. Cf. also Amos 6:6, *wl' nḥlw ʿl šbr ywsp* ("They do not care about the breach of Joseph"), and Jer. 22:13, *zrʿw ḥytm wqwṣym qṣrw nḥlw l' yw'ylw* ("they have sown wheat and have reaped thorns, they exerted themselves but did not profit").

pointed out the correspondence of the Hebrew סבל to the Ugaritic *zbl* ("to be sick").[41] The same correspondence exists between the expressions *anāhu* and *marāṣu* on the figurative level. The notion of exerting oneself for the suzerain is also expressed in the Akkadian inscription of Idrimi, the king of Alalah, in the middle of the second millennium B.C.E.[42] "I sent a messenger to the lord and told him about the exertion of my forefathers (*adbub manahāte ša abūtēya*) for them . . . and they had made a sworn valid alliance (*māmītu*) with me. On the account of our vassal service (exertion, *manahāte*) he received my tribute (*šulmu*) . . . I made many offerings"[43] (lines 41–55).

In light of all this, we may properly understand Psalms 132:1—*zkr ldwd ʾt kl ʿnwtw*—which the Septuagint and the Syriac misunderstood by reading *ʿanwātō* ("his humility"), which does not fit the context. In line with what we have seen above, it has to be understood as "his submissiveness[44] or devotion." To introduce God's promise to David, the psalmist depicts the devotion of David to God, which found expression in his deep concern for the ark. This is what is meant by the opening prayer, "Remember to David all his submissiveness."[45] *Zkr l* here is the semantic equivalent of *ʿšt l* in the

41. M. Held, "The Root ZBL/SBL in Akkadian, Ugaritic and Biblical Hebrew," (Speiser Memorial Volume), *JAOS* 88 (1968), p. 93.

42. Cf. E. L. Greenstein and D. Marcus, "The Akkadian Inscription of Idrimi," *The Journal of the Ancient Near Eastern Society of Columbia University* 8 (1976), pp. 59–96.

43. The reference to the covenant with the ancestors of the suzerain and the sending of gifts to him was a stereotype in the oath of the vassals; see my "Initiation of Political Friendship in Ebla," in H. Hauptmann and H. Waetzoldt, eds., *Wirtschaft und Gesellschaft von Ebla,* Heidelberger Studien zum Alten Orient 2 (Heidelberg, 1988), pp. 345–48.

44. Cf. *wʿn ʾnk ʾrṣt ʿzt* ("I subjugated mighty countries") in the Azittawada inscription (*KAI* 26:18); cf. the Mesha inscription (*KAI* 181:5) and Exod. 10:3: *ʿd mty mʾnt lʿnt mpny,* which has to be rendered, "how long will you refuse to surrender before me." Cf. also Gen. 15:13; 16:6; Exod. 1:11; Num. 24:24; 2 Sam. 7:10; 1 Kings 11:39; Nah. 1:12.

45. The notion that the promise of dynasty to David is to be seen as a reward for his devotion seems to lie behind the juxtaposition of chapters 6 and 7 in the second book of Samuel.

quoted Aramaic gift deed, which means "to take favorable thought."[46] The Akkadian *hasāsu,* the equivalent of the Hebrew זכר,[47] likewise means "to think about" or "to consider"[48] and, in fact, occurs in this sense in the neo-Assyrian grant quoted above. After describing the loyalty of his servant, upon whom he bestows the grant, the Assyrian emperor says, *ṭābtašu ahsusma ukîn ši-ri-[ik]-su*[49] (I took thought of his kindness and established his gi[ft])." The establishing of God's grant to the Patriarchs is expressed by הקים, which is the semantic equivalent of *ukîn* in the Assyrian grant.[50]

David's exertion, for which he was granted dynasty, is expressed in Psalms 132 by *ʿnh,* which corresponds to the discussed *anāhu, marāṣu* and *ʿml*.[51]

In the Deuteronomic historiography, however, David's devotion is expressed, as in the neo-Assyrian grants,[52] in a more abstract way—"walking in truth," "acting with wholeheartedness and integrity," etc. The phraseological correspondence between the Deuteronomic literature and the neo-Assyrian documents is very salient in the description of the benevolence of God toward the Patriarchs and toward David. Thus, the Assyrian king, before announcing the grant, says, "I am the king . . . who returns kindness to the one who serves in

46. Cf. H. L. Ginsberg, "Lexicographical Notes," *Hebräische Wortforschung: Festschrift W. Baumgartner,* Suppl. *VT* 15 (Leiden, 1967), pp. 81–82.

47. See, e.g., *EA* 228:18–19: *lihsusmi* glossed by *yazkurmi;* cf. M. Held, "Studies in Comparative Semite Lexicography," *Studies in Honor of B. Landsberger on his Seventy-Fifth Birthday,* Assyriological Studies 15 (Chicago, 1965), p. 399. On the root *zkr* cf. P. A. H. de Boer, *Gedenken und Gedächtnis in der Welt des A.T.* (Leipzig, 1962); B. S. Childs, *Memory and Tradition in Israel* (London, 1962); W. Schottroff, *"Gedenken" im Alten Orient und im Alten Testament* (Neukirchen, 1967).

48. See Y. Muffs, *Aramaic Papyri* (n. 20), p. 134.

49. See n. 12.

50. Compare the Latin *foedus firmare* ("to establish a pact"), cf. J. J. Rabinowitz, *Jewish Law* (New York, 1956), pp. 1–2.

51. See n. 36. For the correspondence of *ʿml* to *ʿnh,* see Gen. 41:51–52; Deut. 26:7, etc.

52. See n. 34 above.

obedience (lit., to the reverential) and (to the one who) guards the royal command."[53] This phrase is close to the biblical phrase, "the God . . . who keeps his gracious promise (*hbryt whḥsd*) to those who are loyal to him (lit., who love him) and guard his commandments" (Deut. 7:9–12), which appears in connection with the fulfillment of God's promise to the Patriarchs. A similar phrase occurs in the context of the promise of dynasty to David: "who keeps his gracious promise (*hbryt whḥsd*) to your servants who serve you wholeheartedly" (*hhlkym lpnyk bkl lbm,* 1 Kings 8:23; cf. 3:6). The grant par excellence is an act of royal benevolence arising from the king's desire to reward his loyal servant.[54] It is no wonder, then, that the gift of the land to Abraham and the assurance of dynasty to David were formulated in the style of grants to outstanding servants.

The grant and the treaty alike are named *bryt,* a word which conveys the general idea of an obligation involving two parties, similar to *riksu* in Akkadian and *išhiul* in Hittite. However, in the more developed and therefore more reflective stage of Deuteronomy one can find a distinction between the term for grant and the term for treaty. As we have seen, the Deuteronomic sources refer to the Abrahamic and Davidic covenants as *hbryt whḥsd* ("the gracious covenant"), in contradistinction of the covenants of Sinai and the Plains of Moab, which referred to *bryt* only.

The Unconditional Gift. Although the grant to Abraham and David is close in its formulation to the neo-Assyrian grants and therefore might be late, the promises themselves are much older and reflect the Hittite pattern of the grant. "Land" and

53. *ana pālihi nāṣir amāt šarrūtišu utirru gimilli dumqi,* Postgate, *Royal Grants* (no. 8), numbers 9–11.

54. Cf. F. Thureau-Dangin, "Un acte de donation," *RA* 16 (1919), p. 118: "Ces titres de propriété sont généralement des actes royaux de donation dont le bénéficiare est, soit un enfant de roi, soit un prêtre temple, soit quelque serviteur que le roi veut récompenser."

"house" (dynasty), the objects of the Abrahamic and Davidic covenants, respectively, are indeed the most prominent gifts of the suzerain in the Hittite and Syro-Palestinian political reality, and like the Hittite grants, the grant of "land" to Abraham and the grant of "house" to David are unconditional. Thus we read in the pact[55] of Hattušili III (or Thudhalya IV) with Ulmi-Tešup of Tarhuntašša:[56] "After you, your son and grandson will possess it, nobody will take it away from them. If one of your descendants sins (*u̯aštai-*) the king will prosecute him at his court. Then when he is found guilty . . . if he deserves death he will die. But nobody will take away from the descendant of Ulmi-Tešup *either his house or his land* in order to give it to a descendant of somebody else."[57] In a similar manner Muršili II reinforces the right of Kupanta-Kal to the "house and the land in spite of his father's sins."[58] A similar wording occurs in the royal decree of Tudhaliya IV and Puduhepa for the descendants of Šahurnuvaš, a Hittite high official, where we read:[59] "No-

55. In fact, this document can also be considered as a grant and, according to V. Korošec ("Einige juristische Bemerkungen zur Šahurunuva-Urkunde," *Münchener Beiträge zur Papyrusforschung und antiken Rechtsgeschichte* 35 (1945), p. 221, n. 5), is something between a grant and a treaty. Cf. also E. von Schuler, "Staasverträge und Dokumente hethitischen Rechts," *Historia,* Einzelschriften 7 (1964), p. 40.

56. *KBo* 4:10, obv. 8–14; cf. the treaty with Tarhuntašša between Thudhalya IV and Kurunta, written on a bronze tablet and edited by H. Otten, *Die Bronzetafel aus Boğazköy,* Studien zu den Boğazköy-Texten Beiheft 1 (Wiesbaden, 1988), para. 20. The connection between this treaty and the Davidic covenant has been seen by R. de Vaux, "Le roi d'Israël, vassal de Yahve," *Mélanges E. Tisserant* 1 (Rome, 1964), pp. 119–33.

57. Cf. (*KBo* 4:10), rev. 21 ff.: "Now as for what I, the sun, have given to Ulmi-Tešup . . . I have engraved on an iron tablet and in future no one shall take it away from any descendant of Ulmi-Tešup, nor shall any one litigate with him about it; the king shall not take it, but [it shall belong] to his son. To another man's descendant they shall not give it." It seems that this iron tablet was the original gift-deed.

58. J. Friedrich, *MVAeG* 31 (n. 4), (1926), no. 3:7–8 (pp. 112–15), 21–22 (pp. 134–37).

59. *KUB* 26, 43 and 50. Cf. V. Korošec, "Einige juristische Bemerkungen" (n. 55) for analysis of this document.

body in the future shall take away[60] this house from Umanava (or Tešup-manava), her children, her grandchildren and her offspring. When anyone of the descendants of U-manava provokes the anger of the kings . . . whether he is to be forgiven[61] of whether he is to be killed, one will treat him according to the wish of his master but his house they will not take away and they will not give it to somebody else."[62]

A striking parallel to these documents is found in a will of Nuzi,[63] where it says: "Tablet of Zigi . . . in favor of his wife and his sons . . . All my lands . . . to my wife Zilipkiashe have been given . . . and Zilipkiashe shall be made parent of the sons.[64] As long as Zilipkiashe is alive the sons of Zigi shall serve/respect her (*ipallahšunuti*).[65] When Zilipkiashe dies the

60. *ziladuu̲a arha lē kuiski dāi;* cf. the same formula in *KBo* 4:10, obv. 11. Cf. *urram šerram mamman la ileqqê ištu qati* PN in the grants from Ugarit written in Akkadian (PRU 3 passim), and *šḥr. ʿlmt bnš bnšm* (or *mnk mnkm* = whoever you are) *lʾ yqhṇn. bd* PN in the Ugaritic version of the grants. Compare the conveyance formula from Elephantine, *mḥr ʾw ywm ʾḥrm lʾ ʾhnṣl mnky lmntn l ʾḥrnn* ("on a future day I will not take it away from you in order to give it to the others"). (L. A. Cowley, *The Aramaic Papyri of the Fifth Century* B.C. (Oxford, 1923), pp. 7:18–19. On the correspondence between *urram šerram* and *mḥr ʾw ywm ʾḥr,* see J. J. Rabinowitz, *Jewish Law* (n. 48), (1956), p. 161. The Hebrew *mḥr* and therefore *ywm ʾḥrwn* also mean future; cf. Gen. 30:33; Exod. 13:14; Deut. 6:20; Josh. 4:6, 21; 22:24, 27 for *mḥr,* and Isa. 30:8 for *ywm ʾḥrn*. Cf. also the neo-Assyrian formula *ina šerta ina lidiš* ("some time in the future"); see Y. Muffs, *Aramaic Papyri* (n. 20), pp. 206–07.

61. *duddunu* means "to forgive"; cf. A. Goetze, "Critical Reviews of *KBo* 14 (by H. G. Güterbock)," *JCS* 18 (1964), p. 93. Cf. also F. Imparati, "Conassione de Terre," *RHA* 32 (1974), pp. 96 ff.

62. Cf. the Abban deed from Alalah, *ana šanim ul inaddin* ("he shall not give it to any one else," D. J. Wiseman, "Abban and Alalah," *JCS* 12 [1958] 1:63), and the Nuzi deed *mimma ana nakari la inandin* ("she shall not give anything [from the inheritance] to strangers," HSS 5 73:27–28). Compare the deed from Elephantine quoted above (n. 60): *lmntn l ʾḥrnn* ("to give it to the others").

63. *Excavations at Nuzi I,* HSS 5 73:1–28; cf. E. A. Speiser, "New Kirkuk Documents," *AASOR* 10, no. 20 (1930), pp. 51–52.

64. Read *a-na a-bu-ti ša mārē īteppuš* (ll. 10–11), with P. Koschaker, "Review of Scheil, *MDP* XXII," *OLZ* 35 (1932), pp. 399 f.

65. *ipallahšunuti* has to be translated as "she shall respect them," but as

sons of Zigi shall receive their inheritance portions, each according to his allotment.[66] Whoever among my sons will not obey Zilipkiashe, Zilipkiashe shall put him in the house of de[tention],[67] their mark (on the head) shall be applied to him and (they) will be put in (their) fetters,[68] but (their) right shall not be annuled[69] . . . and Zilipkiashe shall not give away anything to strangers."

The same concept lies behind the promise of the house to David and his descendants in 2 Sam. 7:8–16 where we read: "I will establish the throne of his kingdom forever, I will be his father and he shall be my son, when he sins I will chastise him with the rod of men and with human afflictions but my grace will not be removed . . . your house and your kingdom will be

---

Speiser pointed out (see., e.g., *Introduction to Hurrian, AASOR* 20 (New Haven, 1941), pp. 206 f.) this grammatical confusion is characteristic of the Hurrian scribes (cf. also Speiser, "A Significant New Will from Nuzi," *JCS* 17 (1963), p. 66 to lines 21 f.).

66. *u mārū ša Zigi attamannu kī emūqišu zitta ileqqū* (lit., "and the sons of Zigi, *whoever you are,* shall receive his inheritance portion according to his allotment." *attamannu* here is the equivalent of the Ugaritic *mnk* (mn + ka) quoted in note 58. Cf. the Canaanite and Aramaic inscriptions: *KAI* 13:3 (*my 'th*), 225:5 (*mn 't*), 259:2 (*wmn zy 't*), and Zech. 4:7: *my 'th hr hgdwl lpny Zrbbl lmyšr* ("whoever you are big mountain before Zerubabel, you will become a plain.").

67. *ina bit nu-[pa-ri] inandin;* cf. E. Cassin, "Nouvelles données sur les relations familiales à Nuzi," *RA* 57 (1963), p. 116, and M. Burrows and E. A. Speiser, eds., *One Hundred New Selected Nuzi Texts, AASOR* 16 (1935–36) (New Haven, 1936), p. 3, line 40: *ina (bīt) nupāri ittadanni;* p. 12, line 12: *bīt nupāri; nupāru* occurs in parallel with *bīt kīlī* in texts from Nuzi; see E. Cassin, "Nouvelles données," *RA* 57 (1963), p. 116.

68. *abbutašunu umaššaršu u ina kurṣišunu (GIR-šu-nu) Išakkan.* On the meaning of *abbutu* in this context, see E. Cassin, "Nouvelles données," *RA* 57 (1963), p. 116; E. Cassin, "Pouvoir de la femme et structures familiales," *RA* 63 (1969), pp. 133 f.; E. Speiser, "New Will from Nuzi" (n. 65), *JCS* 17 (1963) pp. 65 ff.

69. *kirbana la iheppe* (lit. "lump [clod] of earth [symbolizing tablet of rights] will not be broken"); cf. E. Cassin, "L'influence babylonienne à Nuzi," *JESHO* 5 (1962), p. 133; M. Malul, *Studies in Mesopotamian Legal Symbolism,* AOAT (1988), pp. 80 ff.

steadfast before me forever, your throne shall be established forever."

The phrase "I will be his father and he shall be my son" is an adoption formula[70] and actually serves as the judicial basis for the gift of the eternal dynasty. This comes to the fore in Psalms 2 where we read, "he (God) said to me: you are my son, this day[71] have I begotten you. Ask me and I will give you nations for your patrimony and the ends of the earth for your possession" (vv. 7–8).

Similarly we read in Psalms 89:[72] "I have found David my servant . . . with whom my hand shall be established, my arm shall hold him *ʾšr ydy tkwn ʿmw ʾp zrwʿy tʾmṣnw*[73] . . . I will smash his adversaries before him and will defeat his enemies . . . he will call me 'you are my father'[74] my God . . . and I will make him as my first born, the highest of the earthly kings. I will keep my grace forever and my covenant shall endure for him. Should his children forsake my law and will

70. Cf. C. Kuhl, "Neue Dokumente zum Verständnis von Hos. 2, 4–15," *ZAW* 52 (1934), pp. 102 ff.

71. *hywm* ("this day") indicates the formal initiation of a legal contract; cf. Ruth 4:9–10, 14; Gen. 25:31, 33; see G. M. Tucker, "Witnesses and 'Dates' in Israelite Contracts," *CBQ* 28 (1966), pp. 42–45. Compare S. E. Loewenstamm, "The Formula *mĕ ʿattā wĕʿad ʿōlām*," *Comparative Studies in Biblical and Ancient Oriental Literatures*. AOAT 204 (Neukirchen, 1980), pp. 166 ff., for the formula *ištu ūmi annīm* (from today) in the Akkadian documents from Alalah and Ugarit.

72. On the relationship of this Psalm to Nathan's oracle, see N. M. Sarna, "Psalm 89: A Study in Inner Biblical Exegesis," in A. Altman, ed., *Biblical and other Studies* (Philip W. Lown Institute of Advanced Judaic Studies, Brandeis University, 1963), pp. 29–46.

73. *ḥzq* and *ʾmṣ*, verbs connoting strength (cf. the pair *ḥzq* and *wʾmṣ*), when intensified by Hiphʿil or Piʿel, express the concept of keeping and holding; cf. Ps. 80:18—*thy ydk ʿl ʾyš ymynk ʿl bn ʾdm ʾmṣt lk* ("May your hand be on the man at your right, upon the man you held with you"); cf. also Isa. 41:10—*ʾmṣtyk ʾp ʿzrtyk ʾp tmktyk bymyn ṣdqy* ("I have taken hold of you and helped you. I kept you with my victorious right hand"). For an understanding of *ʾmṣ* in Ps. 80:18 and Isa. 41:10 I am indebted to the late Prof. H. L. Ginsberg.

74. Cf. Jer. 3:4, 19, and see below.

not follow my decrees . . . I will punish their rebellion with the rod and their sin with afflictions. But I will never annul my grace with him and shall not betray my pact (*wlʾ ʾšqr bʾmwnty*)[75] (with him). I will not profane my covenant and alter what came out of my lips."

"House" (dynasty), land, and peoples are then given to David as a fief, and as was the rule in the second millennium this gift could be legitimized only by adoption.[76] That this is really the case here may be learned from the treaty between Šupilluliuma and Mattiwaza.[77] Mattiwaza (or Kurtiwaza), in describing how he established relations with Šuppiluliuma, says: "(The great king) grasped me with [his ha]nd . . . and said: when I will conquer the land of Mittanni I shall not reject you, I shall make you my son,[78] I will stand by (to help in war) and will make you sit on the throne of your father . . . the word which comes out of his mouth will not turn back."[79] A similar adoption imagery is to be found in the bilingual of Hattu-

75. Cf. Sefire, p. 3, line 7—*šqrtm bʿdyʾ ʾln* ("You will have been false to this treaty"); see W. Moran, "Recensiones, G. W. Ahlström, *Psalm 89*," *Biblica* 42 (1961), p. 239. *ʾmwnh* here and in v. 50 has the same meaning as *ʾmnh* in Neh. 10:1 (cf. J. C. Greenfield, "Stylistic Aspects of the Sefire Treaty Inscriptions," *Acta Orientalia* 29 [1965], p. 8). *ʾmwnh* in 2 Kings 12:16 and 22:7 also, in my opinion, means pact or contract, and the reason for not calling to account the people in charge of the work was that they were bound by the oath to deal honestly. On the loyalty oath of craftsmen, see D. B. Weisberg, *Guild Structure and Political Allegiance in Early Achaemenid Mesopotamia* (New Haven, 1967).

76. Cf., e.g., Yarimlim of Alalah, who is named son of Abban (see Wiseman, *AT* *444a, [n. 7] seal impression) but actually was the son of Hammurabi (*AT* *1:9; cf. *444b). According to A. Alt, "Bemerkungen zu den Verwaltungs-und Rechtsurkunden von Ugarit und Alalach," *Die Welt des Orients,* Band 3, Heft 1–2 (1964), pp. 14 ff., Abban adopted Yarimlim in order to create the legal basis for installing him as king of Haleb.

77. Weidner, *Politische Dokumente* (n. 4), no. 2, lines 24 ff. (pp. 40–41).

78. *ana mārūtija ēppuškami. Ana marūti epēšu* means to adopt as a son; cf. E. A. Speiser, "New Kirkuk Documents Relating to Family Laws," *AASOR* 10 (1930), pp. 7 ff. Cf. also below.

79. *amātu ša ina pīšu uṣṣu ana kutallišu ul itār.*

šili I.[80] In this document, which actually constitutes a testament, we read:[81] "Behold, I declared for you the young Labarna: He shall sit on the throne, I, the king called him my son";[82] "he is for you the offspring of my Sun" (he is for you the offspring of his majesty).[83] On the other hand, when he speaks of his rejected daughter he says, "She did not call me father, I did not call her 'my daughter,' "[84] which reminds us of Psalms 89:27: "He will say to me: 'you are my father . . . and I will appoint (*ntn*) him as my first born' " (compare Jer. 3:4, 19, and see below, pp. 246–47).

Hattušili I himself is similarly described as adopted and legitimized by the sun goddess of Arinna: "She put him into her bosom, grasped his hand and ran (in battle) before him."[85] According to Psalms 89, David is also grasped and held by God's hand, as a result of which he succeeds in the battles with his enemies (vv. 22–26).[86] If the emendation of Psalms 2:7 is

80. F. Sommer and A. Falkenstein, *Die hethitisch-akkadische Bilingue des Hattušili I (Labarna II),* Abhandlungen der bayerischen Akademie der Wissenschaften, Phil.-hist. Abt. N.F. 16, 1938.

81. *u a-nu-um-ma TUR-am la-ba-ar-na [aq-b]i-a-ak-ku-nu-ši-im šu-u li-it-ta-ša-ab-mi LUGAL-ru [al]-si-šu-ma DUMU(?)-am* (in Hittite, [*nu-uš-ma-aš TUR-la-an] la-ba-ar-na-an te-nu-un [a-pa-a-aš-ua-aš-ša-an e-ša-ru LUGAL-ša-an-za] DUMU-la-ma-an hal-zi-ih-hu-un* (1/2; 2–4). The Akkadian *qabû* is equivalent to the Hittite *te* and the Hebrew *'mr.* In this context they have the same connotation as *'mr 'ly* in Ps. 2:7, "proclaim" or "declare." The newly appointed king is not the real son of Hattusili but the son of his sister, who is being adopted.

82. Compare 1/2:37: "Behold, Muršili is now my son."

83. 2:44: NUMUN ^{d}UTU^{si} .KU .NU. Compare the Akkadian *ana marūti nadānu* in the sense of adopting; see S. M. Paul, "Adoption Formulae," *Eretz Israel* 14, *H. L. Ginsberg Volume* (1978), p. 34 (Hebrew).

84. 3:24–25.

85. [5] *ana sūnišu iškunšu u qāssu iṣbatsu, ina pānišu irtup alakam, KBo* 10, 1 Vs. 13–14 (cf. H. Otten, "Keilschrifttexte," *MDOG* 91 [1958], p. 79 and A. Goetze, "Review of *KBo* X," *JCS* 16 [1962], p. 125). For the corresponding Hittite restoration (*KBo* 10, 2 Vs. 1:28–30), see H. A. Hoffner, "Birth and Name-Giving in Hittite Texts," *JNES* 27 (1968), p. 201, note 27.

86. According to H. L. Ginsberg (private communication), Isa. 41:9 ff., which also deals with grasping the hand and helping against enemies,

correct, then the idea of the heir placed into the bosom of his adoptant also occurs in connection with David.[87] It is also not without significance that the promise of Šupilluliuma to Kurtiwaza, as well as God's promise to David (v. 35), are accompanied by the declaration that the suzerain will not alter his word. Psalms 132:12 also says that "the lord swore to David in truth from which he will not turn away."

The notion of sonship within the promise of dynasty comes then to legitimize the grant of dynasty. It has nothing to do with mythology; it is a purely forensic metaphor. The metaphor is taken from the familial sphere,[88] as may be seen from the quoted Nuzi will. In this document, the father decrees that in case of disorder the rebellious son might be chained and confined but his inheritance rights will not be canceled. The same concept is reflected in 2 Samuel 7, where the phrase *hwkḥ bšbṭ* ("chastening with the rod") is used, which in other places occurs in a didactic context (cf., e.g., Prov. 13:24, 23:14). Furthermore, on the basis of the comparison with the familial documents from Nuzi, the phrase "rod of men" (*ʾnšym*) and afflictions of the sons of man (*bny ʾdm*) may now be properly

---

refers to the election of Abraham (cf. end of v. 8), which supports our view about the common typology of the Davidic and Abrahamic covenants. On "grasping the hand" in Deutero-Isaiah and the corresponding neo-Babylonian royal imagery, see S. Paul, "Deutero-Isaiah and Cuneiform Royal Inscriptions," *JAOS* 88 (1968), p. 182, n. 19.

87. *ʾspw ʾl ḥyqy, ʾmr ʾylyw* ("I will gather him to my bosom, I will say to him") instead of *ʾsprh ʾl ḥq, yhwh ʾmr ʾly* ("I will recite the law, YHWH said to me"). Cf. H. Gunkel, *Psalmen,* HKAT (Göttingen, 1929) ad loc., which follows Torczyner. For *ʾsp* in the sense of adoption, see Ps. 27:10.

88. Cf. Ruth 4:6 and see Hoffner, "Birth," etc., *JNES* (n. 85). We must admit however, that putting into the bosom as such does not necessarily indicate adoption; it may just as well signify care and protection. T. Jacobsen ("Parerga Sumerologica," *JNES* 2 [1943], p. 120) denies that nourishing by the goddess or placing on her knee in Sumero-Akkadian literature implies adoption. Similarly, giving birth on one's knees in the Old Testament (Gen. 16:2; 30:3; 50:23) does not necessarily imply adoption; see J. Tigay, "Adoption," *Encyclopedia Judaica* 2, cols. 298–301.

understood. In the so-called *tuppi šīmti* documents from Nuzi published[89] and analyzed by Speiser,[90] we find often, in connection with the provisions about obedience to the adoptive father,[91] phrases such as "If PN_1 (the adopted child) fails to show respect for PN_2 (the adoptive father) then just as a man treats his son too shall PN_2 treat PN_1."[92] Another document says that "just as one treats the citizen of Arrapha, so should PN_1 treat PN_2: he shall put fetters upon his feet, place a mark on his hand, and put him in the house of detention."[93] The intention is clear: the son given into adoption has the duties of a son (i.e., respecting his parents) but has also the privileges of a son: he has to be treated like the son of a free citizen and not like a slave. This is implied in another document of this collection, where the father says that the adoptive parent "may act as though she were I."[94] This kind of privilege for the adopted can be traced back to the Old Babylonian period. In a document of adoption by manumission, the master of the manumitted slave says, "If Zugagu will say to his father Sinabušu 'you are not my father' they will impose upon him the punish-

89. E. R. Lacheman, *Excavations at Nuzi VIII: Family Law Documents,* HSS 19 (Cambridge, Mass., 1962).

90. E. A. Speiser, "A Significant New Will from Nuzi," *JCS* 17 (1963), pp. 65–71; cf. also E. Cassin, "Nouvelles données sur les relations familiales à Nuzi," *RA* 57 (1963), pp. 113–19.

91. This means, of course, anybody who assumes parenthood of the children (*ana abbūti*) as, for instance, the wife or the daughter of the one who draws the will.

92. *šumma* PN_1=PN_2 *lā [ipal]lahšu u kīme awēlu māršu huddumumma ippuš kinannama huddumumma ippuš* (JEN 572:26–31). Cf. the analysis of this passage by Speiser (n. 90), pp. 68–69. According to Speiser, *huddumumma epēšu* means to discipline. Cassin (n. 90), p. 116 translates it as "enfermer."

93. *kīme māršu ša awīl Arraphe ippušu, kinannama* PN_1=PN_2 *ippuššuma, kurṣa ina šēpešu išakkan, abbuta ina qaqqadišu išakkan, ina bīt kīlī inandin* (*Nuzi VIII,* HSS 19, 39:16–23) (n. 89); cf. Speiser (n. 90), p. 69; E. Cassin, "Pouvoir," *RA* 63 (1969), p. 134 (n. 68).

94. *k[īma] yâši eteppuš* (*Nuzi VIII,* HSS 19, 19:31–32) (n. 89); cf. Speiser, "New Will from Nuzi," (n. 90), p. 70 and n. 22 for the grammatical problem involved.

ment of the free born,"[95] i.e., he will not be enslaved but disciplined as the son of a free citizen.[96]

What is meant, then, in 2 Samuel 7:14, is that when David's descendants sin they will be disciplined like rebellious sons by their father,[97] but they will not be alienated. One must say that this lenient approach toward rebellious sons was not the rule in familial relationship in the ancient Near East. On the contrary, in most cases rebelliousness brought about the dissolution of sonship, be it sonship by birth or by adoption.[98] Among the quoted adoption documents from Nuzi we find that the adoptive parent may chastise the disobedient son but may also disinherit him if he wants.[99] Similarly, we find that the Hittite suzerain did not always grant land unconditionally. In a land

95. *PN ana PN abišu ula abi atta iqabbīma, aran mārū awīlē immidušu* (M. Schorr, *Urkunden* [n. 10], 1913, 23:23–27, p. 46).

96. Contrary to Schorr (ibid.), who understands it as deprivation of freedom, i.e., enslavement.

97. B. Jacob ("Das hebräische Sprachgut im Christlich-Palästinischen," (*ZAW* 22 (1902), pp. 91–92) interprets *bšbṭ ʾnšym wbngʿy bny ʾdm* ("Schlage wie sie die Kinder vom Vater erhalten d.h. aus Liebe und daher mit Maassen," which generally fits our understanding of the phrase. However, his interpretation of *ʾdm* and *ʾnšym* as "parents," literally (on the basis of the Palestinian Syriac *ʾnšwtʾ*), is not warranted. It might as well be understood as "human" (cf. Hos. 11:4, *bḥbly ʾdm ʾmškm bʿbtt ʾhbh* ("I drew them with human cords, with bands of love.")

98. Cf., e.g., CH, 168–69 and the discussion in G. R. Driver and J. C. Miles' *The Babylonian Laws* 1 (Oxford, 1952), pp. 348–49, 395–405. These laws apply to the real son as well as the adopted, as may be learned from a Nuzi document (*Nuzi I,* HSS 5 [n. 63], p. 7), where it is stated that the adopted son might be disinherited following repeated trials (11.25 ff.), which is similar in attitude to CH, 168–69, according to which the son is to be disinherited only after being brought up before the judges for the second time. Compare Deut. 21:18–21, where the rebellious son is to be condemned to death only after being previously chastised. For dissolution of sonship as a result of disobedience, cf. also RS 8.145 (F. Thureau-Dangin, "Trois contrats de Ras-Shamra," *Syria* 18 [1937], pp. 249–50).

99. PN *kurṣi inandinšu abbuta umaššarsu, ina bīt kīlī inandin, šumma hašihšu kirba[na] iheppe u ukaššašu k[īma] yâši eteppuš* ("PN may put fetters upon him, apply the slave mark to him, put him in the house of detention or, if it pleases her, break the clump of clay to disinherit him [*kuššudu*], she may act as though she were I" (*Nuzi VIII,* HSS 19, 19:28–32) (n. 89).

grant of Muršili II to Abiradda, the Hittite suzerain guarantees the rights of DU-Tešup, Abiradda's son, to throne, house, and land, only on the condition that DU-Tešup will not sin (*u̯aštai-*) against his father.[100] The unconditional promise is therefore a special privilege and apparently given for extraordinarily loyal service.

In connection with David, this privilege is also reflected in that David is given the right of the first born. As is now known to us from Nuzi, Alalah, Ugarit and Palestine,[101] the father had the right to select a "firstborn" as well as to make all his heirs share alike,[102] and was not bound by the law of primogeniture.[103] Needless to say, the selection of the firstborn elevated the chosen son to a privileged position in the family and thus entitled him to a double share in the inheritance. Indeed, the phrase *bkwr ʾtnhw* (Ps. 89:28) means "I will *appoint* him or make him firstborn," which speaks for a given right and not one acquired by nature. The titles "son" and "firstborn" are also attested among Mesopotamian kings; see M. J. Seux, *Éphithètes royales Akkadiennes et Sumériennes,* pp. 42–44.

In fact, not only David is named the firstborn to God; Israel itself is called by God "my son the firstborn Israel" (Exod.

100. F. Hrozny, *Hethitische Keilschrifttexte aus Boghazköi,* Boghazköi Studien 3 (Leipzig, 1919), pp. 142–44, vs. 2:10–18; J. Friedrich, "Aus dem hethitischen Schrifttum, 2 Heft," *Der Alte Orient* 24:3 (1925), p. 20, lines 10–18; cf. also E. Cavaignac, "L'affaire de Iaruvatta," *RHA* 6 (Jan. 1932), p. 196; H. Klengel, "Der Schiedsspruch des Muršili II," *Orientalia,* N.S. 32 (1963), pp. 35–36, 41–42.

101. Cf. I Mendelsohn, "On the Preferential Status of the Eldest Son," *BASOR* 156 (Dec. 1959), pp. 38–40 and the references there.

102. Cf., e.g., *ina libbišunu ša māriya rabi yānu* ("there is none among them who shall be the oldest,") *Nuzi VIII* (n. 89) HSS 19 23:5–6; cf. 17:12–13; see Speiser, "New Will from Nuzi," *JCS* 17 (1963), p. 66 (n. 65) and the discussion on p. 70.

103. This is prohibited in the Deuteronomic Code (21:15–17). The Deuteronomic Law stands in clear contradiction to Gen. 48:13–20, where Joseph, the son of the loved woman Rachel, is given the double share while Reuben, the son of the "unloved" Leah (cf. Gen. 29:33—*śnwʾh*), is repudiated as the firstborn.

4:22; cf. Jer. 31:8), and as the adoption of David is supposed to legitimize the inheritance of nations, i.e., the Davidic empire, the adoption of Israel by God is supposed to validate the gift of land. Though this is not expressed explicitly in the Pentateuch it is clearly indicated in a prophetic text (Jer. 3:19), where we read, "I said I will surely[104] put you among the sons (I will adopt you as a son, *w'nky 'mrty 'yk ('k) 'šytk bbnym*)[105] and give you a pleasant land, the goodliest heritage of the host of nations, and I said you shall call me my father[106] and you will not turn away from me." The phrase *'šytk bbnym* ("I will put you among the sons") undoubtedly alludes to adoption, as Ehrlich indicated, and as such anticipates the inheritance of the land.[107]

The use of familial metaphors to express relationships belonging to the royal-national sphere should not surprise us, since the whole diplomatic vocabulary of the second millennium B.C.E.[108] is rooted in the familial sphere. For instance,

104. Read *'akh* instead of *'ēykh;* cf. A. Ehrlich, *Randglossen zur hebr. Bibel,* ad loc.

105. Cf. the new JPS translation of *The Torah* (Philadelphia, 1978): "I had resolved to adopt you as my son." Cf. in the Azitawadda inscription, *w'p b'bt pʿln kl mlk* ("and every king made me his father [his suzerain]"); see N. H. Tur-Sinai (Torczyner), *The Language and the Book II,* 2d ed. (Jerusalem, 1964), p. 76 (Hebrew). The Greek *poieīsthai* (the Hebrew *pʿl,* the Akkadian *epēšu*) or *thesthai* (the Hebrew *śym, šyt*) are the verbs used for adoption. *wyśymw bnym* in Ezra 10:44 implies adoption (cf. S. Feigin, "Some Cases of Adoption in Israel," *JBL* 50 [1931], pp. 196 ff., though we do not accept his restoration). For the Akkadian *ana abbūti epēšu* as adoption see the discussion by S. M. Paul, "Adoption Formulae" (n. 83), pp. 33, n. 23.

106. Inheritance of land in connection with divine sonship (*bny 'l*) occurs in Deut. 32:8 (Septuagint and Qumran). Compare the cone of Enmetena of Lagash, "Enlil, the king of all the lands, the father of all the gods, marked off the boundary for Ningirsu (god of Lagash) and Shara (god of Umma) by his steadfast word" (Cone A, 1–7); cf. F. Thureau-Dangin, *Die sumerischen und akkadischen Königinschriften* (Leipzig, 1907), p. 36; J. S. Cooper, *Presargonic Inscriptions* (New Haven, 1986), p. 55.

107. Cf. above, p. 241.

108. Cf. J. Munn-Rankin, "Diplomacy in Western Asia in the Early Second Millennium B.C.," *Iraq* 18 (1956), pp. 68 ff.

the relationship between the states is defined as *abbūtu* = fathership (suzerainty); *mārūtu* = sonship (vassalship); *ahhūtu* = brotherhood (parity relationship). The phrase *itti nakrīya lū nakrata itti salmīya lū salmata,* "with my enemy be an enemy, with my friend be a friend," which is so common in the Hittite-Ugaritic treaties,[109] is already found in the Elamite treaty of the third millennium B.C.E.[110] This phrase is found in an Old Babylonian marriage contract in which we read *zenî ša* PN_1 PN_2 *izenni salāmiša isallim* = "PN_2 (the second wife) will be angry with whom PN_1 (the first wife) will be angry, she will be on good terms with whom PN_1 will be on good terms.[111] Similarly, we read in a Mari adoption document, *damaqišunu idammiq lemenišunu ilemmin* ("their joy will be his joy, their sorrow will be his sorrow").[112] The close relationship of familial and political alliances has also been seen long ago by N. Glueck,[113] who says, "Allies had the same rights and obligations as those who were blood relatives."

Thus, the gift of land to Abraham and the gift of kingship to David are formulated in the way Hittite grants used to be formulated, particularly those grants bestowing gifts upon privileged vassals. Contrary to the prevalent law in the Hittite

109. Cf. *PRU* 4, pp. 36, 49 passim. From the Hittites it passed to the Greeks; see my article "Covenant Terminology," (n. 12) *JAOS* 93 (1973), p. 198 and note 103.

110. Cf. W. Hinz, "Elams Vertrag mit Naram-Sin von Akkade," *ZA* 24 (1967), pp. 66 ff. See also the text in *Baghdader Mitteilungen* 2 [1963], p. 54 [W 19900], 147, which according to F. R. Kraus ("*Baghdader Mitteilungen* 2 (1963) herausgegeben vom Deutschen Archäologischen Institut, Abteilung Baghdad," *Bibliotheca Orientalis* 22 [1965], p. 289) is part of a treaty, where we read: *[lu a-n]a-ki-ir [is-l]i-mu lu-u a-sa-li-im.*

111. M. Schorr, *Urkunden des altbabylonischen Zivil—und Prozessrechts,* VAB 5 (Leipzig, 1913), 4:21–23; cf. 5:7–8; Schorr's translation is wrong and Ungnad's is incorrect; see p. 11 there. Cf. *CAD* v. 21 (Z) *zenû* b.

112. ARM 8, 1:4–5. R. Yaron, "Varia on Adoption," *Journal of Juristic Papyrology* 15 (1965), pp. 173–75, discussed this text in the context of some of the above-mentioned texts and reached similar conclusions.

113. *Hesed in the Bible* (n. 17) (Cincinnati, 1967), p. 46.

kingdom,[114] in Ugarit,[115] and in Alalah,[116] according to which the property of the condemned is to be confiscated, in the cited documents the property of the condemned cannot be taken away.

It was the Deuteronomist, the redactor of the Book of Kings, who put the promise of David under a condition (1 Kings 2:4; 8:25; 9:4 f.), as did Deuteronomy with the promise to the Patriarchs.[117] The exile of Northern Israel, the destruction of Jerusalem, and the disruption of the dynasty refuted, of course, the claim of the eternity of the Abrahamic and Davidic covenants, thereby necessitating a reinterpretation of the covenants. This was done by making them conditional, i.e., by asserting that the covenant is eternal only if the donee keeps his loyalty to the donor. It is true, even in the predeuteronomic documents, that the loyalty of David's sons and the sons of the Patriarchs is somehow presupposed,[118] but it is never formulated as the condition for national existence as in the Deuteronomic literature. In the JE source, Israel is never threatened with destruction for violating the law. The non-observance of the covenant will certainly bring punishment (Exod. 33:33; 34:12) but no annihilation. Even the parenetic section of Exodus 19:5–6, which sounds like a condition, is in fact a prom-

114. Cf., e.g., Friedrich, *Staatsverträge* (n. 4), no. 3, 7C:13–17 (pp. 112 ff.); V. Korošec, "Juristische Bemerkungen," (n. 53), pp. 218 ff., although the different attitudes toward the condemned do not reflect a historical development, as Korošec puts it, but might be explained as a double standard: to the privileged on the one hand and to the unprivileged on the other.

115. *PRU* 3, 16.249:22–29 (pp. 97–98); 16.145 (p. 169, *bēl arni*).

116. *AT* no. 17 (p. 40—*bēl mašikti*). See S. E. Loewenstamm, "Notes on the Alalah Tablets," *Comparative Studies in Biblical and Ancient Oriental Literatures,* AOAT 20 (Neukirchen, 1980), pp. 23–26.

117. It is significant that in spite of frequent references to the promise of the Patriarchs, Deuteronomy never mentions the eternity of this promise (*ʿd ʿwlm, ldwrwtm, bryt ʿwlm*), in contrast to JE and P; see below.

118. Cf. Gen. 18:19. This is an expectation and not a condition.

ise and not a threat: "If you will obey me faithfully and keep my covenant you shall be treasured possession (*sglh*).[119] Indeed all the earth is mine but you shall be to me a kingdom of priests and a holy nation."[120] The observance of loyalty in this passage is not a condition for the fulfillment of God's grace, as in Deuteronomy (cf. 7:12 f., 11:13 f.), but a prerequisite for high and extraordinary status.

The priestly code also, in spite of the curses and the threat of exile in Leviticus 26, does not end with the breach of the covenant; on the contrary, it has God saying: "Even when they are in the land of their enemies I will not reject them or spurn them so as to destroy them, violating my covenant with them

119. For the meaning of *sglh* and its Akkadian equivalent *sikiltum,* see M. Greenberg, "Hebrew *segullā:* Akkadian *sikiltu,*" *JAOS* 71 (1951), pp. 172 ff. Cf. now *PRU* 5, 60 (18.38), 11.7–12 (p. 84), where the Ugaritic vassal is called the *sglt* of his suzerain, which is rendered by C. Virolleaud as *propriété*. The *sglt* in the Ugaritic text now elucidates the *sglh* in the Pentateuch. It seems that *sglt* and *sglh* belong to the treaty and covenant terminology and that they are employed to distinguish the special relationships of the suzerains to their vassals. On the basis of Ugaritic, Biblical and also Alalahian evidence (cf. the seal impression in D. J. Wiseman, *AT,* pl. 3, where the king Abban is said to be the *sikiltum* of the goddess), we may safely say that the basic meaning of the root *sakālu* is to set aside a thing or certain property either with good intention (as Israel is set aside from other nations) or with an evil purpose, as in CH 141 and other Babylonian sources. Cf. the discussion by M. Held, in "A Faithful Lover in an Old Babylonian Dialogue," *JCS* 15 (1961), pp. 11–12. For the Ugaritic text, cf. also H. B. Huffmon and S. B. Parker, "A Further Note on the Treaty Background of Hebrew *yadaʿ*," *BASOR* 184 (1966), pp. 36 ff.; E. E. Loewenstamm, "*Am Segulla,*" *Hebrew Languages Studies Presented to Z. ben-Hayyim* (Jerusalem, 1983), pp. 321–28.

120. As a reward for her loyalty, Israel will in turn be God's most precious possession—she will be God's priesthood. A similar idea is indeed expressed in the consolation prophecy in Isa. 61:6: "And you shall be called the priests of YHWH. You will be named servants of our God, you shall eat the wealth of the nations and in their splendor you shall excel." For a thorough discussion of this passage see W. L. Moran, "A Kingdom of Priests," in J. McKenzie, ed., *The Bible in Current Catholic Thought* (1962), pp. 7–20.

(*lhpr bryty 'tm*). I will remember in their favor[121] the covenant with the ancients (*wzkrty lhm bryt r'šnym*)" (Lev. 26:44–45). Deuteronomy, however, concludes chapter 28 with the threat that the people will be sent back to Egypt, and no allusion to the grace of the covenant is made.[122]

The Covenant with Abraham in Genesis 15[123]. In light of our analysis we properly understand the nature of the covenant in Genesis 15: God as the suzerain commits himself and swears, as it were, to keep the promise.[124] It is he, accompanied by a smoking kiln and a blazing torch (*tnwr ʿšn wlpyd 'š*),[125] who passes between the parts as though he were invoking the curse upon himself.

A similar oath occurs in the Abban-Yarimlim deed, where Abban, the donor, takes the oath by cutting the neck of a lamb (*kišād 1 immeru iṭbuh*), saying "(may I be cursed) if I take back what I gave you."[126] In another document, which completes

121. Cf. above, pp. 234–35.

122. Deut. 30:1–10 and 4:29–31 are of a later origin and revolve around the Deuteronomic doctrine of return to God; cf. H. W. Wolff, "Das Kerygma des deuteronomistischen Geschichtswerks," *ZAW* 73 (1961), pp. 180 ff., and recently M. Weinfeld, *Deuteronomy 1–11,* Anchor Bible (New York, 1991), pp. 216–17.

123. See the bibliography in C. Westermann, *Genesis* I BK 14 (Neukirchen, 1979), pp. 247–50.

124. On the covenant with Abraham in Gen. 15 as representing an oath, cf. Lohfink, *Die Landverheissung* (n. 1), pp. 11–23.

125. Compare the Sinaitic theophany where God appears in fire and smoke; cf. Exod. 19:18, "for YHWH had come down upon it in fire ('š) and the smoke (ʿšn) rose like the smoke of a kiln." In the commentary of the Syrian church father Ephrem (quoted by T. Zachariae; see J. C. Greenfield, "An Ancient Treaty Ritual and its Targumic Echo," *Salvacion en la Palabra, Targum - Derash - Berith: Homenaje al Profesor A. Diez Macho* [Madrid, 1985], p. 395), we find the tradition "that the Chaldeans would solemnize a pact by passing through the dissecting parts holding torches."

126. D. J. Wiseman, "Abban and Alalah," *JCS* 12 (1958), p. 126, lines 39–42; cf. n. 10 above. In the continuation Abban states that if Yarimlim

the data of this gift, we read: "On that day Abban in exchange for Irridi gave the city. . . . On that day Yarimlim delivered (or brought up) to Ištar . . . ,"[127] which seems to reflect a situation similar to that of the covenant in Genesis 15, i.e., that the inferior party delivers the animals while the superior swears the oath.

In Alalah as in Genesis 15 the animals slaughtered at the scene of the covenant are considered sacrificial offerings.[128] That the act of cutting the neck of the animal is of sacrificial nature may be learned from another covenantal description in Alalah, where we read, "the neck of a sacrificial lamb was cut in the presence of PN the general."[129] A later Alalahian cove-

---

betrays him he will forfeit his territory, thus making the gift conditional. We must, however, keep in mind that the deed of Abban to Yarimlim is not a deed of grant but rather of exchange. Alalah was given to Yarimlim in place of the destroyed Irridi. The gift of Alalah is therefore not a reward for loyal service as is the case in grants but part of a political arrangement between two parties.

127. *ina ūmišu Yarimlim . . . [ana [d]] Ištar ušēlî,* reading with *CAD* E, p. 130[c]. According to Lohfink (*Landverheissung* [n. 1], pp. 93 ff.) the tradition of Gen. 15:7 ff. reflects an incubation dream in a sanctuary (Hebron or Shechem). If true, this might be an additional parallel with the Alalah covenant.

128. Cf. *Jubilees* 14:9 ff.; Pseudo-Philo, *Biblical Antiquities* 23:6–7; Apocalypse of Abraham 9–15; Josephus, *Antiquities* 1, § 183–85; see C. T. Begg, "Rereadings of the 'Animal Rite' of Gen. 15 in Early Jewish Narratives," *CBQ* 50 (1988), pp. 36–46. For the sacrificial nature of the offerings brought to the ceremony in Gen. 15, see E. Loewenstamm, "Zur Traditionsgeschichte des Bundes zwischen den Stücken," *VT* 18 (1968), pp. 500 ff. (in English in *AOAT* 204, [1980], pp. 273–80). However, in view of the evidence presented here, we cannot accept his opinion that the sacrifice is a late element in the tradition of Gen. 15.

129. AT* 54:16–18: GÚ SILÁ *a-sa-ki* IGI PN UGULA UKÚ.UŠ *ṭa-bi-ih* (cf. A. Draffkorn "King Abba-AN" (n. 7), *JCS* 13 (1959), p. 95, n. 11). The presence of the general at this transaction may be paralleled with Gen. 21:22 f. and the Yahwistic counterpart in 26:26 ff., where the covenant between Abimelech and Abraham and Isaac, respectively, is made in the presence of Phicol the general. For *Ahuzzat mereʿehu,* who joins Phicol in 26:26, cf. Jonathan D. Safran, "Ahuzzath and the Pact of

nantal text[130] tells us about offerings[131] in connection with the oath of the vassal Idrimi to his Hurrian suzerain.[132] The ancient covenant in Exodus 24 is wholly based upon sacrifices, and the secular Patriarchal covenants are also ratified by sacrifices (Gen. 21:27).[133]

In Greece, too, sacrifices were offered at the covenant ceremony.[134] Thus we read in the *Iliad* 3:103–07 that for the covenant with the Achaeans the Trojans bring two lambs and a ram and prepare libations (3:268 ff.). Furthermore, as in Genesis 15:9, in Greece three animals (*trityes*), a bull, a ram, and a boar, were usually taken for the covenantal rite.[135] The offerings of the *lustrum* in Rome also consisted of three animals (*souvetaurilia*), a boar, a sheep and a bull (*sus, ovis, taurus*), and accord-

---

Beer-Sheba," in M. Cogan, ed., *Beer-Sheva* 2: *Presented to S. Abramsky on his Retirement* (Jerusalem, 1985), pp. 121–30 (Hebrew). According to Safran, *mrʿhw* is equivalent to *merhum* in Mari, who is in charge of the pasture lands.

130. S. Smith, *The Statue of Idri-mi* (London, 1949); for a thorough investigation of this inscription see E. L. Greenstein and D. Marcus, "The Akkadian Inscription of Idrimi," *The Journal of the Ancient Near Eastern Society of Columbia University* 8 (1976), pp. 59–96.

131. See lines 55–56—SISKUR *(niqê) ušarbi* (I multiplied offerings); compare lines 89–90.

132. E. Szlechter, "Les tablettes juridiques datées du règne d'Abî-ešuẖ conservées au Musée d'art et d'histoire de Genève," *JCS* 7 (1953), p. 92, 5:16–17; A. Goetze, "Critical Review of S. Smith *The Statue of Idri-mi*," *JCS* 4 (1950), p. 228, n. 20.

133. We are told there that Abraham gave seven lambs to Abimelech as a "witness" (*ʿdh*) or as Speiser (*Genesis,* Anchor Bible, ad loc.) translates, a "proof" for his rights on the well. A similar procedure is found in an old Babylonian act of partition where one of the partners gives to the other two lambs as a proof of the agreement (E. Szlechter, *JCS* 7 [1953], p. 92, 5:16–17). Compare also A. Goetze, *JCS* 4 (1950), p. 228, n. 20.

134. Cf. P. Stengel, *Die griechische Kultusaltertümer,* 3d ed. (Berlin, 1920), p. 119, n. 7; 137; M. P. Nillson, *Geschichte des griechischen Religion* 1, 3d ed. (Munich, 1967), pp. 139 ff.; W. Burkert, *Griechische Religion* (Stuttgart, 1977), pp. 133 ff.

135. Cf. P. Stengel, *Griechische Kultusaltertümer* (n. 134), pp. 119, 137 f.

ing to Dionysius of Halicarnassus, the triple sacrifice consisted of a bull, a ram and a goat,[136] as in Genesis 15:9.

This tradition of covenantal sacrifices goes back to the third millennium B.C.E. In the treaty between Lagash and Umma, recorded on the stele of the vultures, we hear about sacrificing a bull[137] and two doves.[138] The doves remind us of the pigeon and the turtledove in Genesis 15, whereas the NINDA + GUD (fattened bull), which equals Akkadian *bīru*, is in many cases three years old[139] and may therefore be paralleled with

136. It was pointed out that the later Greeks sometimes performed such sacrifices and the knowledge of such sacrifices may have misled the scribe of the work of Dionysius; see E. Cary, *Dionysius Halicarnassensis*, (Loeb Classical Library, Harvard University Press, 1939), pp. 338–39.

137. Rev. 1:37–40, *Utu lugal ni-sig*[10]*-ga-ra larsam (ki) e-babbar* NINDÁ + GUD-*še an-ku*, which is translated by E. Sollberger (*Le système verbal dans les inscriptions "royales" presargoniques de Lagaš*, [Geneva, 1952], example 161), a Utu, le roi étincelant, à Larsa dans l'Ebabbar, j'y ai fait le sacrifice (alimentaire). Compare id., *Inscriptions royales Sumériennes et Akkadiennes* (Paris, 1971), p. 54. The passage is not altogether clear; some scholars take the phrase to mean that the doves were offered *like sacrificial bulls* (see J. S. Cooper, *Presargonic Inscriptions* [New Haven, 1986], p. 36 and the references there, pp. 33–34), but in the other paragraphs the doves are being released and not sacrificed. Cf. also G. Steiner, "Der Grenzvertrag Zwischen Lagaš und Umma," *Acta Sumerologica* 8 (1986), pp. 219 ff. C. T. Begg ("The Covenantal Dove in Ps. 84:19–20," *VT* 37 [1987], pp. 78–80), interprets Ps. 84:19–20, where *twr* (dove) is mentioned next to *běrit* (covenant), on the basis of Gen. 15:9, 17.

138. "Two doves on whose eyes he had put kohl (and) on whose heads he had strewn cedar he released them to Enlil at Nippur (with the plea): 'As long as days exist . . . if the Ummaite . . . breaks his word . . .' "

139. Cf. *bīru* B, *CAD*, vol. 2 (B) p. 266. The three-year-old bull in 1 Sam. 1:24 (Septuagint and Qumran) and the three-year animals in Gen. 15 do not therefore reflect precisely a Shilonite tradition, as Loewenstamm contends (loc cit). It seems that the three-year-old animal was considered of good quality in general; cf., e.g., 1 *immeru ša šullušītu damqu* ("one three-year-old sheep of good quality" (C. J. Gadd, *Tablets from Kirkuk*, *RA* 23 [1926], p. 154, no. 47.15); *šullušīta enza* ("a three-year old she goat") in connection with a feast (*Anatolian Studies* 6 [1956], p. 152:15, 44); *l alpu šulušša ešru sa . . . PN ana Ebabbara iddinu* ("the three-year old ox, the tithe which PN has given to Ebabbara") (J. N. Strassmaier, *Inschriften von Nabonidus, König von Babylon* [Leipzig, 1889], no. 1071:1). For cattle

Genesis 15:9. An offering of a similar kind, though in a different context (lustration), is found in Leviticus 14:4, 49, where two birds are taken, along with cedar wood, crimson stuff, and hyssop.

Release of birds for lustration is very common in Mesopotamia and Anatolia.[140] Especially instructive are the Hittite lustrations, where we find, as in Leviticus, cords of red wool, etc., put on the head of the substitute like a crown.[141]

In the covenantal ceremony of Genesis 15, as in the treaty between Lagash and Umma, it is very difficult to distinguish between the sacrifice proper and the lustration; we may have a combination of both here. Indeed, the rite of passing between the pieces of the victims originated in Asia Minor and had been propagated in the sphere of Hittite influence; cf. E. J. Bickerman, "Couper une alliance," *Archives d'histoire du droit Oriental* 5 (1950–51), 141 ff. Cf. also S. Henninger, "Was bedeutet die rituelle Teilung eines Tieres in zwei Hälften?" *Biblica* 34 (1953), pp. 344–53. Especially interesting for our discussion is the case in which a man, a goat, a puppy, and a little pig were cut, and the soldiers had to pass between the pieces (see O. Masson, "A propos d'un rituel Hittite pour la lustration d'une armée: le rite de purification par le passage entre les deux parties d'une victime," *RHR* 137 (1950) pp. 5–25). An oath accompanied by passing between the pieces is found in Greece: electing a candidate for office is done by passing between the pieces of the sacrifice while walking toward the altar (Plato, *Laws* 753d).

In Mari we encounter a ritual accompanying the covenant (*ARM* 2:37) that also does not look sacrificial. For the covenant between the Haneans and the land of Idamaraṣ, the pro-

---

and sheep and their ages in Mesopotamia, cf. *MSL* 5, vol. 1 and esp. p. 67 there. For the age adjective *šuluššu,* compare also *ʿglt šlšyh* (Isa. 15:5, Jer. 48:34) and see Mishnah Parah 1:1 *šlšyt*.

140. Cf. David P. Wright, *The Disposal of Impurity: Elimination Rites in the Bible and in the Hittite and Mesopotamian Literature* (Atlanta, 1986), pp. 80–83.

141. Ibid., p. 56.

vincial tribes brought a young dog and a she-goat, which the king of Mari did not permit but gave the command to use a donkey foal (*hayaru*) instead. The "killing of a donkey foal" (*hayaram qatālum*) for a covenant ceremony was so common that this phrase was tantamount to "making a covenant."[142] In the ceremony of Genesis 15, the passing between the parts symbolizes the self-curse, similar to the act of "seizing the throat," but this does not nullify the sacrificial nature of the ceremony. On the contrary, the ritual adds solemnity to the oath. It is only in the covenantal ceremonies of the first millennium that the sacrificial element gradually disappears and gives way to the dramatic act. Thus, the neo-Assyrian treaty and the Deuteronomic covenant become binding and valid not by virtue of the treaty ritual but by the oath-imprecation (the *māmītu*)[143] that accompanies the ceremony. The ritual itself—if it was performed—served only a symbolic and dramatic end: to tangibly impress upon the vassal the consequences that would follow inevitably should he infringe the covenant. The treaty between Ashurnirari V and Mati'ilu of Bit-Agusi[144] even states explicitly that the ram is brought forward in the treaty ceremony not for sacrificial purposes but to serve as a palpable example of the punishment awaiting the transgressor of the treaty (Drohritus): "This ram was not taken from its flock for sacrifice (UDU .SISKUR), it has been brought to conclude the treaty of Ashur-nirari, king of Assyria, with Mati'ilu, if Mati'ilu [shall violate] the covenant and oath to the

142. Cf. M. Held, "Philological Notes on the Mari Covenantal Rituals," *BASOR* 200 (1970), pp. 32–40.

143. Cf. M. Weinfeld, *Deuteronomy and the Deuteronomic School,* 1972, pp. 102–4.

144. See E. Weidner, "Der Staatsvertrag Aššurniräris VI von Assyrien mit Mati'ilu von bit Agusi," *AfO* 8 (1932), pp. 17–34; E. Reiner, *ANET,* 3d ed. pp. 532–33; R. Borger, "Assyrische Staatsverträge," in O. Kaiser, *Texte aus der Umwelt des Alten Testaments,* Band 1 Lieferung 2 (Gütersloh, 1983), pp. 155–58; S. Parpola and K. Watanabe, *Neo-Assyrian Treaties and Loyalty Oaths,* State Archives of Assyria 2 (Helsinki, 1988), pp. 8–13.

gods, then just as this ram, which was taken from its flock and to its flock will not return, and not behold its flock again, so Mati'ilu with his sons, (ministers), the men of his land, shall be taken from his land, and to his land he shall not return, and not (behold) his country again" (col. 1, ll. 10 ff.).

Like Saul, who cut a yoke of oxen into pieces and proclaimed, "Whoever does not come after Saul and Samuel, so shall it be done to his oxen" (1 Sam. 11:7),[145] Bar Ga'yah declared in his treaty with Mati''el, "[As] this calf is cut apart so shall Mati''el be cut apart."[146] Zedekiah's covenant with the people on the manumission of the slaves (Jer. 34:8–22) is to be understood in an analogous manner. Hence, those passing between the two parts of the calf (v. 18) must have accepted the consequences ensuing from a violation of the oath-imprecation: "So may it befall me if I shall not observe the words of the covenant."[147] Dramatic acts of this sort were not, however, performed only with animals. In the Sefire treaty,[148] in the vassal treaties of Esarhaddon,[149] and in Hittite military oath-taking ceremonies[150] similar acts were performed with wax images and other objects.[151] Generally speaking, however, it appears that this act was not a requisite part of the ceremony. Many Hittite and Assyrian treaties make no men-

145. Compare the Mari letter (*ARM* 2, 48), where it is proposed to cut off the head of a culprit and circulate it among the cities of Hana so that the troops may fear and quickly assemble.

146. *[w'yk zy] ygzr 'glh znh kn ygzr mt''l;* see J. A. Fitzmyer, *The Aramaic Inscriptions of Sefire* 1, Biblica et Orientalia 19 (Rome, 1967), A:39–40.

147. See W. Rudolph, *Jeremia,* 2d ed. HAT (1985), p. 205.

148. 1A:35–42.

149. D. J. Wiseman, *Vassal Treaties* (n. 11), lines 608–11.

150. J. Friedrich, "Der hethitische Soldateneid," *ZA* 35 (1924), p. 163, 1:41–45, 2:1–3; see now N. Oettinger, *Die militärischen Eide der Hethiter,* Studien zu den Bogazköy Texten 22 (Wiesbaden, 1976).

151. This type of symbolism was also employed in Babylonian magic; see E. Reiner, *Šurpu: A Collection of Sumerian and Akkadian Incontations* 3, *AfO* 11 (Graz, 1958), pp. 60–112.

tion of such acts, and neither does the book of Deuteronomy. Apparently the oath-imprecation, which was recorded in the treaty document, was believed to be enough to deter the treaty party from violating the stipulations of the treaty.

Distinction should therefore be made between the covenant in Genesis 15 (which, like the covenants of Alalah and Mari, preserves the sacrificial element alongside the symbolic one), and the covenant in Jeremiah 34, in which the ceremony, although performed before God, seems to be nothing more than a self-curse dramatized by a symbolic act. Another difference between Genesis 15 and Jeremiah 34 is that while in Genesis 15, as in the Abban deed, it is the superior party who places himself under oath, in Jeremiah 34, as in the treaty of Ashurnirari V, the vassals are the parties who commit themselves to their masters.

The Legal Formulae in the Covenant with Abraham. It has already been indicated that the legal formulae expressing the gift of land to Abraham are identical to the legal formulae of conveyance of property in the ancient Near East.[152] Especially instructive in this case are the formulations of conveyance in perpetuity. For example, the formulae, "for your descendants forever" (*lzrʿk ʿd ʿwlm*—Gen. 13:15) and "for your descendants after you throughout their generations" (*lzrʿk ʾḥryk ldrtm*[153]—Gen. 17:7–8)[154] are identical to the conveyance and

152. Cf. J. J. Rabinowitz, *Jewish Law* (New York, 1956), pp. 130–31; id., "The Susa Tablets," *VT* 11 (1961), pp. 55 ff.

153. As Loewenstamm indicated in his article "The Divine Grants of Land to the Patriarchs," *JAOS* 94 (1971), pp. 509–10 (AOAT 204 [1980], pp. 423–25), there are two types of legal declarations in the grant formulae: (1) the land is given to the patriarch and to his seed (Gen. 13:15; 17:8; 26:3; 28:4, 13; 35:12), and (2) the land is given to the patriarch's seed (Gen. 12:7; 15:18; 24:7; 48:4). The former type represents the standard formula of the royal grant, but it is inappropriate in Genesis, where the patriarchs are sojourners in the land and only their descendants are the legal possessors of it. On the formulation of the land promise in the Priestly code vs. the one in the Deuteronomic source, see M. Z. Brettler, "The Promise

donation formulae from Susa,[155] Alalah,[156] Ugarit[157] and Elephantine.[158] In Assyria and Babylonia proper we meet with different clichés in this context, such as *ana arkat ūmē*[159] or *ana ṣāt ūmē,*[160] which, though not as close to *ʿd ʿwlm* or *ldrtm* as the expressions of the peripheral documents (*adi dāris,*[161] etc.), nevertheless render the same idea of perpetuity.

The proclamation of the gift of land in Genesis 15 is also styled according to the prevalent judicial pattern. In the gift-

---

of the Land of Israel to the Patriarchs in the Pentateuch," *Shnaton* 5–6 (1981–82), pp. VII–XXIV.

154. *dwr* (*dūru*) with the pronominal suffix is also attested in old Babylonian documents pertaining to conveyance in perpetuity. Cf., e.g., *eqlam ana durišu idna* ("give the field as his permanent property") (TCL 7, 16:13; cf. F. R. Kraus, *Briefe aus dem British Museum* [*Altbabylonische Briefe*], in *Umschrift und Ubersetzung* 7 [Leiden, 1977] to which one might compare Lev. 25:30, "that house shall be established forever to him that bought it throughout *his generation*" *ldrtyw* (i.e., for his permanent property).

155. Cf. *ana dūr u pala ana šêršêri . . . kīma abu ana māri išâmu, PN ana darāti išâm* (*MDP* 22, 45:10–21) ("forever and for all times, for the offspring . . . like a father, who bequeathes to his son, so shall PN bequeath forever."

156. *mārmārišu ana dāria marianni:* "his descendants will have the status of *mariannu* forever," (*AT* 15:8–9); cf. S. Smith, "A Preliminary Account of the Tablets from Atchana," *The Antiquaries Journal* 19 (1939), p. 43.

157. Cf. *PRU* 3, p. 160, 16.132:27–38: *u ittadinšu ana* *ᵐAdalšeni [u] ana mārēšu adi dārīti* ("and gives it to Adalšeni and his sons forever"); cf. 16.248:14 (p. 48: *ana dāri dūri*), 16.182 + 199:9 (p. 148: *ana dārīti/ana dāri dūri*), 16.146:10–12 (p. 146: *eqlatu ṣāmid ana dārīti*). In Ugaritic the formula is *wlbnh ʿd ʿlm* (*PRU* 2, 16.382, pp. 20–21).

158. Cf. A. Cowley, *The Aramaic Papyri of the Fifth Century* B.C. (Oxford, 1923), 8:9, (p. 22): *ʾnty šlyṭh bh mn ywmʾ znh wʿd ʿlm wbnyky ʾḥryky* ("you have rights over it from this day forever and your children after you"); ibid., 25:9 (p. 85). Cf. R. Yaron, *The Law of the Elephantine Documents* (Jerusalem, 1961), pp. 82 f., 165 (Hebrew).

159. F. Steinmetzer, "Die Bestallungsurkunde Königs Šamas-šum-ukîn von Babylon," *Archiv orientální* 7 (1935), pp. 314–18, 2:9.

160. *ana ṣāti irenšu* ("he granted to him in perpetuity,") *BBSt* 8 (n. 5), 1:13; cf. also 34:6.

161. Cf. *CAD* vol. 3 (D), p. 198.

deed of Abban to Yarimlin we read, "On that day (*ina ūmišu*) Abban gave the city. . . ." Similarly, we read in Genesis 15:18, "On that day (*bywm hhwʾ*) Yahweh concluded a covenant with Abraham saying: 'To your offspring I give this land.'" The phrase "on that day" in these instances certainly has legal implications.[162] The delineation of the borders and the specification of the granted territories in vv. 18–21 indeed constitute an important part of the grant documents in the ancient Near East.[163]

The formulation of the priestly covenant with Abraham, "to be unto you a God" (*lhywt lk lʾlhym*—Gen. 17:7, 8) and the priestly formulation of the covenant with Israel, "I will be your God and you shall be my people" (*whyyty lkm lʾlhym wʾtm thyw ly lʿm*—Lev. 26:12, Exod. 6:7; cf. Deut. 29:12), is taken from the sphere of marriage/adoption legal terminology,[164] as is its Davidic counterpart in 2 Samuel 7:14.[165]

The covenant with Abraham and the covenant with David are indeed based on a common pattern, and their literary formulation may have the same historical and literary antecedents.[166] The promise of the land to Abraham is preceded by

162. Cf. note 71 above.

163. Cf. *BBSt* (n. 5) (passim) and also Cowley, *Aramaic Papyri* (n. 158), 8:3 ff.; 13:13 f.; 25:4 f. On this point see my *Deuteronomy and the Deuteronomic School* (n. 2), pp. 69 ff.

164. Cf. Y. Muffs, "Studies in Biblical Law IV (The Antiquity of P)," Lectures at the Jewish Theological Seminary, (New York, 1965). For the use of *verba solemnia* in marriage and adoption in Mesopotamia see S. Greengus, "The Old Babylonian Marriage Contract," *JAOS* 89 (1969), pp. 514 ff. On the prophetic vs. pentateuchal imagery of the covenantal relationship between God and the people, see my *Deut. and the Deuteronomic School,* (n. 2), pp. 81 ff.

165. The tradition of the covenant with Abraham is very ancient and reflects the covenant customs in Mari and Alalah, but the literary formulation of this covenant is more recent and seems to be from the time of the United Monarchy; cf. R. E. Clements, *Abraham and David,* Studies in Biblical Theology, 2d. ser. 5 (London, 1967).

166. Cf. K. McCarter, *II Samuel,* Anchor Bible (New York, 1984), p. 205.

the promise of progeny (Gen. 15:4–5), and the latter is formulated in the way the promise of the dynasty is phrased in 2 Sam. 7:12: *ʾšr yṣʾ mmʿyk*. Similarly, the promise of a great name to Abraham (*wʾgdlh šmk*—Gen. 12:2) sounds like 2 Sam. 7:9: "David will have a name like the name of the great ones of the earth" (*kšm hgdlym ʾšr bʾrṣ*). As I have shown elsewhere,[167] the greatness of the name has political significance,[168] which also finds expression in the Genesis traditions apparently crystalized under the impact of the united monarchy.[169]

The priestly source in Genesis goes even further and combines the promise of land with the promise of dynasty. To the promise of progeny he adds, "Kings shall come out from you" (17:6, 16; 35:11), which sounds like a promise of dynasty.

The Grant of Hebron to Caleb. On the basis of the grant typology, discussed here, we may properly understand the nature of some other promises and bestowals in the Old Testament. Thus, the accounts of the conquest inform us about the gift of Hebron to Caleb (Josh. 14:13–14, Judg. 1:20; cf. Num. 14:24, Deut. 1:36).[170] The reason for the gift was the faithfulness of Caleb during his mission with the spies: "Because he filled up after the lord" (*yʿn ky mlʾ ʾḥry YHWH ʾlhy yśrʾl*—Jos. 14:14; cf. vv. 8, 9 and Num. 14:24, 32:11–12, Deut. 1:36),

167. "Political Greatness: The Realization of the Promise to the Patriarchs," *Eretz-Israel* vol. 24 (1993), A. Malamut volume (in press).

168. Cf. *šumam rabêm* in connection with military victories in ARM 1, 69:14–16.

169. The extent of the promised land in Gen. 15:19–21, and especially the Kenites, Kenizzites and Kadmonites mentioned there, also point to a Davidic background; cf. B. Mazar, "Historical Background of the Book of Genesis," *JNES* 28 (1969), pp. 79 f.

170. Joshua is secondary in this tradition (cf. Num. 14:24; Deut. 1:36). The promise of land to Joshua was incorporated later, when the conquest was nationalized and the original account of spying out the south (to Hebron and the Valley of Eshkol, Num. 13:22–23) was expanded by an alleged excursion to the northern part of the country (to Rehob at Lebo-Hamath, v. 21). See Commentaries and J. Liver, "*Caleb,*" in *Encyclopedia Miqraʾit* 4, cols. 106–110 (Hebrew).

a phrase which is semantically equivalent to *hyh tmym* (be perfect, i.e., wholly devoted) of the Abrahamic covenant and *hyh šlm* of the Davidic covenant. Furthermore, as in the Abrahamic-Davidic covenants and in the grants of the ancient Near East, in the Caleb gift we also find the conventional formulae of conveyance in perpetuity: "to you and your descendants forever" (*lk.. wlbnyk ʿd ʿwlm*—Josh. 14:9).

Granting a city or a territory to the one who excelled in the king's expedition is indeed very common in the *kudduru* documents,[171] and the case of Caleb has therefore to be considered as a grant, although we don't know whether the grant reflects an authentic historical fact of the times of the conquest or is rather a back projection of later times. Granting a city to a vassal who proved loyal to the overlord is found in connection with the city *Ṣiglag,* which was given to David by Achish, the Philistine king (1 Sam. 27:6).[172]

Clements[173] suggested that Hebron was the birthplace of the traditions of the Abrahamic and Davidic covenants. The tradition about the grant to Caleb is certainly rooted in Hebron. It therefore seems plausible that the tradition of the grant of Hebron to Caleb had been transmitted by the same circle which transmitted the tradition of the Abrahamic-Davidic covenants.

The Grant of Priesthood and Priestly Revenues. The documents of grant in the ancient Near East also include grants of status—*maryannu*-ship,[174] priesthood,[175] etc. The priesthood of Aaron in Israel had also been conceived as an eternal grant.

171. Cf., e.g., King, *BBSt* (n .5), pp. 31 ff., 43 ff., 96 ff.

172. Cf. J. Tigay, "Psalm 7:5 and Ancient Near Eastern Treaties," *JBL* 89 (1970), p. 183, n. 34.

173. See note 1.

174. Cf. S. Smith, *The Antiquaries Journal* 19 (1939), ATT/8/49 (p. 43): *mār mārēšu ana dāria maryanni u šangi ša Enlil* ("his grandsons in perpetuity are [will be] *maryannu* and priests of Enlil").

175. Cf., e.g., Schorr, *Urkunden* (n. 10), VAB 5, no. 220; F. Thureau-Dangin, "Un acte de donation de Mardouk - zâkir - šumi," *RA* 16 (1919), pp. 141 ff. and the Alalah text in the previous note.

Thus we read in Num. 25:12–13: "Phinehas, son of Eleazar son of Aaron the priest, has turned back my wrath from the Israelites by displaying among them his passion for me . . . say, therefore, I grant him my pact of friendship (*bryt šlwm*). It shall be for him and his descendants after him a pact of priesthood forever (*bryt khnt ʾwlm*)." As in other grants, here the grant is given for showing one's zeal and devotion for the master; and like the other grants, the gift of priesthood is given in perpetuity.[176] In biblical texts that do not follow the rigid distinction (of the Priestly code) between priests and Levites but rather adopt the Deuteronomic attitude of priests and Levites being one group, the grant applies to the whole tribe of Levi. Thus, we read in Malachi 2:4 f.: "that my covenant might be with Levi . . . my covenant was with him of life and well being (*ḥyym whšlwm*)." In the continuation, an indication of the loyalty and devotion of Levi is also found, which is similar in its phraseology to the descriptions of the loyalty of Abraham and David:[177] "he walked with me [he served me] with integrity and equity" (*bšlm wbmyšwr hlk ʾty*—v. 6).[178] The eternal covenant with Levi is also mentioned alongside the covenant with David in Jeremiah 33:17 ff.

Priestly revenues in the ancient Near East were also subject to grants and royal bestowals. This is also reflected in Israel. The holy donations assigned to the Aaronide priesthood are formulated in the manner of royal grants:[179] "All the sacred donations of the Israelites, I grant them to you and your sons as a prerequisite,[180] a due for all time" (*lkl qdšy bny yśrʾl lk nttym lmšḥh wlbnyk lḥq ʿwlm*—Num. 18:8; cf. Lev. 7:34 ff.), and in

176. Cf. above, pp. 233–39.

177. Cf. above, pp. 230–31.

178. See note 30 above.

179. Following the translation of *The Torah,* Jewish Publication Society of America (1962).

180. On the priestly revenue as a royal grant see Y. Muffs, "Joy and Love as Metaphorical Expressions of Willingness and Spontaneity in Cuneiform, Ancient Hebrew and Related Literatures," in J. Neusner, ed., *Christianity, Judaism and other Greco-Roman Cults: For Morton Smith at Sixty* 3 (Leiden, 1975), pp. 14 ff.

slightly different formulations, "all the sacred gifts that the Israelites set aside for YHWH I give to you, to your sons . . . as a due forever, it shall be as everlasting salt covenant . . . for you and your offspring as well" (v. 19).

Similarly, the tithe, which according to Numbers 18:21 f., belongs to the Levites, was also given to them as a grant for the services that they perform (*ḥlp ʿbdtm ʾšr hm ʿbdym*). Grants of the tithe of a city to royal servants are actually known to us from Ugarit, as we read, for instance, in the grant of Ammistamru II:[181] "(From this day) Ammištamru granted everything whatsoever (that belongs to the city) to Yaṣiranu . . . forever for his grandsons: his grain, and his wine of its tithe." Yaṣiranu receives here the right to collect the tithe.[182]

The connection of the Aaronites and the Levites to Hebron has been pointed out,[183] and we may therefore suppose that the "Sitz im Leben" of the grant to Aaron and the Levites is rooted in Hebron, as are the other grant traditions discussed.

As has been shown, the grants to Abraham, Caleb, David, Aaron, and the Levites have much in common with the grants from Alalah, Nuzi, the Hittites, Ugarit, and middle-Babylonian *kudurru's,* i.e., in documents from the second half of the second millennium B.C.E. This fact and the possible link of the mentioned Israelite grants to Hebron, the first capital of David's kingdom, may lead us to the contention that it was Davidic scribes who stood behind the formulation of the covenant of grant in Israel.

181. GN *qadu gabbi mimmi šumsiša iddin ana PN . . . ana dāriš ana mārē mārēšu: šêšu, šikarsu ša maʾšarišu* (*PRU* 3, 16.153): 4–11 (pp. 146–47). As in Ugarit, in Israel the tithe is taken from grain and wine (and also oil).

182. Cf. M. Heltzer, *The Rural Community in Ancient Ugarit* (Wiesbaden, 1976), pp. 50–51.

183. Cf. the dissertation by M. D. Rehm, "Studies in the History of the Pre-Exilic Levites," announced in the *Harvard Theological Review* 61 (1968), pp. 648–49. Cf. also B. Mazar, "Cities of Priests and Levites," SVT 7 (1959), pp. 197 ff.

Bibliography

Abel, F. M. *Les livres des Maccabées*. Paris, 1949.

Abramsky, S. "The Attitude towards the Amorites and Jebusites in the Book of Samuel: Historical Foundation and the Ideological Significance" (in Hebrew). *Zion, Jubilee Volume* 50 (1985): 27–58.

Aharoni, Y. "The Conquests of David According to Psalms 60 and 108" (in Hebrew). In *Bible and Jewish History: Dedicated to the Memory of S. Liver,* ed. B. Uffenheimer, 13–17. Tel Aviv, 1972.

———. *The Land of the Bible: A Historical Geography*. 2d ed. Trans. and ed. A. F. Rainey. London, 1979.

———. "The Settlement and the Inheritance." In *The History of the People of Israel: The Patriarchs and the Judges* (in Hebrew), ed. B. Mazar, 200–217. Jerusalem: 1967.

———. *The Settlement of the Israelite Tribes in Upper Galilee* (in Hebrew). Jerusalem, 1957.

———. "Tel-Masos: Historical Considerations." *Tel-Aviv* 2 (1975): 114–24.

Albright, W. F. "The Israelite Conquest of Canaan in the Light of Archaeology." *BASOR* 74 (1939): 11–23.

Alföldi, A. *Early Rome and the Latins*. Ann Arbor, 1966.

Alt, A. "Ägyptische Tempel in Palästina und die Landnahme der Philister." In vol. 1 of *Kleine Schriften,* 216–30. Munich, 1953.

———. "Jerusalems Aufstieg." In vol. 3 of *Kleine Schriften,* 243–57. Munich, 1959.

———. "Josua." In vol. 1 of *Kleine Schriften,* 176–92. Munich, 1953.

———. "Die Landnahme der Israeliten in Palästina." In vol. 1 of *Kleine Schriften,* 89–125. Munich, 1953.

———. "Neues über Palästina aus dem Archiv Amenophis' IV." In vol. 3 of *Kleine Schriften,* 158–75. Munich, 1959.

———. "Die Ursprünge des Israelitischen Rechts." In vol. 1 of *Kleine Schriften,* 279–332. Munich, 1953.

———. "Bemerkungen zu den Verwaltungs- und Rechtsurkunden von Ugarit und Alalach." *Die Welt des Orients* 3/1–2 (1964): 3–17.
Altman, A. "The Development of the Office of 'Judge' in Pre-Monarchic Israel." In *Proceedings of the Seventh World Congress of Jewish Studies: Studies in Bible and the Ancient Near East,* (in Hebrew), 11–21. Jerusalem, 1981.
———. "The Revolutions in Byblos and Amurru during the Amarna Period and their Social Background." In *Bar-Ilan Studies in History,* 3–24. Ramat Gan, 1978.
Aptowitzer, V. "Les premiers possesseurs de Canaan, légends apologétiques et exégétiques." *RÉJ* 82 (1926): 282 ff.
Archi, A. "Città Sacre d'Asia Minore." *La Parola del Passato* 20 (1975): 329–44.
Artzi, P. "*ʿAmarna: teʿudot ʾel ʿamarna.*" *Encyclopedia Miqraʾit* 6 (1971): cols. 242–54.
———. " 'Vox Populi' in the El-Amarna Tablets." *Revue d'assyriologie* 58 (1964): 159–66.
Asheri, D. "The Dating of the Fall of Troy in Greek Historiography from Herodotus to Timaeus." In vol. 2 of *Isac Leo Seeligmann Volume, Essays on the Bible and the Ancient World* (in Hebrew), ed. A. Rofé and Y. Zakovitch, 509–23. Jerusalem, 1983.
Astour, M. C. "The Amarna Age Forerunners of Biblical Anti-Royalism." In *For Max Weinreich on his Seventieth Birthday: Studies in Jewish Languages, Literature and Society,* 6–17. New York: 1964.
———. *Hellenosemitica.* Leiden, 1965.
Auld, A. G. *Joshua, Moses and the Land.* Edinburgh, 1980.
———. "Judges I and History: A Reconsideration." *VT* 25 (1975): 261–85.
Austin, R. G. *P. Vergili Maronis Aeneidos* 2. Oxford, 1964.
Baltzer, K. *Das Bundesformular.* 2d ed. Wissenschaftliche Monographien zum Alten und Neuen Testament 4. Neukirchen, 1964.
Begg, C. T. "The Covenantal Dove in Ps. 74:19–20." *VT* 37 (1987): 78–80.
Beyerlin, W. "Gattung und Herkunft des Rahmens im Richterbuch." In *Tradition and Situation: Festschrift A. Weiser,* 1–29. Göttingen, 1963.
———. "Geschichte und heilsgeschichtliches Traditionsbildung im Alten Testament (Richter VI–VIII)." *VT* 13 (1963): 1–25.
Bickerman, E. J. "Couper une alliance." *Archives d'histoire du droit Oriental* 5 (1950–51): 141 ff. Vol. 1 of *Studies in Jewish and Christian History,* 1–32. Leiden, 1976.

Bin Gorion, M. J. (Berdichewski), *Sinai und Garizim*. Berlin, 1926.
Biram, A. "Hosea 2:16–25." In *E. Urbach Volume* (in Hebrew), 116–39. Jerusalem, 1955.
———. "*Mas ʿobed.*" *Tarbiz* 23 (1944): 137–42.
Biran, A. "Notes and News, Tel Dan, 1984." *IEJ* 35 (1985): 186–89.
Boer, P. A. H. de. *Gedenken und Gedächtnis in der Welt des A.T.* (Franz Delitzsch—Vorlesungen, 1960) Leipzig, 1962.
Borderuil, P., and D. Pardee. "Le rituel funéraire ougaritique RS.34.126." *Syria* 59 (1982): 121–28.
Borger, R. "Assyrische Staatsverträge." In *Rechts- und Wirtschaftsurkunden. Hist.-chron. Texte,* ed. O. Kaiser, 155–77. Texte aus der Umwelt des Alten Testaments 1. Gütersloh, 1983.
———. "Zu den Asarhaddon—Verträgen aus Nimrud." *ZA* 20 (1961): 173–96.
Breasted, J. H., ed. Vol. 3 of *Ancient Records of Egypt*. New York, 1906.
Brettler, M. Z. "The Promise of the Land of Israel to the Patriarchs in the Pentateuch." *Shnaton* 5–6 (1981–82): VII–XXIV.
Bright, J. *Early Israel in Recent History Writing*. London, 1956.
Brinkman, S. A. "The Foundation-Legends in Vergil." *Classical Journal* 54 (1958–59): 25–33.
Brock, S. P. Vol. 2 of *Pseuduepigrapha Veteris Testamenti Graece*. Leiden, 1967.
Bron, F. *Recherches sur les inscriptions phéniciennes de Karatepe*. Geneva, 1979.
Brueggemann, W. *The Land: Place as Gift, Promise and Challenge in Biblical Faith*. Philadelphia, 1977.
Bruston, C. "La mort et la sépulture de Jacob." *ZAW* 7 (1887): 202–10.
Buber, M. *Kingship of God*. Trans. R. Scheimann. London, 1967.
———. *Königtum Gottes*. Berlin, 1932.
Budde, K. *Das Buch der Richter. KHC* 7 (1897): Feiburg I.B.
Bunnens, G. *L'éxpansion phénicienne en Méditerranée*. Brussels, 1979.
Burkert, W. *Griechische Religion*. Stuttgart, 1977.
Burrows, M., and E. A. Speiser, eds. *One Hundred New Selected Nuzi Texts. AASOR* 16. New Haven, 1936.
Callaway, J. A. "New Evidence on the Conquest of ʿAi." *JBL* 87 (1968): 312–20.
Cary, E. *Dionysius of Halicarnassus*. Loeb Classical Library. 1937.
Cassin, E. "L'influence babylonienne à Nuzi," *JESHO* 5 (1962): 113–38.

———. "Nouvelles données sur les relations familiales à Nuzi." *RA* 57 (1963): 113–19.

———. "Pouvoir de la femme et structures familiales," *RA* 63 (1969): 121–48.

Cavaignac, E. "L'affaire de laruvatte." *RHA* 6 (1932): 189–200.

———. "Daddassa-Dattasa." *RHA* 10 (1933): 65–76.

Childs, B. S. *Memory and Tradition in Israel*. London, 1962.

———. "A Study of the Formula 'Until this Day'" *JBL* 82 (1962): 279–92.

Christman-Franck, L. "Le rituel des funérailles royales hittites." *RHA* 29 (1971): 61–111.

Clements, R. E. *Abraham and David*. Studies in Biblical Theology, 2d ser. 5. London, 1967.

Cogan, M., and H. Tadmor. "Aḥaz and Tiglath-Pileser in the Book of Kings: Historiographic Considerations." *Eretz Israel* 14 (*H. L. Ginsberg Volume,* 1978): 55–61.

Colson, F. H. *Philo*. Loeb Classical Library 9. Cambridge, Mass., 1929–62.

Cook, A. B. Vol. 3 of *Zeus, A Study in Ancient Religion*. Cambridge, 1940.

Cooke, G. "The Israelite King as the Son of God." *ZAW* 73 (1961): 202–25.

Cooper, J. S. *Presargonic Inscriptions*. New Haven, 1986.

Cornell, T. S. "Aeneas and the Twins: The Development of the Roman Foundation Legend." *Proceedings of the Cambridge Philological Society* 21 (1975): 1–32.

Cowley, L. A. *The Aramaic Papyri of the Fifth Century* B.C. Oxford, 1923.

Cross F. M. "The Ammonite Oppression of the Tribes of Gad and Reuben: Missing Verses from 1 Samuel 11 Found in 4Q Samuel[a]." In *History, Historiography and Interpretation: Studies in Biblical and Cuneiform Literatures,* ed. H. Tadmor and M. Weinfeld, 148–58. Jerusalem, 1983.

———. *Canaanite Myth and Hebrew Epic*. Cambridge, Mass., 1973.

Crüsemann, F. *Der Widerstand gegen das Königtum*. Wissenschaftliche Monographien zum Alten und Neuen Testament 49. Neukirchen, 1978.

Daube, D. *Studies in Biblical Law*. Oxford, 1949.

Davies, W. D. *The Gospel and the Land*. London, 1974.

Dillmann, A. *Exodus and Leviticus*. Kurzgefasstes exegetisches Handbuch zum Alten Testament. Leipzig, 1877.

———. *Numeri*. Kurzgefasstes exegetisches Handbuch zum Alten Testament. Leipzig, 1886.

Donner, H., and W. Röllig, eds. *Kanaanäische und aramäische Inschriften*. Wiesbaden, 1969.

Draffkorn, A. "Was King Abba-AN of Yamḫad a Vizier for the King of Hattuša?" *JCS* 13 (1959): 94–97.

Draffkorn, A. E. "Ilāni/Elohim." *JBL* 76 (1957): 216–24.

Driver, G. R. "Confused Hebrew Roots." In *Gaster Anniversary Volume*, 73–83. London, 1936.

Driver, G. R., and J. C. Miles. *The Babylonian Laws*. Vols. 1–2. Oxford, 1952.

Driver, S. R. *Deuteronomy*. ICC. Edinburgh, 1902.

———. *Introduction to the Literature of the Old Testament*. New York, 1956.

Edgerton, W. F., and J. A. Wilson. *Historical Records of Ramses III: The Text of Medinet Habu*. Chicago, 1936.

Ehrlich, A. *Randglossen zur hebräischen Bibel*. Leipzig, 1908–14.

Eisele, W. "Der Telepinus-Erlass." Diss., Munich, 1970.

Eissfeldt, O. *Die Quellen des Richterbuches*. Leipzig, 1925.

———. "Zwei verkannte militärtechnische Termini," *VT* 5 (1955): 232–38.

Elgavish, J. "Shiqmonah, Tel." In vol. 4 of *Encyclopedia of Archaeological Excavations in the Holy Land*, cols. 1101--09. Jerusalem, 1978.

Epstein, J. N. *Introduction to the Tannaitic Literature* (in Hebrew). Jerusalem, 1964.

———. *Introduction to the Text of the Mishnah* (in Hebrew). Jerusalem, 1964.

Ericksen, W. *Papyrus Harris I*. Brussels, 1933.

Feigin, S. "Some Cases of Adoption in Israel." *JBL* 50 (1931): 186–200.

Fensham, F. C. "Covenant, Promise and Expectation in the Bible." *Theologische Zeitschrift* 23 (1967): 305–22.

Fenton, T. "Comparative Evidence in Textual Study: M. Dahood on 2 Sam. 1:21 and *CTA* 19 (1 Aqht) I, 44–45." *VT* 29 (1979): 162–70.

Finkelstein, I., ed. "Excavations at Shiloh 1981–1984: Preliminary Report." *Tel-Aviv* 12 (1985): 123–80.

Finkelstein, I., S. Bonimowitz and Z. Lederman. "Excavations at Shiloh, 1981–1983 (in Hebrew)." *Qadmoniot* 17 1/65 (1984): 15–25.

Finkelstein, I., and A. Brandl. "A Group of Metal Objects from Shiloh." *The Israel Museum Journal* 4 (1985): 17–26.

———. *The Archaeology of the Israelite Settlement* (in Hebrew). Jerusalem, 1988.

Finkelstein, J. J. "The Genealogy of the Hammurapi Dynasty." *Journal of Cuneiform Studies* 20 (1966): 95–118.

Fitzmyer, J. A. *The Aramaic Inscriptions of Sefire*. Biblica et Orientalia 19. Rome, 1967.

———. *The Genesis Apocryphon of Qumran Cave 1*. 2d rev. ed. Rome, 1971.

Flusser, D. "The Parables of Jesus" (in Hebrew). In *Jewish Sources in Early Christianity: Studies and Essays*, 150–202. Jerusalem, 1979.

Fontenrose, J. *The Delphic Oracle*. Berkeley, 1978.

Fratelli and Palombi, eds. *Enea nel Lazio, Archeologia e Mito, Bimillenario Virgiliano*. Rome, 1981.

Freedman, D. N. "Divine Commitment and Human Obligation." *Interpretation* 18 (1964): 419–31.

———. "The Poetic Structure of Deuteronomy 33." In *The Bible World: Essays in Honor of C. H. Gordon*, 28–30. New York, 1980.

———. *Pottery, Poetry and Prophecy: Studies in Early Hebrew Poetry*. Winona Lake, Ind., 1980.

Friedman, R. E. ed. *The Poet and the Historian: Essays in Literary and Historical Biblical Criticism*. Harvard Semitic Studies 26. Chico, Calif., 1983.

Friedrich, J. "Aus dem hethitischen Schriftum, 2 Heft." *Der Alte Orient* 24/3 (1925): 1–32.

———. "Der hethitische Soldateneid." *ZA* 35 (1924): 161–92.

———. *Staatsverträge des Hatti Reiches in hethitischer Sprache*. *MVAeG* 31 (1926); 34 (1934).

Fritz, V. "Die sogennante Liste der besiegten Könige in Josua 12." *ZDPV* 85 (1969): 136–61.

Gadd, C. J. *Tablets from Kirkuk*. *RA* 23 (1926).

Gafni, I. "The Status of Eretz Israel in Reality and in Jewish Consciousness following the Bar-Kokhva Uprising." In *The Bar-Kokhva Revolt: A New Approach*, ed. A. Oppenheimer and U. Rappaport, 224–32. Jerusalem, 1984.

Galil, G. "The Genealogies of the Tribe of Judah." Diss., The Hebrew University, Jerusalem, 1983.

Galinsky, G. K. *Aeneas, Sicily and Rome*. Princeton, 1969.

———. "The 'Tomb of Aeneas' at Lavinium." *Vergilius* 20 (1974): 2–11.

Gardiner, A. Vol. 1 of *Ancient Egyptian Onomastica.* Oxford, 1947.
Gaster, T. H. *Myth, Legend and Custom in the Old Testament.* New York, 1969.
Gelb, J. "Review of D. J. Wiseman, *The Vassal Treaties of Esarhaddon.*" *Bibliotheca Orientalis* 19 (1962): 159–62.
Ginsberg, H. L. *The Israelian Heritage of Judaism.* New York, 1982.
———. "Lexicographical Notes." In *Hebräische Wortforschung: Festschrift W. Baumgartner,* 71–82. SVT 15. Leiden, 1967.
———. *Qohelet.* Tel-Aviv, 1961.
———. *Studies in Qohelet.* New York, 1950.
———. "An Ugaritic Parallel to 2 Sam 1:21." *JBL* 57 (1938): 209–13.
Ginzberg, L. *The Legends of the Jews.* Vols. 1–7. New York, 1909–28.
Giveon, R. "An Inscription of Rameses III from Lachish." *Tel-Aviv* 10 (1983): 176–77.
Glueck, N. *Hesed in the Bible.* (Cincinnati, 1967).
Goetze, A. *Die Annalen des Muršiliš. MVAeG* 38. Leipzig, 1931.
———. "Critical Reviews of *KBo X* (by H. G. Güterbock and H. Otten)." *JCS* 16 (1962): 24–30.
———. "Critical Reviews of *KBo XIV* (by H. G. Güterbock)." *JCS* 18 (1964): 92–94.
———. "Critical Reviews of S. Smith, *The Statue of Idri-mi.*" *JCS* 4 (1950): 226–31.
———. *Hattušiliš. MVAeG* 29/3. Leipzig, 1925.
Goitein, S. D. "The City of Adam in the Book of Psalms" (in Hebrew). *Bulletin of the Israel Exploration Society* (*Yediot*) 13 (1947): 86–88.
Gordon, C. H. "Vergil and the Near East." *Ugaritica* 7 (1969): 266–88.
Gottwald, N. K. *The Tribes of Yahweh.* New York, 1979.
Graham, J. "Foundation." CAH^2 3:143–52. Cambridge, 1982.
Gray, G. B. *Numbers.* ICC. Edinburgh, 1903.
Greenberg, M. "Another Look at Rachel's Theft of the Teraphim." *JBL* 81 (1962): 239–48.
———. "The Design and the Themes of Ezekiel's Program of Restoration." *Interpretation* 38 (1984): 181–208.
———. "Hebrew *s*ᵉ*gullā:* Akkadian sikiltu." *JAOS* 71 (1951): 172–74.
———. "*Herem.*" In vol. 8 of *Encyclopedia Judaica,* cols. 344–50. Jerusalem, 1972.
———. "*Pršt hšbt* in Jeremiah." In *Studies in the Book of Jeremiah* (in Hebrew), ed. B. Z. Luria, 23–52. Jerusalem, n.d.
Greenfield, J. C. "An Ancient Treaty Ritual and Its Targumic Echo."

In *Salvación en la Palabra: Targum-Derash-Berith Homenaje al Profesor A. Diez Macho*, 391–97. Madrid, 1988.

———. "Un rite religieux araméen et ses paralleles." *RB* 80 (1973): 46–52.

———. "Stylistic Aspects of the Sefire Treaty Inscription." *Acta Orientalia* 29 (1965): 1–18.

Greengus, S. "The Old Babylonian Marriage Contract." *JAOS* 89 (1969): 505–32.

Greenstein, E. L., and D. Marcus. "The Akkadian Inscription of Idrimi." *The Journal of the Ancient Near Eastern Society of Columbia University* 8 (1976): 59–96.

Grinz, Y. M. *Judith*. Jerusalem, 1957.

Güdemann, M. "Tendenz und Abfassungszeit der letzten Capitel des Buches der Richter." *Monatsschrift für die Geschichte und Wissenschaft des Judentums* 18 (1869): 357–68.

Gunkel, H. *Psalmen*. In vol. 4 of HKAT. Göttingen, 1929.

Güterbock, H. *Siegel aus Bogazköy*. AfO Beiheft 5. Berlin, 1940.

———. *Vokabulare, Mythen und Kultinventare*. *KBo* 26. Berlin, 1978.

Gutman, Y. Vol. 2 of *The Beginnings of the Jewish-Hellenistic Literature*. Jerusalem, 1963.

Halbe, J. "Gibeon und Israel." *VT* 25 (1975): 613–41.

———. *Das Privilegrecht Jahwes Ex. 34:10–26, Gestalt und Wesen, Herkunft und Wirken in vordeuteronomischer Zeit*. FRLANT 114. Göttingen, 1975.

Halperin-Amaru, B. "Land Theology in Josephus' *Jewish Antiquities*." *JQR* 71 (1981): 202–29.

Hanhart, R. "Das Land in der spätnachexilischen Prophetie." In *Das Land Israel in biblischer Zeit,* ed. G. Strecker. Göttingen, 1983.

Haran, M. "Behind the Scenes of History: Determining the Date of the Priestly Source." *JBL* 100 (1981): 321–33.

———. "The Gibeonites, the Nethinim and the Sons of Solomon's Servants." *VT* 11 (1961): 159–69.

———. "The Law Code of Ezekiel XL–XLVIII and its Relation to the Priestly School." *HUCA* 50 (1979): 45–72.

———. "Shechem Studies" (in Hebrew). *Zion* 38 (1973): 1–32.

———. "Shiloh and Jerusalem: The Origin of the Priestly Tradition in the Pentateuch" (in Hebrew). *Tarbiz* 31 (1962): 317–25 (Printed in English in *JBL* 81 (1962), 14–24).

———. "*Sugyot miqra'* Problems in the Composition of the Former Prophets" (in Hebrew). *Tarbiz* 37 (1968): 1–14 Vol. 1 of *Likkutei Tarbiz,* 155–68.

Harvey, J. "Le 'Rib-pattern': Requisitoire prophétique sur la rupture de l'alliance." *Biblica* 43 (1962): 172–96.
Held, M. "A Faithful Lover in the Old Babylonian Dialogue." *JCS* 15 (1961): 1–26.
———. "Philological Notes on the Mari Covenantal Rituals." *BASOR* 200 (1970): 32–40.
———. "The Root ZBL/SBL in Akkadian, Ugaritic and Biblical Hebrew." *JAOS* 88 (*E. A. Speiser Memorial Volume*) (1968): 90–96.
———. "Studies in Comparative Semitic Lexicography." In *Studies in Honor of B. Landsberger on His Seventy Fifth Birthday,* 395–406. Assyriological Studies 15. Chicago, 1965.
Heltzer, M. "A New Approach to the Question of the Alien Wives in the Books of Ezra and Nehemiah" (in Hebrew). *Shnaton* 10 (1986–89): 83–92.
———. *The Rural Community in Ancient Ugarit*. Wiesbaden, 1976.
Henninger, S. "Was bedeutet die rituelle Teilung eines Tieres in zwei Hälften?" *Biblica* 34 (1953): 344–53.
Herdner, A. *Corpus des tablettes en cunéiformes alphabétiques*. Paris, 1963.
Herzog, R. *Heilige Gesetze von Kos*. Berlin, 1928.
Hinz, W. "Elams Vertrag mit Narām-Sîn von Akkade." *ZA* N.F. 24 (1967): 66–96.
Hoffner, H. "The Arzana House." In *Anatolian Studies Presented to H. G. Güterbock,* 113–21. Istanbul: Nederlands Historisch-Archaeologisch Instituut in Het Nabije Oosten. Istanbul, 1974.
———. "Birth and Name-Giving in Hittite Texts." *JNES* 27 (1968): 198–203.
Hölscher, G. "Zum Ursprung der Rahabsage." *ZAW* 38 (1919–20): 54–57.
Horbury, W. "Extirpation and Excommunication." *VT* 35 (1985): 19–38.
Horsfall, N. M. "Enea." In vol. 2 of *Enciclopedia Virgiliana,* 221–29. Rome, 1985.
———. "Stesichorus at Bovillae." *JHS* 99 (1979): 26–48.
———. "Virgil's Roman Chronography." *Classical Quarterly* 24 (1974): 111–16.
Hrozny, F. *Hethitische Keilschrifttexte aus Boghazköi*. Boghazköi Studien 3. Leipzig, 1919.
Huffmon, H. B. "The Covenant Lawsuit in the Prophets." *JBL* 78 (1959): 285–95.
Huffmon, H. B., and S. B. Parker. "A Further Note on the Treaty Background of Hebrew *yada*ʿ." *BASOR* 184 (1966): 36–38.

Imparati, F. "Conassione de Terre." *RHA* 32 (1974): 96–120.

Ishida, T. *The Royal Dynasties in Ancient Israel*. Berlin, 1977.

———. "The Structure and Historical Implication of the Lists of the Pre-Israelite Nations." *Biblica* 60 (1979): 461–90.

Jacob, B. "Das hebräische Sprachgut im Christlich-Palästinischen." *ZAW* 22 (1902): 83–113.

Jacobsen, T. "Early Political Development in Mesopotamia." *Zeitschrift für Assyriologie* 52 (1957): 91–140.

———. "Parerga Sumerologica." *JNES* 2 (1943): 117–21.

Jacoby, F. *Die Fragmente der griechischen Historiker*. Berlin, 1923–58.

Japhet, S. "Conquest and Settlement in Chronicles." *JBL* 98 (1979): 205–18.

———. *The Ideology of the Book of Chronicles and its Place in Biblical Thought*. Frankfurt, 1989.

Kallai, Z., and H. Tadmor. "Bīt Ninurta = Beth Horon: On the ble: Territorial Models in Biblical Historiography" (in Hebrew). *Eretz Israel* 12 (*N. Glueck Vol.*, 1975): 27–34.

———. "Conquest and Settlement of Trans-Jordan: A Historiographical Study." *ZDPV* 99 (1983): 110–18.

———. *Historical Geography of the Bible*. Jerusalem, 1986.

———. "Judah and Israel: A Study in Israelite Historiography." *IEJ* 28 (1978): 251–61.

———. "The Settlement Traditions of Ephraim: A Historiographical Study." *ZDPV* 102 (1986): 68–74.

———. "*Timnat-ḥeres*." In vol. 8 of *Encyclopedia Miqra'it*, cols. 602–3. Jerusalem, 1982.

Kallai, Z., and H. Tadmor. "Bīt Ninurta = Beth Horon: On the History of the Kingdom of Jerusalem in the Amarna Period" (in Hebrew). *Eretz-Israel* 9 (*W. F. Albright Vol.*, 1969–70): 138–47.

Kaufmann, Y. *Commentary on the Book of Judges* (in Hebrew). Jerusalem, 1959.

———. *The History of the Israelite Religion* (in Hebrew). Vols 1–4. Tel Aviv, 1948–56.

Kempinski, A. "Some Observations on the Hyksos (15th) Dynasty and its Canaanite Origins." In *Pharaonic Egypt, the Bible and Christianity,* ed. S. Israelit Groll, 129–37. Jerusalem, 1985.

Kempinski, A., and S. Košak. "The Išmeriga-Vertrag." *Die Welt des Orients* 5 (1970): 191–217.

Kempinski, A., O. Zimchoni, E. Gilboa and N. Rösel. "Excavations at Tel Masos" (in Hebrew). *Eretz Israel* 15 (*Y. Aharoni Vol.*, 1981): 154–80.

King, L. W. *Babylonian Boundary Stones and Memorial Tablets*. London, 1912.

Kittel, R. *Geschichte des Volkes Israel*. Gotha, 1917.

———. "Die pentateuchischen Urkunden in den Büchern Richter und Samuel." *ThStKr* 65 (1892): 41–47.

Klengel, H. "Der Schiedssprung des Muršili II," *Orientalia* N.S. 32 (1963): 32–55.

Klima, J. "Untersuchungen zum elamischen Erbrecht." *Archív orientální* 28 (1960): 5–54.

Knudtzon, J. A., ed. *Die El-Amarna Tafeln*. Leipzig, 1915.

Kochavi, M. "The Israelite Settlement in Canaan in the Light of Archaeological Survey." *Proceedings of the International Congress on Biblical Archaeology*. (April 1984): 54–60.

———. " 'Khirbet Rabud'—Debir." *Tel-Aviv* 1 (1974): 2–33.

Kohler, J., and A. Ungnad. *Assyrische Rechtsurkunden*. Leipzig, 1913.

Korošec, V. "Einige juristische Bemerkungen zur Šahurunuva-Urkunde." *Münchener Beiträge zur Papyrusforschung und antiken Rechtsgeschichte* 35 (1945): 221 ff.

———. *Hethitische Staatsverträge*. Leipzig, 1931.

Koschaker, P. "Review of Scheil, *MDP* XXII." *OLZ* 35 (1932): 318–21.

Kraeling, E. *The Brooklyn Museum Papyri*. New Haven, 1953.

Kraus, F. R. *Altbabylonische Briefe*. Heft 1. Leiden, 1964.

———. "*Baghdader Mitteilungen* 2 (1963)." *Bibliotheca Orientalis* 22 (1965): 287–93.

Kuhl, C. "Neue Dokumente zum Verständnis von Hosea 2:4–15." *ZAW* 52 (1934): 102–09.

Lacheman, E. R. *Excavation at Nuzi VIII: Family Law Documents*. HSS 19. Cambridge, Mass., 1962.

Landsberger, B. *Sam'al: Studien zur Entdeckung der Ruinenstätte Karatepe*. Ankara, 1948.

Langlamet, F. *Gilgal et les récits de la traversée du Jourdain*. Cahiers de la *Revue Biblique* 11. Paris, 1969.

———. "Israël et 'l'habitant du pays' " *RB* 76 (1969): 321–50.

Laroche, E. "Un point d'histoire: Ulmi-Teshub." *RHA* 8/48 (1947–48), 40–48.

Latte, K. "Ein Sakrales Gesetz aus Kyrene." *Archiv für Religionswissenschaft* 26 (1928): 41–51.

Leschhorn, W. *Gründer der Stadt*. Stuttgart, 1984.

Lewy, J. H. *Studies in Jewish Hellenism* (in Hebrew). Jerusalem, 1969.

Lieberman, S. Vol. 8 of *Tosefta ki-Fshuṭah*. New York, 1973.
———. "Notes." In E. S. Rosenthal, ed., *P'raqim—Yearbook of the Schocken Institute for Jewish Research of the Jewish Theological Seminary of America* (in Hebrew), ed. E. S. Rosenthal, 1:97–107. Jerusalem, 1967–68.
Licht, J. "The Biblical Claim about the Foundation" (in Hebrew). *Shnaton* 4 (1980): 98–128.
Lipinski, E. *Le poème royal du Ps 89:1–5, 2–38*. Paris, 1969.
Liver, J. "*Caleb*." In vol. 4 of *Encyclopedia Miqra'it* (in Hebrew), cols. 106–10. Jerusalem, 1962.
Loewenstamm, S. E. "*ʿAm Segulla*." *From Babylon to Canaan: Studies in the Bible and Its Oriental Background,* 268–79. Jerusalem, 1992.
———. "The Death of the Patriarchs in Genesis." *From Babylon to Canaan: Studies in the Bible and Its Oriental Background,* 77–108. Jerusalem, 1992.
———. "The Divine Grants of the Land to the Patriarchs." *JAOS* 91 (1971): 509–10. (Later published in AOAT 204, 423–25. Neukirchen, 1980.)
———. "The Formula of *meʿatta weʿad ʿolam*." In *Comparative Studies in Biblical and Ancient Oriental Literatures,* 166–70. Vol. 204 of AOAT. Neukirchen, 1980.
———. "*ḥrm*." In vol. 3 of *Encyclopedia Miqra'it,* cols. 290–92. Jerusalem, 1965.
———. "Notes on the Alalaḫ Tablets." In *Comparative Studies in Biblical and Ancient Oriental Literatures,* 23–26. Vol. 204 of AOAT. Neukirchen, 1980.
———. "The Settlement of Gad and Reuben as related in Num. 32:1–38—Background and Composition." *From Babylon to Canaan: Studies in the Bible and Its Oriental Background,* 109–30. Jerusalem, 1992.
———. "Zur Traditionsgeschichte des Bundes zwischen den Stücken." *VT* 18 (1968): 500–506. AOAT 204, 273–80. Neukirchen, 1980.
Lohfink, N. "Die Bedeutung von heb. *yrš* qal und hif." *Biblische Zeitschrift* N.F. 26 (1982): 14–33.
———. *Das Hauptgebot: Eine Untersuchung literarischer Einleitungsfragen zu Dtn. 5–11*. Rome, 1963.
———. "*ḥeraem*." In vol. 3 of *Theologisches Wörtebuch zum Alten Testament,* ed. G. J. Botterweck and H. Ringgren, 192–213. Stuttgart, 1978.

———. *Die Landverheissung als Eid.* Stuttgarter Bibelstudien 28. Stuttgart, 1967.

———., ed. *Das Deuteronomium, Entstehung, Gestalt und Botschaft.* Leuven, 1985.

Maisler, B. *Untersuchungen zur alten Geschichte und Ethnographie Syriens und Palästinas.* Giessen, 1930.

Malamat, A. "The Danite Migration and the Pan-Israelite Exodus-Conquest—A Biblical Narrative Pattern." *Biblica* 51 (1970): 1–16.

———. *Israel in Biblical Times* (in Hebrew). Jerusalem, 1983.

———. "The Kingdom of David and Solomon and its Relation with Egypt: A Superpower in the Making." In *Israel in Biblical Times,* 167–94. Jerusalem, 1983.

Malkin, I. *Religion and Colonization in Ancient Greece.* Leiden, 1987.

———. "What is a Name? The Eponymous Founders of Greek Colonies." *Athenaeum,* n. ser. 63 (1985): 114–30.

———. "What Were the Sacred Precincts of Brea?" *Chiron* (1984): 43–48.

Malten, A. L. "Aineias." *Archiv für Religionswissenschaft* 29 (1931): 53 ff.

Malul, M. *Studies in Mesopotamian Legal Symbolism* AOAT 220. Neukirchen, 1988.

Masson, O. "A propos d'un rituel Hittite pour la lustration d'une armée: Le rite de purification par le passage entre les deux parties d'une victime." *RHR* 137 (1950): 5–25.

Mazar, A. "Giloh: An Early Israelite Settlement Site Near Jerusalem." *IEJ* 31 (1981): 1–36.

Mazar, B. "Biblical Archaeology Today: The Historical Aspect." In *Biblical Archaeology Today: Proceedings of the International Congress on Biblical Archaeology: Jerusalem, April 1984,* 16–20. Jerusalem, 1985.

———. "The Cities of the Priests and the Levites." In *Congress Volume, Oxford 1959,* 193–205. SVT 7. Leiden, 1960.

———. "The Exodus from Egypt and the Conquest of the Land." In *The History of the People of Israel* (in Hebrew), 187–99. Vol. 2, *The Patriarchs and the Judges.* Jerusalem, 1967.

———. "The Historical Background of the Book of Genesis." In *The Early Biblical Period: Historical Studies,* ed. S. Ahituv and B. A. Levine, 49–62. Jerusalem, 1986. (First published in *JNES* 28 (1969), 73–83.)

———. "Josephus Flavius, the Historian of Jerusalem." In *Josephus*

Flavius—Collected Papers (in Hebrew), ed. U. Rappaport, 1–5. Jerusalem, 1982.

———. "Lebo-ḥamath and the Northern Border of Canaan." In *The Early Biblical Period: Historical Studies* 189–202. Jerusalem, 1986. (First published in Hebrew in *BIES* (*Yediot*) 12 (1946): 91–102.)

———. "The Sanctuary at Arad and the Family of Ḥobab, Moses' Father-in-Law." *JNES* 24 (1965): 297–303.

McCarter, K. *II Samuel*. Anchor Bible. New York, 1984.

McCarthy, D. J. *Treaty and Covenant*. 2d ed. Analecta Biblica 21a. Rome, 1978.

Meiggs, R., and D. Lewis. *A Selection of Greek Historical Inscriptions to the End of the Fifth Century B.C.* Oxford, 1969.

Mendels, D. "Hecataeus of Abdera and a Jewish 'patrios politeia' of the Persian Period (Diodorus Siculus LX, 3)." *ZAW* 95 (1983): 96–110.

———. *The Land of Israel as a Political Concept in Hašmonean Literature*. Texte und Studien zum antiken Judentum 15. Tübingen, 1987.

Mendelsohn, I. "On the Preferential Status of the Eldest Son." *BASOR* 156 (1959): 38–40.

Mendenhall, G. E. "Covenant Forms in Israelite Tradition." *Biblical Archaeologist* 17 (1954): 50–76.

———. "The Hebrew Conquest of Palestina." *BA* 25 (1962): 66–87.

———. *The Tenth Generation: The Origin of the Biblical Tradition*. Baltimore, 1973.

Meritt, B. D. "Inscriptions of Colophon." *American Journal of Philology* 56 (1935): 358–97.

Meyer, E. *Ursprung und Anfänge des Christentums* Vol. 2, *Die Entwicklung des Judentums und Jesus von Nazaret*. Berlin, 1925.

Milgrom, J. "Profane Slaughter and a Formulaic Key to the Composition of Deuteronomy." *HUCA* 47 (1976): 1–17.

———. "Religious Conversion and the Revolt Model for the Formation of Israel." *JBL* 101 (1982): 169–76.

Milik, J. T. "Fragment d'une source du Psautir (4Q Ps. 89) et fragments des Jubilés, de Document de Damas, d'un phylactere dans la grotte 4 de Qumran." *RB* 73 (1966): 94–106.

Momigliano, A. "How to Reconcile Greeks and Trojans?" In *Mededelingen der Koninklijke Nederlandse Akademie van Westenschappen. Afd. Letterkunde,* 231–54. N.S. 45/9 Amsterdam, 1982.

Montgomery, J. A. "Archival Data in the Book of Kings." *JBL* 53 (1934): 46–52.

Moran, W. L. "The End of the Unholy War and the Anti-Exodus." *Biblica* 44 (1963): 333–42.

———. "A Kingdom of Priests." In *The Bible in Current Catholic Thought,* ed. J. McKenzie, 7–20. New York, 1962.

———. "Recensiones, G. W. Ahlström, *Psalm 89.*" *Biblica* 42 (1961): 237–39.

Muffs, Y. "Abraham the Noble Warrior: Patriarchal Politics and Laws of War in Ancient Israel." *JJS* 33 (1982): 81–108.

———. "Joy and Love as Metaphorical Expressions of Willingness and Spontaneity in Cuneiform, Ancient Hebrew and Related Literatures." In vol. 3 of *Christianity, Judaism and other Greco-Roman Cults: For Morton Smith at Sixty,* ed. J. Neusner, 1–36. Leiden, 1975.

———. "Studies in Biblical Law IV (The Antiquity of P.)." *Lectures at the Jewish Theological Seminary.* New York, 1965. Mimeograph.

———. *Studies in the Aramaic Legal Papyri from Elephantine.* Leiden, 1969.

Munn-Rankin, J. "Diplomacy in Western Asia in the Early Second Millennium B.C." *Iraq* 18 (1956): 68–110.

Musil, A. *Arabia Petrae* 2: *Edom,* 1, Vienna, 1907.

Na'aman, N. *Borders and Districts in Biblical Historiography.* Jerusalem, 1968.

———. "The Brook of Egypt and the Assyrian Policy on the Egyptian Border" (in Hebrew). *Shnaton* 3 (1978–79): 138–58.

———. "The Inheritance of the Cis-Jordanian Tribes of Israel and the 'Land that yet Remaineth' " (in Hebrew). *Eretz Israel* 16 (*Orlinsky Vol.* 1982): 152–58.

———. "Pastoral Nomads in the Southwestern Periphery of the Kingdom of Judah" (in Hebrew). *Zion* 52 (1987): 261–78.

———. "Shiḥor of Egypt and Assyria which is in Front of Egypt." In *Biblical Studies: Y. M. Grintz Memorial Volume* (in Hebrew), 215–21. Tel Aviv, 1982.

———. "Society and Culture in Late Bronze Age." In vol. 1 of *The History of Eretz Israel* (in Hebrew), ed. I. Ephʿal, 212–41. Jerusalem, 1982.

———. "*Yenoʿam.*" *Tel-Aviv* 4 (1977): 168–77.

Neufeld, E. "Insects as Warfare Agents in the Ancient Near East." *Orientalia* 49 (1980): 30–57.

Nilsson, M. P. *Geschichte der griechischen Religion.* 3d ed. Munich, 1974.

Noetscher, F. *'Das Angesicht Gottes Schauen' nach biblischer und babylonischer Auffassung*. Würzburg, 1924.
Norden, E. *Die germanische Urgeschichte in Tacitus Germania*. Leipzig, 1920.
Noth, M. "The Background of Judges 17–18." In *Israel's Prophetic Heritage: Essays in Honor of J. Muilenburg*, 68–85. London, 1962.
———. *Das Buch Josua*. 2d ed. HAT. Tübingen, 1953.
———. "Gilead und Gad." *ZDPV* 75 (1959): 14–73.
———. *Überlieferungsgeschichtliche Studien*. Halle, 1943.
Oded, B. *Mass Deportation and Deportees in the Neo-Assyrian Empire*. Wiesbaden, 1979.
———. "*qnt*." In vol. 7 of *Encyclopedia Miqra'it*, cols. 203–04. Jerusalem, 1976.
O'Doherty, E. "The Literary Problem of Judges 1:1–3:6." *CBQ* 18 (1956): 1–7.
Oettinger, N. *Die militärischen Eide der Hethiter*. Studien zu den Bogazköy Texten 22. Wiesbaden, 1976.
Otten, H. *Die Bronzetafel aus Boğazköy ein Staatsvertrag Tuthalijas IV*. Studien zu den Boğazköy-Texten Beiheft 1. Wiesbaden, 1988.
———. "Keilschrifttexte." *MDOG* 91 (1958): 73–84.
Otto, E. *Das Mazzotfest in Gilgal*. Stuttgart, 1975.
Ottosson, N. *Gilead: Tradition and History*. Lund, 1969.
Parke, H. W., and D. E. W. Wormell. *A History of the Delphic Oracle*. Oxford, 1956.
Parker, R. *MIASMA, Pollution and Purification in Early Greek Religion*. Oxford, 1983.
Parpola, S., and K. Watanabe. *Neo Assyrian Treaties and Loyalty Oaths*. State Archives of Assyria 2. Helsinki, 1988.
Paul, S. M. "Adoption Formulae" (in Hebrew). *EI* 14 (*H. L. Ginsberg Volume*, 1978): 31–36.
Paul, S. M. "Deutero-Isaiah and Cuneiforn Royal Inscriptions." *JAOS* 88 (1968): 180–86.
Podlecki, A. J. "Cimon, Skyros and 'Theseus' Bones.'" *JHS* 91 (1971): 141–43.
Poebel, A. *Das appositionell bestimmte Pronomen der 1 Pers. Sing. in der westsemitischen Inschriften und im A.T.* Assyriological Studies no. 3. Oriental Institute, Chicago, 1932.
Postgate, J. N. *Neo-Assyrian Royal Grants and Decrees*. Rome, 1969.
Prawer, Y. "Jerusalem as Conceived in Christianity and Judaism in the Early Middle Ages" (in Hebrew). *Cathedra* 17 (1980): 40–72.
Printz, F. *Gründungsmythen und Sagenschronologie*. Zetemata 72. Munich, 1981.

Pritchard, J. B., ed. *Ancient Near Eastern Texts Relating to the old Testament*. 2d ed. Princeton, 1969.
Rabinowitz, J. J. *Jewish Law*. New York, 1956.
———. "The Susa Tablets, the Bible and the Aramaic Papyri." *VT* 11 (1961): 55–76.
Rad, G. von. *Studies in Deuteronomy*. London, 1953.
———. *Theologie des Alten Testaments*. 2d ed. Munich, 1957.
Rainey, A. F. "*ʿbr hnhr.*" In vol. 6 of *Encyclopedia Miqra'it,* cols. 43–48. Jerusalem, 1971.
Rehm, M. D. "Studies in the History of the Pre-Exilic Levites." Diss. announced in *Harvard Theological Review* 61 (1986): 648–49.
Reiner, E. Vol. 3 of *Šurpu: A Collection of Sumerian and Akkadian Incantations*. AfO Beih. 11. Graz, 1958.
Reiner, E. "Treaty Between Ashurnirari V of Assyria and Matiʾilu of Arpad." In *ANET,* 3d ed., ed. J. B. Pritchard, 532–33.
Reviv, H. "Governmental Authority in Shechem in the Period of El Amarna and the Time of Abimelech" (in Hebrew). *BIES* (*Yediot*) 27 (1963–64): 270–75.
———. "On the Events in the Land of Shechem in the El Amarna Period" (in Hebrew). *Tarbiz* 33 (1964–65): 1–7.
Riemschneider, K. *Die hethitischen Landschenkungsurkunden,* Mitteilungen des Instituts für Orientforschung 6. Berlin, 1958.
Rofé, A. "The Composition of the Introduction of the Book of Judges" (in Hebrew). *Tarbiz* 35 (1966–67): 201–13.
———. "The End of the Book of Joshua According to the Septuagint" (in Hebrew). *Shnaton* 2 (1977): 217–27.
Rösel, N. "Judges 1 and the Problem of the Settlement of the 'Leah Tribes.'" In *Proceedings of the Eighth World Congress for Jewish Studies* (in Hebrew), 17–20. Jerusalem, 1982.
Rouillard, H., and J. Tropper. "*trpym* rituels de guérison et culte des ancêstres d'après 1 Sam. 19:11–17 et les textes parallèles d'Assur et de Nuzi." *VT* 37 (1987): 340–61.
Rudolph, W. "*Der 'Elohist' von Exodus bis Josua*. Berlin, 1938.
———. *Jeremia*. 2d ed. HAT. Tübingen, 1958.
Safrai, S. "And All is According to the Majority of Deeds" (in Hebrew). *Tarbiz* 53 (1983): 33–40.
———. "The Land of Israel in Tannaitic Halacha." In *Das Land Israel in biblischer Zeit,* ed. G. Strecker, 201–15. Göttingen, 1983.
Safran, J. D. "Aḥuzzath and the Pact of Beer-Sheba." In vol. 2 of *Beer-Sheva, Presented to S. Abramsky on his Retirement* (in Hebrew), ed. M. Cogan, 121–30. Jerusalem, 1985.

Sandars, N. K. *The Sea Peoples, Warriors of the Ancient Mediterranean 1250–1150 B.C.* London, 1978.

Sarna, N. M. "Psalm 89: A Study in Inner Biblical Exegesis." In *Biblical and other Studies,* ed. A. Altman, 29–46. Philip W. Lown Institute of Advanced Judaic Studies. Brandeis University, Boston, 1963.

Sasson, J. M. *The Military Establishments at Mari*. Rome, 1969.

Schaefer, H. *Probleme der alten Geschichte, Gesammelte Abhandlungen und Vorträge*. Göttingen, 1963.

Schaller, B. "Philon von Alexandria und das 'Heilige Land'" In *Das Land Israel in biblischer Zeit, Jerusalem Symposium, 1981,* ed. G. Strecker, 172–87. Göttingen, 1983.

———. *Das Testament Hiobs*. Gütersloh, 1979.

Schmid, F. B. "Studien zur griechischen Ktisissagen." Diss., Freiburg, 1947.

Schmidt, F. "Jewish Descriptions of the Settled Land during the Hellenistic and Roman Periods." In *Greece and Rome in Eretz Israel: Collected Essays* (in Hebrew), ed. A. Kasher, G. Fuks and U. Rappaport, 85–97. Jerusalem, 1989.

Schorr, M. *Urkunden des altbabylonischen Zivil-und Prozessrechts*. VAB 5. Leipzig, 1913.

Schottroff, W. *"Gedenken" im Alten Orient und Alten Testament*. Neukirchen, 1967.

Schuler, E. von. *Hethitische Dienstanweisungen*. AfO Bech. 10. Graz, 1957.

———. *Die Kaskäer.* Berlin, 1965.

———. "Staasverträge und Dokumente hethitischen Rechts." In *Neuere Hethiterforschung, Historia,* ed. G. Walser, 34–53. Einzelschriften 7 (1964).

Seeligmann, I. L. "Aetiological Elements in Biblical Historiography" (in Hebrew). *Zion* 26 (1960–61): 141–61.

———. "From Historic Reality to Historiosophic Conception in the Bible." In vol. 2 of *P'raqim, Yearbook of the Schocken Institute for Jewish Research* (in Hebrew), ed. E. S. Rosenthal, 274–313. Jerusalem, 1969–74.

———. "*ger.*" In vol. 2 of *Encyclopedia Miqra'it,* cols. 546–49. Jerusalem, 1954.

———. "Indications of Editorial Alteration and Adaptation in the Masoretic Text and the Septuagint." *VT* 11 (1961): 201–21. In Hebrew in vol. 1 of *Likkutei Tarbiz,* 290–91. Jerusalem, 1979.

———. "Menschliches Heldentum und göttliche Hilfe." *Theologische Zeitschrift* 19 (1963): 385–411.

Seux, M. J. *Éphithètes royales Akkadiennes et Sumériennes*. Paris, 1967.

Shalit, A. *Antiquities of the Jews by Josephus* (in Hebrew). Jerusalem, 1955.

Singer, Rev. S., ed. *The Standard Prayer Book*. New York, 1943.

Smend, R. *Jahwekrieg und Stammesbund*. Forschungen zur Religion und Literatur des Alten und Neuen Testaments. Göttingen, 1963.

Smith, P. M. "Aeneadae as Patrons in Iliad XX." *Harvard Studies in Classical Philology* 85 (1981): 17–58.

Smith, S. "A Preliminary Account of the Tablets from Atchana." *The Antiquaries Journal* 19 (1939): 38–48.

———. *The Statue of Idri-mi*. London, 1949.

Soden, W. von. *Grundriss der akkadischen Grammatik*. Analecta Orientalia 33. Rome, 1952.

Soggin, J. A. *Joshua*. OTL. London, 1972.

———. *Judges*. OTL. London, 1981.

Sollberger, E. *Inscriptions royales Summériennes et Akkadiennes*. Paris, 1971.

———. *Le système verbal dans les inscriptions "royales" presargoniques de Lagaš*. Geneva, 1952.

Sommela, P. "Das Heroon des Aeneas und die Topographie des antiken Lavinium." *Gymnasium* 81 (1974): 197–273.

Sommer, F., and A. Falkenstein. *Die hethitisch-akkadische Bilingue des Hattušili I (Labarna II)* Abhandlungen der bayerischen Akademie der Wissenschaften: Phil.-hist. Abt. N. F. 16. Munich, 1938.

Speiser, E. A. *Introduction to Hurrian*. AASOR 20. New Haven, 1941.

———. *New Kirkuk Documents Relating to Family Laws*. AASOR 10. New Haven, 1930.

———. "A Significant New Will from Nuzi." *JCS* 17 (1963): 65–71.

Steiner, G. "Der Grenzvertrag Zweischen Lagaš und Umma." *Acta Sumerologica* 8 (1986): 219 ff.

Steinmetzer, F. X. *Die babylonischen Kudurru (Grenzsteine) als Urkundenform* Studien zur Geschichte und Kultur des Altertums 11. Paderborn, 1922.

———. "Die Bestallungsurkunde Königs Šamaš-sum-ukîn von Babylon," *Archív orientální* 7 (1935): 314–18.

Stengel, P. *Die griechische Kultusaltertümer*. 3d ed. Berlin, 1929.

Stern, M. Vol. 1 of *Greek and Latin Authors on Jews and Judaism*. Jerusalem, 1976.

Strassmaier, J. N. *Inschriften von Nabonidus König von Babylon*. Leipzig, 1889.

Strecker, G. "Das Land Israel in Früh Christlischer Zeit." In *Das Land Israel in biblischer Zeit,* ed. G. Strecker, 188–200. Göttingen, 1983.

Stroumsa, G. "Old Wine and New Bottles: On Patristic Soteriology and Rabbinic Judaism." In *The Origins and Diversity of Axial Ages Civilizations,* ed. S. M. Eisenstadt, 252–60. Albany, 1986.

Studer, G. L. *Das Buch der Richter.* Bern, 1835.

Sturtevant, H. E., and C. Bechtel. *A Hittite Chrestomathy.* Philadelphia, 1935.

Szlechter, E. "Les tablettes juridiques datées du règne d'Abî-ešuḫ." *JCS* 7 (1953): 81–99.

Tadmor, H. "Royal City and Holy City in Assyria and Babylonia." In *Town and Community* (in Hebrew), 179–206. Jerusalem, 1967.

Tadmor, H., and M. Weinfeld, eds. *History, Historiography and Interpretation*. Jerusalem, 1983.

Thureau-Dangin, F. "Un acte de donation de Mardouk-zâkir-šumi." *RA* 16 (1919): 117–56.

———. *Die sumerischen und akkadischen Königsinschriften* VAB 1. Leipzig, 1907.

———. "Trois contracts de Ras-Shamra." *Syria* 18 (1937): 245–55.

Tigay, J. H. "Adoption." In vol. 2 of *Encyclopedia Judaica,* cols. 298–301. Jerusalem, 1971.

———. "Psalm 7:5 and Ancient Near Eastern Treaties." *JBL* 89 (1970): 178–86.

Toeg, A. "Exodus 22:4—The Text and the Law in the Light of the Ancient Sources" (in Hebrew). *Tarbiz* 39 (1970): 223–31.

Tucker, G. M. "Witnesses and 'Dates' in Israelite Contracts." *CBQ* 28 (1966): 42–45.

Tufnell, O. *Lachish: The Bronze Age*. London, 1958.

Tur-Sinai (Torczyner), N. H. *The Language and the Book* (in Hebrew). 2d ed. Jerusalem, 1964.

Urbach, E. E. "Inheritance Laws and After-life." In vol. 1 of *Proceedings of the Fourth World Congress of Jewish Studies* (in Hebrew), 133–41. Jerusalem, 1967.

———. *The Sages: Their Concepts and Beliefs*. Jerusalem, 1975.

Ussishkin, D. "Excavations at Tel Lachish, 1978–1983: Second Preliminary Report." *Tel-Aviv* 10 (1983): 97–175.

Vaux, R. de. *The Early History of Israel to the Period of the Judges*. Trans. D. Smith. London, 1971.

———. "Le pays de Canaan." *Journal of the American Oriental Society* 88 (1968): 23–30.

———. "Le roi d'Israäl, vassal de Yahve." In vol. 1 of *Mélanges E. Tisserant,* 119–33. Rome, 1964.

Virgilio, B. "I termini de colonizzazione in Erodoti e nella tradizione preerodotea," *Atti Della Academia Delle Scienze di Torino II,* Cl. de scienze mor., stor. e fil 106 (1972), 345–401.

Volz, P., and W. Rudolph. *Der Elohist als Erzähler—ein Irrweg der Pentateuchkritik*. Giessen, 1933.

Wacholder, B. Z. *Eupolemus: A Study of Judeo-Greek Literature*. Cincinnati, 1974.

Wagner, S. "Die Kundschaftergeschichten im A. T." *ZAW* 76 (1964): 255–69.

Weidner, E. *Politische Dokumente aus Kleinasien: Die Staatsverträge akkadischer Sprache aus dem Archiv von Boghazköi*. Boghazköi Studien 8. Leipzig, 1928.

———. "Der Staatsvertrag Aššurnirāris VI von Assyrien mit Matiʾilu von bît Agusi." *AfO* 8 (1932): 12–34.

Weill, R. *La fin du moyen empire égyptien*. Paris, 1918.

Weinfeld, M. "The Awakening of National Consciousness in Israel in the Seventh Century B.C.E." In *ʿOz le-David, Jubilee Volume in Honor of D. Ben Gurion,* 396–420. Jerusalem, 1964.

———. "Bond and Grace—Covenantal Expression in the Bible and in the Ancient Near East" (in Hebrew). *Leshonenu* 36 (1972): 85–105.

———. "Chieftain." In vol. 5 of *Encyclopedia Judaica,* cols. 420–21.

———. *Commentary of the Book of Genesis* (in Hebrew). Tel Aviv, 1975.

———. "The Counsel of the 'Elders' to Rehoboam and Its Implication." *Maʿarab, A Journal for the Study of the Northwest Semitic Languages and Literatures* 3/1 (1982): 25–54.

———. "Covenant Davidic." In the Supplementary Volume of *Interpreter's Dictionary of the Bible,* 188–92. Nashville, 1976.

———. "The Covenant of Grant in the Old Testament and in the Ancient Near East." *JAOS* 90 (1970): 186–202.

———. "Covenant Terminology in the Ancient Near East and Its Influence on the West." *JAOS* 93 (1973): 190–99.

———. *Deuteronomy and the Deuteronomic School*. Oxford, 1972.

———. "Deuteronomy 1–11." Anchor Bible. New York, 1991.

———. "The Emergence of the Deuteronomic Movement: The His-

torical Antecedents." In *Das Deuteronomium, Entstehung, Gestalt und Botschaft,* ed. N. Lohfink, 76–98. Leuven, 1985.
———. "The Extent of the Promised Land: The Status of Transjordan." In *Das Land Israel in biblischer Zeit,* ed. G. Strecker, 59–75. Göttingen, 1983.
———. "God the Creator in Genesis 1 and in the Prophecy of Second Isaiah" (in Hebrew). *Tarbiz* 37 (1968): 105–32.
———. "The Heavenly Praise in Unison." In *Meqor Ḥayyim. Festschrift für G. Mollin,* 427–37. Graz, 1983.
———. "*Ḥilul kbisha* and *mirmas regel.*" In *Meḥqerey Lašon, Hebrew Language Studies Presented to Zeev Ben Ḥayyim* (in Hebrew), 195–200. Jerusalem, 1983.
———. "Holy People and Great Nation" (in Hebrew). *Molad* 21 (1964): 662–65.
———. "Inheritance of the Land—Privilege vs. Obligation: The Concept of the 'Promise of the Land' in the Sources of the First and Second Temple Periods" (in Hebrew). *Zion* 49 (1984): 115–37.
———. "Initiation of Political Friendship in Ebla." In *Wirtschaft und Gesellschaft von Ebla,* ed. H. Hauptmann and H. Waetzoldt, 345–48. Heidelberger Studien zum Alten Orient 2. Heidelberg, 1988.
———. "Jeremiah and the Spiritual Metamorphosis of Israel." *ZAW* 88 (1976): 17–56.
———. *Justice and Righteousness in Israel and in the Nations* (in Hebrew). Jerusalem, 1985.
———. "The Loyalty Oath in the Ancient Near East." *Ugarit-Forschungen* 8 (1976): 379–414.
———. "Old Testament—The Discipline and Its Goals." SVT 32. In *Vienna Congress 1980,* 423–34. Leiden, 1981.
———. "The Pattern of the Israelite Settlement in Canaan." SVT 40. In *Jerusalem Congress 1986,* 270–84. Leiden, 1988.
———. "The Pattern of the Israelite Settlement in Canaan: The Model and Its Nature" (in Hebrew). *Cathedra* 44 (1987): 3–20.
———. "Recent Publications." *Shnaton* 5–6 (1981–82): 233–34.
———. Review article on *Gibeon and Israel,* by J. Blenkinsopp. *IEJ* 26 (1976): 60–64.
———. "The Tithe in the Bible—Its Royal and Cultic Background" (in Hebrew). *Beer Sheva* 1 (1973): 122–31.
———. "The Tradition about Moses and Jethro at the Mountain of God" (in Hebrew). *Tarbiz* 56 (1978): 449–60.
———. "The Tribal League at Sinai." In *Ancient Israelite Religion:*

Essays in Honor of Frank Moore Cross, ed. P. D. Miller and S. D. McBride, 303–14. Philadelphia, 1987.

———. "Zion and Jerusalem as Religious and Political Capital: Ideology and Utopia." In *The Poet and the Historian: Essays in Literary and Historical Biblical Criticism,* ed. R. E. Freedman, 75–115. Harvard Semitic Studies 26. Chico, Calif., 1983.

Weinfeld, M., and R. Meridor. "The Punishment of Zedekiah and That of Polymestor." In the I. L. Seeligmann Volume 1 of *Studies in the Bible and the Ancient Near East* (in Hebrew), ed. Y. Zakovitch and A. Rofé, 229–33. Jerusalem, 1983.

Weinstock, S. "Penates." In vol. 39 of *Real-Encyclopädie der classischen Altertumswissenschaft,* ed. A. E. Pauly and G. Wissowa, cols. 429 ff. Stuttgart, 1937.

Weippert, M. *Die Landnahme der israelitischen Stämme in der neuren wissenschaftlichen Diskussion.* Göttingen, 1961.

Weisberg, D. B. *Guild Structure and Political Allegiance in Early Achaemenid Mesopotamia.* New Haven, 1967.

Weiser, A. *Samuel 7–12.* FRLANT 81. Göttingen, 1962.

Weisman, Z. *The Narrative Cycle of the Jacob Stories and Their Integration in the History of the Nation* (in Hebrew). Jerusalem, 1986.

———. "Toward an Explanation of "ʿ*lzh*" (in Hebrew). *Beit Miqra* 34 (1968): 49–52.

Weiss, M. "Some Problems of the Biblical 'Doctrine of Retribution' " (in Hebrew). *Tarbiz* 32 (1963–64): 1–18.

Westermann, C. Vol. 1 of *Genesis.* BKAT 14. Neukirchen, 1979.

Whittaker, C. R. "The Western Phoenicians: Colonization and Assimilation." *Proceedings of the Cambridge Philological Society* 20 (1974): 58–79.

Wilamowitz, U. von. "Apollon." *Hermes* 38 (1903): 575–86.

———. "Heilige Gesetze: Eine Urkunde aus Kyrene." In *Sitzungsberichte Akademie Berlin, Phil-hist. Klasse,* 155–76. Berlin, 1927.

Williamson, H. G. M. *1 and 2 Chronicles.* The New Century Bible Commentary. London, 1982.

Windisch, H. "Zur Rahabgeschichte (zwei Parallelen aus der classischen Literatur)." *ZAW* 37 (1917–18): 188–98.

Wiseman, D. J. "Abban and Alalah." *JCS* 12 (1958): 124 ff.

———. *The Alalaḫ Tablets.* London, 1954.

———. *The Vassal Treaties of Esarhaddon.* Iraq 20. London, 1958.

Wolff, H. W. "Das Kerygma des deuteronomistischen Geschichtswerks." *ZAW* 73 (1961): 171–86.

Wolfson, H. A. *Philo.* Cambridge, Mass., 1947.

Wright, D. P. "Deuteronomy 21:1–9 as a Rite of Elimination." *CBQ* 49 (1987): 387–403.

———. *The Disposal of Impurity: Elimination Rites in the Bible and in Hittite and Mesopotamian Literature.* Atlanta, 1986.

Wright, G. E. "The Lawsuit of God: A Form-Critical Study of Deuteronomy 32." In *Israel's Prophetic Heritage: Essays in Honor of J. Muilenburg,* 26–67. New York, 1962.

Wüst, F. R. "Amphiktyonie, Eidgenossenschaft, Symmachie." *Historia* 3 (1954–55): 129–53.

Yadin, Y. *Hazor.* Schweich Lectures, 1970. London, 1972.

———. *The Temple Scroll* (in Hebrew). Jerusalem, 1977. (Later published in English, 1983.)

Yaron, R. *The Law of the Elephantine Documents* (in Hebrew). Jerusalem, 1961.

———. "Varia on Adoption." *Journal of Juristic Papyrology* 15 (1965): 171–83.

Zawadzki, T. "Quelques remarques sur l'étendue et l'accroissement des domaines des grands temples en Asia Mineure." *Eos* 46 (1952–53): 83–96.

Zertal, A. "An Early Iron Age Cultic Site on Mount Ebal: Excavation Seasons 1982–1987." *Tel-Aviv* 13–14 (1986–87): 105–65.

Index of Texts

Apocrypha and Pseudepigrapha

Qumran Texts

Rabbinic Literature

Tosefta

Classical Sources

Mesopotamian, Hittite, and Syrian Sources

Index of Subjects

Index of Scholars

Compositor: Keystone Typesetting
Text: 10/12 Bembo
Display: Bembo
Printer: Braun-Brumfield, Inc.
Binder: Braun-Brumfield, Inc.